THE

AMERICAN LAWYER,

AND

BUSINESS-MAN'S FORM-BOOK;

CONTAINING

FORMS AND INSTRUCTIONS

For
Contracts,
Arbitration and
Award, Assignments,
Chattel Mortgages, Bills
of Sale, Bill of Lading, Bonds,
Exchange, Drafts, Promissory Notes,
Orders, Receipts, Due-Bills, Conveyances,
Deeds, Mortgages, Indentures, Satisfactions,
Releases, Dower, Leases, Landlord's and Tenant's
Agreements, Composition with Creditors, Charter of
Vessels, Building, Letters of Credit and License, Marriage,
Articles of Partnership, Power of Attorney, Wills and Codicils,
Trust Forms, Barter, Liabilities of Common Carriers and of Minors,
*Naturalization, Pre-Emption Rights on Public Lands, Rights to Military
Bounty Land, Copyright Laws, Regulations and Forms for obtaining Patents,
Customhouse Regulations, Domestic and Foreign Rates of Postage, A System of
Book-Keeping, Interest Tables, Equation Time Table, Interest and Mensuration Rules,
Weights and Measures of different Countries, Value of Gold and Silver Coins, &c., &c.*

TOGETHER WITH

THE LAWS OF THE VARIOUS STATES

ON

HOUSEHOLD AND HOMESTEAD EXEMPTIONS FROM EXECUTION, DEEDS, ACKNOWLEDGMENT OF DEEDS, MECHANICS' LIEN, COLLECTION OF DEBTS, LIMITATION OF ACTIONS, REGULATING CONTRACTS, CHATTEL MORTGAGES, RIGHTS OF MARRIED WOMEN, DOWER, RATES OF INTEREST, USURY, AND WILLS;

AND

A MAP AND SEAL FOR EACH STATE IN THE UNION.

BY DELOS W. BEADLE, A. M.,
ATTORNEY AND COUNSELLOR AT LAW.

NEW YORK:
PUBLISHED BY PHELPS, FANNING, & CO.,
195 BROADWAY.
CINCINNATI: A. RANNEY, 34 EAST THIRD ST.
1852.

Stereotyped by C. C. Savage,
13 Chambers Street, N. Y.

Printed by Grossman & Son,
69 Ann St., New York.

TO THE PURCHASER.

This book which we now offer you is emphatically a manual for the guidance of any and every man in business transactions, in a manner prescribed by law and the usages of trade. But in addition to this, it embodies an array of practical information which makes it a most valuable reference-book to the business man; and we assume that the world is not in possession of its equal in point of FULLNESS and CORRECTNESS. It has been prepared by a lawyer of high character and standing in the city of New York, whose professional reputation is a sufficient guaranty for its accuracy, assisted by a business-man well acquainted with the wants of the community, which this work is intended to supply.

In presenting its claims to public favor, we do not address ourselves as is usual "to the Reader," but "to the Purchaser," for we do not expect any man to read it through, but to use it as a reference-book, not only that his business may be done in a *form* that shall secure his legal rights, but also to ascertain what protection the *laws* of the states afford him in the prosecution of his business. When we ask the business-man to purchase it, we expect him to inquire, "WILL IT PAY?" we answer—

IT WILL PAY THE CITY WHOLESALE MERCHANT.

Your customers are scattered throughout the country, and it is important for you to know the laws of the various States for the Collection of Debts, the kinds of Property Exempt from Attachment, Customhouse Regulations, Foreign Weights and Measures, Liabilities of Common Carriers, Forms of Power of Attorney and of Revoking the same, Agreements, and many other things which the index will show.

IT WILL PAY THE CITY RETAILER.

We give Forms of Articles of Copartnership, of Leases, Assignment of Policy of Insurance, Notes, Orders, Receipts, Value of Coins, &c.; besides important information on various subjects.

IT WILL PAY THE COUNTRY MERCHANT.

We give you Forms for Bills of Sale, Contracts, Letters of Credit, Shipping Bills, Agreement for Sale of Personal Property, Bonds, Book-Keeping, Chattel Mortgages, and a large number of other items adapted to your daily wants.

IT WILL PAY THE ATTORNEY.

Our book, emanating from one whose legal acumen will not be questioned, gives the profession the State Laws for the Collection of Debts, Laws Regulating Conveyances, the Limitation of Actions, Property Exemptions, Rates of Interest, Acknowledgments of Deeds, Statutes of Fraud, Wills, and a long array of forms for drafting business papers.

It will Pay the Farmer.

We give you Forms for Deeds, Mortgages, Satisfaction of Mortgages, Bills of Sale, Cultivation of Land, Sale of Animals with Warranty, Homestead and other Exemptions, Instructions for obtaining Public Lands of the government, and numerous other forms and information which might be as important to a farmer as his plough.

It will Pay the Mechanic.

Turn to the Lien Laws for the benefit of mechanics, Liabilities of Minors, Indentures for an Apprentice, Articles of Partnership, forms and rules prescribed for securing Patents, Contracts, Assignments: the index will exhibit other subjects equally useful to you.

It will Pay the Emigrant.

We give you the Laws and Forms regulating Naturalization, Right of settling on United States Public Land, Homestead and other Property Exempt from Sale for Debts in the different States, Rates of Postage to Foreign Countries, Value of Gold and Silver Coins, besides business forms, &c.

It will Pay Every Man.

Look at the array of subjects already mentioned, besides Forms for holding Property in Trust, Promissory Notes, Compounding with Creditors Landlord and Tenant's Agreements, Rights of Married Women, Dower Rights to Military Bounty Land, Interest Tables, &c., together with another item giving great interest to this work, being a well-delineated

Map of each State in the Union, and a Map of the U. S.

which Maps alone are worth three times what is asked for the whole work.

The special State Laws have been compiled at great labor and expense, from the latest statutes of the various States, so far as they could be reached, and will be found more complete and reliable than anything now before the public.

If we have now made it plain that it will be a valuable book to you, we ask you to buy it, not simply to promote our interest, but because we give you in return that information which every man ought to have at his command.

The Publishers.

January 1, 1851.

INDEX.

THE

AMERICAN LAWYER.

AGREEMENTS.

An agreement or contract is the mutual consent of two or more persons respecting anything done or to be done.

When reduced to writing, the memorandum or articles containing the agreement, signed by the parties thereto, is usually called an agreement.

It is advisable, in all cases, to reduce the agreements and contracts of parties to writing; not only because, in case of dispute, the instrument is a more reliable and satisfactory source of evidence than the memory of witnesses, but because, by statute, many agreements are void unless put into writing and subscribed by the party to be charged.

But care must be taken to put the whole and exact contract in writing, as verbal evidence will not be admitted to alter or vary a written instrument. If erasures or interlineations are made, the fact should be stated on the paper, that they were so done before the parties signed it.

In all agreements or contracts there must be a consideration flowing from the promisor to the promisee, such as the payment of money, the sale and delivery of property — something whereby the promisee is benefited or the promisor put to inconvenience; and this consideration should be expressed.

Contracts which militate against the public good can not

be enforced—as a contract not to exercise one's trade or calling at all, a contract to erect a public nuisance, &c.

It is understood, in every contract for work or labor, that it shall be executed in a suitable and workmanlike manner, whether it is so expressed in the contract or not.

If it is desired by both parties to an agreement to waive the performance of a part of it, let it be so endorsed on the back of the agreement, and signed by the party who so consents to waive it.

The law of the state where the contract is made regulates the construction of the contract; the law of the state where the contract is sought to be enforced regulates the remedy.

Amounts and dates should always be written out, and not expressed in figures: thus, two thousand dollars, instead of $2,000.

The words in *italics*, and names in capitals, are merely inserted to show how the forms may be filled out. They should be always omitted in drawing a paper, and such words inserted as correspond with the facts in hand, and the actual agreement of the parties.

Fraud destroys every contract into which it enters.

No. 1.—General Form of Agreement.

This Agreement, made this *first* day of *May*, one thousand eight hundred and *fifty*, between JOHN DOE, of the *village* of *Black Rock*, in the county of *Erie*, and state of *New York*, of the first part, and RICHARD ROE, of the *city* of *Buffalo*, in *said county and state*, of the second part—*

Witnesseth, that the said JOHN DOE, in consideration of the covenants on the part of the party of the second part hereinafter contained, doth covenant and agree to and with the said RICHARD ROE, that [*here insert the agreement on the part of John Doe*].

And the said RICHARD ROE, in consideration of the covenants on the part of the party of the first part, doth covenant

* To avoid repetition, we have referred in the succeeding forms to certain numbers, for the introductory matter of the form. For example, in No. 5, the first part of No. 1 is to be copied in that form as far as the star.

and agree to and with the said JOHN DOE, that [*here insert the agreement on the part of Richard Roe*].

† **In witness whereof,** we have hereunto set our hands and seals, the day and year first above written.

Signed, sealed, and delivered, in presence of
JOHN SMITH,
JAMES SHORT.

JOHN DOE *(seal)*.
RICHARD ROE *(seal)*.

[*When required, this clause may be inserted:*]

And it is further agreed between the parties hereto, that the party that shall fail to perform this agreement on his part, will pay to the other the full sum of *fifty* dollars, as liquidated, fixed, and settled damages.‡

No. 2.—Agreement for the Sale and Delivery of Personal Property.

This Agreement, made this *first* day of *July*, one thousand eight hundred and *fifty*, between JOHN DOE, of the *village* of *New Albany*, in the county of *Floyd*, and state of *Indiana*, of the first part, and RICHARD ROE, of the *city* of *Buffalo*, in the county of *Erie*, and state of *New York*, of the second part—

Witnesseth, that the said JOHN DOE, in consideration of the covenants on the part of the said RICHARD ROE, doth covenant to and with the said RICHARD ROE, that he will deliver to the said RICHARD ROE, at *his storehouse* in *New Albany aforesaid*, *one thousand* bushels of wheat, of good merchantable quality, on or before the *first* day of *September next.*

And the said RICHARD ROE, in consideration of the covenants on the part of the said JOHN DOE, doth covenant and agree to and with the said JOHN DOE, that he will pay to the said JOHN DOE at the rate of *one dollar* for each bushel of wheat so delivered, immediately on the completion of the delivery thereof.

† This form of witnessing and signing may be adopted in every legal instrument, except where a different form is particularly given or directed to be used.

‡ When it is desired to fix the damages for the violation of the contract, this clause may be inserted before the witnessing clause. It has the advantage of making certain the amount of damages to be paid, instead of leaving it to be settled by a suit at law, or an agreement between the parties, *after* the contract has been violated.

In witness whereof, the said parties have hereunto set their hands and seals the day and year first above written.

Signed, sealed, and delivered, in presence of
JOHN SMITH,
JAMES SHORT.

JOHN DOE *(seal)*.
RICHARD ROE *(seal)*.

The foregoing form can be used for any description of personal property.

No. 3.—Agreement for Building.

Contract for Building, made the *tenth* day of *July*, one thousand eight hundred and *fifty*, by and between JOHN DOE, of *Brooklyn*, in the county of *Kings*, and state of *New York*, of the first part, and RICHARD ROE, of *New York*, in the county of *New York*, and state of *New York*, of the second part, in these words: the said party of the second part covenants and agrees to and with the said party of the first part, to make, erect, build, and finish, in a good, substantial, and workmanlike manner, *a three-story brick dwelling-house*, on the lot of land situated [*here insert description of lot*], agreeable to the draught, plan, and explanation,* hereto annexed, of good and substantial materials, by the *first* day of *January* next. And the said party of the first part covenants and agrees to pay unto the said party of the second part, for the same, the sum of *two thousand* dollars lawful money of the United States, as follows: the sum of *one thousand* dollars *when the building is enclosed and the roof put on, and the remaining one thousand* dollars *when the building is completed.*

And for the true and faithful performance of all and every of the covenants and agreements above mentioned, the parties to these presents covenant and agree, each with the other, that the sum of *one thousand* dollars, as fixed, settled, and liquidated damages, shall be paid to the other by the failing party.

In witness whereof, &c. [*as in No.* 1].

* The draughts and explanations should be all signed by the parties to the agreement, in order that they may be identified.

No. 4.—Agreement for the Sale of Land.

Articles of Agreement, made the *fifth* day of *March*, one thousand eight hundred and *fifty*, between JOHN DOE, of *Rochester*, in the county of *Monroe*, and state of *New York*, of the first part, and RICHARD ROE, of *Newburgh*, in the county of *Orange*, and state of *New York*, of the second part, witnesseth, that the said party of the first part, for and in consideration of the sum of *fifty* dollars, to him in hand paid, has contracted and agreed to sell to the said party of the second part, all that certain piece or parcel of land, situate in the town of *Newburgh*, in *Orange* county, and state of *New York*, and which is bounded and described as follows, to wit: beginning at, &c. [*here insert description of the land*].*

And the said party of the first part agrees to execute and deliver to the said party of the second part a warranty deed, for the said land: Provided, and upon condition nevertheless, that the said party of the second part, his heirs or assigns, pay to the said party of the first part, his heirs or assigns, for the same land, the sum of *five hundred* dollars lawful money of the United States of America, payable as follows: the sum of *two hundred and fifty dollars on the first day of June next, and the further and remaining sum of two hundred and fifty dollars on the first day of August in the year* one thousand eight hundred and *fifty-two*, together with lawful interest on the same, from the date hereof: And the said party of the second part, for himself, his heirs, executors, and administrators, doth covenant and agree, to and with the said party of the first part, his heirs and assigns, that the said party of the second part will pay the said several sums as they severally become due, with the interest thereon, without deduction of any taxes or assessments whatever. And it is further agreed between the parties to these presents, that if default be made in fulfilling this agreement, or any part thereof, on the part of the said party of the second part, then, and in such case, the said party of the first part, his heirs and assigns, shall be at liberty to consider this contract as forfeited and annulled, and to dispose of the said land to any other person, in the same manner as if this contract had never been made.

In witness whereof, &c. [*as in No. 1*].

* In describing land, buildings, &c., care should be had to make the description as complete as possible, so as to be readily identified on examination.

No. 5.—Agreement for the Hiring of a Clerk or Workman.

This Agreement, &c. [*as in No.* 1 *to the* *]—

Witnesseth, that the said John Doe has agreed to enter the service of the said Richard Roe as clerk [*or journeyman*], and covenants and agrees, to and with the said Richard Roe, that he will faithfully, honestly, and diligently, apply himself and perform the duties of a clerk [*or journeyman*] in the store [*or shop*] of the said Richard Roe, and faithfully obey all the reasonable wishes and commands of the said Richard Roe, for and during the space of *one year* from the *first* day of *December next*, for the compensation of *five hundred* dollars per annum, payable *quarterly*.

And the said Richard Roe covenants with the said John Doe, that he will receive him as his clerk [*or journeyman*] for the term of *one year* aforesaid, and will pay him for his services as such clerk [*or journeyman*] the sum of *five hundred* dollars annually, in *quarter yearly* payments.

In witness whereof, &c. [*as in No.* 1].

No. 6.—Agreement for making and delivering Boots.

This Agreement, &c. [*as in No.* 1 *to* *]—

Witnesseth, that the said John Doe, in consideration of the covenants on the part of the party of the second part, to be performed, doth covenant and agree, to and with the said Richard Roe, that he will, within [*here insert the time*] from the date hereof, make and deliver to the said Richard Roe, *ten thousand* pairs of boots, made from *calfskin*, of the first quality, and of the following sizes [*here insert sizes*].

And the said Richard Roe covenants to pay to the said John Doe *two* dollars for each pair upon the completion of the delivery of the said *ten thousand* pairs, if the same are delivered within [*insert the time agreed upon*] from the date hereof as aforesaid.

In witness whereof, &c. [*as in No.* 1].

No. 7.—Agreement for making Flour-Barrels.

This Agreement, &c. [*as in No.* 1 *to the* *]—

Witnesseth, that JOHN DOE, in consideration of the agreement on the part of RICHARD ROE, to be performed, covenants with the said RICHARD ROE, that he will make and deliver to the said RICHARD ROE, during the term of *one year* next ensuing from the date hereof, *one thousand* merchantable flour-barrels in each *week*, said flour-barrels to be made of good, hard, well-seasoned white-oak stuff, and the hoops to be of black ash.

And the said RICHARD ROE, in consideration thereof, agrees to pay to the said JOHN DOE at the rate of *twenty* cents for each barrel, such payment to be made on each thousand barrels immediately on the delivery thereof, until the whole quantity is made and delivered.*

In witness whereof, &c. [*as in No.* 1].

No. 8.—Agreement to sell and deliver Cord-Wood.

This Agreement, &c. [*as in No.* 1 *to the* *].

Witnesseth, that the said JOHN DOE agrees to sell to the said RICHARD ROE *one thousand* cords of wood, all of it to be well seasoned, and to be of *beech and maple* only, and to deliver the same, securely corded, at the *factory* of the said RICHARD ROE in the *town* aforesaid, for the price of *two* dollars per cord, on the *first* day of *June* next.

And the said RICHARD ROE, in consideration thereof, agrees to pay to the said JOHN DOE, for the said wood, at the rate of *two* dollars for each cord of wood, immediately upon the completion of the delivery thereof.

In witness whereof, &c. [*as in No.* 1].

No. 9.—Agreement to sell Shares of Stock.

This Agreement, &c. [*as in No.* 1 *to* *]—

Witnesseth, that, in consideration of the agreement of RICHARD ROE, hereinafter contained, the said JOHN DOE agrees to sell, transfer, and convey, to the said RICHARD ROE,

* The time and rate of payment may be altered to correspond with the special agreement between the parties.

on the *tenth* day of *July* next, *one thousand* shares of the *Glenville Manufacturing Company*, now owned by the said John Doe, and standing in his name on the books of said company, and to execute and deliver to the said Richard Roe all necessary assignments, transfers, and conveyances, to assure and convey the same to the said Richard Roe, his executors, administrators, and assigns, for ever.

In consideration of which, the said Richard Roe, agrees with the said John Doe to pay to him *one hundred* dollars for each share of the said capital stock, on the said *tenth* day of *July* next.

In witness whereof, &c. [*as in No.* 1].

No. 10.—Agreement to sell Goods in Store.

This Agreement, &c. [*as in No.* 1 *to* *]—

Witnesseth, that in consideration of the covenants on the part of the said Richard Roe, hereinafter contained, the said John Doe doth covenant with the said Richard Roe, that he will take of the said Richard Roe all his stock of goods, wares, and merchandise, now being in his store in the *village* of *Cooperstown*, together with all the fixtures thereto belonging; an account of such stock of goods, wares, and merchandise, to be taken by the parties hereto in the presence of each other: and the said John Doe agrees to pay for them at the invoice price; but if any of said goods be damaged, such damaged goods, together with the fixtures aforesaid, to be valued by two disinterested persons, one of whom is to be selected by each of the parties hereto, and to pay for the same the value or price that the said appraisers may agree to set upon them as a fair valuation of the same; and that in *five days* after the value of said goods, wares, merchandise, and fixtures, can be ascertained as aforesaid, said value is to be paid by the said John Doe to the said Richard Roe.

And the said Richard Roe, in consideration thereof, agrees to sell to the said John Doe the said goods, wares, and merchandise, at the invoice price, and the fixtures and such goods as may be damaged at such price as the appraisers appointed as aforesaid may fix and determine; and make, execute, and deliver, to the said John Doe, a good and sufficient bill of sale and conveyance thereof.

In witness whereof, &c. [*as in No.* 1].

No. 11.—Agreement to cultivate Land on Shares.

This Agreement, &c. [*as in No.* 1 *to* *]—

Witnesseth, that the said JOHN DOE agrees with the said RICHARD ROE, that he will properly plough, harrow, till, fit, and prepare for sowing, all that certain field of ground belonging to the said RICHARD ROE, which field lies, &c. [*here insert description of the field*], containing about *fifty* acres, and to sow the same with good *winter wheat*, finding one half of the seed *wheat* necessary therefor, on or before the *first* day of *September* next; and that he will at the proper time cut, harvest, and thrash, the said *wheat*, and properly winnow and clean the same, and deliver the one half part of the said *wheat* to the said RICHARD ROE, at his *barn, on his premises*, in the town of *Washington* aforesaid, *near his dwelling-house*, within *ten* days after the same shall have been cleaned; and will carefully stack the one half part of the straw on the premises of the said RICHARD ROE, near to his barn aforesaid.

And the said RICHARD ROE, in consideration of the foregoing agreement, promises and agrees, to and with the said JOHN DOE, that he may enter in and upon the said field for the purpose of tilling and sowing the same, and of harvesting the crop; and free ingress and egress have and enjoy for the purposes aforesaid; and that he will furnish to the said JOHN DOE one half part of the seed *wheat* necessary to sow the same, on or before the *first* day of *September* next, and permit the said JOHN DOE to thrash and clean the *wheat* upon the premises of the said RICHARD ROE.

In witness whereof, &c. [*as in No.* 1].

No. 12.—Agreement for the Sale of Horse.

This Agreement, &c. [*as in No.* 1 *to the* *]—

Witnesseth, that the said JOHN DOE hereby agrees to sell to the said RICHARD ROE his *dark-bay* horse, *with a white star in the forehead, and black mane and tail*, and to warrant the said horse to be well broken, to be kind and gentle, both under the saddle and in single and double harness, to be sound in every respect and free from vice—for the sum of *one hundred* dollars, to be paid by the said RICHARD ROE on the *tenth* day of *May* next.

In consideration whereof, the said Richard Roe agrees to purchase the said horse, and to pay therefor to the said John Doe the sum of *one hundred* dollars, on the *tenth* day of *May* next.

In witness whereof, &c. [*as in No.* 1].

No. 13.—Agreement for Sale and Purchase of Fruit-Trees.

This Agreement, &c. [*as in No.* 1 *to* *]—

Witnesseth, that the said John Doe agrees to sell and deliver to the said Richard Roe, at his dwelling-house in *Springfield* aforesaid, *five hundred* apple-trees, *two hundred and fifty* peach-trees, *two hundred* plum-trees, *one hundred* pear-trees, and *fifty* nectarine-trees, all in good order for transplanting, in the month of *May* next, for the following prices, namely: for each hundred apple-trees, *twenty* dollars; for each hundred peach-trees, *fifteen* dollars; for each hundred plum-trees, *thirty* dollars; for each hundred pear-trees, *twenty-five* dollars; and for each fifty nectarine-trees, *ten* dollars.*

And the said Richard Roe, in consideration thereof, agrees to purchase the trees aforesaid, in the quantity aforesaid, and at the prices aforesaid; and to pay to the said John Doe the price therefor in cash upon the delivery of the said trees.

In witness whereof, &c. [*as in No.* 1].

No. 14.—Agreement for Barter.

This Agreement, &c. [*as in No.* 1 to *]—

Witnesseth, that the said John Doe, in consideration of the agreement of the said Richard Roe, hereinafter contained, agrees to deliver to the said Richard Roe, on or before the *first* day of *October* next, *one thousand bushels of potatoes*, at the *dwelling-house* of the said Richard Roe.

And the said Richard Roe, in consideration thereof, agrees to deliver to the said John Doe, at *his dwelling-house*, on or before the *first* day of *October* next, *two hundred and fifty bushels of good, clean, merchantable wheat.*

In witness whereof, &c. [*as in No.* 1].

* The number of trees and the price may be varied to correspond with the agreement between the parties.

No. 15.—Agreement for the Sale of Animals.

This Agreement, &c. [*as in No.* 1 *to* *]—

Witnesseth, that in consideration of the agreement of the said RICHARD ROE, hereinafter contained, the said JOHN DOE agrees to sell and deliver, on the *first* day of *June* next, to the said RICHARD ROE, at his *store* in *Bennington*, one yoke of *four-year old oxen*.

And the said RICHARD ROE, in consideration thereof, agrees to pay to the said JOHN DOE *sixty* dollars immediately upon the delivery thereof.

In witness whereof, &c. [*as in No.* 1].

No. 16.—Apprentice's Indenture.*

This Indenture witnesseth, that JAMES DOE, of the *town* of *Cooperstown*, in the county of *Otsego*, and state of *New York*, now aged *eighteen* years, by and with the consent of JOHN DOE his *father*, hath voluntarily, and of his own free will and accord, put and bound himself apprentice to RICHARD ROE, of the *city* of *Rochester*, in the county of *Monroe*, and state of *New York*, to learn the art, trade, and mystery of *a hatter*, and as an apprentice, to serve from this date, for and during and until the full end and term of *three years* next ensuing; during all which time, the said apprentice his master faithfully, honestly, and industriously shall serve, his secrets keep, all lawful commands everywhere readily obey, and at all times protect and preserve the goods and property of said master, and not suffer or allow any to be injured or wasted; he shall not buy, sell, or traffic with his own goods, or the goods of others, nor be absent from his said master's service day nor night, without leave, and in all things behave himself as a faithful apprentice ought to do, during the said term. And the said master shall use and employ the utmost of his endeavors to teach, or cause him, the said apprentice, to be taught or instructed, in the art, trade, and mystery of a *hatter, and of making and finishing hats in all its branches.*†

* An indenture is an instrument, under seal, indented or notched at the top, "*instar dentium*," like the teeth of a saw. Most of the states have special regulations in regard to the rights and duties of the parties, which should be observed.

† The conditions in regard to board and lodgings, and the rate of wages with the time of payment, should here be inserted, according to the terms of agreement made between the parties.

And for the true performance of all and singular the covenants and agreements aforesaid, the parties bind themselves each unto the other, firmly by these presents.

In witness whereof, the parties aforesaid have hereunto set their hands and seals, the *tenth* day of *July*, in the year one thousand eight hundred and *fifty*.

Sealed and delivered in the presence of JOHN SMITH, PETER JONES.

JAMES DOE *(seal)*.
RICHARD ROE *(seal)*.

I do hereby consent to, and approve of, the binding of my *son*, JAMES DOE, as in the above indenture mentioned.

COOPERSTOWN, *July* 10, A. D. 1850. JOHN DOE.

No. 17.—Servant's Indenture.

This Indenture witnesseth, that JOHN DOE, now aged *seventeen* years, of the *city* of *Boston*, in the county of *Suffolk*, and state of *Massachusetts*, by and with the consent of WILLIAM DOE, his father, hath voluntarily, and of his own free will and accord, put and bound himself servant to RICHARD ROE, of *the same place*, and as a domestic servant, to serve from the date hereof, for and until the full end and term of *his minority;* during all which time, the said servant his master faithfully, honestly, and industriously shall serve, all lawful commands everywhere readily obey, protect and preserve the goods and property of his said master, and not suffer or allow any to be injured or wasted; he shall not be absent from service without leave, and in all things and at all times behave as a faithful servant ought to do. And the said RICHARD ROE shall and will furnish and provide the said servant, during the continuance of the said term, with suitable and sufficient board, lodging, and washing; *and in case of sickness, with medical attendance, care, and medicines.*

And for the true performance of all and singular the covenants and agreements aforesaid, the said parties bind themselves, each unto the other, firmly by these presents.

In witness whereof, &c. [*as in No.* 16].

I do hereby consent to, and approve of, the binding of my *son*, JOHN DOE, as in the above indenture mentioned.

BOSTON, *November* 1, 1850. WILLIAM DOE.

ARBITRATION.

ARBITRATION is an agreement by parties who have a controversy, to submit that controversy or difference to the decision of a third party.

When the matters in difference are simply those of fact or opinion merely, it is often more expeditious and satisfactory to submit them to the decision of mutual friends than to the regularly-constituted authorities.

The agreement to refer matters in difference to the decision of a third party, is called a *submission.*

The decision of the arbitrators is called an *award.*

The award should be specific and distinct, containing the decision of the arbitrators in as clear and concise language as possible.

When the arbitration is under a rule of court, the award should be sealed up and delivered to the court without delay.

The following oath should be taken by the persons chosen as arbitrators, before entering upon the examination of the matters in dispute:—

WE, the undersigned, arbitrators, appointed by and between JOHN DOE and RICHARD ROE, do swear fairly and faithfully to hear and examine the matters in controversy between the said JOHN DOE and RICHARD ROE, and to make a just award according to the best of our understanding.

JOHN JONES,
HENRY SMITH,
THOMAS SHARPE.

Sworn to, this *fifteenth* day of October, A. D. 185–, before me—

JOHN RICHTER, *Justice of the Peace*

Oath to be administered to a witness by arbitrators:—

You do solemnly swear that the evidence you shall give to the arbitrators here present in a certain controversy submitted to them by and between JOHN DOE and RICHARD ROE, shall be the truth, the whole truth, and nothing but the truth; so help you God.

No. 18.—Form of Submission.

Know all Men by these Presents, that whereas a controversy is now existing between John Doe, of the *city* of *New York*, in the county of *New York*, and state of *New York*, and Richard Roe, of *the same place*, concerning *the sale, warranty, and soundness, of a certain horse, which it is alleged was sold by the said* John Doe *to* Richard Roe *aforesaid, upon a warranty that the said horse was sound in every respect, and which horse, it is alleged, is not and was not at the time of such sale sound in every respect:*

Now, therefore, we the said John Doe and Richard Roe do hereby submit the said controversy to the decision and arbitration of John Jones, Henry Smith, and Thomas Sharpe, all of *New York aforesaid*, or to any two of them; and do covenant each with the other that we will in all things faithfully keep, observe, and abide by, the decision and award that they or any two of them may make in writing in the premises under their hands, ready to be delivered on or before the *first* day of *October* next.

And it is further agreed between the parties hereto, that the party that shall fail to keep, abide by, and observe the decision and award that shall be made according to the foregoing submission, will pay to the other the sum of *two hundred* dollars, as liquidated, fixed, and settled damages.

Witness our hands and seals, this *tenth* day of *October*, one thousand eight hundred and *fifty*.

Sealed and delivered in the presence of
John Smith,
John Stone.

JOHN DOE *(seal)*.
RICHARD ROE *(seal)*.

No. 19.—Arbitration Bond.

Know all Men by these Presents, that I, John Doe, of the *city* of *New York*, in the county of *New York*, and state of *New York*, am held and firmly bound unto Richard Roe, of *the same place*, in the sum of *five hundred* dollars, lawful money of the United States of America, to be paid to the said Richard Roe, his executors, administrators, or assigns; for which payment, well and truly to be made, I bind myself, my heirs, executors, and administrators, each and every of them firmly by these presents. Sealed with my *seal.* Dated the *twelfth* day of *October*, one thousand, eight hundred, and *fifty*.

The condition of the above obligation is such, that if the above-bounden JOHN DOE shall well and truly submit to the decision of JOHN JONES, HENRY SMITH, and THOMAS SHARPE, or the majority of them named, selected and chosen *arbitrators*, as well by and on the part and behalf of the said JOHN DOE as of the said RICHARD ROE, between whom a controversy exists, to hear all the proofs and allegations of the parties of and concerning *the sale, warranty, and soundness, of a certain horse, which it is alleged is unsound, and that it was sold by the said* JOHN DOE *to the said* RICHARD ROE *with warranty that it was in every respect sound*—and all matters relating thereto; and that the award of the said *arbitrators* be made in writing, subscribed by them or the majority of them, and attested by a subscribing witness, ready to be delivered to the said parties on or before the *first* day of *November* next. But before proceeding to take any testimony therein, the *arbitrators* shall be sworn "faithfully and fairly to hear and examine the matters in controversy between the parties to these presents, and to make a just award according to the best of their understanding." And the said parties to these presents do hereby agree, that judgment in the *supreme* court of the said state shall be rendered upon the award which may be made pursuant to this submission, to the end that all matters in controversy in that behalf, between them, shall be finally concluded—then the above obligation to be void, otherwise to remain in full force and virtue.

Signed, sealed, and delivered, in presence of PETER PENNY, HIRAM JONES.	JOHN DOE *(seal)*. RICHARD ROE *(seal)*.

Another bond should be executed by Richard Roe to John Doe, similar to this in every respect, except reversing the names.

No. 20.—Award of Arbitrators.

To all to whom these Presents shall come or may concern, Greeting: We, John Jones, Henry Smith, and Thomas Sharpe, to whom was submitted as *arbitrators* the matters in controversy existing between John Doe and Richard Roe, both of the *city* of *New York*, in the county of *New York*, and state of *New York*, as by the condition of their respective bonds of submission, executed by the said parties respectively, each unto the other, and bearing date the *twelfth* day of *October*, one thousand eight hundred and *fifty*, more fully appears.

Now, therefore, know ye, that we the *arbitrators* mentioned in the said bonds, having been first duly sworn according to law, and having heard the proofs and allegations of the parties, and examined the matters in controversy by them submitted, do make this award in writing: that is to say, the said John Doe *did sell to the said* Richard Roe *a certain horse on the fifteenth day of September last, warranting him to be sound in every respect, for the price of one hundred and fifty dollars; the said horse is and was at the time of such sale unsound, and worth only the sum of forty dollars; and the said* John Doe *should pay to the said* Richard Roe *one hundred and ten dollars for the difference in price, and thirty dollars for the expenses of keeping him, besides the costs of this arbitration.*

In witness whereof, we have hereunto subscribed these presents, this *first* day of *November*, one thousand eight hundred and *fifty*.

In the presence of
Peter Penny,
Hiram Jones.

JOHN JONES,
HENRY SMITH,
THOMAS SHARPE.

ASSIGNMENTS.

An *assignment* is a transfer of one man's interest in property to another, enabling the person to whom it is assigned to have the same control over the thing assigned as though he were the original owner.

An assignment made with the intent to hinder, delay, or defraud creditors or other persons, is void.

An assignment may be made for the benefit of the one to whom it is made; or partly for his benefit and partly in trust for the benefit of others; or wholly in trust for the benefit of others.

If there be reserved in an assignment any profit, benefit, or advantage, to the one making the assignment, this will be conclusive evidence of fraud; and the assignment would be at once set aside on the application of creditors prejudiced by it.

But the assignee may employ the assignor in settling up the claims and such like business necessary to be done.

An assignment, like any other conveyance, of an interest in lands, should be immediately acknowledged and properly recorded.

An assignment to a near relation is always looked upon with great suspicion by the courts; and, unless made with entire good faith, and for a valuable consideration, will be set aside on the application of creditors upon whom it operates as a fraud.

No. 21.—General Form of Assignment.

Know all Men by these Presents, that I, John Doe, within named, in consideration of *fifty* dollars, to me in hand paid* by Richard Roe, of the *city* of *Boston*, in the county of *Suffolk*, and state of *Massachusetts*, the receipt whereof is

* It will hardly be necessary to caution a prudent person against parting with the possession of an instrument acknowledging the receipt of the consideration, until it has actually been paid.

hereby acknowledged, have sold and assigned, and by these presents do sell and assign, to the said Richard Roe, the within instrument in writing, and all my right, title, and interest in and to the same, authorizing him, in my name or otherwise, but at his own expense, to enforce the same according to the tenor thereof.

In witness whereof, I have hereunto set my hand and seal, this *first* day of *July*, one thousand eight hundred and *fifty*.

JOHN DOE *(seal)*.

Sealed and delivered in presence of
John Smith,
John Stone.

The foregoing form to be endorsed on the instrument assigned.

No. 22.—Assignment of Bond.

Know all Men by these Presents, that I, John Doe, of the *city* of *Rochester*, in the county of *Monroe*, and state of *New York*, of the first part, for and in consideration of the sum of *one thousand* dollars, lawful money of the United States of America, to me in hand paid by Richard Roe, of the *city* of *Brooklyn*, in the county of *Kings*, and state of *New York*, of the second part, at or before the ensealing and delivery of these presents, the receipt whereof is hereby acknowledged, have bargained, sold, and assigned, and by these presents do bargain, sell, and assign, unto the said party of the second part, his executors, administrators, and assigns, a certain written bond or obligation and conditions thereof, bearing date the *first* day of *January*, one thousand eight hundred and *fifty*, executed by John Smith, of the *city* of *New York*, in the county of *New York*, and state of *New York*, to me, conditioned for the payment of *twelve hundred* dollars, on the *first* day of *May next*, with interest, and all sum and sums of money due, or to grow due thereon. And the said party of the first part doth covenant with the said party of the second part, that there is now due on the said bond or obligation, according to the conditions thereof, for principal and interest, the sum of *twelve hundred and forty-two* dollars, and doth hereby authorize the said party of the second part, in his name to ask, demand, sue for, recover, receive, and enjoy, the money due, and that may grow due thereon, as aforesaid.

In witness whereof, I have hereunto set my hand and seal, this *fifth* day of *July*, one thousand eight hundred and *fifty*.

JOHN DOE *(seal)*.

Sealed and delivered in the presence of
PETER PEPPER,
JOHN STONE.

No. 23.—Assignment of Mortgage.

Know all Men by these Presents, that I, JOHN DOE, of the *town* of *White Plains*, in the county of *Westchester*, and state of *New York*, of the first part, in consideration of the sum of *two thousand* dollars, lawful money of the United States, to me in hand paid by RICHARD ROE, of *the same place*, of the second part, at or before the ensealing and delivery of these presents, the receipt whereof is hereby acknowledged, have granted, bargained, sold, assigned, transferred, and set over, and by these presents do grant, bargain, sell, assign, transfer, and set over, unto the said party of the second part, a certain indenture of mortgage, bearing date the *tenth* day of *April*, in the year one thousand eight hundred and *fifty*, made by HIRAM SMITH, of the *town* of *White Plains*, in the county of *Westchester*, and state of *New York*, to secure the sum of *two thousand* dollars, together with the bond or obligation therein described, and the money due and to grow due thereon, with the interest. **To have and to hold** the same unto the said party of the second part, his executors, administrators, and assigns, for his sole use, benefit, and behoof, for ever, subject only to the proviso in the said indenture of mortgage mentioned: and I do hereby make, constitute, and appoint, the said party of the second part my true and lawful attorney, irrevocable, in my name or otherwise, but at his proper costs and charges, to have, use, and take, all lawful ways and means for the recovery of the said money and interest; and in case of payment, to discharge the same as fully as I might or could do if these presents were not made.

And I covenant, for myself, my heirs, executors, and administrators, that I am the true and lawful owner of the said bond and mortgage, and that I have just right, full power and authority to sell, assign, and dispose of the same; and that there is now owing thereon the said principal sum of *two thousand* dollars, together with the interest thereon, from the *first* day of *August last past.*

In witness whereof, &c. [*as in No.* 22].

No. 24.—Assignment of Mortgage to be endorsed thereon.*

I, John Doe, in consideration of *five hundred* dollars, to me in hand paid by Richard Roe, of the *city* of *Hartford*, in the county of *Hartford*, and state of *Connecticut*, the receipt whereof is hereby acknowledged, do hereby assign, transfer, convey, and set over, unto the said Richard Roe, the within indenture of mortgage and the bond accompanying the same, and all my right, title, and interest, in and to the same, and do authorize the said Richard Roe, in my name or otherwise, but at his own costs and charges, to collect and obtain payment of the same. And I covenant that there is now owing for principal upon the said bond and mortgage the sum of *five hundred* dollars, and interest from the *first* day of *July*, one thousand eight hundred and *fifty;* and that I am the owner thereof, and have good right to sell the same.†

In witness whereof, &c. [*as in No.* 22].

No. 25.—Assignment to be endorsed on Mortgage when intended as Collateral Security.

I, John Doe, in consideration, &c. [*as in No.* 24 *to* †]. But this assignment is upon this express condition, that if the said John Doe, his heirs, executors, administrators, or assigns, shall well and truly pay or cause to be paid unto the said Richard Roe the sum of *five hundred* dollars, on or before the *first* day of *July*, one thousand eight hundred and *fifty-eight*, with interest thereon from the date hereof—then this assignment to be void:

But if the said Richard Roe, his executors, administrators,

* The regulations of the respective states, in regard to acknowledging and recording interests in landed property, will be found described on pages 150 to 341.

or assigns, shall collect the money secured by the bond and mortgage hereby assigned; then, after taking therefrom the said sum of *five hundred* dollars, with interest thereon from the date hereof, and the amount of the costs and charges properly incurred in and about the collecting thereof, he or they shall pay over the surplus (if any) to the said JOHN DOE, his executors, administrators, or assigns.

In witness whereof, we have hereunto set our hands and seals, this *first* day of *October*, one thousand eight hundred and *fifty*.

Signed, sealed, and delivered, in presence of
JOHN SMITH,
JAMES SHORT.

JOHN DOE *(seal).*
RICHARD ROE *(seal).*

No. 26.—Assignment of a Debt.

Know all Men by these Presents, that I, JOHN DOE, of the *city* of *New Orleans*, in the *parish* of *Orleans*, and state of *Louisiana*, in consideration of *one thousand* dollars to me in hand paid by RICHARD ROE, of *the same place*, the receipt whereof I hereby acknowledge, have sold, transferred, and assigned, unto the said RICHARD ROE, a certain debt due and owing to me from JOHN SMITH, of the *city* of *Cincinnati*, in the county of *Hamilton*, and state of *Ohio*, for [*here state the consideration or cause of indebtedness*], amounting to *twelve hundred* dollars:

And I do hereby authorize the said RICHARD ROE, in my name or otherwise, but at his own costs, to sue for, collect, and receive, sell and transfer, settle and discharge, the said debt.

And I do covenant that the said sum of *twelve hundred* dollars is justly owing and due to me from the said JOHN SMITH, and that I have neither done nor will do anything to lessen or discharge the said debt, or hinder the said RICHARD ROE or his assigns from collecting the same.

In witness whereof, &c. [*as in No.* 22].

No. 27.—Assignment of Judgment.

This Indenture, made the *first* day of *October*, one thousand, eight hundred and *fifty*, between JOHN DOE, of the *town* of *Winchester*, in the county of *Cheshire*, and state of *New Hampshire*, of the first part, and RICHARD ROE, of the *same place*, of the other part: WHEREAS, the said party of the first part, on the *first* day of *June*, one thousand eight hundred and *fifty*, recovered by judgment in the *superior court of the state of New Hampshire*, against JOHN SHORT, the sum of *ten thousand* dollars:

Now this Indenture witnesseth, that the said party of the first part, in consideration of *ten thousand* dollars, to him duly paid, hath sold, and by these presents doth assign, transfer, and set over, unto the said party of the second part, and his assigns, the said judgment, and all sum and sums of money that may be had or obtained by means thereof, or on any proceedings to be had thereupon. And the said party of the first part doth hereby constitute and appoint the said party of the second part, and his assigns, his true and lawful attorney irrevocable, with power of substitution and revocation, for the use and at the proper costs and charges of the said party of the second part, to ask, demand, and receive, and to sue out executions, and take all lawful ways for the recovery of the money due or to become due on the said judgment; and on payment, to acknowledge satisfaction, or discharge the same: and attorneys one or more under him for the purpose aforesaid, to make and substitute, and at pleasure to revoke; hereby ratifying and confirming all that his said attorney or substitute shall lawfully do in the premises. And the said party of the first part doth covenant that there is now due on the said judgment the sum of *ten thousand* dollars, and that he will not collect or receive the same, or any part thereof, nor release or discharge the said judgment, but will own and allow all lawful proceedings therein, the said party of the second part saving the said party of the first part harmless of and from any costs in the premises.

In witness whereof, the party of the first part hath hereunto set his hand and seal the day and year first above written. JOHN DOE *(seal)*.

Sealed and delivered in the presence of
JOHN SMITH,
PETER JONES.

No. 28.—Assignment of Lease.

Know all Men by these Presents, that I, John Doe, of the *city* of *Boston,* in the county of *Suffolk,* and state of *Massachusetts,* for and in consideration of the sum of *one hundred* dollars, lawful money of the United States, to me duly paid by Richard Roe, of the *same place,* have sold, and by these presents do grant, convey, assign, transfer, and set over, unto the said Richard Roe, a certain indenture of lease, bearing date the *first* day of *April,* in the year one thousand eight hundred and *fifty,* made by James Smart, of the *city* of *Boston aforesaid,* to me for the term of *twenty years,* reserving unto the said James Smart the yearly rent of *two hundred* dollars, payable *quarterly,* with all and singular the premises therein mentioned and described, and the buildings thereon, together with the appurtenances. **To have and to hold** the same unto the said Richard Roe, his executors, administrators, and assigns, from the *first* day of *May next ensuing,* for and during all the rest, residue, and remainder, yet to come of and in the term of *twenty years* mentioned in the said indenture of lease: subject, nevertheless, to the rents, covenants, conditions, and provisions, therein also mentioned. [And I do hereby covenant, grant, promise, and agree, to and with the said Richard Roe, that the said assigned premises now are free and clear of and from all former and other gifts, grants, bargains, sales, leases, judgments, executions, back rents, taxes, assessments, and encumbrances whatsoever.]

In witness whereof, &c. [*as in No.* 22].

Instead of the clause within brackets, the following may be used:—

And I do hereby covenant and agree, to and with the said Richard Roe, that the said assigned premises are free and clear of and from all other gifts, grants, bargains, sales, leases, and encumbrances, by me suffered, made, or created.

No. 29.—Assignment of Policy of Insurance.*

Know all Men by these Presents, that I, John Doe, of the *city* of *St. Louis*, in the county of *St. Louis*, and state of *Missouri*, for and in consideration of the sum of *five hundred* dollars, lawful money of the United States, to me in hand paid by Richard Roe, of the *same place*, the receipt whereof is hereby acknowledged, do hereby sell, assign, transfer, convey, and set over, unto the said Richard Roe all my right, title, interest, claim, and demand, in and to the within named policy of insurance, and all sum and sums of money, interest, benefit, and advantage whatever, now due or which may hereafter arise, or to be had or made, by virtue thereof, to have and to hold the same unto the said Richard Roe, his heirs and assigns, for ever.

In witness whereof, &c. [*as in No.* 22].

No. 30.—Assignment for the Benefit of all Creditors equally.

Know all Men by these Presents, that I, John Doe, of the *town* of *Milford*, in the county of *New Haven*, and state of *Connecticut*, for value received, have sold, and by these presents do grant, sell, assign, and convey, unto Richard Roe, of the *same place*, all the accounts, debts, dues, notes, bills, bonds, and demands, enumerated and specified in the schedule hereunto annexed, and marked "*Schedule A*;"† to have and to hold the same, unto the said Richard Roe and his assigns:

In trust to collect, sue for, demand, receive, and recover, all such sums of money as may be due, owing, and payable thereon; and after paying all reasonable and proper costs, charges, and expenses, to pay to each and all of my creditors the full sum that may be due and owing to them from me, of whom the said Richard Roe is one, and a full and complete list of whom, with the true amount due to each, is contained in the schedule hereto annexed, marked "*Schedule B*;" and if the proceeds of the said notes, accounts, bonds,

* This assignment must be endorsed on the insurance policy, and approval of the insurers attested by the signature of one of the principal officers of the insurance company.

† The schedules should state the assignment to which they belong, and be dated and signed by the parties, for the purpose of identification.

and so forth, be not sufficient fully and entirely to pay off and satisfy each and all of my creditors, then to pay them *pro rata* in proportion to the amount due and owing to each. And if the proceeds as aforesaid shall be more than sufficient to pay and satisfy every one of my creditors, then to pay and return to me the balance that may be left, if any, after paying all my creditors as aforesaid.

And I do hereby nominate, constitute, and appoint, the said RICHARD ROE my true and lawful attorney, irrevocable, in my name or otherwise, for the purpose aforesaid, to ask, demand, sue for, collect, receive, and recover, all and singular such sum or sums of money as now are or hereafter may become due, upon, for, or on account of any of the property, effects, things in action, or demands above assigned; giving and granting unto my said attorney full power and authority to do and perform every act, deed, and thing, requisite and necessary in the premises; as fully, to all intents and purposes, as I might or could do, if this assignment had not been made; with full power of substitution and revocation, hereby ratifying and confirming all that my said attorney or his substitute may lawfully do or cause to be done, in the premises, by virtue hereof.

In witness whereof, &c. [*as in No.* 22].

No. 31.—Assignment by a Firm for the Benefit of Preferred Creditors.

This Indenture, made this *first* day of *July*, in the year one thousand eight hundred and *fifty*, between JOHN DOE and RICHARD DOE, of the *city* of *Philadelphia*, in the county of *Philadelphia*, and state of *Pennsylvania*, copartners, known as, and doing business under the name, style, or firm, of JOHN DOE and BROTHER, of the first part, and JAMES SMITH, of the *city* of *Philadelphia aforesaid*, of the second part:

WHEREAS, the said firm or copartnership are justly indebted in sundry dues and considerable sums of money, and have become unable punctually to pay and discharge the same, and are desirous of making a fair, just, and equitable distribution of all their property and effects among their creditors—

Now, therefore, this Indenture witnesseth, that the said parties of the first part, in consideration of the premises and of the sum of *one* dollar to them in hand paid by the said party of the second part, the receipt whereof is hereby acknowledged, have granted, bargained, covenanted, released, sold, assigned, transferred, and set over, and by these presents do grant, bargain, covenant, release, assign, transfer, and set over, unto the said JAMES SMITH, of the second part, and to his heirs and assigns for ever, all and singular the lands, tenements, hereditaments, and appurtenances, situate, lying, and being within the state of *Pennsylvania;* and all goods, wares, merchandise, chattels, notes, bills, bonds, judgments, evidences of debt, securities and vouchers for and affecting the payment of money, claims, demands, things in action, and property of every name and nature whatsoever, of and belonging to the said parties of the first part (and which are more particularly and fully enumerated and described in the schedule hereto annexed, marked "*Schedule A*"). **To have and to hold** the same and every part and parcel thereof with the appurtenances thereunto belonging, to the said party of the second part, his heirs, executors, administrators, and assigns:

In trust, nevertheless, for and upon the following uses and purposes, namely: the said party of the second part to take possession of all and singular the lands, tenements, and hereditaments, property and effects, hereby assigned, and sell and dispose of the same upon such terms and conditions as in his judgment may appear best and most for the interest of all the parties concerned, and convert the same into cash; and to collect all and singular the said notes, bills, bonds, judgments, evidences of debt, securities, claims, demands, things in action, and property, or so much thereof as may prove collectible, and thereupon execute, acknowledge, and deliver, all conveyances, receipts, and instruments, necessary and proper in the premises, for the purposes aforesaid. And by and with the avails and proceeds of such sales and collections to pay or cause to be paid—

First, all the just and reasonable expenses, costs, commissions, and charges, of executing and carrying out the objects of this assignment; and all rents, assessments, and taxes, due or to become due on the lots, lands, tenements, and hereditaments aforesaid, until the same shall be sold and disposed of according to this assignment.

Secondly, to pay and discharge in full the several and respective debts, notes, bonds, obligations, and sums of money due or to grow due from the said parties of the first part, or for which they are jointly liable to the said party of the second part, and the several other persons and firms specified in the schedule hereto annexed, marked "*Schedule B;*" together with all interest-moneys now due or to grow due thereon; and if the said proceeds and avails shall not be sufficient to pay and discharge the same in full, then such proceeds and avails shall be distributed *pro rata* among the said several persons and firms named in Schedule B aforesaid, in proportion to the amount of their respective claims.

Thirdly, to pay and discharge all the other copartnership debts, demands, and liabilities whatsoever, now existing, whether now due, or hereafter to become due, provided that there be sufficient funds for that purpose; and should they prove insufficient, then the same shall be applied *pro rata* to the payment of such debts, demands, and liabilities, in proportion to their respective amounts.

Fourthly, to pay and discharge all the private and individual debts of the parties of the first part, or either of them, whether now due or to grow due, provided there be sufficient funds for that purpose; and should they prove insufficient, then the same to be applied *pro rata* to the payment of the said debts in proportion to their respective amounts.

Lastly, to return the full surplus of the said proceeds and avails, if any there shall be, to the said parties of the first part, their executors, administrators, and assigns.

And for the better execution of these presents, and of the several trusts hereby reposed, the said parties of the first part do hereby nominate, constitute, and appoint, the said party of the second part, their and each of their true and lawful attorney, irrevocable, with full power and authority to do, transact, and perform all acts, deeds, matters, and things, which are or may be necessary in the premises, as fully and completely as they, the said parties of the first part, or either of them, might or could do, were these presents not executed; with full power of substitution and revocation, hereby ratifying and confirming all and every thing whatsoever that our said attorney or his substitute shall lawfully do or cause to be done in the premises.

In witness whereof, &c.

Sealed and delivered in the presence of
JOHN SMITH,
PETER JONES.

JOHN DOE *(seal)*.
RICHARD DOE *(seal)*.

No. 32.—Assignment of the Partnership Property by one Partner to the other, to wind up the Concern.

This Indenture, made this *tenth* day of *October*, one thousand eight hundred and *fifty*, between John Doe, of the *town* of *Concord*, in the county of *Merrimack*, and state of *New Hampshire*, and Richard Roe, of the *same place*.

Whereas, a copartnership has heretofore existed between the said John Doe and Richard Roe, under the style and name of Doe and Roe, which said copartnership has been this day dissolved by mutual consent:

Now, therefore, this Indenture witnesseth, that the said John Doe has sold, assigned, transferred, and set over, and by these presents does sell, transfer, assign, and set over, unto the said Richard Roe, his half part of all the goods, wares, merchandise, property, and effects, and stock in trade, belonging to the said copartnership, and also all the accounts, notes, bills, bonds, things in action, claims and demands due and owing to the said firm.

To have and to hold the same unto himself and his assigns, in trust to sell the said property and effects in such manner as he may think proper, but not on a longer credit than *ninety days;* and to collect, demand, sue for, and receive, all sums of money due or to become due upon the said bills, notes, bonds, accounts, claims, and demands; and with the moneys thus collected, realized, and obtained, to pay off and discharge all the debts and obligations of the said firm, if the same shall be sufficient therefor; and of the balance, if any there shall be, after satisfying all the claims and demands against the firm, to pay over the one half part to the said John Doe or his legal representatives.

And the said John Doe doth hereby make, constitute, and appoint the said Richard Roe, his true and lawful attorney, irrevocable, in the name of the late firm or otherwise, to sell the said property and effects of the late firm, and all the interest of the said John Doe in and to the same; and also ask, demand, sue for, collect, and receive, any and all debts, claims, and demands, due or to become due and owing to the said late firm, to compound the same and prosecute suits for the recovery thereof in his discretion; to defend any and all suits that may be brought against the said firm; and to make, execute, deliver, and acknowledge, all necessary deeds, conveyances, releases, receipts, and discharges, in the premises, and generally to do any and every act and thing requisite and necessary to secure a full, entire, complete, and speedy settlement of all the business and affairs of the late firm of Doe and Roe, hereby ratifying and confirming any and every thing which the said Richard Roe may lawfully do in the premises.

And the said Richard Roe, for himself, his heirs, executors, and administrators, covenants with the said John Doe, his heirs, executors, and administrators, that he will sell the aforesaid property to the best of his ability, and for the best price he can obtain therefor; and will use all diligence to collect all the debts, claims, and demands, due the said late firm, and that he will faithfully apply the proceeds of such sales and claims in accordance with the above-recited trust.

And the said John Doe, for himself, his heirs, executors, and administrators, covenants with the said Richard Roe, that if, after the entire proceeds of said property and effects, claims and demands, of the said late firm, have been faithfully applied to the payment of the debts, liabilities, and obligations, of the said late firm, there shall remain any debt or liability unsatisfied, that then he, the said John Doe, his heirs, executors, or administrators, will pay and satisfy the moiety or one half part of any and every such debt or liability; and the said Richard Roe, his heirs, executors, or administrators, from the one half part thereof save harmless and keep indemnified.

In witness whereof, &c. [*as in No.* 25].

No. 33.—Assignment of a Patent-Right.

Whereas I, John Doe, of the *town* of *Greenfield*, in the county of *Franklin*, and state of *Massachusetts*, did obtain letters-patent of the United States for certain improvements in *clocks*, which letters-patent bear date the *first* day of *April*, one thousand eight hundred and *fifty*; and whereas, Richard Roe, of the *town* of *Portsmouth*, in the county of *Rockingham*, and state of *New Hampshire*, is desirous of purchasing from me all the right, title, and interest, which I have in and to the said invention, in consequence of the grant of letters-patent therefor:

Now this Indenture witnesseth, that for and in consideration of the sum of *one thousand* dollars, lawful money of the United States, to me in hand paid, the receipt whereof is hereby acknowledged, I have assigned, sold, and set over, and do hereby assign, sell, and set over, unto the said Richard Roe, all the right, title, and interest, which I have in the said invention, as secured to me in the said letters-patent [for, to, and in the several states of *Ohio* and *Michigan*, and in no other place or places]:

The same to be held and enjoyed by the said Richard Roe, for his own use and behoof, and for the use and behoof of his legal representatives, to the full end of the term for which the said letters-patent are or may be granted, as fully and entirely as the same would have been held and enjoyed by me had this assignment and sale not been made.

In testimony whereof, I have hereunto set my hand and affixed my seal, this *first* day of *October*, one thousand eight hundred and *fifty*.

JOHN DOE *(seal)*.

Sealed and delivered in presence of
John Smith,
John Stone.

This form can be used for the assignment of a partial right in a patent, by *omitting* the words (in the first paragraph) "purchasing from me all the right, title, and interest, which I have in and to the said invention, in consequence of the grant of letters-patent therefor," and *inserting* the words "acquiring an interest therein," and by *adding* the words in brackets.*

* This assignment must be recorded in the patent-office within three months from the date of the same. For fees, see "Patents."

AFFIDAVIT.

An *affidavit* is a written statement, subscribed by the party making it, and sworn to or affirmed before the proper officer.

A *deposition* is the testimony of a witness under oath, reduced to writing.

No. 34.—Form of Affidavit.

State of *Illinois*,
County of *Kane*, } to wit:

John Doe, of the town of *Geneva*, in the *county aforesaid*, being duly sworn, says [*here state the facts*], and further says not.

JOHN DOE.

Sworn to this *tenth* day of *October*, A. D. 1850, before me, John Jones, *Commissioner of Deeds.*

If the matters embraced in the affidavit are not within the deponent's own knowledge, but have been communicated to him by others in whose assertion he places confidence, the affidavit should be in this form:—

State of *Illinois*,
County of *Kane*, } to wit:

John Doe, of the *town* of *Geneva*, in the *county aforesaid*, being duly sworn, says that he has been informed, and believes it to be true, that [*here insert what he has been informed of*]; and further says not.

JOHN DOE.

Sworn to this *tenth* day of *October*, A. D. 1850, before me, John Jones, *Commissioner of Deeds.*

BILLS OF EXCHANGE.

A *bill of exchange* is a written request from one person to another, desiring him to pay a sum of money to a third person, absolutely and at all events. They are seldom used except in drawing upon a person who is abroad in a foreign country.

The person who draws the bill is called the *drawer;* the person on whom it is drawn is called the *drawee.* After the drawee has accepted the bill, he is called the *acceptor.*

A bill or note drawn payable to order must have the name of the person to whose order it is made payable written on it before it can be negotiated to a third person; and he whose name is thus written on it is liable to pay the bill or note, if not paid, and he have due notice of the same.

In accepting a bill of exchange or draft, write the word "accepted," together with the date when accepted, and the name of the party or firm accepting, across the face or on the back of the bill or draft.

Acceptance acknowledges the genuineness of the signature of the drawer; and the acceptor would be liable to a holder in good faith, although the signature of the drawer were a forgery.

When a bill is drawn payable so many days after sight, it should be presented for acceptance on the next day after it is received. If you keep the bill without presenting it for acceptance, to the injury of the drawer, you must bear the loss yourself.

The drawee of a bill has twenty-four hours' time within which to make up his mind whether he will accept the bill; but if he refuses to return it after the expiration of that time, he is to be considered as having accepted it.

If the drawee refuses to accept a bill presented for acceptance, or to pay a bill presented for payment, it should be immediately protested, and notice sent to all the endorsers on the bill; otherwise the endorsers will not be liable.

Three days of grace, as they are called, are allowed on bills of exchange that are not drawn payable at sight; that is, they are not due until the third day after the time mentioned in the bill. If the third day happens to fall on Sunday, they are then due the day before, that is, on Saturday.

A bill drawn at sight is payable on presentation: at least it is advisable to protest it first for non-payment, and then demand acceptance; and if acceptance is refused, protest it also for non-acceptance.

A person becoming surety for a note or bill of exchange, should be notified of its non-payment in the same manner as an endorser. A check ought to be presented for payment within twenty-four hours of the time of receiving it.

If the drawer of a check payable on demand have no funds in the bank at the time it is drawn, it is a fraud.

The holder of a check is not obliged to accept part payment thereof, although tendered by the bank: he has a right to have the whole, and may decline any less sum.

If the drawee of a bill or maker of a note be out of the state or at sea, the same must be presented at his usual place of business, or at his place of residence, unless some other place is specified therein.

Any material alteration of a bill of exchange, drafts, &c.—such as an alteration in the date, in the amount, or the time of payment—discharges all the parties thereto who do not assent to the making of the alteration.

See "PROMISSORY NOTES," &c.

No. 35.—Set of Foreign Bills of Exchange.

No. 100. New York, October 10th, 1850.

Exch^ge for £1000.

Ten Days after sight of this **First** of Exchange (second and third unpaid), pay to the order of John Doe, One Thousand Pounds sterling, value received, and charge the same without further advice, to account of

Your obed't serv't,

Richard Roe.

To Peter Jones,

Liverpool.

No. 35.—Set of Foreign Bills of Exchange.

No. 100. New York, October 10th, 1850.

Exch^ge for £1000.

Ten Days after sight of this **Second** of Exchange (first and third unpaid), pay to the order of John Doe, One Thousand Pounds sterling, value received, and charge the same without further advice, to account of

Your obed't serv't,

Richard Roe.

To Peter Jones,
Liverpool.

No. 35.—Set of Foreign Bills of Exchange.

No. 100. New York, October 10th, 1850.

Exch^{ge} for £1000.

Ten Days after sight of this **Third** of Exchange (first and second unpaid), pay to the order of John Doe, One Thousand Pounds sterling, value received, and charge the same without further advice, to account of

Your obed't serv't,

Richard Roe.

To Peter Jones,
Liverpool.

No. 36.—Ordinary Bill of Exchange or Draft at a certain Time after Sight.

$250:: *New Orleans, Sept.* 12, 1850.

Ten Days after sight,* pay to the order of *John Jones, Two Hundred and Fifty* Dollars, Value received, and charge the same to account of

To *Richard Roe,*
Detroit,
Michigan.

Yours, &c.,
John Doe,
New Orleans, La.

No. 37.—Bill or Draft at a certain Time after Date.

$110.$\frac{25}{100}$ *Chicago, July* 10*th*, 1850.

Twenty Days after date, pay to the order of *James Smith, One Hundred and Ten* $\frac{25}{100}$*th* Dollars, Value received, and charge the same to account of

To *Richard Roe,*
Buffalo,
New York.

Yours, &c.,
John Doe,
Chicago, Ill.

No. 38.—Check or Draft on a Bank.

PRINTERS' BANK.

No. 50. New York, *May 14, 1850.*

Cashier of the **PRINTERS' BANK,**

Pay to *C. C. Savage* or *Bearer*

Four Hundred and Twenty Dollars

$ 420.:: *H. Phelps.*

* For a bill payable *at sight*, instead of the words, "ten days after sight," insert "at sight." A check made payable to *order* must be endorsed before used.

BILLS OF SALE AND CHATTEL MORTGAGES.

A *bill of sale* is a written instrument, transferring the ownership of personal property therein mentioned from one person to another.

The things included in the bill of sale should be delivered into the entire and continued possession of the purchaser; else the sale will be presumed to be fraudulent as to the creditors of the vendor.

A *chattel mortgage* is a written instrument, transferring the ownership of personal property therein mentioned conditionally. The usual condition is, that it is to become the property of the one to whom it is mortgaged, if the mortgager fail to make payment of money in the manner specified in the mortgage.

As to the validity and registering of these mortgages, see the respective states.

No. 39.—General Form of Bill of Sale.

Know all Men by these Presents, that I, John Doe, of the *city* of *Detroit,* in the county of *Wayne,* and state of *Michigan,* of the first part, for and in consideration of the sum of *five hundred* dollars, lawful money of the United States, to me in hand paid, at or before the ensealing and delivery of these presents, by Richard Roe, of the *same place,* of the second part, the receipt whereof is hereby acknowledged, have bargained and sold, and by these presents do grant and convey, unto the said party of the second part, his executors, administrators, and assigns, *one dark-bay colt, sixteen hands high, one single harness, one light single wagon, one cow, two pigs, and three geese.* **To have and to hold** the same unto the said party of the second part, his executors, administrators, and assigns, for ever.

And I do for myself, my heirs, executors, and administrators, covenant and agree, to and with the said party of the second part, to warrant and defend the sale of the said *goods and chattels* hereby sold unto the said party of the second part, his executors, administrators, and assigns, against all and every person and persons whomsoever.

In witness whereof, I have hereunto set my hand and seal, this *first* day of *July*, one thousand eight hundred and *fifty*.

JOHN DOE *(seal)*.

Sealed and delivered in the presence of
JOHN SMITH,
PETER JONES.

No. 40.—Bill of Sale of Horse, with Warranty.

Know all Men by these Presents, that I, JOHN DOE, of the *town* of *Racine*, in the county of *Racine*, and state of *Wisconsin*, of the first part, for and in consideration of the sum of *one hundred and fifty* dollars, lawful money of the United States, to me in hand paid at or before the ensealing and delivery of these presents, by RICHARD ROE, of the *same place*, of the second part, the receipt whereof is hereby acknowledged, have bargained and sold, and by these presents do grant and convey unto the said RICHARD ROE, his executors, administrators, and assigns, *one dark-bay* horse, *with a white star in the forehead, and a black mane and tail.* **To have and to hold** the same unto the said RICHARD ROE, his executors, administrators, and assigns, for ever.

And I do hereby warrant the said horse to be sound in every respect, to be free from vice, to be well broken, and kind and gentle in single and in double harness, and under the saddle; and I covenant for myself, my heirs, executors, and administrators, with the said RICHARD ROE, to warrant and defend the sale of the said horse unto tho said RICHARD ROE, his executors, administrators, and assigns, against all and every person and persons, lawfully claiming or to claim the same, whomsoever.

In witness whereof, I have hereunto set my hand and seal, this *fifth* day of *July*, one thousand eight hundred and *fifty*.

JOHN DOE *(seal)*.

Sealed and delivered in the presence of
PETER PEPPER,
JOHN STONE.

No. 41.—Bill of Sale of Registered or Enrolled Vessel.

Know all Men by these Presents, that I, John Doe, of the *city* of *San Francisco*, in the state of *California*, owner of the *ship or vessel* called the *America*, of the burden of *one thousand* tons or thereabouts, now lying at the port of *Sacramento*, in the *state aforesaid*, for and in consideration of the sum of *fifty thousand* dollars, lawful money of the United States, to me in hand paid by Richard Roe, of the *place first aforesaid*, at or before the ensealing and delivery of these presents, the receipt whereof I hereby acknowledge, have granted, bargained and sold, and by these presents do grant, bargain, and sell, unto the said Richard Roe, his executors, administrators, and assigns, all the hull or body of the said *ship or vessel*, together with the masts, bowsprit, sails, boats, anchors, cables, spars, and all other necessities thereunto appertaining and belonging; the certificate of the registry *or enrolment* of which said *ship or vessel* is as follows, to wit [*here copy the whole of the certificate of registry or enrolment.*] **To have and to hold** the said *ship or vessel*, and appurtenances thereunto belonging, unto the said Richard Roe, his executors, administrators, and assigns, to his and their proper use, benefit, and behoof, for ever.

And I, the said John Doe, for myself, my heirs, executors, and administrators, do covenant with the said Richard Roe, his executors, administrators, and assigns, that I am the sole, true, and lawful owner of the said ship *America*, and her appurtenances; and that I have full power, good right, and lawful authority, to sell and dispose of the said ship and her appurtenances in manner aforesaid. And I do further covenant, for myself, my heirs, executors, and administrators, that I, the said ship *America* and her appurtenances, as aforesaid, against the lawful claims of all persons whomsoever, claiming or to claim the same, will for ever warrant and defend.

In witness whereof, I have hereunto set my hand and seal, this *first* day of *July*, one thousand eight hundred and *fifty*.

JOHN DOE *(seal)*.

Sealed and delivered in the presence of
John Smith,
John Jones.

No. 42.—Form of Chattel Mortgage.

To all to whom these Presents shall come, KNOW YE that JOHN DOE, of the *town* of *Princeton*, in the county of *Middlesex*, and state of *New Jersey*, of the first part, for securing the payment of the money hereinafter mentioned, and in consideration of the sum of *one* dollar to me duly paid by RICHARD ROE, of the *city* of *Trenton*, in the county of *Huntingdon*, and state of *New Jersey*, of the second part, at or before the ensealing and delivery of these presents, the receipt whereof is hereby acknowledged, have bargained and sold, and by these presents do grant, bargain, and sell, unto the said party of the second part, *all my household furniture*, and all other goods and chattels mentioned in the schedule hereunto annexed,* and now in the *house in which I reside in the town aforesaid.* **To have and to hold** all and singular the goods and chattels above bargained and sold, or intended so to be, unto the said party of the second part, his executors, administrators, and assigns, for ever.

And I, the said party of the first part, for myself, my heirs, executors, and administrators, all and singular the said goods and chattels above bargained and sold, unto the said party of the second part, his heirs, executors, administrators, and assigns, against me, the said party of the first part, and against all and every person or persons whomsoever, shall and will warrant, and for ever defend: **upon condition,** that if I, the said party of the first part, shall and do well and truly pay unto the said party of the second part, his executors, administrators, or assigns, *the sum of three hundred dollars on the first day of August next*—then these presents shall be void.

And I, the said party of the first part, for myself, my executors, administrators, and assigns, do covenant and agree, to and with the said party of the second part, his executors, administrators, and assigns, that in case default shall be made in payment of the said sum above mentioned, then it shall and may be lawful for, and I the said party of the first part do hereby authorize and empower the said party of the second part, his executors, administrators, and assigns, with the aid and assistance of any person or persons, to enter my dwelling-house, store, and other premises, and such other place or places as the said goods or chattels are or may be, and take

* Annex a schedule, specifying all the articles mortgaged, adapted to the wants of the case. The plan of one is appended to this mortgage.

and carry away the said goods and chattels, and to sell and dispose of the same for the best price he can obtain; and out of the money arising therefrom, to retain and pay the said sum above mentioned, and all charges touching the same, rendering the overplus (if any) unto me or to my executors, administrators, or assigns. And until default be made in the payment of the said sum of money, I am to remain and continue in the quiet and peaceable possession of the said goods and chattels, and the full and free enjoyment of the same.

In witness whereof, I, the said party of the first part, have hereunto set my hand and seal the *first* day of *September*, one thousand eight hundred and *fifty*.

JOHN DOE (*seal*).

Sealed and delivered in the presence of
JOHN STONE,
JOHN SMITH.

Schedule referred to in the foregoing Mortgage.

IN THE PARLOR.

No. 1.—Two mahogany sofas.
" 2.—Fourteen mahogany chairs.
" 3.—One large looking-glass.
" 4.—One centre-table.
" 5.—One card-table.

IN THE DINING-ROOM.

" 6.—One dining-table.
" 7.—Ten cane-bottomed chairs.
" 8.—One sideboard.
" 9.—One clock.
" 10.—One lounge.
" 11.—One book-case.

[*And so on through the list in each room.*]

September 1, 1850.

JOHN DOE.

Witness { JOHN STONE,
JOHN SMITH.

BILLS OF LADING.

A *bill of lading* is a receipt from the agent or master of a vessel, that he has received the goods named therein, and an agreement for the safe carriage of the same to the port of destination, and delivery to the person to whom they are consigned. Two or three bills are usually signed, one to be retained by the agent of the vessel, and another to be forwarded to the party to whom they are shipped.

See article, "LIABILITIES OF COMMON CARRIERS."

No. 43.—Bill of Lading.

Shipped, in good order and well conditioned, by JOHN DOE, on board the *ship* called the *United States*, whereof RICHARD ROE is master, now lying in the port of *New York*, and bound for *Havre, France*. To say: *five packages of merchandise*, being marked and numbered as in the margin, and are to be delivered in the like order and condition at the port of *Havre, France* (the dangers of the seas only excepted), unto JACQUES MONTALEMBERT, or to his assigns, he or they paying freight for the said *packages* the sum of *five* dollars, with *fifty cents* primage and average accustomed.

J. M.
Havre, France.

In witness whereof, the master or purser of said vessel hath affirmed to *two* bills of lading, both of this tenor and date; one of which being accomplished, the other to stand void.

Dated in *New York*, the *first* day of *October*, one thousand eight hundred and *fifty*.

RICHARD ROE, *Master*

BONDS.

A *bond* is a written instrument under seal, acknowledging some liability, duty, or obligation, with a penalty for non-fulfilment. Fraud vitiates every instrument into which it enters.

The maker of the bond is called the *obligor*, the person to whom it is made the *obligee*.

As to what is sufficient to constitute a seal, see the respective states, titles, deeds, &c.

The amount of money first named in a bond for the payment of money is called the *penal sum*, and is usually double the amount of the condition, in order to cover interest and cost of recovery, should the conditions of payment not be complied with.

No. 44.—Bond for the Payment of Money.

Know all Men by these Presents, that I, JOHN DOE, of the *town* of *Jamaica*, in the county of *Queens*, and state of *New York*, am held and firmly bound unto RICHARD ROE, of the *city* of *Brooklyn*, in the county of *Kings*, and state of *New York*, in the sum of *two thousand four hundred* dollars, lawful money of the United States, to be paid to the said RICHARD ROE, his executors, administrators, or assigns: for which payment, well and truly to be made, I bind myself, my heirs, executors, and administrators, and each of them, firmly by these presents. Sealed with my seal. Dated the *first* day of *December*, one thousand eight hundred and *fifty*.—*

The condition of the above obligation is such, that if the above bounden JOHN DOE or his heirs, executors, or administrators, shall well and truly pay, or cause to be paid, unto the above-named RICHARD ROE, his executors, administrators, or assigns, the just and full sum of *twelve hundred dollars on the first day of May next, with interest thereon at the rate of seven per cent. per annum*—then the above obligation to be void, otherwise to remain in full force and virtue.

JOHN DOE *(seal)*.

Sealed, &c., in presence of JOHN JONES and JOHN SMITH.

No. 45.—Bond, conditioned that if the Interest is *not paid within a certain Time after it is due, the whole Sum, Principal and Interest, shall, at the option of the Obligee, be due immediately.*

Know all Men by these Presents, that I, JOHN DOE, of the *city* of *Portland*, in the county of *Cumberland*, and state of *Maine*, am held and firmly bound unto RICHARD ROE, of the *same place*, in the sum of *two thousand eight hundred* dollars, lawful money of the United States, to be paid to the said RICHARD ROE, his executors, administrators, or assigns: for which payment, well and truly to be made, I bind myself, my heirs, executors, and administrators, and every of them, firmly by these presents. Sealed with my seal. Dated the *tenth* day of *August*, one thousand eight hundred and *fifty*.

The condition of the above obligation is such, that if the above-bounden JOHN DOE, or his heirs, executors, or administrators, shall well and truly pay, or cause to be paid, unto the above-named RICHARD ROE, his executors, administrators, or assigns, the just and full sum of *one thousand four hundred* dollars on the *tenth* day of *March*, which will be in the year one thousand eight hundred and *fifty-six*, and the interest thereon, to be computed from the date hereof, at and after the rate of *six* per cent. per annum, and to be paid *quarter yearly* —then the above obligation to be void, else to remain in full force and virtue.

And it is hereby expressly agreed, that should any default be made in the payment of the said interest, or of any part thereof, on any day whereon the same is made payable, as above expressed, and should the same remain unpaid and in arrear for the space of *ten* days, then and from thenceforth, that is to say, after the lapse of the said *ten* days, the aforesaid principal sum of *one thousand four hundred* dollars, together with all arrearage of interest thereon, shall, at the option of the said RICHARD ROE, his executors, administrators, and assigns, become and be due and payable immediately thereafter, although the period above limited for the payment thereof may not then have expired, anything herein before contained to the contrary thereof in any wise notwithstanding.

Sealed and delivered in the presence of JOHN JONES, JOHN SMITH. } JOHN DOE *(seal)*.

5*

No. 46.—Bond of a Corporation.

Know all Men by these Presents, that *the president and directors of the Ascutney Bank, at* the *city* of *Cleveland,* in the county of *Cuyahoga,* and state of *Ohio,* are held and firmly bound unto John Doe, of the *village* of *Parkman,* in the county of *Geauga,* and state of *Ohio,* in the sum of *ten thousand* dollars, lawful money of the United States, to be paid to the said John Doe, his executors, administrators, or assigns: for which payment, well and truly to be made, *the president and directors of the said Ascutney Bank* bind themselves and their successors firmly by these presents. Sealed with their corporate seal. Dated the *fifth* day of *July,* one thousand eight hundred and *fifty.*

The condition of the above obligation is such, that if the above-bounden *president and directors of the Ascutney Bank* shall well and truly pay, or cause to be paid, unto the above-named John Doe, the sum of *five thousand* dollars on the *first* day of *August next,* with interest thereon at the rate of *five* per cent. per annum—then the above-written obligation to be void, otherwise to remain in full force and virtue.

RICHARD ROE, President *(corporate seal).*

Sealed and delivered in the presence of
John Jones,
John Smith.

No. 47.—Bond to be given to a Sheriff, to indemnify *him for levying upon Goods, &c., when claimed by another than the Judgment Debtor.*

Know all Men by these Presents, that we, John Doe and Richard Roe, both of the *city* of *Madison,* in the county of *Jefferson,* and state of *Indiana,* are held and firmly bound unto John Smith, sheriff of the said county of *Jefferson,* in the sum of *one thousand* dollars, lawful money of the United States, to be paid to the said John Smith, or to his certain attorney, executors, administrators, or assigns: for which payment, well and truly to be made, we bind ourselves, our and each of our heirs, executors, and administrators, jointly and severally, firmly by these presents. Sealed with our seals

Dated the *tenth* day of *June*, one thousand eight hundred and *fifty*.

Whereas, the above-bounden JOHN DOE and RICHARD ROE did obtain judgment in the *supreme court* against JOHN JONES for *three hundred* dollars, damages and costs, whereupon execution has been issued, directed, and delivered to the said JOHN SMITH, commanding him, that of the goods and chattels of the said JOHN JONES, he should cause to be made the damages and costs aforesaid. And whereas, certain goods and chattels that appear to belong to the said JOHN JONES are claimed by JAMES SHORT, of the said *city* of *Madison:*

Now, therefore, the condition of this obligation is such, that if the above-bounden JOHN DOE and RICHARD ROE shall well and truly save, keep and bear harmless, and indemnify the said JOHN SMITH, and all and every person and persons aiding and assisting him in the premises, of and from all harm, let, trouble, damage, costs, suits, actions, judgments, and executions, that shall or may at any time arise, come, or be brought against him, them, or any of them, as well for the levying and making sale under and by virtue of such execution, of all or any goods or chattels which he or they shall or may judge to belong to the said JOHN JONES, as well as in entering any shop, store, building, or other premises, for the taking of any such goods and chattels—then this obligation to be void, else to remain in full force and virtue.

Signed, sealed, and delivered, in presence of
PETER PENNY,
HIRAM JACOBS.

JOHN DOE *(seal)*.
RICHARD ROE *(seal)*.

No. 48.—Bond to Executors.

Know all Men by these Presents, that I, JOHN DOE, of the *village* of *Clinton*, in the county of *Oneida*, and state of *New York*, am held and firmly bound unto RICHARD ROE, of the *city* of *Utica*, in the county of *Oneida*, and state of *New York*, and PETER SMITH, of the *village* of *Clinton*, in the county of *Oneida*, and state of *New York*, executors of the last will and testament of PETER HAMILTON, late of the *village* of *Clinton*, in the county of *Oneida*, and state of *New York*, now deceased, and the survivor of them, his or their assigns, in the penal sum of *five thousand* dollars, lawful money of the United States, to be paid to the said executors, *or the* survivor of them, his or their assigns: for which payment, well and truly to be made, I bind myself, my heirs, executors and administrators, and every of them, firmly by these pres ents. Sealed with my seal. Dated this *first* day of *May* one thousand eight hundred and *fifty*.

Now, the condition of this obligation is such, that if the above-bounden obligor, his heirs, executors, or administrators, shall well and truly pay, or cause to be paid, unto the said Richard Roe and Peter Smith, as such executors as aforesaid, or the survivor of them, his or their assigns, the sum of *two thousand five hundred* dollars on the *first* day of *May*, one thousand eight hundred and *fifty-three*, with interest thereon at the rate of *seven* per cent. per annum—then this obligation to be void, otherwise to remain in full force, virtue, and effect.

JOHN DOE *(seal)*.

Sealed and delivered in presence of
John Smith,
John Stone.

No. 49.—Bond for a Deed.

Know all Men, &c. [*as in No.* 44 *to the* *]—

Now, the condition of this obligation is such, that if the above-bounden obligor shall, on the *tenth* day of *December next*, make, execute, and deliver, unto the said Richard Roe (provided that the said Richard Roe shall on or before that day have paid to the said obligor the sum of *twelve hundred* dollars, the price by said Richard Roe agreed to be paid therefor), a good and sufficient conveyance in fee simple, with the usual covenants, of all that certain piece or parcel of land [*here describe the land*]—then this obligation to be void, otherwise to remain in full force, virtue, and effect.

JOHN DOE *(seal)*.

Sealed and delivered
in the presence of
John Smith,
Peter Jones.

No. 50.—Bond of Treasurer or Trustee of an Association.

Know all Men by these Presents, that we, JOHN DOE, as principal, and RICHARD ROE and IRA STEARNS as sureties, all of the *city* of *Richmond*, in the county of *Henrico*, and state of *Virginia*, are held and firmly bound unto HENRY HIGGINS and THOMAS SHARPE, both of the *city* of *Richmond* aforesaid, in the sum of *one thousand* dollars, lawful money of the United States, to be paid unto the said HENRY HIGGINS and THOMAS SHARPE, or their successors in office, or their certain attorneys, executors, administrators, or assigns; to which payment, well and truly to be made, we jointly and severally bind ourselves, our heirs, executors, and administrators, firmly by these presents. Sealed with our seals, and dated the *twenty-fifth* day of *December*, one thousand eight hundred and *fifty*.

The condition of this obligation is such, that whereas the above-named JOHN DOE has been chosen by an *association*, known as the *Union Association*, treasurer [*or one of the trustees*] of said *association*, by reason whereof, and as such treasurer [*or trustee*], he will receive into his hands and possession divers sums of money, goods and chattels, and other things, the property of said *association;* and is bound to keep true and accurate accounts of said property, and of his receipts and disbursements for and on account of said *association:*

Now, therefore, if the said JOHN DOE shall well and truly perform all and singular the duties of treasurer [*or trustee*] of said *association*, for and during his official term, and until he shall deliver all the property which he may receive as such treasurer [*or trustee*] to his successor in said office, or to such other person as the said *association* or its authorized officers may direct, according to the provisions of the constitution, by laws, rules, and regulations, of said *association* now existing, or which may be by said *association* adopted; and shall keep true and just accounts of all property belonging to the said *association* that may come to his hands; and shall exhibit and submit to the said *association*, or to the persons by them thereunto appointed, his said accounts and the vouchers therefor, whenever he shall be thereto properly requested; and shall, at the expiration of his term of office, by any cause whatever, deliver up to his successor in office all the property of the said *association* that may be found to remain in his hands, and his books of accounts, and the vouchers thereunto belonging —then this obligation shall be null and void, otherwise to remain in full force and virtue.

Signed, sealed, and delivered, in presence of JOHN SMITH, JAMES SHORT.	JOHN DOE *(seal)*. RICHARD ROE *(seal)*. IRA STEARNS *(seal)*.

No. 51.—Bottomry Bond.

Know all Men by these Presents, that I, JOHN DOE, now master and commander of the *bark* or vessel called the *Isidore*, of the burden of *five hundred* tons or thereabouts, now lying at the port of *Baltimore*, am held and firmly bound unto RICHARD ROE, of the *city* of *Baltimore*, in the county of *Baltimore*, and state of *Maryland*, in the sum of *two thousand* dollars, lawful money of the United States, to be paid to the said RICHARD ROE, or to his certain attorney, executors, administrators, or assigns: for which payment, well and truly to be made, I bind myself, my heirs, executors, and administrators, and also the said vessel, her tackle, apparel, and furniture, firmly by these presents. Sealed with my seal, at the *city* of *Baltimore*, this *first* day of *November*, one thousand eight hundred and *fifty*.

Whereas, the above-bounden JOHN DOE has been obliged to take up and borrow, and has received of the said RICHARD ROE, for the use of the said vessel, and for the purpose of fitting the same for sea, the sum of *one thousand* dollars, lawful money of the United States, which sum is to be and remain as a lien and bottomry on the said vessel, her tackle, apparel, and furniture, at the rate or premium of *twenty-five* per cent. for the voyage; in consideration whereof, all risks of the seas, rivers, enemies, fires, pirates, &c., are to be on account of the said RICHARD ROE: And for the better security of the said sum and premium, the said master doth, by these presents, hypothecate and assign over to the said RICHARD ROE, his heirs, executors, administrators, and assigns, the said vessel, her tackle, apparel, and furniture. And it is hereby declared that the said vessel *Isidore* is thus hypothecated and assigned over for the security of the money so borrowed.

and taken up as aforesaid, and shall be delivered for no other use or purpose whatever, until this bond is first paid, together with the premium hereby agreed to be paid thereon.

Now, the condition of this obligation is such, that if the above-bounden JOHN DOE shall well and truly pay, or cause to be paid, unto the said RICHARD ROE, his certain attorney, executors, administrators, and assigns, the just and full sum of *one thousand* dollars, lawful money as aforesaid, being the sum borrowed, and also the premium aforesaid, at or before the expiration of *ten* days after the arrival of the said vessel at the port of *New York*—then this obligation, and the said hypothecation, to be void and of no effect, otherwise to remain in full force and virtue. Having signed and executed *two* bonds of the same tenor and date, one of which being accomplished, the other to be void and of no effect.

JOHN DOE *(seal)*.

Sealed and delivered in the presence of
PETER PEPPER,
JOHN STONE.

NOTE.—*Bottomry* is the act of borrowing money, and pledging the keel or *bottom* of the ship (that is, the ship itself) as security for the repayment of the money. The contract of bottomry is in the nature of a mortgage—the owner of a ship borrowing money to enable him to carry on a voyage, and pledging the ship as security for the money: but if the ship is lost, the lender loses the money; if she arrives safe, he is to receive back the money lent, with the interest agreed upon, although it may exceed the legal rate of interest. The tackle of the ship is also liable as well as the ship itself, and the borrower is likewise personally responsible if the ship arrive.

Respondentia is where the money is borrowed upon goods shipped, instead of the ship itself.

COMPOSITION WITH CREDITORS.

This is a contract between a debtor who is able only to pay a portion of his debts, with his creditors, whereby they agree to accept a certain sum less than the original claim; and, upon the receipt thereof, not to prosecute or trouble the debtor on account of his debt.

No. 52.—Form for Composition with Creditors.

Know all Men by these Presents, that whereas John Doe is justly indebted unto us, John Jones, Henry Smith, and Thomas Sharpe, creditors of the said John Doe, in divers sums of money, which he has become unable fully to pay and discharge: therefore we, the said creditors, do consent and agree with the said John Doe to demand less than the full amount of our respective claims, and to accept of *ten* cents for every dollar owing to each of us the said creditors of the said John Doe, in full satisfaction and discharge of our several claims and demands; the said sum of *ten* cents on a dollar to be paid to each of us, our heirs, executors, and administrators, within the space of *thirteen* months from the date hereof. And we, the creditors aforesaid, do further severally and respectively covenant and agree with the said John Doe, that he may, within the said time of *thirteen* months from the date hereof, sell and dispose of his goods and chattels, wares and merchandise, at his own free will and pleasure, for the payment of the *ten* cents on the dollar of each of our respective debts; and that neither of us will, at any time hereafter, sue, arrest, or attach the said John Doe, or his goods and chattels, for any debt now due and owing to us or any of us, provided the said John Doe does well and truly pay, or cause to be paid, the said *ten* cents for every dollar of each of our several and respective claims against him. And all and each of the covenants and agreements herein contained shall extend to and bind our several executors, administrators, and assigns.

In witness whereof, &c. [*as in No.* 25].

CONTRACTS.

A *contract* is an agreement, between two or more parties, for the performance of some certain thing by them respectively agreed upon. For forms of contracts, see under the head "AGREEMENTS."

A *charter-party* is a contract of affreightment in writing, by which the owner of a vessel lets the whole or a part of her to another for the conveyance of goods on a particular voyage, in consideration of the payment of freight.

No. 53.—Form of Charter-Party.

This Charter-Party, made and concluded upon in the *city* of *New York*, the *tenth* day of *October*, in the year one thousand eight hundred and *fifty*, between JOHN DOE, *agent for the owner and master* of the *brig Eagle*, of the *city* of *New York*, of the burden of *four hundred* tons or thereabouts, register measurement, now lying in the harbor of *Mobile*, in the state of *Alabama*, of the first part, and RICHARD ROE, *merchant*, of the *city* of *Mobile*, in the state of *Alabama*, of the second part, **Witnesseth**, that the said party of the first part, for and in consideration of the covenants and agreements hereinafter mentioned, to be kept and performed by the said party of the second part, doth covenant and agree on the freighting and chartering of the said vessel unto the said party of the second part, for a voyage from the port of *Mobile*, in the state of *Alabama*, to *Liverpool*, *England*, on the terms following, that it is to say:

First. The said party of the first part does engage that the said vessel in and during the said voyage shall be kept tight, stanch, well fitted, tackled, and provided with every requisite, and with men and provisions necessary for such a voyage.

Second. The said party of the first part does further engage that the whole of said vessel (with the exception of the cabin, the deck, and the necessary room for the accommodation of the crew, and the stowage of the sails, cables, and provisions) shall be at the sole use and disposal of the said party of the second part during the voyage aforesaid; and that no goods or merchandise whatever shall be laden on board, otherwise than from the said party of the second part, or his agent, without his consent, on pain of forfeiture of the amount of freight agreed upon for the same.

Third. The said party of the first part does further engage to take and receive on board the said vessel, during the aforesaid voyage, all such lawful goods and merchandise as the said party of the second part or his agents think proper to ship.

And the said party of the second part, for and in consideration of the covenants and agreements to be kept and performed by the said party of the first part, does covenant and agree with the said party of the first part, to charter and hire the said vessel as aforesaid, on the terms following, that is to say:

First. The said party of the second part does engage to provide and furnish to the said vessel *a sufficient cargo of freight for ballast from one port to another on her voyage.*

Second. The said party of the second part does further engage to pay to the said party of the first part, or his agent, for the charter or freight of the said vessel during the voyage aforesaid, in the manner following, that is to say:

For the voyage to Liverpool, the sum of four thousand dollars, lawful money of the United States, on the delivery of the freight aforesaid in the port of Liverpool. It is further understood and agreed that the said party of the second part, or his agent, is to pay all foreign port-charges, pilotage, and dues incurred by the vessel on her voyage, exclusive of the before-mentioned sum of four thousand dollars; the said party of the second part, or his agent, to furnish the said party of the first part sufficient money in the port aforesaid free of charge for the same.

It is further agreed between the parties to this instrument, that the said party of the second part shall be allowed for the loading and discharging of the vessel at the respective ports aforesaid, lay days as follows, that is to say: *in the port of Mobile twenty lay days, and customary despatch in the port of Liverpool.* And in case the vessel is longer detained, the said party of the second part agrees to pay to the said party of the first part at the rate of *fifty* Spanish milled dollars per day, day by day, for every day so detained, provided such detention shall happen by default of said party of the second part, or his agent.

It is also further understood and agreed, that the cargo or cargoes shall be received and delivered alongside of the vessel, within reach of her tackles, or according to the custom and usages at the ports of loading and discharging.

It is also further understood and agreed, that this charter shall commence when the vessel is ready to receive cargo at her place of loading, and notice thereof is given to the party of the second part, or his agent; *and the said party of the first part agrees to proceed with all despatch from Mobile direct to Liverpool, and there discharge the cargo aforesaid.*

To the true performance of all and every of the foregoing covenants and agreements, the said parties each to the other do hereby bind themselves, their heirs, executors, administrators, and assigns (especially the said party of the first part the vessel, her freight, tackle, and appurtenances; and the said party of the second part the merchandise to be laden on board), each to the other in the penal sum of *eight thousand* dollars.

In witness whereof, the said parties have hereunto interchangeably set their hands and seals the day and year first above written.

Sealed and delivered in the presence of
JOHN SMITH,
JOHN STONE.

JOHN DOE *(seal)*.
RICHARD ROE *(seal)*.

DEEDS AND MORTGAGES.

Strictly speaking, every instrument under seal is a deed; but, in ordinary language, a conveyance of lands is intended.

There should be a good consideration for a deed, which may be money, goods, services, or marriage.

A deed in *fee simple* is a conveyance of the absolute and entire ownership of the land.

A *warranty deed* is a conveyance in which the grantor agrees to be answerable for any defect whatever that there may be in the title.

A *quit-claim deed* is one whereby the grantor conveys away all the title (if any) that he may perchance have in the land.

A *trust-deed* is a conveyance by which the grantee takes the estate upon some trust, or for some special purpose, therein specified.

A *mortgage* is a deed of lands conditionally, and is usually given to secure the payment of money, by pledging the land of the grantor therefor. It is usual to execute a bond, bearing date on the same day with the mortgage, specifying the amount to be paid, the time when it is to be paid, and the interest agreed upon, to secure which the mortgage is given. In some states a promissory note is used instead of a bond. The description of the premises should be exact, so that they may be readily identified.

These instruments should always be sealed, subscribed by the person whose estate is conveyed, and by that person acknowledged before the proper officer.

If it be impossible to acknowledge the instrument at the time of execution, it is advisable always (and in some states requisite) that it should be witnessed by two subscribing witnesses.

The person to whom the conveyance is made should immediately have the instrument recorded in the proper office.

When a deed, mortgage, or release, is executed to two or more persons, the whole name of each should be given; and also when they are the grantors, each should sign his individual name. Never sign as a firm.

As to acknowledgments, and the rights of the wife, see the respective states. For form of satisfaction of mortgages, see "RELEASE AND SATISFACTION."

No. 54.—Simple Deed, with Warranty.

This Indenture, made the *fifth* day of *December*, in the year one thousand eight hundred and *fifty*, between JOHN DOE, of the *city* of *Detroit*, in the county of *Wayne*, and state of *Michigan*, of the first part, and RICHARD ROE, of the *same place*, of the second part—*

Witnesseth, that the said party of the first part, for and in consideration of the sum of *ten thousand* dollars, lawful money of the United States, to him duly paid before the delivery hereof, hath bargained and sold, and by these presents doth grant and convey to the said party of the second part, his heirs and assigns, for ever, all that certain piece or parcel of land, lying and being in the county of *Shiawassee*, and state of *Michigan*, and which is known and described as follows, to wit:—

The north half of the northeast quarter of section number ten of town number eight north, in range number six east, containing eighty acres more or less, together with all and singular the tenements, hereditaments, and appurtenances, and all the estate, title, and interest, of the said party of the first part therein. And the said party of the first part doth hereby covenant and agree with the said party of the second part, that at the time of the delivery hereof, the said party of the first part is the lawful owner of the premises above granted, and seized thereof in fee simple absolute, and that he will warrant and defend the above-granted premises in the quiet and peaceable possession of the said party of the second part, his heirs and assigns, for ever.

In witness whereof, I have hereunto set my hand and seal, this *fifth* day of *December*, one thousand eight hundred and *fifty*.

JOHN DOE *(seal)*.

Sealed and delivered in the presence of
JOHN SMITH, PETER JONES.

No. 55.—Simple Deed, without Warranty.

This Indenture, &c. [*as in No.* 54 *to the* *]—

Witnesseth, that the said JOHN DOE, for and in consideration of *one thousand* dollars, lawful money of the United States, to him in hand paid by the said RICHARD ROE, the receipt whereof is hereby acknowledged, hath granted, bargained, and sold, and by these presents doth grant, bargain, sell, convey, and confirm, unto the said RICHARD ROE, his heirs, executors, administrators, and assigns, for ever, all and singular that certain piece or parcel of land situate in the *town* of *Andover*, in the county of *Windham*, and state of *Vermont* [*here describe the land*], together with all and singular the tenements, hereditaments, and appurtenances, thereunto belonging; and the reversions, remainders, rents, issues, and profits thereof, and all the estate, title, and interest, of the said JOHN DOE, to the said premises, or any part thereof.

In witness whereof, &c. [*as in No.* 54].

No. 56.—Quit-claim Deed by Husband and Wife.*

This Indenture, made the *tenth* day of *April*, in the year one thousand, eight hundred and *fifty*, between JOHN DOE, of the *city* of *Nashville*, in the county of *Davidson*, and state of *Tennessee*, and SUSAN his wife, parties of the first part, and RICHARD ROE, of the *town* of *Lebanon*, in the county of *Wilson*, and state of *Tennessee*, party of the second part—†

Witnesseth, that the said parties of the first part, for and in consideration of the sum of *two thousand* dollars, lawful money of the United States, to them in hand paid by the said party of the second part, at or before the ensealing and delivery of these presents, the receipt whereof is hereby acknowledged, have remised, released, and quit-claimed, and by these presents do remise, release, and quit-claim, unto the said party of the second part, and to his heirs and assigns, for ever, all that certain piece or parcel of land lying and being situated in the *town*, &c. [*here describe the land*], together with all and singular the tenements, hereditaments,

* It will be understood that the forms in which the wife is included are also correct for a single person, by the omission of those parts which refer to the wife and her interest in the property.

and appurtenances, thereunto belonging or in anywise appertaining, and the reversion and reversions, remainder and remainders, rents, issues, and profits thereof; and also all the estate, right, title, interest, dower and right of dower, property, possession, claim, and demand whatsoever, as well in law as in equity, of the said parties of the first part, of, in, or to the above-described premises, and every part and parcel thereof with the appurtenances. **To have and to hold** all and singular the above mentioned and described premises, together with the appurtenances, unto the said party of the second part, his heirs, and assigns, for ever.

In witness whereof, the said parties of the first part have hereunto set their hands and seals the day and year first above written.

JOHN DOE *(seal)*.
SUSAN DOE *(seal)*.

Sealed and delivered in the presence of
JOHN SMITH,
JOHN JONES.

No. 57.—Deed, by Husband and Wife, with full Covenants (or Warranty).

This Indenture, &c. [*as in No.* 56 *to the* †]—

Witnesseth, that the said parties of the first part, for and in consideration of the sum of *twelve hundred* dollars, lawful money of the United States, to them in hand paid by the said party of the second part, at or before the ensealing and delivery of these presents, the receipt whereof is hereby acknowledged, and the said party of the second part, his heirs, executors, and administrators, for ever released and discharged from the same, by these presents, have granted, bargained, sold, aliened, remised, released, conveyed, and confirmed, and by these presents do grant, bargain, sell, alien, remise, release, convey, and confirm, unto the said party of the second part, and to his heirs and assigns, for ever, all that, &c. [*here describe the property*], together with all and singular the tenements, hereditaments, and appurtenances, thereunto belonging or in any wise appertaining, and the reversion and reversions, remainder and remainders, rents, issues, and profits thereof; and also all the estate, right, title, interest, dower and right of dower, property, possession, claim, and demand whatsoever, as well in law as in equity, of the said parties of the first part, of, in, and to the same, and every part and parcel thereof, with the appurtenances. To have and to hold the above granted, bargained, and described premises, with the appurtenances, unto the said party of the second part, his heirs and assigns, to his and their own proper use, benefit, and behoof, for ever.

And the said JOHN DOE, for himself, his heirs, executors, and administrators, doth covenant, grant, and agree, to and with the said party of the second part, his heirs and assigns, that the said JOHN DOE, at the time of the sealing and delivery of these presents, was lawfully seized in his own right of a good, absolute, and indefeasible estate of inheritance, in fee simple, of and in all and singular the above granted and described premises, with the appurtenances, and has good right, full power, and lawful authority, to grant, bargain, sell, and convey the same, in manner aforesaid: and that the said party of the second part, his heirs and assigns, shall and may, at all times hereafter, peaceably and quietly have, hold, use, occupy, possess, and enjoy the above-granted premises, and every part and parcel thereof, with the appurtenances, without any let, suit, trouble, molestation, eviction, or disturbance, of the said parties of the first part, their heirs or assigns, or of any other person or persons lawfully claiming or to claim the same: and that the same now are free, clear, discharged, and unencumbered, of and from all former and other grants, titles, charges, estates, judgments, taxes, assessments, and encumbrances, of what nature or kind soever: and also that the said parties of the first part and their heirs, and all and every person or persons whomsoever, lawfully or equitably deriving any estate, right, title, or interest, of, in, or to the herein before-granted premises, by, from, under, or in trust for them or either of them, shall and will, at any time or times hereafter, upon the reasonable request, and at the proper costs and charges in the law, of the said party of the second part, his heirs and assigns, make, do, and execute, or cause to be made, done, and executed, all and every such further and other lawful and reasonable acts, conveyances, and assurances in the law, for the better and more effectually vesting and confirming the premises hereby granted or so intended to be, in and to the said party of the second part, his heirs and assigns, for ever, as by the said party of the second part, his heirs or assigns, his or their counsel learned in the law, shall be reasonably advised or required. And the said JOHN DOE, his heirs, the above described and hereby granted and released premises, and every part and parcel thereof, with the appurtenances, unto the said party of the second part, his heirs and assigns, against the said parties of the first part and their heirs, and against all and every person and persons whomsoever, lawfully claiming or to claim the same, shall and will warrant and by these presents for ever defend.

In witness whereof, &c. [*as in No.* 56].

No. 58.—Deed by Executors.

This Indenture, made the *twentieth* day of *March*, one thousand eight hundred and *fifty*, between JOHN DOE, of the *city* of *Memphis*, in the county of *Shelby*, and state of *Tennessee*, and RICHARD ROE, of the *town* of *Raleigh*, of the county and state *aforesaid*, executors of the last will and testament of JOHN SMITH, late of *Raleigh*, in the county of *Shelby*, and state of *Tennessee*, deceased, parties of the first part, and JOHN JONES, of *Raleigh*, in the county of *Shelby*, and state of *Tennessee*, *farmer*, party of the second part—

Witnesseth, that the said parties of the first part, by virtue of the power and authority to them given in and by the said last will and testament, and for and in consideration of the sum of *eight hundred* dollars *and twenty-five cents*, lawful money of the United States, to them in hand paid at or before the ensealing and delivery of these presents, by the said party of the second part, the receipt whereof is hereby acknowledged, and the said party of the second part, his heirs, executors, and administrators, for ever released and discharged from the same by these presents, have granted, bargained, sold, aliened, released, conveyed, and confirmed, and by these presents do grant, bargain, sell, alien, release, convey, and confirm, unto the said party of the second part, his heirs and assigns for ever, all that certain piece or parcel of land, situate, lying, and being in the *town* of *Raleigh*, in the county of *Shelby*, and state of *Tennessee*, and which is known and described as follows [*here insert description of land*]; together with all and singular the edifices, buildings, rights, members, privileges, advantages, hereditaments, and appurtenances, to the same belonging, or in any wise appertaining; and the reversion and reversions, remainder and remainders, rents, issues, and profits thereof: and also all the estate, right, title, interest, claim, and demand whatsoever, both in law and equity, which the said testator had in his lifetime, and at the time of his decease, and which the said parties of the first part, or either of them, have or hath, by virtue of the said last will and testament, or otherwise, of, in, and to the same, and every part and parcel thereof, with the appurtenances. **To have and to hold** the said premises above mentioned and described, and hereby granted and conveyed, or intended so to be, with the appurtenances unto the said party of the second part, his heirs and assigns, to his and their only proper use, benefit, and behoof, for ever.

And the said parties of the first part, for themselves severally and respectively, and for their several and respective heirs, executors, and administrators, do severally, and not jointly, nor the one for the other or others of them, nor for the heirs, executors, administrators, or acts or deeds of the other or others of them, but each and every of them, for himself only and for his and their heirs, executors, and administrators, and their several and separate acts and deeds only, covenant, grant, promise, and agree to and with the said party of the second part, his heirs and assigns, that the said party of the second part, his heirs and assigns, shall and lawfully may from time to time, and at all times for ever hereafter, peaceably and quietly have, hold, use, occupy, possess, and enjoy, all and singular the said hereditaments and premises hereby granted and conveyed, or intended so to be, with their and every of their appurtenances, and receive and take the rents, issues, and profits thereof, to and for his and their own use and benefit, without any lawful let, suit, hinderance, molestation, interruption, or denial whatsoever, of, from, or by them the said parties of the first part, their heirs or assigns; or of, from, or by any other person or persons whomsoever lawfully claiming, or who shall or may lawfully claim hereafter, by, from, or under them, or either of them, or by, from, or under their or either of their right, title, interest, or estate: and that free and clear, and freely and clearly discharged, acquitted, and exonerated, or otherwise well and sufficiently saved, defended, kept harmless and indemnified by them, the said parties of the first part, their heirs and assigns, of, from, and against all and all manner of former and other gifts, grants, bargains, sales, mortgages, judgments, and all other charges and encumbrances whatsoever, had, made, committed, executed, or done, by them the said parties of the first part, or by, through, or with, their or either of their acts, deeds, means, consent, procurement, or privity.

In witness whereof, the said parties to these presents have hereunto interchangeably set their hands and seals the day and year first above written.

Signed, sealed, and delivered, in presence of HENRY HIGGINS, JAMES SHORT.	JOHN DOE *(seal)*. RICHARD ROE *(seal)*. JOHN SMITH *(seal)*.

No. 59.—Trust-Deed.

This Indenture, &c. [*as in No.* 54 *to* *]—

Whereas, the said JOHN DOE is desirous to make provision *for his daughter* JANE DOE, now of the age of *twenty-two years*, against future contingencies, and for her maintenance and support; and whereas, the said JOHN DOE is desirous that his said *daughter* should enjoy the proceeds, rents, issues, and income, of the real estate hereinafter more particularly described, during the term of her natural life, free from the control, liabilities, or interference, of any *husband* that she now has or may hereafter have:

Now, therefore, this Indenture witnesseth, that the said JOHN DOE, in consideration of the premises, and of the sum of *one dollar*, lawful money of the United States, to him in hand paid by the said party of the second part, the receipt whereof is hereby acknowledged, hath bargained, sold, aliened, remised, released, conveyed, and confirmed, and by these presents doth bargain, sell, alien, remise, release, convey, and confirm, unto the said party of the second part, all that certain lot, piece, or parcel of land situate, lying, and being in the *town* of, &c. [*here describe the premises*]; together with all and singular the tenements, hereditaments, and appurtenances thereunto belonging or in any wise appertaining; and the reversion and reversions, remainder and remainders, rents, issues, and profits thereof; and also all the estate, right, title, interest, property, possession, claim, and demand whatsoever, as well at law as in equity, of the said party of the first part, of, in, or to the above-described premises, and every part and parcel thereof, with the appurtenances. **To have and to**

hold all and singular the above mentioned and described premises, together with the appurtenances, unto the said RICHARD ROE, his successors and assigns—

In Trust,* and to and for the several uses, intents, and purposes, hereinafter mentioned, namely:

First. In trust to lease the same, and to take, collect, and receive the rents, issues, and profits thereof; and out of the same to keep the said premises in good order and repair, and properly insured, and pay all taxes, assessments, and charges, that may be imposed thereon.

Secondly. In trust to pay the residue of such rents, issues, and income, to my *daughter* JANE DOE, upon her sole and separate receipt, to the intent and purpose that she may enjoy, possess, and have the same, free from the control, interference, or liabilities, of any *husband* she now has or may hereafter have, during the term of her natural life.

Thirdly. In trust to convey the said land and premises to such person or persons as she, the said JANE DOE, by her last will and testament, or by an instrument in the nature of a last will and testament, subscribed by her in the presence of two credible witnesses, notwithstanding her coverture, may direct and appoint.

And the said JOHN DOE hereby declares, that upon the decease of his said daughter JANE DOE, the said trusts shall cease and determine, and the land and premises above described, shall belong, in fee simple absolute, to such person or persons as the said JANE DOE shall, as aforesaid, direct and appoint; and in default of such appointment, shall revert to the said JOHN DOE, the grantor herein named, and to his heirs, to his and their sole use, benefit, and behoof, for ever.

And the said party of the second part doth hereby signify his acceptance of this trust, and doth hereby covenant and agree, to and with the said party of the first part, faithfully to discharge and execute the same according to the true intent and meaning of these presents.

In witness whereof, &c. [*as in No.* 54].

* It will be understood that only the general idea of the manner in which a trust should be drawn can be given: the condition for which the trust is granted must depend on the nature of the property and intention of the grantor.

No. 60.—Short Form of Mortgage, with Power of Sale.

This Indenture, made the *thirtieth* day of *November*, in the year one thousand eight hundred and *fifty*, between JOHN DOE, of the *town* of *Wheatland*, in the county of *Monroe*, and state of *New York*, of the first part, and RICHARD ROE, of the *village* of *Scottville*, in the county of *Monroe*, and state of *New York*, of the second part—

Witnesseth, that the said party of the first part, in consideration of the sum of *one thousand* dollars, lawful money of the United States, to him duly paid, has sold, and by these presents does grant and convey, to the said party of the second part, all that certain piece or parcel of land, &c. [*here describe the land*], with the appurtenances, and all the estate, title, and interest, of the said party of the first part therein.

This Grant is intended as a security for the payment of *one thousand* dollars, on the *first* day of *January*, one thousand eight hundred and *fifty-five*, with interest thereon, payable *semi-annually*, at the rate of *seven* per cent. per annum, which payments, if duly made, will render this conveyance void. And if default shall be made in the payment of the principal or interest above mentioned, then the said party of the second part, and his assigns, are hereby authorized to sell the premises above granted, or so much thereof as will be necessary to satisfy the amount then due, with the costs and expenses allowed by law.

In witness whereof, &c. [*as in No.* 54].

No. 61.—Mortgage by Husband and Wife, with Interest and Insurance Clause.

This Indenture, made the *sixth* day of *July*, in the year one thousand eight hundred and *fifty*, between JOHN DOE, of the *city* of *Charleston*, in the *district* of *Charleston*, and state of *South Carolina*, and JANE his wife, parties of the first part, and RICHARD ROE, of the *same place*, party of the second part:

Whereas, the said JOHN DOE is justly indebted to the said party of the second part in the sum of *one thousand four hundred* dollars, lawful money of the United States, secured to be paid by his certain bond or obligation bearing even date with these presents, in the penal sum of *two thousand eight hundred* dollars, lawful money as aforesaid, conditioned for the payment of the said first-mentioned sum of *one thousand four hundred* dollars, lawful money as aforesaid, to the said party of the second part, his executors, administrators, or assigns, on the *tenth* day of *March*, which will be in the year of our Lord one thousand eight hundred and *fifty-six*, and the interest thereon, to be computed from *the date hereof*, at and after the rate of *six* per cent. per annum, and to be paid *quarter yearly:* And it is thereby expressly agreed, that should any default be made in the payment of the said interest, or of any part thereof, on any day whereon the same is made payable, as above expressed, and should the same remain unpaid and in arrear for the space of *ten* days, then and from thenceforth, that is to say, after the lapse of the said *ten* days, the aforesaid principal sum of *one thousand four hundred* dollars with all arrearage of interest thereon, shall, at the option of the said party of the second part, his executors, administrators, or assigns, become and be due and payable immediately thereafter, although the period above limited for the payment thereof may not then have expired, anything therein before contained to the contrary thereof in any wise notwithstanding: as by the said bond or obligation, and the condition thereof, reference being thereunto had, may more fully appear.*

Now this Indenture witnesseth, that the said parties of the first part, for the better securing the payment of the said sum of money mentioned in the condition of the said bond or obligation, with interest thereon, according to the true intent and meaning thereof, and also for and in consideration of the sum of *one dollar*, to them in hand paid by the said party of the second part, at or before the ensealing and delivery of these presents, the receipt whereof is hereby acknowledged, have granted, bargained, sold, aliened, released, conveyed, and confirmed, and by these presents do grant, bargain, sell, alien, release, convey, and confirm, unto the said party of the second part, and to his heirs and assigns for ever, all that certain lot, piece, or parcel of ground, situate, lying, and being in the *district aforesaid*, and which may be better known and described as follows, namely: *Beginning at a*

* Bond No. 45 has been drawn to correspond with this mortgage, and should accompany it, to make the papers complete.

*post planted on the northerly side of the highway leading from the said city of Charleston to Palmetto bridge distant two hundred and fifty feet easterly from the easterly side of John Smith's stone mill; thence running north twenty-five degrees east thirty chains, to a stone there planted; thence east sixty-five degrees south thirty-five chains; thence south twenty-five degrees west twenty-five chains, to the said northerly side of the said highway; thence westerly along the northerly side of the highway thirty-six chains, more or less, to the place of beginning, containing by admeasurement ten acres more or less:** together with all and singular the tenements, hereditaments, and appurtenances, thereunto belonging or in any wise appertaining; and the reversion and reversions, remainder and remainders, rents, issues, and profits thereof: and also all the estate, right, title, interest, dower and right of dower, property, possession, claim, and demand whatsoever, as well in law as in equity, of the said parties of the first part, of, in, and to the same, and every part and parcel thereof, with the appurtenances. **To have and to hold** the above granted and described premises, with the appurtenances, unto the said party of the second part, his heirs and assigns, to his and their own proper use, benefit, and behoof, for ever: PROVIDED ALWAYS, and these presents are upon this express condition, that if the said parties of the first part, their heirs, executors, or administrators, shall well and truly pay unto the said party of the second part, his executors, administrators, or assigns, the said sum of money mentioned in the condition of the said bond or obligation, and the interest thereon, at the time and in the manner mentioned in the said condition, according to the true intent and meaning thereof, that then these presents, and the estate hereby granted, shall cease, determine, and be void:

And the said JOHN DOE, for himself, his heirs, executors, and administrators, doth covenant and agree to pay unto the said party of the second part, his executors, administrators, or assigns, the said sum of money, and interest, as mentioned above, and expressed in the condition of the said bond.

[And it is also agreed by and between the parties to these presents, that the said parties of the first part shall and will keep the buildings erected and to be erected upon the lands

* This form of describing property is that usually adopted in the older states. The description in No. 54 applies to lands which have been surveyed by the general government.

above conveyed, insured against loss and damage by fire, by insurers and in an amount approved by the said party of the second part, and assign the policy and certificates thereof to the said party of the second part; and in default thereof, it shall be lawful for the said party of the second part to effect such insurance, and the premium and premiums paid for effecting the same shall be a lien on the said mortgaged premises, added to the amount of the said bond or obligation, and secured by these presents, and payable on demand with interest at the rate of *seven* per cent. per annum.]*

In witness whereof, the parties to these presents have hereunto set their hands and seals the day and year first above written.

Signed, sealed, and delivered, in presence of
PETER PENNY,
HIRAM JACOBS.

JOHN DOE *(seal)*.
JANE DOE *(seal)*.

No. 62.—Mortgage to Executors.

This Indenture, made the *tenth* day of *April*, in the year one thousand eight hundred and *fifty*, between JOHN DOE, of the *city* of *Savannah*, in the county of *Chatham*, and state of *Georgia*, of the first part, and RICHARD ROE and JOHN JONES, both of the *town* of *Milledgeville*, in the county of *Baldwin*, and state of *Georgia*, executors of the last will and testament of JOHN SMITH, late of *Milledgeville aforesaid*, of the second part:

Whereas, the said JOHN DOE is justly indebted to the said parties of the second part in the sum of *ten thousand* dollars, lawful money of the United States, secured to be paid by his certain bond or obligation, bearing even date with these presents, in the penal sum of *twenty thousand* dollars, lawful money as aforesaid, conditioned for the payment of the said first-mentioned sum of *ten thousand* dollars, on the *first* day of *January*, in the year one thousand eight hundred and *fifty six*, with interest thereon at the rate of *six* per cent. per annum, payable *semi-annually*, as by the said bond or obligation and the condition thereof, reference being thereunto had, may more fully appear.

* This insurance clause may be omitted at pleasure.

Now this Indenture witnesseth, that the said party of the first part, for the better securing the payment of the said sum of money mentioned in the condition of the said bond or obligation, with interest thereon, according to the true intent and meaning thereof, and also for and in consideration of the sum of *one dollar* to him in hand paid by the said parties of the second part, at or before the ensealing and delivery of these presents, the receipt whereof is hereby acknowledged, has granted, bargained, sold, aliened, released, conveyed, and confirmed, and by these presents doth grant, bargain, sell, alien, release, convey, and confirm, unto the said parties of the second part, and the survivors and survivor, and their assigns, for ever, all that, &c. [*here describe the property mortgaged*]; together with all and singular the tenements, hereditaments, and appurtenances, thereunto belonging or in any wise appertaining, and the reversion and reversions, remainder and remainders, rents, issues, and profits thereof: and also all the estate, right, title, interest, property, possession, claim, and demand whatsoever, as well in law as in equity, of the said party of the first part, of, in, and to the same, and every part and parcel thereof, with the appurtenances. **To have and to hold** all and singular the above granted, bargained, and described premises, with the appurtenances, unto the said parties of the second part, the survivors and survivor, and their assigns, to their only proper use, benefit, and behoof, for ever: PROVIDED ALWAYS, and these presents are upon this express condition, that if the said party of the first part, his heirs, executors, or administrators, shall well and truly pay unto the said parties of the second part, the survivors or survivor, or their assigns, the said sum of money mentioned in the condition of the said bond or obligation, and the interest thereon, at the time and in the manner mentioned in the said condition, according to the true intent and meaning thereof, that then these presents, and the estate hereby granted, shall cease, determine, and be null and void.

And the said JOHN DOE, for himself, his heirs, executors, and administrators, doth covenant and agree to pay unto the said parties of the second part, the survivors or survivor, or their assigns, the said sum of money, and interest, as mentioned above, and expressed in the condition of the said bond.

In witness whereof, &c. [*as in No.* 54].

No. 63.—Mortgage to secure a Note.

This Indenture, made the *twelfth* day of *October*, in the year of our Lord one thousand eight hundred and *fifty*, between John Doe, of *Iowa City*, in the county of *Johnson*, and state of *Iowa*, of the first part, and Richard Roe, of the *town* of *Galena*, in the county of *Jo Daviess*, and state of *Illinois*, of the second part:

Witnesseth, that the said party of the first part, in consideration of the sum of *seven hundred and ten* dollars, lawful money of the United States, to him in hand paid, the receipt whereof is hereby acknowledged, hath granted, bargained, sold, aliened, remised, released, conveyed and confirmed, and by these presents doth grant, bargain, sell, alien, remise, release, convey, and confirm, unto the said party of the second part, and to his heirs and assigns for ever, all that, &c. [*here describe the property mortgaged*], together with all and singular the tenements, hereditaments, and appurtenances, thereunto belonging or in any wise appertaining, and the reversion and reversions, remainder and remainders, rents, issues, and profits thereof; and also all the estate, right, title, interest, claim, and demand whatsoever, as well in law as in equity, of the said party of the first part, of, in, and to the same. **To have and to hold** the above granted and described premises, with the appurtenances, unto the said party of the second part, his heirs and assigns, to his and their own proper use, benefit, and behoof, for ever: Provided always, and these presents are upon this condition, that if the said party of the first part shall well and truly pay his certain promissory note, bearing *even date herewith*, given to the said party of the second part for the sum of *seven hundred and ten* dollars, lawful money as aforesaid, according to the tenor of said note, then these presents shall become void, and the estate hereby granted shall cease and utterly determine.

In witness whereof, the said party of the first part to these presents has hereunto set his hand and seal the day and year first above written.

JOHN DOE *(seal).*

Sealed and delivered in the presence of
John Smith,
John Jones.

No. 64.—Mortgage on Lease, with Covenant to Insure.

This Indenture, made the *seventh* day of *November*, in the year one thousand eight hundred and *fifty*, between John Doe, of the *city* of *New York*, in the county of *New York*, and state of *New York*, and Richard Roe, of the *same place*, parties of the first part, and John Smith, of the *village* of *Williamsburgh*, in the county of *Kings*, and state of *New York*, of the second part:

Whereas, John Jones did, by a certain indenture of lease, bearing date the *first* day of *August*, in the year one thousand eight hundred and *fifty*, demise, lease, and to farm let, unto the said parties of the first part, and to their executors, administrators, and assigns, all and singular the premises hereinafter mentioned and described, together with their appurtenances: **To have and to hold** the same unto the said parties of the first part, and to their executors, administrators, and assigns, for and during and until the full end and term of *twenty-one* years, from the *first* day of *August last*, and fully to be complete and ended, yielding and paying therefor unto the said John Jones, and to his heirs, executors, administrators, or assigns, the yearly rent or sum of *one hundred* dollars: and whereas, the said parties of the first part are justly indebted to the said party of the second part, in the sum of *five hundred* dollars, lawful money of the United States, secured to be paid by their certain bond or obligation bearing even date with these presents, in the penal sum of *one thousand* dollars, lawful money as aforesaid, conditioned for the payment of the first-mentioned sum of *five hundred* dollars, as by the said bond or obligation and the condition thereof, reference being thereunto had, may more fully appear:

Now this Indenture witnesseth, that the said parties of the first part, for the better securing the payment of the said sum of money mentioned in the condition of the said bond or obligation, with interest thereon, according to the true intent and meaning thereof, and also for and in consideration of the sum of *one dollar*, to them in hand paid by the said party of the second part, at or before the ensealing and delivery of these presents, the receipt whereof is hereby acknowledged, have granted, bargained, sold, assigned, transferred, and set over, and by these presents do grant, bargain, sell, assign, transfer, and set over, unto the said party of the second part, all that certain piece, parcel, or lot of land, situate in the *city* of *New York*, in the county of *New York*, and state of *New York*, and which is known and described as follows, namely [*here describe the land*], together with all and singular the edifices, buildings, rights, members, privileges, and appurtenances, thereunto belonging or in any wise appertaining: and also all the estate, right, title, interest, term of years yet to come and unexpired, property, possession, claim, and demand whatsoever, as well in law as in equity, of the said parties of the first part, of, in, and to the said demised premises, and every part and parcel thereof, with the appurtenances: and also the said indenture of lease, and every clause, article, and condition, therein expressed and contained. **To have and to hold** the said indenture of lease, and other hereby granted premises, unto the said party of the second part, his executors, administrators, and assigns, to his and their only proper use, benefit, and behoof, for and during all the rest, residue, and remainder, of the said term of years yet to come and unexpired: subject, nevertheless, to the rents, covenants, conditions, and provisions, in the said indenture of lease mentioned: PROVIDED ALWAYS, and these presents are upon this express condition, that if the said parties of the first part shall well and truly pay unto the said party of the second part the said sum of money mentioned in the condition of the said bond or obligation, and the interest thereon, at the time and in the manner mentioned in the said condition, according to the true intent and meaning thereof, that then and from thenceforth these presents, and the estate hereby granted, shall cease, determine, and be utterly null and void, anything herein before contained to the contrary in any wise notwithstanding.

And the said parties of the first part do hereby covenant, grant, promise, and agree to and with the said party of the second part, that they shall well and truly pay unto the said party of the second part, the said sum of money mentioned in the condition of the said bond or obligation, and the interest thereon, according to the condition of the said bond or obligation; and that the said premises hereby conveyed now are free and clear of all encumbrances whatsoever, and that they have good right and lawful authority to convey the same in manner and form hereby conveyed: and if default shall be made in the payment of the said sum of money above mentioned, or in the interest which shall accrue thereon, or of any part of either, that then and from thenceforth it shall be lawful for the said party of the second part, and his assigns, to sell, transfer, and set over, all the rest, residue, and remainder, of the said term of years then yet to come, and all other the right, title, and interest, of the said parties of the first part, of, in, and to the same, at public auction: and as the attorney of the said parties of the first part, for that purpose by these presents duly authorized, constituted, and appointed, to make, seal, execute, and deliver to the purchaser or purchasers thereof, a good and sufficient assignment, transfer, or other conveyance in the law, for the same premises, with the appurtenances; and out of the money arising from such sale, to retain the principal and interest which shall then be due on the said bond or obligation, together with the cost and charges of advertisement and sale of the same premises, rendering the overplus of the purchase money (if any there shall be) unto the said parties of the first part, or their assigns; which sale, so to be made, shall be a perpetual bar, both in law and equity, against the said parties of the first part, and against all persons claiming or to claim the premises, or any part thereof, by, from, or under them, or any of them.

[And it is also agreed by and between the parties to these presents, that the said parties of the first part shall and will keep the buildings erected and to be erected upon the lands above conveyed, insured against loss and damage by fire, by insurers, and in an amount approved by the said party of the second part, and assign the policy and certificates thereof to the said party of the second part; and in default thereof, it shall be lawful for the said party of the second part to effect such insurance, and the premium and premiums paid for effecting the same shall be a lien on the said mortgaged premises, added to the amount of the said bond or obligation, and secured by these presents, and payable on demand, with interest, at the rate of *seven* per cent. per annum.]*

In witness whereof, the parties of the first part to these presents have hereunto set their hands and seals the day and year first above written.

Sealed and delivered in the presence of John Gates, John Stone.	JOHN DOE *(seal)*. RICHARD ROE *(seal)*.

* This clause can be omitted when not required.

DOWER.

Dower is the interest which the law allows a wife in the lands of her husband, in the event of her surviving him. It is generally the right to have the one third part in value of the lands of her husband set off to her for her use during her natural life, but which she can not dispose of for a longer period than her life. The rights of the wife in personal property depend on the statute regulations of the states.

If the husband by his will devise a legacy to her in lieu of her dower, she has the right to choose which she will take, the dower or the legacy.

In case of an exchange of lands, the widow must elect whether she will take her dower in the lands given in exchange or in those taken in exchange.

An *assignment of dower* is a conveyance, by the heirs, of a certain part of the lands to the widow for life, in lieu and satisfaction of her dower interest in the whole.

Never take a conveyance of real estate from a married man without seeing that his wife joins in the conveyance, and properly acknowledges it, according to the laws of your state, before the proper officer. If she be not twenty-one years of age, she can not bar her right of dower, in which case it will be of no use for her to join in the conveyance.

As to acknowledgments by the husband and wife, see the respective states.

A female wishing to secure the property she may possess, so as to enjoy the benefit of it after marriage, free from the control and liabilities of her husband, can effect her purpose by conveying it to a third person in trust for her benefit.

If a husband wishes to convey property to a wife, he can do so by conveying to some friend in trust for her benefit. Such a conveyance would be set aside on the application of creditors whose rights were prejudiced by it, but they will secure the property to the wife against everybody else.

No. 65.—Assignment of Dower.

This Indenture, made the *thirtieth* day of *November*, in the year one thousand eight hundred and *fifty*, between JOHN DOE, of the *town* of *Morristown*, in the county of *Morris*, and state of *New Jersey*, and RICHARD DOE, of the *town* of *Rahway*, in the county of *Essex*, and state of *New Jersey*, sole heirs of WILLIAM DOE, late of *Morristown aforesaid*, now deceased, parties of the first part, and SUSAN DOE, of *Morristown aforesaid*, widow and relict of the said WILLIAM DOE, deceased, of the other part:

Whereas, the said WILLIAM DOE was seized at the time of his decease in fee simple of certain lands and tenements, which, upon his decease aforesaid, descended to the said JOHN DOE and RICHARD DOE, his sole heirs at law—

Now this Indenture witnesseth, that the said JOHN DOE and RICHARD DOE have set off and assigned, and by these presents do set off and assign, unto the said SUSAN DOE, all that, &c. [*here describe the premises assigned*]: **To have and to hold** the same, with all the tenements and appurtenances thereunto belonging, unto the said SUSAN DOE, for and during the term of her natural life, as and for her dower, and in lieu of and full satisfaction of all her dower and claim of dower, in the lands of which the said WILLIAM DOE died seized.

And the said SUSAN DOE hereby signifies her acceptance of the premises so set off and assigned to her, as and for her dower and in full satisfaction of all her dower and claim of dower in the lands whereof the said WILLIAM DOE, her late husband, died seized.

In witness whereof, the parties to these presents have hereunto set their hands and seals the day and year first above written.

Signed, sealed, and delivered, in presence of HENRY HIGGINS, JAMES SHORT.	JOHN DOE *(seal)*. RICHARD DOE *(seal)*. SUSAN DOE *(seal)*.

No. 66.—Release of Dower.

To all to whom these Presents shall come, SUSAN DOE, of the *city* of *Pittsburgh*, in the county of *Allegany*, and state of *Pennsylvania*, widow and relict of JOHN DOE, late of the *same place*, deceased, sends greeting: KNOW YE, that the said SUSAN DOE, the party of the first part to these presents, for and in consideration of the sum of *five hundred* dollars, lawful money of the United States, to her in hand paid at or before the ensealing and delivery of these presents, by RICHARD DOE, of the *city* of *Wheeling*, in the county of *Ohio*, and state of *Virginia*, of the second part, the receipt whereof is hereby acknowledged, hath granted, remised, released, and for ever quit-claimed, and by these presents doth grant, remise, release and for ever quit-claim, unto the said party of the second part, his heirs and assigns for ever, all the dower and thirds, right and title of dower and thirds, and all other right, title, interest, property, claim, and demand whatsoever, in law and equity, of her, the said party of the first part, of, in, and to all that certain piece or parcel of land, &c. [*here describe the premises*]; so that she, the said party of the first part, her heirs, executors, administrators, or assigns, nor any other person or persons, for her, them, or any of them, shall not have, claim, challenge, or demand, or pretend to have, claim, challenge, or demand, any dower or thirds, or any other right, title, claim, or demand whatsoever, of, in, and to the same, or any part or parcel thereof, in whosoever hands, seisin, or possession, the same may or can be, and thereof and therefrom shall be utterly barred and excluded for ever by these presents.

In witness whereof, the said party of the first part to these presents hath hereunto set her hand and seal, the *first* day of *November*, in the year of our Lord one thousand eight hundred and *fifty*.

SUSAN DOE (*seal*).

Sealed and delivered in the presence of
PETER PEPPER,
JOHN STONE.

LANDLORD AND TENANT.

A *landlord* is one who lets or leases property.

A *tenant* is the person to whom it is leased.

A *lease* is a contract whereby the owner of property conveys the use of it to another for a limited time, at a stipulated rent or consideration, payable at specified periods. In drawing a lease, care should be had that all the conditions and liabilities on which the premises are granted and taken are clearly specified in it.

An *under-lease* is the contract whereby a tenant leases his leasehold property to some third person, who is called an *under-tenant.*

Leases should be in writing, They are of four kinds, namely :—

—— *Lease for years ;*
—— *Lease for life ;*
—— *Lease at will ;*
—— *Lease by sufferance ;*

A *lease for years* is a lease for a certain number of years specified in the lease.

A *lease for life* is a lease for either the life of the tenant, or of some other person or persons.

A *lease at will* is where the tenantry exists only during the will of either of the parties.

A *lease by sufferance* is when the tenant's lease has expired, and he continues to remain in possession. He is then tenant by the *sufferance* of the landlord.

No. 67.—Short Form of Lease.

This Indenture, made the *first* day of *April*, in the year one thousand eight hundred and *fifty*, between John Doe, of the *city* of *New York*, in the county of *New York*, and state of *New York*, of the first part, and Richard Roe, of the *same place*, of the second part—*

Witnesseth, that the said party of the first part hath letten, and by these presents doth grant, demise, and to farm let, unto the said party of the second part, all that, &c. [*here describe the premises intended to be let*], with the appurtenances, for the term of *twenty years*, from the *first* day of *May*, one thousand eight hundred and *fifty*, at the yearly rent or sum of *two hundred* dollars, to be paid in equal *quarter yearly* payments. And it is agreed that if any rent shall be due and unpaid, or if default shall be made in any of the covenants herein contained, then it shall be lawful for the said party of the first part to re-enter the said premises, and to remove all persons therefrom.

And the said party of the second part doth covenant to pay to the said party of the first part the said yearly rent as herein specified, namely, in *quarter yearly* payments *on the first day of August, November, February, and May*, in each and every year: and that at the expiration of the said term, the said party of the second part will quit and surrender the premises hereby demised in as good state and condition as reasonable use and wear thereof will permit, damages by the elements excepted: and the said party of the first part doth covenant that the said party of the second part, on paying the said yearly rent, and performing the covenants aforesaid, shall and may peaceably and quietly have, hold, and enjoy, the said demised premises for the term aforesaid.

In witness whereof, we have hereunto set our hands and seals, this *first* day of *April*, one thousand eight hundred and *fifty*.

Sealed and delivered in the presence of John Smith, Peter Jones.	JOHN DOE *(seal)*. RICHARD ROE *(seal)*.

No. 68.—Lease: Tenant to pay Taxes, and not to underlet without Consent of the Landlord, under his Hand and Seal.

This Indenture, &c. [*as in No.* 67 *to* *]—

Witnesseth, that the said party of the first part, in consideration of the rents and covenants hereinafter reserved and contained, on the part and behalf of the said party of the second part, to him, his executors, administrators, and assigns, to be paid, kept, and performed, hath granted, demised, and to farm let, and by these presents doth grant, demise, and to farm let, unto the said party of the second part, all that, &c. [*here describe the property*]. **To have and to hold** the said above mentioned and described premises unto the said party of the second part, his executors, administrators, and assigns, from the *first* day of *May*, in the year of our Lord one thousand eight hundred and *fifty*, for and during, and until the full end and term of *five* years, from thence next ensuing, and fully to be complete and ended; yielding and paying for the same unto the said party of the first part, or to his heirs or assigns, the rent or sum of *three hundred* dollars, lawful money of the United States, yearly and every year, during the said term, in equal *quarter yearly* payments, to be made on the first day of *August*, *November*, *February*, *and May*, in each and every year, during the term hereby demised, the first payment to be made on the first day of *August* next: PROVIDED ALWAYS, that if it shall happen that the said yearly rent or any part thereof, shall not be paid on any day on which the same ought to be paid, as aforesaid, then, and at all times thereafter, it shall and may be lawful for the said party of the first part, his heirs and assigns, into the said demised premises, or any part thereof, in the name of the whole, to re-enter and to re-possess, have, and enjoy the same again, as of his or their former estate and interest therein, anything herein contained to the contrary in any wise notwithstanding.

And the said party of the second part, for himself, his executors, administrators, and assigns, doth by these presents covenant and grant, to and with the said party of the first part, his heirs and assigns, in manner following, that is to say: that he, the said party of the second part, his executors, administrators, and assigns, shall and will, during the term hereby demised, well and truly pay unto the said party of the first part, his heirs or assigns, the said yearly rent hereby reserved, at the days and times herein before limited for the payment thereof, without fraud or delay.

And also, that he, the said party of the second part, his executors, administrators, or assigns, shall and will, at his and their own proper costs and charges, bear, pay, and discharge, all such duties, taxes, assessments, and payments, extraordinary as well as ordinary, as shall during the time hereby demised be laid, levied, assessed, or imposed on, or grow due or payable out of, or for, or by reason of the said demised premises, or any part thereof: and also, that he, the said party of the second part, himself, his executors, administrators, or assigns, or any of them, shall not, nor will, at any time or times hereafter, during the term hereby granted, lease, let, or demise, all or any part of the said premises hereby demised, nor assign, transfer, or make over the same, or this present lease, or any of his or their term or time therein to any person or persons whomsoever, without the consent of the said party of the first part, his heirs or assigns, in writing, under his or their seal, for that purpose first had and obtained, anything herein before contained to the contrary thereof in any wise notwithstanding: and also that he, the said party of the second part, his executors, administrators, or assigns, or some or one of them, shall and will, on the last day of the term hereby demised, or other sooner determination of the estate hereby granted, well and truly deliver up the said hereby demised premises, in good and sufficient order, into the possession of the said party of the first part, his heirs or assigns, without fraud or delay.

And provided further, and this present lease is upon this express condition, that if the said party of the second part, his executors, administrators, or assigns, at any time during the term hereby granted, shall fail in the performance of any or either of the covenants, conditions, or provisoes, in these presents contained, which, on the part and behalf of the said party of the second part, his executors, administrators, and assigns, are or ought to be observed, performed, fulfilled, and kept; then, and at all times thereafter, it shall and may be lawful for the said party of the first part, his heirs and assigns, into the said demised premises, or any part thereof, in the name of the whole, to re-enter and re-possess, have, and enjoy the same again, as of their former estate and interest therein, anything herein contained to the contrary in any wise notwithstanding.—**In witness whereof,** &c. [*as in No.* 67].

No. 69.—Agreement to Let, with Covenant not to Underlet.

This Agreement, made the *sixteenth* day of *February*, in the year one thousand eight hundred and *fifty-one*, between JOHN DOE, of the *city* of *Brooklyn*, in the county of *Kings*, and state of *New York*, of the first part, and RICHARD ROE, of the *same place*, of the second part—

Witnesseth, that the said party of the first part hath agreed to let, and hereby doth let, and the said party of the second part hath agreed to take, and hereby doth take, *that certain lot or parcel of land lying and being situated on the north side of Franklin street, known and at present numbered as twenty-one, in the third ward of the city of Brooklyn aforesaid, together with the two-story brick dwelling and other appurtenances thereunto belonging*, for the term of *one year*, to commence on the *first* day of *May*, one thousand eight hundred and *fifty-one*, and to end on the *first* day of *May*, one thousand eight hundred and *fifty-two*.

And the said party of the second part hereby covenants and agrees to pay unto the said party of the first part the *yearly* rent or sum of *three hundred* dollars, payable *quarterly* on the *first days of August, November, February, and May, in each year*, and to quit and surrender the premises at the expiration of the said term, in as good state and condition as reasonable use and wear thereof will permit, damages by the elements excepted. And the said party of the second part further covenants that he will not assign, let, or underlet, the whole or any part of the said premises, without the written consent of the said party of the first part, under the penalty of forfeiture and damages; and that he will not occupy the said premises, nor permit the same to be occupied for any business deemed extra-hazardous without the like consent, under the like penalty: and the said party of the second part further covenants that he will permit the said party of the first part or his agent to enter said premises for the purpose of making repairs or alterations, and also to show the premises to persons wishing to hire or purchase; and on and after the first day of February next will permit the usual notice of "to let" or "for sale" to be placed upon the walls of said premises, and remain thereon, without hinderance or molestation: and also, that if the said premises or any part thereof shall become vacant during the said term, the said party of the first part may re-enter the same, by either force or otherwise, without being liable to any prosecution therefor; and re-let the said premises as the agent of the said party of the second part, and receive the rent thereof, applying the same, first to the payment of such expense as he may be put to in re-entering, and then to the payment of the rent due by these presents; and the balance (if any) to be paid over to the said party of the second part.

And the said party of the second part hereby further covenants that if any default be made in the payment of the said rent, or any part thereof, at the times above specified, or if default be made in the performance of any of the covenants or agreements herein contained, the said hiring, and the relation of landlord and tenant, at the option of the said party of the first part, shall wholly cease and determine; and the said party of the first part shall and may re-enter the said premises, and remove all persons therefrom; and the said party of the second part hereby expressly waives the service of any notice in writing of intention to re-enter.

In witness whereof, &c. [*as in No.* 67].

In consideration of the letting of the premises above mentioned to the above-named Richard Roe, I do hereby covenant and agree, to and with the party of the first part above named, and his legal representatives, that if default shall at any time be made by the said Richard Roe in the payment of the rent and performance of the covenants above contained on his part to be paid and performed, that I will well and truly pay the said rent, or any arrears thereof, that may remain due unto the said party of the first part, and also all damages that may arise in consequence of the nonperformance of said covenants, or either of them, without requiring notice of any such default from the said party of the first part.

Witness my hand and seal, this *sixteenth* day of *February*, one thousand eight hundred and *fifty-one*.

THOMAS SHARPE.

Witness { John Stone,
John Smith.

No. 70.—Tenant's Agreement.*

This is to Certify, that I have hired and taken of JOHN SMITH, of the *village* of *Smithtown*, in the county of *Saginaw*, and state of *Michigan, a house and lot known as number twenty-one, Smith street, in the village of Smithtown aforesaid*, for the term of *one year* from the *first* day of *June*, one thousand eight hundred and *fifty*, at the yearly rent of *two hundred* dollars, payable *quarter yearly*. And I hereby promise to make punctual payment of the rent in manner aforesaid, and quit and surrender the premises at the expiration of the said term, in as good state and condition as reasonable use and wear thereof will permit, damages by the elements excepted, and engage not to let or underlet the whole or any part of the said premises, without the written consent of the landlord, under the penalty of forfeiture and damages; and also not to occupy the said premises for any business deemed extra-hazardous without the like consent, under the like penalty.

Given under my hand and seal, the *tenth* day of *May*, one thousand eight hundred and *fifty*. JOHN DOE *(seal)*.

Witness { JAMES SHORT,
JOHN JONES.

No. 71.—Landlord's Agreement.

This is to Certify, that I have let and rented unto JOHN DOE, of the *village* of *Smithtown*, in the county of *Saginaw*, and state of *Michigan*, my *house and lot known as number twenty-one, Smith street, in the village of Smithtown aforesaid*, for the term of *one year* from the *first* day of *June*, one thousand eight hundred and *fifty*, at the yearly rent of *two hundred* dollars, payable *quarter yearly*. The premises are not to be used or occupied for any business deemed extra-hazardous, on account of fire, nor shall the same or any part thereof be let or underlet without the written consent of the landlord, under the penalty of forfeiture and damages.

Given under my hand and seal, the *tenth* day of *May*, one thousand eight hundred and *fifty*. JOHN SMITH.

Witness { JAMES SHORT,
JOHN JONES.

* If a surety is required, as security for the payment of the rent, the one appended to No. 69 can be added.

No. 72.—Agreement for Letting, with Mortgage on Personal Property to secure the Rent.

This Agreement, made the *seventh* day of *July*, in the year one thousand eight hundred and *fifty*, between JOHN DOE, of the *city* of *Boston*, in the county of *Suffolk*, and state of *Massachusetts*, of the first part, and RICHARD ROE, of the *same place*, of the second part—

Witnesseth, that the said party of the first part hath agreed to let, and hereby doth let, and the said party of the second part hath agreed to take, and hereby doth take [*here describe the premises*], for the term of *three years*, to commence on the *first* day of *August*, one thousand eight hundred and *fifty*, and to end on the *thirty-first* day of *July*, one thousand eight hundred and *fifty-three*.

And the said party of the second part hereby covenants and agrees to pay unto the said party of the first part the *yearly* rent or sum of *four hundred* dollars, payable *quarter yearly*, that is to say, on the *first day of November, February, May, and August*, of each and every year, and to quit and surrender the premises at the expiration of the said term, in as good state and condition as reasonable use and wear thereof will permit, damages by the elements excepted; and not assign, let, or underlet, the whole or any part of the said premises, or occupy the same for any business deemed extra-hazardous, without the written consent of the said party of the first part, under the penalty of forfeiture and damages.

And the said party of the second part hereby further covenants, that if any default be made in the payment of the said rent, or any part thereof, at the times above specified, the said party of the first part shall and may re-enter the said premises, and remove all persons therefrom.

And the said party of the second part, for the consideration aforesaid, and for the sum of *one dollar* to him paid by the said party of the first part, doth grant, bargain, and sell, unto the said parties of the first part, all and singular the goods and chattels mentioned in the schedule hereto annexed.* **To have and to hold** the said goods and chattels for ever: UPON CONDITION, that if the said party of the second part shall well and truly pay, or cause to be paid, unto

* See page 50 for plan of schedule.

the said party of the first part the rent above reserved punctually, at the several times when the same shall become due as aforesaid, then the said bargain and sale shall be null and void. But in case default shall be made in the payment of the said rent, or any part thereof, at the several times mentioned as aforesaid, and shall remain unpaid five days after the same becomes due and payable, then it shall be lawful for the said party of the first part to take possession of the said goods and chattels, wherever the same may be found, and to sell the same at public sale (first giving three days' notice of the time and place of such sale), or so much thereof as may be necessary to pay the rent due, and the balance of rent for the whole unexpired term, whether due or not due, and all costs and expenses that may have accrued on account thereof, rendering the remaining goods and chattels, and the surplus money from said sale, if any there shall be, unto the said party of the second part.

And it is further agreed between the parties to these presents, that in case the said party of the second part shall sell, assign, or dispose of, or attempt to sell, assign, or otherwise dispose of the said goods and chattels, or shall attempt to remove the same from the premises hereby demised to the said party of the second part, it shall and may be lawful for the said party of the first part to take possession of the same, and retain them in his possession until the said rent shall be paid, or until default in the payment thereof. But until default be made in the payment of the said rent, the said goods and chattels (unless the said party of the second part shall sell, or attempt to sell or remove the same, as aforesaid) shall remain in the possession of the said party of the second part.

In witness whereof, the parties to these presents have hereunto set their hands and seals the day and year first above written.

Signed, sealed, and delivered, in presence of
PETER PENNY,
HIRAM JACOBS.

JOHN DOE *(seal)*.
RICHARD ROE *(seal)*.

LETTER OF CREDIT.

This is a letter frequently given by a person of known responsibility to a friend, to enable that friend to procure goods on time. It is usually somewhat in this form:—

No. 73.—Form of Letter of Credit.

Hamilton, Canada West,
October 15, 1850.

Messrs. John Smith & Co.—*Gentlemen:* Please deliver to Richard Roe, of *this place*, goods, silks, and merchandise, to any amount not exceeding *five thousand* dollars, and I will hold myself accountable to you for the payment of the same, in case Mr. Roe should fail to make payment therefor.

You will please to notify me of the amount for which you may give him credit; and if default should be made in the payment, let me know it immediately.

I am, gentlemen, your most ob't servant,

JOHN DOE.

Messrs. John Smith & Co.,
No — *Broadway, New York.*

LETTER OF LICENSE.

A *letter of license* is an agreement by creditors to permit a debtor, when he is not able to pay his debts at the time due, to carry on his business without molestation. It does not release the debts, or prevent creditors who have not signed it from collecting their claims in the usual method.

No. 74.—Agreement not to sue a Debtor.

Know all Men by these Presents, that whereas John Doe, of the *city* of *Baltimore*, in the county of *Baltimore*, and state of *Maryland*, is justly indebted to us, RICHARD ROE, JOHN JONES, THOMAS SHARPE, and HENRY SMITH, in divers sums of money, which the said JOHN DOE is unable to pay:

Now, therefore, we do hereby grant unto the said JOHN DOE full liberty and license to attend to, follow, and negotiate, any business or affairs whatsoever, without any suit, trouble, or hinderance from us, or any of us, for the space of *two years* from the date hereof.

And we and each of us, for ourselves, our and each of our heirs, executors, administrators, and assigns, for and in consideration of the agreement and covenant of the said JOHN DOE hereinafter contained, do covenant and agree with the said JOHN DOE, that we will not, nor will either or any of us, at any time during the said space of *two years*, sue, prosecute, arrest, molest, or trouble the said JOHN DOE, in respect or on account of any debts now by him due to us or any or either of us.

And the said JOHN DOE, in consideration of the foregoing covenant and agreement, for himself, his heirs, executors, or administrators, covenants and agrees with the creditors aforesaid, that he will faithfully apply all moneys, property, and effects, that he may earn or procure during the said term of *two years*, to the payment of his debts owing to the creditors aforesaid, in proportion to the amount due and owing to each.

In witness whereof, we have hereunto set our hands and seals, this *first* day of *April*, one thousand eight hundred and *fifty*.

RICHARD ROE,
JOHN JONES,
THOMAS SHARPE,
HENRY SMITH.

Witness { JOHN STONE,
JOHN SMITH.

MARRIAGE.

MARRIAGE is a civil contract entered into by persons capable of consenting thereto.

It can not be entered into by idiots or lunatics. When procured by force or fraud, it is also void. Marriage is likewise prohibited between near relations.

The parties must be of the age of consent, which is generally fourteen in males and twelve in females.

No peculiar ceremonies are requisite by the common law to the valid celebration of the marriage rite, but it is advisable that the contract should be entered into in the presence of some clergyman or civil magistrate. In all cases be sure to take a certificate of the marriage: it is of much importance to have that certificate in case of necessity.

No. 75.—Form of Marriage.

The parties having joined hands, say: "By this act of joining hands, you do now assume toward each other the relation of husband and wife, and do solemnly promise, as such, to love, honor, and cherish each other, so long as you both shall live.

"I therefore pronounce you to be henceforth husband and wife."

No. 76.—Marriage Certificate.

State of *Massachusetts*,
County of *Franklin*,
Town of *Deerfield*.

I do hereby Certify, that on the *first* day of *July*, in the year of our Lord one thousand eight hundred and *fifty*, *at the house of* JOHN JONES, in *said town*, JOHN DOE, of the *city* of *Boston*, in the county of *Suffolk*, and state of *Massachusetts*, and HARRIET E. JONES, of the *city aforesaid*, to me personally known [*or proved by the oath of John Jones aforesaid*] to be the persons described in this certificate, were by me joined together with their mutual consent in the bonds of wedlock; and I did first ascertain that the said parties were of sufficient age to consent to the same: which marriage took place in the presence of JOHN SMITH and JOHN STONE, subscribing witnesses hereto.

Witness my hand and seal, this *first* day of *July*, one thousand eight hundred and *fifty*. HENRY HOPE,

Pastor of First —— *Church in Deerfield.*

Marriage celebrated in presence of us, } JOHN SMITH, JOHN STONE.

JUDGMENT NOTE.

THIS note enables the holder, in some of the states, to enter up judgment thereon without suit, if it be not paid when it is due.

No. 77.—Form of Judgment Note.

$1,000. **For Value received,** I promise to pay to RICHARD ROE, or order, the sum of *one thousand* dollars, thirty days after date; and I hereby nominate, constitute, and appoint the said RICHARD ROE, or any attorney-at-law of this state, my true and lawful attorney, irrevocable, for me and in my name to appear in any court of record of this state, at any time after the above promissory note becomes due, and to waive all process and service thereof, and to confess judgment in favor of the holder hereof for the sum that may be due and owing hereon, with interest and costs, and waiving all errors, &c.

In witness whereof, I have hereunto set my hand and seal, at the *city* of *Chicago*, in the county of *Cook*, and state of *Illinois*, this *first* day of *July*, one thousand eight hundred and *fifty*.

JOHN DOE *(seal).*

Sealed and delivered in the presence of
JOHN SMITH,
JOHN JONES. }

PROMISSORY NOTES.

A *promissory note* is an absolute engagement in writing to pay a specified sum at a certain time to a person named, or to his order, or to the bearer.

The signer of the note is called the *maker ;* the one to whom it is made payable, the *payee ;* and he to whom the payee makes it payable by endorsement, is called the *endorsee ;* he who endorses the note, the *endorser*.

A consideration must be given for a note to make it valid, as between the maker and payee; but any one who has given value for it, before it had become due, and not knowing that it was originally made without consideration, can recover on it against all the antecedent parties to the note.

The words "value received" should be inserted in a promissory note, so as to express a consideration for the promise.

But he who receives a promissory note for a consideration before given, for instance as security for a precedent debt, does not *give value* for it, and is in no better position than the payee.

A negotiable note is one that is transferable without, or is made transferable by endorsement. A note negotiable by the laws of the state where it is made is negotiable elsewhere.

The most usual methods of drawing notes are on demand, or at a certain time after date; either payable only to the person named, or to his order, or to bearer, or in a specified commodity. A note payable to the person named, where the words, *to order*, or *to bearer*, are omitted, is not negotiable; if payable to order, it is negotiable by the payee endorsing it by writing his name on the back of the note, in which case the payee is liable to the holder if it is not paid by the maker, provided he have due notice thereof. If payable to bearer, the holder can demand payment without endorsing it.

Any payee who desires to transfer a note by endorsement, without incurring any responsibility, can do so by endorsing the note in this manner: "Without recourse to me, JOHN DOE." If he wishes to make it payable to a third party specially, he can do so by endorsing it thus: "Pay the within to JOHN JONES, or order, JOHN DOE;" John Jones must then endorse it in order to transfer it to another person.

A note running thus, "I promise to pay," and signed by two parties is joint and several, and may be collected of either party; if it is desired to make only a joint note, write it thus, "We jointly and not severally promise."

If a note is made payable to the order of two or more persons who are not partners, they must each and all endorse it, in order to make a valid transfer.

A note negotiated after it is due is subject to any offset the maker of the note may have against the person to whom it is made payable.

The words "without defalcation or discount," must be inserted in notes in New Jersey and Pennsylvania. In those states a note in which these words are not inserted is subject to the same disabilities as a note that is past due.

Promissory notes are entitled, like bills of exchange, to three days of grace, and payment should be demanded on the last day of grace. Custom, and the statute in some states, make a note falling due on Sunday payable the day previous.

Demand of payment should be made of the maker on the day when the note is due, and if not paid, notice should be immediately given to all the endorsers, if this is not done they will be discharged from their liability.

If the words "with interest" are omitted in a note, it will not draw interest before the time at which it is due. If it is not paid when due, it will draw legal interest from that time. If the note is payable on demand, it will draw interest from the time payment is demanded. If a note is made payable in a specified commodity payment must be offered at the time required, otherwise the holder can demand its value in money. (This rule is equally applicable in all contracts for barter.) The holder of a note need not accept a sum less than the whole amount due, but if he does, he should credit the amount received on the back of the note. The rate of interest allowed on money past due, is the legal rate of the state in which the paper is drawn.

When a note has been lost it is advisable to give the fact all the publicity possible, so that the public may be prevented from purchasing it; yet if it get into the hands of one who paid value for it in good faith, it must be paid, unless its negotiation has been accomplished by forgery.

See BILLS OF EXCHANGE, page 40.

No. 78.—Note not Negotiable.

$610:: *New York, November* 9, 1850.

Twenty Days after date, I promise to pay to *Martin W. Goodman, Six Hundred and Ten* Dollars, value received. JOHN DOE.

No. 79.—Note Negotiable by Endorsement.

$250:: *New Orleans, Sept.* 12, 1850.

Ten Days after date, I promise to pay to the order of *John Jones, Two Hundred and Fifty* Dollars, value received.

JOHN DOE.

No. 80.—Note Negotiable without Endorsement.

$125.$\frac{25}{100}$ *Chicago, July* 10*th*, 1850.

Three months after date, I promise to pay to *James Smith*, or bearer, *One Hundred and Twenty-Five* $\frac{25}{100}$*th* Dollars, value received.

JOHN DOE.

No. 81.—Joint Negotiable Note, payable at a Bank.

$200:: *Boston, January* 8, 1851.

Six months after date, for value received, we promise to pay *Henry Reed*, or order, *Two Hundred* Dollars, at the *People's Bank, Boston.* JOHN DOE, RICHARD ROE.

No. 82.—Negotiable Note payable in Merchandise.

$300:: *Philadelphia, Sept.* 12, 1850.

Sixty Days after date, for value received, I promise to pay without defalcation, to *John Jones*, or order, *Three Hundred* Dollars, in merchantable *wheat* at the current price. JOHN DOE.

"Without defalcation" are inserted in notes drawn in Pennsylvania and New Jersey to protect them when due against any offset of the maker.

No. 83.—Negotiable Note on Demand.

$400:25 *New York, November* 4, 1850.

On demand, I promise to pay to the order of *Martin H. Johnson, Four Hundred* $\frac{25}{100}$*th* Dollars, value received. JOHN DOE.

No. 84.—Note on Demand, with Interest from date, not Negotiable.

$150:: *Detroit, June* 10*th*, 1850.

On demand, I promise to pay to *James Smith*, *One Hundred and Fifty* Dollars, with interest from date, value received.

JOHN DOE.

DUE-BILLS.

DUE-BILLS are general informal notes, or memoranda, acknowledging that a certain amount is due to the party to whom they are given. They are frequently given when money or merchandise has been temporarily borrowed, as an evidence of the fact.

No. 85.—Form of Due-Bill.

NEW YORK, *October* 20, 1850.

Due RICHARD ROE, on demand, *twenty-five dollars*, value received.

JOHN DOE.

This form may be varied in the same manner as a note, to express time, amount, kind of payment, and who paid to. The same is also true of *orders*.

ORDERS.

AN *order* is a written request by one person to another, to do an act for his own benefit or accommodation, or that of a third party. It has, of course, no value, unless the party to whom it is addressed is willing to perform the act desired.

No. 86.—Order for Money.

NEW YORK, *November* 10, 1850.

Mr. RICHARD ROE will please pay to JOHN SMITH, or order, *twenty-five dollars*, on demand, and charge the same to the account of

JOHN DOE

No. 87.—Order to sell Merchandise.

BOSTON, *November* 12, 1850.

PLEASE let Mr. THOMAS SHARPE have such merchandise as he may select, to the amount of *one hundred dollars*, and charge the same to the account of

TO RICHARD ROE. JOHN DOE.

No. 88.—Order to deliver Goods.

CHARLESTON, *November* 15, 1850.

Mr. RICHARD ROE: Please deliver to DUNN BROWN, or bearer, the *package of goods* belonging to me, and oblige

Yours,

JOHN DOE.

RECEIPTS.

A *receipt* is not conclusive evidence of payment, but it throws the burden of proof upon him who attempts to impeach it. For this reason, no prudent person will part with a receipt until the payment has actually been made. They may be either in full of all demands, for a special account, in part payment of an account, or for a special purpose. The arrangement of the wording of a receipt is not important, if the object and time be distinctly stated in it.

A general receipt in *full of all demands* is a discharge of all debts, except special debts under seal.

No. 89.—Receipt in Full.

BOSTON, *June* 15, 1850.

Received of RICHARD ROE *fifty-one dollars*, in full of all demands up to this date.

JOHN DOE.

No. 90.—Receipt on Account.

Boston, *July* 1, 1850.

Received of Richard Roe *ten dollars*, to apply on account.

JOHN DOE.

No. 91.—Receipt for a Special Purpose.

Received, *Boston*, *July* 24, 1850, from Richard Roe, *one hundred* dollars, to pay the account of John Doe against him.

PETER PEPPER.

No. 92.—Receipt when Money is paid by a Third Person.

Boston, *July* 25, 1850.

Received of Richard Roe, through Peter Pepper, *one hundred dollars* in full of all demands against Richard Roe up to this date.

JOHN DOE.

No. 93.—Receipt of Interest to be endorsed on a Bond.

Received, *August* 15, 1850, from Richard Roe, *one hundred and twenty* dollars, being the *semi-annual* interest this day due on the within bond.

JOHN DOE.

No. 94.—Receipt in full for a Special Account.

New York, *October* 15, 1850.

Received from Richard Roe *two hundred dollars and twenty-five cents*, in full of all demands for printing to *October* 1, 1850.

JOHN DOE

PARTNERSHIP.

PARTNERSHIP is a voluntary contract between two or more persons, for joining together their money, goods, labor, and skill, or any or all of them, for the purpose of carrying on a lawful business, under an understanding to participate in the profits in certain proportions.

They whose names appear to the world as partners are termed *ostensible* partners.

An ostensible partner who has no interest in the firm is called a *nominal* partner.

A nominal partner is liable for all the debts and contracts of the firm.

One who has an interest in the firm, but whose name is not published to the world as a partner, is called a *dormant* or *silent* partner.

Any one who permits his name to be used in a firm, or who shares the profits of the business, is liable to the world as a partner.

Each individual of a firm is liable to the whole amount of the debts of the concern.

The acts of one partner bind all the others, when done in pursuance of the business of the firm, and in the usual course of that business; but any act not required by the nature of the business will not bind them.

There is a contract of partnership known as a *special partnership*, consisting of one or more persons called *general* partners, who attend to the carrying on of the business of the concern and are liable to the full amount of the debts of the firm, and of one or more persons called *special* partners, who are liable only to the amount of the capital they put into the concern. These special partnerships are wholly regulated by statute, and can only be entered into by conforming strictly to the statute regulations of the state where the partnership is formed. The laws regulating the formation and conduct of special partnerships are so particular, that no prudent man will take any steps in the formation of such a partnership without good legal advice.

No. 95.—Article of Copartnership.

Article of Agreement, made the *first* day of *January*, in the year one thousand eight hundred and *fifty-one*, between JOHN DOE, of the *town* of *Wilmington*, in the county of *New-castle*, and state of *Delaware*, of one part, and RICHARD ROE, of the *same place*, of the other part, as follows:

The said parties above named have agreed to become copartners in the business of *wholesale and retail dry goods and groceries merchants*, and by these presents do agree to be copartners together under and by the name or firm of "DOE and ROE," in the buying, selling, and vending, all sorts of goods, wares, and merchandise, to the said business belonging, and to occupy the *store in the town aforesaid now occupied by said* DOE, their copartnership to commence on the *first* day of *August next*, and to continue *for three years from that day;* and to that end and purpose the said JOHN DOE *furnishes and puts into the concern the stock in his said store, and two thousand dollars in cash, as part of the capital of the said firm; and the said* RICHARD ROE *puts into the said firm the sum of five thousand dollars as his portion of the common stock*—all which it is agreed is to be used and employed in common between them, for the support and management of the said business, to their mutual benefit and advantage.

And it is agreed, by and between the parties to these presents, that at all times during the continuance of their copartnership, they and each of them will give their attendance, and do their and each of their best endeavors, and, to the utmost of their skill and power, exert themselves for their joint interest, profit, benefit, and advantage, and truly employ, buy, and sell merchandise with their joint stock, and the increase thereof, in the business aforesaid: and also, that they shall and will, at all times during the said copartnership, bear, pay, and discharge equally between them, all rents and other expenses that may be required for the support and management of the said business; and that all gains, profit, and increase, that shall come, grow, or arise, from or by means of their said business, shall be divided between them *equally*; and all loss that shall happen to their said joint business by ill commodities, bad debts, or otherwise, shall be borne and paid between them *equally*.

And it is agreed, by and between the said parties, that there shall be had and kept at all times during the continuance of their copartnership, perfect, just, and true books of account, wherein each of the said copartners shall enter and set down, as well all money by them or either of them received, paid, laid out, and expended, in and about the said business, as also all goods, wares, commodities, and merchandise, by them or either of them bought or sold, by reason or on account of the said business, and all other matters and things whatsoever, to the said business and the management thereof in any wise belonging; which said books shall be used in common between the said copartners, so that either of them may have access thereto, without any interruption or hinderance of the other. And also, the said copartners, once in each and every *year*, that is to say, on the *first day of August in each year*, or oftener if necessary, shall make, yield, and render, each to the other, a true, just, and perfect inventory and account of all profits and increase by them, or either of them, made, and of all losses by them, or either of them, sustained; and also of all payments, receipts, disbursements, and of all other things by them made, received, disbursed, acted, done, or suffered, in their said copartnership and business; and the same account so made, shall and will clear, adjust, pay, and deliver, each to the other, at the time, their just share of the profits so made as aforesaid.

And the said parties hereby mutually covenant and agree, to and with each other, that during the continuance of the said copartnership, neither of them shall nor will endorse any note, or otherwise become surety for any person or persons whomsoever, without the consent of the other of the said copartners. And at the end or other sooner determination of their copartnership, the said copartners, each to the other, shall and will make a true, just, and final account of all things relating to their said business, and in all things truly adjust the same; and all and every the stock and stocks, as well as the gains and increase thereof, which shall appear to be remaining, either in money, goods, wares, fixtures, debts, or otherwise, shall be divided between them.

In witness whereof, the parties to these presents have hereunto set their hands and seals the day and year first above written.

Signed, sealed, and delivered, in presence of PETER PENNY, HIRAM JACOBS.	JOHN DOE *(seal)*. RICHARD ROE *(seal)*.

No. 96.—Renewal of Partnership, to be endorsed on the Article.

Inasmuch as the partnership formed between the subscribers by the within agreement will expire on the *first* day of *August next*, IT IS HEREBY AGREED that the same be continued, upon the same terms in every respect as is within mentioned, for the further term of *three years* from the said *first* day of *August next*.

Witness our hands and seals, this *first* day of *July*, one thousand eight hundred and *fifty-four*. J. D.
R. R.

No. 97.—Agreement to Dissolve a Partnership, to be endorsed on the Article.

We, the Undersigned, do mutually agree that the partnership formed between us by the within article be and the same is hereby dissolved, except for the purpose of the final liquidation and settlement of the business thereof; and upon such settlement, then wholly to determine.*

Witness our hands, &c. [*as in No.* 96].

* The agreement to dissolve should state whether one or all the partners are authorized to sign the name of the firm in the liquidation and settlement of its business; and if less than the whole, the name or names of those who may do so. See form of ASSIGNMENT by one partner to another, page 36, which can be used for a dissolution.

POWER OF ATTORNEY.

A *power of attorney* is an instrument in writing whereby one person delegates to another authority to do any act for him, with the same binding effect as though it were done by the principal.

Every person who has power, in his own right, to do any act, may delegate the power to do that act to any other person; but an attorney can not substitute another in his place unless express authority is given him to do so.

Every person intrusted with discretionary power in respect to the business of another, should perform the duties himself; for, generally speaking, he can not give to another authority to exercise those discretionary powers.

The authority of an attorney ceases when withdrawn by his principal; but when the attorney has an interest in the execution of the power, it is then irrevocable.

The revocation of a power of attorney takes effect as to third persons from the time they have notice of it.

Powers of attorney, to be used in a foreign country, should be acknowledged before a notary public, and the signature of the notary certified by the consul of the government to which the power of attorney is to be sent.

When intended to be used in another state, they should be duly proved or acknowledged according to the laws of the state where they are executed.

No. 98.—General Power of Attorney.

Know all Men by these Presents, that I, John Doe, of the *city* of *St. Augustine*, in the county of *St. John's*, and state of *Florida*, have made, constituted, and appointed, and by these presents do make, constitute, and appoint Richard Roe, of the *same place*, my true and lawful attorney for me and in my name, place, and stead,* to [*here insert the things* *which the attorney is to do*]; giving and granting unto my said attorney full power and authority to do and perform all and every act and thing whatsoever requisite and necessary to be done in and about the premises, as fully, to all intents and purposes, as I might or could do if personally present, with full power of substitution and revocation, hereby ratifying and confirming all that my said attorney or his substitute shall lawfully do or cause to be done by virtue hereof.

In witness whereof, I have hereunto set my hand and seal, this *first* day of *April*, one thousand eight hundred and *fifty*.

JOHN DOE *(seal)*.

Sealed and delivered in the presence of
JOHN JONES,
JOHN SMITH.

No. 99.—General Customhouse Power.

Know all Men by these Presents, that I, JOHN DOE, of the *city* of *New Orleans*, in the parish of *Orleans*, and state of *Louisiana*, have made, constituted, and appointed, and by these presents do make, constitute, and appoint RICHARD ROE, of the *same place*, my true and lawful attorney, for me and in my name, to receive and enter at the customhouse of the district of *New Orleans*, any goods, wares, or merchandise, imported by me or which may hereafter arrive, consigned to me; to sign my name, to seal and deliver for me, and as my act and deed, any bond or bonds which may be required by the collector of the said district, for securing the duties on any such goods, wares, or merchandise: ALSO, to sign my name to, seal, and deliver for me, and as my act and deed, any bond or bonds requisite for obtaining the debenture on any goods, wares, or merchandise, when exported, and generally to transact all business at the said customhouse in which I am or may hereafter be interested or concerned, as fully as I could if personally present. And I hereby declare, that all bonds signed and executed by my said attorney shall be as obligatory on me as those signed by myself: and this power shall remain in full force until revoked by written notice given to said collector.

In witness whereof, &c. [*as in No.* 98].

No. 100.—Power to transfer Stock.

Know all Men by these Presents, that I, JOHN DOE of the *town* of *Raleigh*, in the county of *Wake*, and state of *North Carolina*, do hereby make, constitute, and appoint RICHARD ROE, of the *same place*, my true and lawful attorney, for me and in my name, to sell, transfer, and assign, all stock of the *Greenville and Roanoke Railroad Company* standing in my name on the books of the said company; with power also, an attorney or attorneys under him for that purpose, to make and substitute with like power, and to do all lawful acts requisite for effecting the premises; hereby ratifying and confirming all that my said attorney or his substitute or substitutes shall do therein by virtue of these presents.

In witness whereof, &c. [*as in No.* 98].

Acknowledgment of the foregoing.

State of *North Carolina*, } ss.
County of *Wake*, }

Be it known, that on the *third* day of *September*, in the year one thousand eight hundred and *fifty*, before me personally came JOHN DOE, to me known to be the person described in, and who executed the foregoing letter or power of attorney, and acknowledged the above letter of attorney to be his act and deed.

In testimony whereof, I have hereunto set my hand, and affixed my seal of office, the day and year last above written.

JOHN JONES,
(Seal of office.) *Notary Public.*

No. 101.—Proxy, or Power to Vote at Election of Directors.

Know all Men by these Presents, that I, JOHN DOE, of the *town* of *Concord*, in the county of *Merrimack*, and state of *New Hampshire*, do hereby constitute and appoint RICHARD ROE, of the *same place*, my true and lawful attorney and agent, for me and in my name, place, and stead, to vote as my proxy at any election of directors of the *Merrimack County Bank*, according to the number of votes I should be entitled to vote if then personally present.

In witness whereof, &c. [*as in No.* 98].

Oath or Affirmation to the foregoing.

I do *swear* [*or affirm*] that the shares on which my attorney and agent in the above proxy is authorized to vote, do not belong, and are not hypothecated to the said *Merrimack County Bank*, and that they are not hypothecated or pledged to any other corporation or person whatever; that such shares have not been transferred to me for the purpose of enabling me to vote thereon at the ensuing election, and that I have not contracted to sell or transfer them upon any condition, agreement, or understanding, in relation to my manner of voting at the said election.

JOHN DOE *(seal)*.

Sworn [*or affirmed*] this *second* day of *October*, A. D. 1850, before me, JOHN RICHTER, *Justice of the Peace.*

No. 102.—Power to Collect Debts.

Know all Men, &c. [*as in No.* 98 *to the* *]—to demand, ask, sue for, collect, and receive, all sums of money, debts, rents, dues, accounts, and other demands of every kind, nature, and description whatever, which are due, owing, or payable to me from any person or persons whomsoever, and to give good and sufficient receipts, acquittances, and discharges therefor; giving and granting, &c. [*as in No.* 98 *from the* † *to the end*].

No. 103.—Power to Sell and Convey Real Estate.

Know all Men, &c [*as in No.* 98 *to the* *]—to enter into and take possession of all the real estate belonging to me, situate in the *town* of *Rutland*, in the county of *Rutland*, and state of *Vermont*, and to bargain, sell, grant, convey, and confirm, the whole or any part thereof, for such price or sum of money or on such terms as he may think best, and for me and in my name to make, execute, acknowledge, and deliver, unto the purchaser or purchasers thereof, good and sufficient conveyances, with warranty, of the same; and to demand, receive, and collect, all sums of money which shall become due and payable to me by reason of such sale or sales; giving and granting, &c. [*as in No.* 98 *from the* † *to the end*].

No. 104.—Substitution to be endorsed on the Power of Attorney.*

Know all Men by these Presents, that I, John Doe, of the *city* of *Louisville*, in the county of *Jefferson*, and state of *Kentucky*, by virtue of the authority to me given by the within power of attorney, do substitute Richard Roe, of the *town* of *Frankfort*, in the county of *Franklin*, and state of *Kentucky*, as attorney in my stead, to do, perform, and execute, every act and thing which I might or could do by virtue of the within power of attorney; hereby ratifying and confirming all that the said substitute may do in the premises by virtue hereof and of the within power of attorney.

In witness whereof, &c. [*as in No.* 98].

No. 105.—Revocation of Power of Attorney.

Whereas I, John Doe, of the *town* of *Little Rock*, in the county of *Pulaski*, and state of *Arkansas*, by my certain power of attorney, bearing date the *fifth* day of *July*, in the year one thousand eight hundred and *fifty*, did appoint Richard Roe, of the *same place*, my true and lawful attorney, for me and in my name, to [*here set out what he was authorized to do, using the precise language of the power of attorney originally given him*], as by the said power of attorney, reference thereunto being had, will more fully appear:

Therefore, know all Men by these Presents, that I, John Doe aforesaid, have countermanded and revoked, and by these presents do countermand and revoke the said power of attorney and all power and authority thereby given to the said Richard Roe.

In witness whereof, I have hereunto set my hand and seal, this *fifth* day of *December*, one thousand eight hundred and *fifty*.

JOHN DOE (*seal*).

Sealed and delivered in the presence of
John Smith,
Peter Jones.

* This power of substitution can only be used when the attorney has had the right expressly granted to him in his appointment by the principal.

10*

RELEASES.

A *release* is a written instrument, under seal, whereby one man discharges another, either from all claims and demands, or from certain demands specified therein.

A covenant not to sue one of two joint obligors will not release the other, and may be pleaded by the one to whom it is given in bar to an action.

A release of one of several joint debtors releases ALL.

No. 106.—Form of Release.

Know all Men by these Presents, that I, JOHN DOE, of the *city* of *Natchez*, in the county of *Adams*, and state of *Mississippi*, in consideration of *forty dollars* to me in hand paid by RICHARD ROE, of the *same place*, have released and for ever discharged, and hereby, for myself, my heirs, executors, and administrators, do release and for ever discharge the said RICHARD ROE, his heirs, executors, and administrators, from all claim, demand, and cause of action, which I now have or may hereafter have against the said RICHARD ROE by reason of any contract which he may have entered into with me for the *purchase of lumber*.

In witness whereof, &c. [*as in No.* 98].

No. 107.—General Release of every Demand.

To all to whom these Presents shall come, or may concern, GREETING: KNOW YE, that I, JOHN DOE, of the *town* of *Montpelier*, in the county of *Washington*, and state of *Vermont*, for and in consideration of the sum of *one hundred* dollars, lawful money of the United States, to me in hand paid by RICHARD ROE, of the *same place*, have remised, released, and for ever discharged, and by these presents do, for myself, my heirs, executors, and administrators, remise, release, and for ever discharge the said RICHARD ROE, his heirs, executors, and administrators, of and from all, and all manner of action and actions, cause and causes of action, suits, debts, dues, sums of money, accounts, reckonings, bonds, bills, specialties, covenants, contracts, controversies, agreements, promises, variances, trespasses, damages, judgments, extents, executions, claims, and demands whatsoever, in law or in equity, which against the said RICHARD ROE I ever had, now have, or which my heirs, executors, or administrators, hereafter can, shall, or may have, for, upon, or by reason of, any matter, cause, or thing whatsoever, from the beginning of the world to the day of the date of these presents.

In witness whereof, &c. [*as in No.* 98].

No. 108.—Release of part of Mortgaged Premises.

This Indenture, made this *first* day of *April*, in the year one thousand eight hundred and *fifty*, between JOHN DOE, of the *town* of *Harrisburgh*, in the county of *Dauphin*, and state of *Pennsylvania*, of the first part, and RICHARD ROE, of the *same place*, of the second part:

Whereas, RICHARD ROE aforesaid, by indenture of mortgage, bearing date the *first* day of *January*, one thousand eight hundred and *forty-five*, for the consideration therein mentioned, and to secure the payment of the money therein specified, did convey certain lands and tenements, of which the lands hereinafter described are part, unto JOHN DOE aforesaid; and whereas, the said party of the first part, at the request of the said party of the second part, has agreed to give up and surrender the lands hereinafter described unto the said party of the second part, and to hold and retain the residue of the mortgaged lands as security for the money remaining due on the said mortgage:

Now this Indenture witnesseth, that the said party of the first part, in pursuance of the said agreement, and in consideration of *four hundred* dollars, lawful money of the United States, to him duly paid at the time of the ensealing and delivery of these presents, the receipt whereof is hereby acknowledged, hath granted, released, quit-claimed, and set over, and by these presents doth grant, release, quit-claim, and set over, unto the said party of the second part all that part of the said mortgaged lands [*here describe the mortgaged premises intended to be released from the lien of the mortgage*], together with the hereditaments and appurtenances thereto belonging; and all the right, title, and interest, of the said party of the first part, of, in, and to the same, to the intent that the lands hereby conveyed may be discharged from the said mortgage, and that the rest of the lands in the said mortgage specified may remain to the said party of the first part, as heretofore. **To have and to hold** the lands and premises hereby released and conveyed to the said party of the second part, his heirs and assigns, to his and their only proper use, benefit, and behoof, for ever, free, clear, and discharged of and from all lien and claim, under and by virtue of the indenture of mortgage aforesaid.

In witness whereof, &c. [*as in No.* 63].

The following is the form to be used for the purpose of discharging a mortgage that has been fully paid. It should be acknowledged before the proper officer, in order that the mortgage may be cancelled of record:—

No. 109.—Satisfaction of Mortgage.

I, John Doe, of the *town* of *Columbus*, in the county of *Franklin*, and state of *Ohio*, **do hereby certify**, that a certain mortgage, bearing date the *tenth* day of *December*, one thousand eight hundred and *forty-seven*, made and executed by Richard Roe, of the *city* of *Cincinnati*, in the county of *Hamilton*, and state of *Ohio*, to me, to secure the sum of *three thousand* dollars, and recorded in the office of *the clerk of the* county of *Hamilton* aforesaid, in liber *thirty* of mortgages, page 610, on the *fifteenth* day of *December* aforesaid, is paid.

Dated the *tenth* day of *December*, one thousand eight hundred and *fifty*. JOHN DOE.

Acknowledgment of the foregoing.

State of *Ohio*,
County of *Hamilton*, } *ss.*

On the *tenth* day of *December*, one thousand eight hundred and *fifty*, before me came John Doe, to me known to be the individual described in, and who executed the above certificate, and acknowledged that he executed the same.

JOHN SMITH, *Justice of the Peace.*

No. 110.—Satisfaction of Mortgage to be executed by a Corporation.

I, John Doe, *President* of the *Northwestern Life Insurance Company. of the city of New York*, a body corporate, **do hereby certify**, that a certain mortgage, bearing date the *tenth* day of *June*, in the year one thousand eight hundred and *forty-eight*, made and executed by Richard Roe, of the *town* of *Jamaica*, in the county of *Queens*, and state of *New York*, to the said corporation, and recorded in the office of the *clerk of the* county of *Queens*, in liber *twenty* of mortgages, page 425, on the *sixteenth* day of *June*, one thousand eight hundred and *forty-eight*, is paid.

In witness whereof, the seal of the said corporation is hereunto affixed, this *tenth* day of *June*, in the year one thousand eight hundred and *fifty*.

JOHN DOE, President *(corporate seal)*.

Witnessed by John Smith, *Secretary*.

Acknowledgment of the foregoing.

State of *New York*,
City and County of *New York*, } *ss.*

On the *tenth* day of *June*, in the year one thousand eight hundred and *fifty*, before me came John Doe, with whom I am personally acquainted, and known to me to be the *president* of the above-named corporation, who being by me duly *sworn*, says that he resides at *No. ten Cliff street, in the said city;* that the seal which is affixed to the above certificate is the corporate seal of the said corporation, and was so affixed by their authority.

JOHN JONES, *Commissioner of Deeds.*

WILLS.

The following forms of wills are inserted for the benefit of those who may be unexpectedly called to draw up a will without being able to procure good legal advice.

It is of the utmost importance that the property bequeathed and the conditions and intentions of the bequest be distinctly defined, for wills are generally construed according to the strict letter of the instrument.

Whenever good legal advice can be obtained, it is advisable to procure it; for the statute regulations respecting wills and devises are so minute and important, yet varied in every state, that there is danger of coming in conflict with some statute provision in attempting to make a will without advice.

The person making his will must be of sound mind, must act freely and voluntarily, and with a deliberate intention of making his will. He may, of course, revoke his will by any act which evidences such an intention.

Generally, infants and married women can not make a will, but in some of the states they are empowered to do so by statute.

By common law, marriage and the birth of a child subsequent to the making of a will in which no provision is made for such an event, will be considered a revocation of the will; at least it can not bar the rights of the wife, and the child so born, from an interest in the estate. The will of an unmarried woman is in many states revoked by her subsequent marriage.

A bequest to a wife will not take away her right of dower, unless it be clearly inconsistent with such right, or it be expressly stated that it is in lieu of such right.

A *codicil* is something in addition to a will, and should be executed in the same manner as the will. It may consist of a further bequest, or of a revocation, in part, of the will.

A bequest to a person witnessing a will is void, though all the rest of the will is valid. Coercion and undue influence, when exercised upon a testator, will invalidate the will.

As to the form of attestation of wills, see the directions under head of wills in the respective states, and page 163.

No. 111.—Short Form of Will.

In the Name of God, Amen. I, John Doe, of the *town* of *Middletown*, in the county of *Middlesex*, and state of *Connecticut*, being of sound mind and memory, and considering the uncertainty of this frail and transitory life, do therefore make, ordain, publish, and declare, this to be my last **Will** and **Testament**: That is to say, First, after all my lawful debts are paid and discharged, the residue of my estate, real and personal, I give, bequeath, and dispose of, as follows, to wit: [To my beloved wife, the land and appurtenances situated thereon, known and described as the Wells farm, lying in the town of Middletown, in the county of Middlesex, and state of Connecticut, together with ten shares of the capital stock of the *Middletown Bank*, now possessed by me, during the term of her natural life; and after her death, to be divided equally among my heirs: To my son George the farm situated and lying on the highway between Middletown and Hartford, known as the Wilcox farm; also all the right and title I now have or may have in the axe-factory situated on what is commonly known as the Millpond, together with the machinery connected therewith: To the *American Bible Society*, instituted in the city of New York in the year one thousand eight hundred and sixteen, the sum of five hundred dollars: I give, bequeath, and devise, all the rest, residue, and remainder of my real and personal estate, to my child now living, or to my children, or their heirs, who may be living at the time of my decease, to be divided equally between them, share and share alike.]

Likewise I make, constitute, and appoint, *my said son* George, *and my brothers* William *and* James Doe, to be executors of this my last will and testament, hereby revoking all former wills by me made.

In witness whereof, I have hereunto subscribed my

name, and affixed my seal, the *third* day of *April*, in the year of our Lord one thousand eight hundred and *fifty*.

JOHN DOE *(seal)*.

The above-written instrument was subscribed by the said John Doe in our presence, and acknowledged by him to each of us: and he at the same time published and declared the above instrument so subscribed to be his last will and testament; and we, at the testator's request, and in his presence, have signed our names as witnesses hereto, and written opposite our names our respective places of residence.

RICHARD ROE, *Middletown, Middlesex Co., Ct*
JOHN SMITH, *Middletown, Middlesex Co., Ct*
JOHN JONES, *Portland, Middlesex Co., Ct.*

No. 112.—Codicil to a Will.

Whereas I, John Doe, of the *town* of *Middletown*, in the county of *Middlesex*, and state of *Connecticut*, have made my last will and testament in writing, bearing date the *third* day of *April*, in the year of our Lord one thousand eight hundred and *fifty*, in and by which I have given and bequeathed to the *American Bible Society*, instituted in the city of New York in the year one thousand eight hundred and sixteen, the sum of five hundred dollars:

Now, therefore, I do, by this my writing, which I hereby declare to be a codicil to my said last will and testament, and to be taken as a part thereof, order and declare that my will is, that only the sum of two hundred and fifty dollars shall be paid to the said *American Bible Society*, as the full amount bequeathed to the said society, and that the residue of the said legacy be given to the person who shall be acting as treasurer at the time of my decease, of the *Young Men's Library*, located in the town of Middletown, to be expended by the society in the purchase of books for the said library: and lastly, it is my desire that this codicil be annexed to and made a part of my last will and testament as aforesaid, to all intents and purposes.

In witness whereof, &c. [*as in No.* 111].

No. 113.—Form of Will, in which the Testator devises all his Property to Trustees for certain Purposes.

The last Will of Me, John Smith, of the *town* of *Columbia*, in the district of *Richland*, and state of *South Carolina*, being of sound mind at the time of making and publishing this my last will and testament, I give and devise all my estate, real and personal, whereof I may die seized or possessed, to John Doe, of the said *town* of *Columbia*, and Richard Roe, of the *same place*, gentlemen: **To have and to hold** the same to themselves, their heirs and assigns for ever, upon the uses and trusts following, namely: In trust to pay all my debts and funeral expenses: [secondly, to pay to my wife Jane, upon her sole and separate receipts, the interest, income, and revenue, of all my said estate, during the term of her natural life: and thirdly, upon the decease of my said wife, to convert all my said estate into money, if such a course shall be thought best by my said trustees, and pay to my daughter Jane the one third part thereof, it seeming to me best to give her so large a share on account of her bodily infirmities and inability to provide for herself, and the remaining two thirds equally to divide between my four sons Peter, John, Henry, and Thomas. If either of my children shall, before such division, have died, leaving lawful issue, such issue to receive the parent's share; but if there be no issue, then such share to fall into the general fund, to be divided among the survivors in the manner before directed.

And I hereby give to my said trustees full power and authority to sell any or all of my real estate at private or public sale, and invest the proceeds, or to lease the same as they may deem best for the interest of my family.

And if my said daughter Jane shall not have attained the age of twenty-one upon the decease of her mother, I hereby nominate, constitute, and appoint my said trustees, guardians of the person and estate of my said daughter Jane during the remainder of her minority, commending her to their fatherly care and protection.

And I hereby nominate, constitute, and appoint my said trustees, John Doe and Richard Roe, executors of this my last will and testament.

In witness whereof, &c. [*as in No.* 111].

LIABILITIES OF MINORS.

Persons of both sexes are *minors* until they are twenty-one years of age.

In Vermont and Ohio, females are of age at eighteen.

Minors can not do any act to the injury of their property, which they may not repudiate or rescind when they arrive at full age.

Every contract entered into by a minor which is clearly to his prejudice, is absolutely void; and a contract which is clearly to his benefit, is good; and one that is uncertain whether prejudicial or advantageous, is voidable only at the election of the minor.

If the contract be voidable only, it is binding on the adult party thereto until it is rescinded by the minor.

A contract for necessaries is binding on an infant, and he may be sued on such a contract, but the articles must be shown to have been necessary for him under the circumstances and condition in which he was placed when they were furnished. The real circumstances of the minor must be looked at, not his ostensible condition. Necessaries for a minor's wife and children are necessaries for him.

Infancy or non-age can not be taken advantage of to protect a fraudulent act. An infant has been held liable for deceit in obtaining a loan of money on the fraudulent affirmation that he was of age.

A father is not bound by the contract of his son, even for articles that are necessary and suitable for the minor, unless an actual authority be proved, or the circumstances be sufficient to imply an authority. What circumstances will be sufficient to infer an authority must always be a question to be determined in each particular case.

The father is liable for necessaries furnished his minor children, but they must be strictly necessaries, such as the father is in duty bound to furnish, and has not provided.

LIABILITIES OF COMMON CARRIERS.

A *common carrier* is one who undertakes to carry goods or packages of any kind, by land or water, for hire, stated or implied, as an employment: owners of stage-wagons, stage-coaches, and railroad-cars, who carry goods for hire; truck-men, teamsters, porters—owners and masters of vessels in the carrying-trade—canal-boatmen, barge-owners, &c., are common carriers.

Owners of steamboats who tow vessels, and private individuals who may agree to convey a man's goods on a special occasion, are not liable as common carriers.

Owners of stages, hackney-coaches, and other vehicles for carrying passengers with their baggage, are liable as common carriers for baggage or luggage intrusted to their care, but not for goods, unless under a special agreement.

Common carriers are liable for the entire value of the goods, *if not delivered to the proper person;* except a pirate or other public enemy destroys or captures them, or the act of God (against which foresight can not provide nor human power withstand) destroys them. They are not liable for inevitable losses caused by lightnings, storms, hurricanes, earthquakes, the ordinary decay of perishable goods, spontaneous combustion, leakage of casks, or the carelessness of shippers. Against all other perils the carrier is held as an insurer. If a mob seize the goods, the carrier is held. Any passenger-line in the habit of carrying goods for hire, is under the carrier laws. If a stage-driver, or person going along in the conveyance, takes money or goods to carry for his own profit, he alone is responsible: it is the same if he went in a railroad-car, steamboat, &c., which takes passengers only.

To make the owner or master of a vessel liable as a common carrier, she must be open to transport anybody's goods to the port agreed on—no matter whether there be one shipper or many, or whether she be in the home, foreign, coasting, river, or ocean service; but a ship that carries only for one or more particular individuals, comes not under the carrier laws, nor does an owner who lets the tonnage to particular shippers. If the owners charter a vessel to certain persons for a voyage at a specified freight, they are common carriers, unless the terms of the charter-party relieve them.

Carriers are responsible for the acts of all persons in their employ: the act of the agent or servant is deemed to be the act of the principal and master. Injuries done to the goods by strangers must be made up by the carrier. He is liable for accidental fires, thefts, robberies: the goods must be delivered as directed, in the same good order in which they were intrusted to him.

The common carrier must receive all such goods as are offered for the place to which he carries, from anybody willing to pay the regular or a reasonable freight-charge: proof of readiness and willingness to pay is enough, though it might be advisable to tender the charges if a suit is intended. The carrier may refuse if he is full, or the goods are dangerous to be carried, or until he is ready to receive them, or if they are goods it is not his custom to carry, or for a good reason. When he takes freight, he must deliver it in a reasonable time; his ship should be seaworthy, and properly furnished and manned, and he must proceed to the port advertised or otherwise agreed on.

A carrier is not liable for loss by a river or canal freezing up, during his voyage, unless he neglected to use due diligence; nor for the leakage of a ship strained in a storm, nor for losses from collision of his ship with another, unless he was negligent; but for losses by theft and robbery, and for all felonies except piracy, he is liable.

The carrier is liable for goods the moment they are delivered to him; any delivery, in which he specially accepts the goods, binds him; acceptance is frequently implied and binding from the usage of business. Where a carrier receives his freight, even at the shipper's warehouse or that of his agent, and takes it in charge, if that be the usage, it binds him.

He is not liable for goods left in the yard of an inn, where several carriers put up, and not actually delivered to him. For goods delivered at a wharf to some unknown person, of which the wharfinger had no knowledge, he was held not liable.

When goods have reached the destined place, they must be delivered to the proper person, or deposited in the proper place, and the consignee, or one entitled to receive them, duly notified. If he accepts the delivery, the carrier is no longer liable. In some instances the local usage, or the custom of particular carrying-trades, in the absence of express directions from the shippers, regulates the delivery; but if there is a special contract, it must be fulfilled.

If the carrier of a line from Boston to New York takes goods to be forwarded to Philadelphia by a particular conveyance, his liability ceases, *as carrier*, when they are safely deposited at New York, and ready for such next conveyance; but if he takes goods to forward to places beyond the extent of his own line, he is answerable as carrier to the place of final destination.

A carrier is answerable for losses from deposites or storage of goods on the route; but if goods are left in his possession beyond a reasonable time, he is only bound to take ordinary care. If he delivers goods under a mistake of his own, or of fraud on the part of others (other than the owners or shippers), he must make good the value to the owner.

No contract, no public or personal notice, will exempt the carrier of goods from losses caused by his or his agents' neglect or fraud; but any notice of the carrier (if the shipper can be proved to have read it or known of its existence, and not otherwise) that he will not take goods of great value, or that he will not pay more than a specified sum unless specially informed of such value and paid in proportion to the risk, is good. An ambiguous notice will be construed against the carrier. Notices at each end of a route will not bind those who ship goods at intermediate places, unless specially made known to them. A personal notice to the principal is binding on all his agents who may forward by the same line. A carrier can not, by any transfer of the goods to another carrier, exempt himself: if he forward in another mode than that understood, he will be liable, in cases where his notice would have otherwise protected him.

If the owner of goods mislead the carrier as to their value, or make false statements calculated to lessen his vigilance, it is a fraud upon him.

Where there is no notice, or special contract of limitation, it is enough for the owner to show the carrier's undertaking the carriage of his goods, and a non-delivery. The carrier must show why he did not deliver; but when there is a notice, the owner must show a want of ordinary prudence in the carrier. A valid seizure of goods because of an illegal act of the owner, will excuse a non-delivery; but the seizure must be valid, or the carrier will be liable. The carrier has legal power sufficient to put any claimant to the proof as to his title to take the goods; if he neglect to use that power, he is liable. In case of stolen goods, the carrier must deliver them to the owner on demand.

When goods are sent by water, and it becomes necessary to throw a part overboard, thereby to save the rest, the loss is to be general. When one shipper's goods are thus destroyed, and those of others saved, the loser may demand a contribution from all the others, and from the ship-owners, and the party entitled to freight, in such equitable amount as will subject him only to his fair proportion of the loss according to the value of goods he had shipped. Land-carriers, when inevitable perils oblige them to incur unusual charges, may demand payment by an equitable contribution.

The carrier has a right to demand payment when he receives the goods: he may refuse to take them if not so paid; but if he take them, to be paid at the end of the route, he may retain them till paid, on his arrival there. He may waive this lien by agreement, in which case his charges become a simple debt. As a general rule, the *consignor* is bound for the freight; but the *consignee*, if he engage to pay, is also. Nautical usages have often become, by the decisions of courts, positive law. Different states have passed local laws to regulate their navigation: if a carrier break any of these rules to the loss of a shipper, he is liable.

In the states of New York and Ohio, special notices and special contracts, by common carriers, are held to be against the policy of the law, and therefore utterly void. The courts also hold that the notice that "all baggage is at the risk of the owner," is a nullity; but the carrier may require the shipper to disclose the nature and value of the property, or make a special acceptance.

Warehousemen, wharfingers, and private carriers, are only bound to use ordinary care and diligence, and are liable but for gross negligence or bad faith.

Common carriers are bound to carry *passengers* safely and properly to their place of destination; to use the utmost skill, care, and diligence; and are responsible for the least neglect. If an accident happen, it falls to the carrier to show that it was not his fault. All who seek a passage are to be treated with impartiality, but must pay in advance if required and submit to reasonable rules for the general convenience and comfort. Persons of coarse, rude conduct, or suspicious or notorious bad character, may be refused.

The conveyance must be suitable for the passage, having skilful, prudent, faithful conductors and servants. If by water, the vessel must be seaworthy, with a competent crew. His baggage must be duly delivered to the passenger, or the carrier must keep it for him a reasonable time.

In case of a coachman, if he be rash, careless, races violently, or by want of caution runs foul of anything, and an accident happen, the proprietors are liable. The baggage he may detain for unpaid fare.

LIABILITY OF SHIP-OWNERS.

The following Act in regard to the liabilities of ship-owners, which was passed by Congress, March, 1851, has so important a bearing on sea-carriage of merchandise, that it is inserted entire. How *far* it will effect the old established principles of common carrier liabilities, stated in the preceding article, remains to be settled by the legal tribunals.

No owner or owners of any ship or vessel shall be subject or liable to answer for or make good to any one or more person or persons any loss or damage which may happen to any goods or merchandise whatsoever, which shall be shipped, taken in, or put on board any such ship or vessel, by reason or by means of any fire happening to or on board the said ship or vessel, unless such fire is caused by the design or neglect of such owner or owners: *Provided*, That nothing in this act contained shall prevent the parties from making such contract as they please, extending or limiting the liability of ship-owners.

If any shipper or shippers of platina, gold, gold-dust, silver, bullion, or other precious metals, coins, jewelry, bills of any bank or public body, diamonds or other precious stones, shall lade the same on board any ship or vessel, without at the time of such lading, giving to the master, agent, owner or owners of the ship or vessel receiving the same, a note in writing of the true character and value thereof, and have the same entered on the bill of lading therefor, the master and owner or owners of the said vessel shall not be liable, as carriers, in any form or manner. Nor shall any such master or owners be liable for any such valuable goods beyond the value and according to the character thereof so notified and entered.

The liability of the owner or owners of any ship or vessel for any embezzlement, loss or destruction, by the master, officers, mariners, passengers, or any other person or persons, of any property, goods, or merchandise, shipped or put on board any such ship or vessel, or for any loss, damage, or injury by collision, or for any act, matter or thing, loss, damage, or forfeiture, done, occasioned, or incurred, without the privity or knowledge of such owner or owners, shall in no case exceed the amount or value of the interest of such owner or owners, respectively, in such ship or vessel, and her freights then pending.

If any such embezzlement, loss, or destruction, shall be suffered by several freighters or owners of goods, wares, or merchandise, or any property whatever, on the same voyage, and the whole value of the ship or vessel, and her freight for the voyage, shall not be sufficient to make compensation to each of them, they shall receive compensation from the owner or owners of the ship or vessel in proportion to their respective losses; and for that purpose the said freighters and owners of the property, and the owner or owners of the ship or vessel, or any of them, may take the appropriate proceedings in any court for the purpose of apportioning the sum for which the owner or owners, of any ship or vessel, may be liable among the parties entitled thereto. And it shall be deemed a sufficient compliance with the requirements of this act, on the part of such owner or owners, if he or they shall transfer his or their interest in such vessel and freight, for the benefit of such claimants, to a trustee, to be appointed by any court of competent jurisdiction, to act as such trustee for the person or persons who may prove to be legally entitled thereto, from and after which transfer, all claims and proceedings against the owner or owners shall cease.

The charterer or charterers of any ship or vessel, in case he or they shall man, victual, and navigate, such vessel at his or their own expense, or by his or their own procurement, shall be deemed the owner or owners of such vessel, within the meaning of this act; and such ship or vessel when so chartered shall be liable in the same manner as if navigated by the owner or owners thereof.

Nothing in the preceding sections shall be construed to take away or affect the remedy to which any party may be entitled, against the master, officers, or mariners, for or on account of any embezzlement, injury, loss, or destruction of goods, wares, merchandise, or other property, put on board any ship or vessel or on account of any negligence, fraud, or other malversation of such master, officers, or mariners, respectively, nor shall anything herein contained lessen or take away any responsibility to which any master or mariner of any ship or vessel may now by law be liable, notwithstanding such master or mariner may be an owner or part owner of such ship or vessel.

Any person or persons shipping oil of vitriol, unslaked lime, inflammable matches, or gunpowder, in a ship or vessel taking cargo for divers persons on freight, without delivering at the time of shipment, a note in writing, expressing the nature and character of such merchandise, to the master, mate, officer, or person in charge of the lading of the ship or vessel, shall forfeit to the United States one thousand dollars.

This act shall not apply to the owner or owners of any canal-boat, barge, or lighter, or to any vessel of any description whatsoever, used in river or inland navigation.

CUSTOMHOUSE REGULATIONS.

Entry of Vessels from Foreign Ports.—It is necessary that three copies of the manifests of vessels from foreign ports should be made out before arrival, in order to be presented to the boarding-officer *upon* arrival. They should include *everything* on board; and, after stating the cargo laden at the port of departure, if there should be any return cargo, it should then be added under that head. If there are any surplus stores, these should then be particularized; and, finally, the passengers' names, individually, with the number of packages of baggage belonging to *each*—the whole to be signed by the master.

Where there are passengers, a separate list, besides the names on each manifest—including the names, ages, sex, occupation, country to which they severally belong, and of which they intend to become inhabitants, and if any have died on the passage—will also be necessary. *Another* list of passengers, similar to the last, is required by the mayor of the port in some of the states.

If any part of the cargo is to be landed at a different port than the first one of entry, it must be so stated in the manifest, as otherwise that privilege will be lost, and the cargo required to be landed at the first port of entry.

The captain should be particular in having his crew mustered by the boarding-officer, upon arrival, in order to the cancelling of the bond given for their safe return. Vessels must report at the customhouse within twelve hours, and enter within forty-eight hours, after arrival. If the captain is not an owner of the vessel, and there should be a resident owner at the port of entry, such owner is required to accompany the captain, in order to swear to the register.

Entry of Vessels coastwise.—Nothing further is required than the clearance from the customhouse at the port of departure, and the register, if she is a registered vessel.

Clearance of Vessels for Foreign Ports.—Every shipper must clear his goods at the customhouse before the vessel can clear. From these shippers' clearances the vessel's manifest is to be made, after the same form, and including all the particulars therein contained. A notarial crew-list and duplicate shipping articles are also required. If there is any change of owner or master, notice thereof should be given, at least the day previous, in order that the register may be endorsed or a new one issued.

Inquiry should also be made, a day or two previous to clearing (in case of vessels last from foreign ports), whether the return of the inward cargo corresponds with the manifest, as delays may otherwise occur in settling discrepancies, which to adjust may and do frequently detain vessels from clearing, when the hurry is great, and consignees are anxious to get their vessels to sea.

If there is any cargo brought in the vessel not to be landed, a permit must be obtained to retain the same on board, several days before clearing, as the officer discharging the vessel can not make his return without it; and, without *his* return, the vessel can not be cleared. When cleared, the captain will receive his register, crew-list, clearance, bill of health, and shipping articles; or, in case of a *foreign* vessel, all that he requires is a clearance and bill of health, upon presenting which to the consul of his nation, he will receive all other necessary papers.

Clearance of Vessels coastwise.—Duplicate manifests, made out from the bills of lading (number of packages in each bill of lading being stated *in writing)*, with the names of the shippers and consignees, and their places of residence, are all that is required.

Laws relative to Invoices.—Invoices must be made out in the currency of the country whence the goods are imported. When the value of such currency is not fixed by law, the invoice must be accompanied by a consular certificate, stating the true value of such currency in Spanish or United States silver dollars; and in default thereof, a bond for the production of such certificate must be given. If no invoice of goods has been received by the consignee or owner, they may be entered by appraisement, the owner or consignee first taking oath that no invoice has been received, and giving bond to produce invoice.

Goods belonging to persons residing in the United States, but absent from the place of importation, may be admitted to entry, the importer or agent first giving bond to produce invoice duly verified by the oath of the owner, administered by a collector of the customs or by a public officer duly authorized to administer oaths.

Goods belonging to a person not residing at the time in the United States, can not be admitted to entry, unless accompanied by an invoice verified by the owner's oath, stating that the goods were actually purchased for his account, and that the invoice contains a true and faithful account of the *cost* of such goods.

If such goods have not been acquired in the usual mode, of bargain and sale—or if they belong in whole or in part to the manufacturer thereof—the oath annexed to the invoice must specify that the invoice contains the actual *fair market value* at the time and place when and where the same were procured or manufactured.

The verification may be made before a consul or commercial agent of the United States. If there is no consul or commercial agent in the country or place of purchase, the oath may be administered by any public officer authorized in such place to administer oaths, which authority must be authenticated by a consul or commercial agent of the United States: if there be no such consul or agent, then by the authentication of a consul of any nation at peace with the United States: if no such consul can be found, then the certificate of two respectable merchants will answer.

Goods owned by persons not residing in the United States, and not accompanied with an invoice verified as required above, may be admitted by the secretary of the treasury, the collector first certifying that no fraud was intended; but before such entry shall be permitted, the importer shall give bond to produce an invoice of such goods, duly verified by the owner, in the mode and to the effect before mentioned.

The owner, consignee, or agent of imports, which have been actually purchased, on entry of the same, must make such addition in the entry to the cost or value given in the invoice as in his opinion may raise the same to the true market value of such imports in the principal markets of the country whence the importation shall have been made, or in which the goods imported shall have been originally manufactured or produced, as the case may be.

No goods, wares, or merchandise, subject to duty, can be imported into the United States on the seaboard in vessels of less than thirty tons' burden, under the penalty of the forfeiture of vessel and cargo.

Invoice must contain the weight, quantity, or measure of goods, or the same will be weighed, gauged, or measured, at the expense of the importer. The number of bushels of wheat is to be ascertained by actual measurement by the standard bushel, and not by weight.

In all cases where there are more goods found on board a vessel than the master thereof has reported in his manifest, he must, with the consent of the officers of the customs, make a post entry for the same, and pay two dollars therefor; and for every disagreement between his manifest and cargo, he is liable to a fine of five hundred dollars. All goods, on examination by the appraisers, not corresponding with the entry made of them, are liable to forfeiture.

Drawback.—To be entitled to drawback, the duties on the importation of the goods exported must have been at least fifty dollars by one vessel, at the same time, and by the same person, and the merchandise be, at the time of exportation, in the same package and same condition, including wrapper and original mark and number, as when imported.

Register Act.—Every owner of a vessel, residing within the limits of the United States, must swear (or affirm) to the register within ninety days after its being granted, or it becomes void, and the vessel and cargo pays foreign tonnage and duty.

All *duties* must be paid in gold or silver coin.

Warehousing.—Goods, wares, or merchandise, entitled to entry for warehousing, are such only as shall have been actually imported after the passage of the act "reducing the duty on imports, and for other purposes," approved July 30, 1846. Where owners, importers, consignees, or agents, desire to warehouse their goods, due entry in writing must be made in each case, and a bond taken with surety or sureties to the satisfaction of the collector, in double the amount of the duties.

Goods, wares, or merchandise, entered for warehousing, must be conveyed from the vessel, or wharf where landed, to the warehouse, under the special superintendence of an inspector of the customs, in drays, carts, or other usual modes of conveyance, to be employed on public account, by the proper officer of the customs, and the expense at the rates usually paid for such service at the port in question is to be defrayed at the time by the person who enters said goods, wares, or merchandise, for warehousing. In cases where goods, wares, or merchandise, imported after the passage of the act of July 30, 1846, are intended to be exported directly from warehouse to a foreign country, entry must be made and bond given, in the manner now required by existing laws relating to exportations for the benefit of drawback. In all such cases the appropriate expenses are to be paid before granting permit for exportation,

Where any goods, duly warehoused, shall remain in store beyond one year, without payment of the duties and charges thereon which in pursuance of the act are required to be appraised and sold, the treasury department prescribes that all such sales shall take place within thirty days after the expiration of the year.

If a part of an importation is to be landed and the duties paid forthwith, and the remainder warehoused, the two entries must be made simultaneously. If no invoice has been received, the goods may be entered in conformity with the second section of the act of March 1, 1823, but can not be entered for warehousing. When the goods have been deposited in the warehouse, the collector shall cause them to be compared with the invoice, and the dutiable value, quantity, and the character thereof, ascertained in the manner provided by law; and after the report of the appraisers has been received by the collector, the importer, agent, or purchaser, may withdraw any entire case or package, or any quantity not less than one ton in weight, if imported in bulk.

When the goods have arrived at the port of destination, they may be deposited in the public store, and the duty paid forthwith. If the duty is not paid forthwith, the entry for warehousing shall be presented to the collector, and accompanied with the transportation certificate and copy from invoice, and shall be verified by the oath of the owner or consignee: the collector will then take a bond with satisfactory security.

When the goods are deposited in warehouse, they must be subjected to the same examination as is required by law on the importation of goods from foreign ports, and must be carefully compared with the copy from the original invoice. If the collector is satisfied that the goods so examined are the identical goods described in the transportation certificate, he will grant a copy thereof and certify thereon, which certificate being presented to the collector at the port whence the goods were transported, the bond may be cancelled.

If the goods are withdrawn from warehouse at the port of original importation, for exportation, then entry must be made, the oath prescribed taken, and bond with satisfactory security given for the delivery of the goods at a foreign port or place: when the bond is received, the collector and naval officer will issue a permit to deliver the goods to the surveyor, and shall direct the surveyor to cause the same to be laden on board for exportation, indicating which are to be weighed, gauged, or measured. The officer under whose inspection the goods are shipped must certify on the entry: to cancel the export bond, the exporter must furnish the proofs required by law.

When goods have been deposited in the public stores, the owner or importer on application therefor shall be entitled to receive a certificate, either for the entire importation, or for each package or parcel thereof, on payment of twenty cents for each certificate—which certificate shall be issued and signed by the collector, or by some person to be designated for that purpose by the collector, with the approbation of the secretary of the treasury, which person shall be entitled to receive from the importer a copy of the warehousing entry, and shall be allowed to retain out of the money received for certificates such reasonable amount as may be fixed by the collector, with the sanction of the secretary of the treasury, as his compensation; and the residue thereof, if any, after deducting the expense of printing, filling up, registering, and cancelling said certificates, shall be paid over to the collector, to be by him placed to the credit of the treasurer of the United States.

When goods are withdrawn from warehouse in quantities less than the entire importation, the expense of weighing, gauging, or measuring, must be paid by the owner, importer, or agent, if it be necessary to weigh, gauge, or measure such portion, in order to ascertain the dutiable value.

The warehouses are opened at sunrise, and closed at sunset.

Recording the Sale or Mortgage of Vessels.—No bill of sale, mortgage, hypothecation, or conveyance, of any vessel or part of any vessel of the United States, shall be valid against any person other than the grantor or mortgagor, his heirs, and devisees, and persons having actual notice thereof; unless such bill of sale, mortgage, hypothecation, or conveyance, be recorded in the office of the collector of customs where such vessel is registered or enrolled: *Provided*, That the lien by bottomry on any vessel created during her voyage, by a loan of money or materials, necessary to repair or enable such vessel to prosecute a voyage, shall not lose its priority or be in any way affected by the provisions of this act. The collectors of the customs shall record all such bills of sale, mortgages, hypothecations, or conveyances, and also all certificates for discharging and cancelling any such conveyances, in a book or books to be kept for that purpose, in the order of their reception, and shall certify on the paper so recorded the time when the same was received, and the number of the book and page where they are recorded.

The owner, or agent of the owner of any vessel of the United States, applying to a collector of the customs for a register or enrolment of a vessel, shall, in addition to the oath now prescribed by law, set forth, in the oath of ownership, the part or proportion of such vessel belonging to each owner, and the same shall be inserted in the register or enrolment; and all bills of sale of vessels registered or enrolled shall set forth the part of the vessel owned by each person selling, and the part conveyed to each person purchasing. This act went into effect Oct. 1, 1850.

As blank forms are prepared according to the regulations of the customhouse, and can be obtained at ports of entry, we shall omit them here. The details of passing goods through the customhouse are so intricate, that it will generally be found advisable to employ a broker to attend to the business.

LIST OF FEES RECEIVABLE BY LAW.

For admeasuring every Vessel, in order to the enrolment, or licensing, and recording the same, if of 5 tons, and less than 20	$0 50
Of 20, and not over 70	0 75
Over 70, and not over 100	1 00
Over 100	1 50
Certificate of Enrolment	0 50
Endorsement on Certificate of Enrolment	0 20
License, and granting the same, including the Bond, if not over 20 tons	0 25
Above 20, and not over 100	0 50
Over 100	1 00
Endorsement on a License	0 20
Certifying Manifest, and granting Permit for licensed Vessels to go from District to District, under 50 tons	0 25
Over 50 tons	0 50

Receiving certified Manifest, and granting Permit on arrival of such Vessel, if under 50 tons 0 25
Over 50 tons 0 50
Certifying Manifest, and granting permission to *registered* Vessels to go from District to District 1 50
Receiving certified Manifest, and granting Permit on arrival of such registered Vessel 1 50
Granting Permit to a Vessel, not belonging to a Citizen of the United States, to go from District to District, and receiving Manifest 2 00
Receiving Manifest, and granting Permit to unload, for last-mentioned Vessel, on arrival at one District from another 2 00
Granting Permit for Vessel carrying on Fishery, to trade at a Foreign Port 0 25
Report and Entry of Foreign Goods imported in such Vessel 0 25
Entry of Vessel of 100 tons and more 2 50
Clearance of Vessel of 100 tons and more 2 50
Entry of Vessel under 100 tons 1 50
Clearance of Vessel under 100 tons 1 50
Post Entry 2 00
Permit to land Goods—all official Certificates, and Orders to deliver or transfer 0 20
Bond, taken officially 0 40
Permit to load Goods for Exportation, entitled to Drawback 0 30
Debenture, or other official Certificate 0 20
Bill of Health 0 20
Official Documents, except Register, required by any Merchant, Owner, or Master of any Vessel, not before enumerated 0 20
Admeasurement and certifying Vessels of 100 tons and under .... 1 c. per ton
Over 100, and not over 200 .... 1 50
Over 200 .... 2 00
Other services to be performed by the Surveyor, in Vessels of 100 tons and more, having on board Merchandise subject to duty 3 00
Like services in Vessels under 100 tons, having similar Merchandise 1 50
All Vessels not having Merchandise subject to duty 0 67
Protection 0 25
Crew-List 0 25
Certificate of Registry and Bond 2 25
Endorsement on Register 1 00
All Orders, Permits, and other Documents, requiring the Collector's signature, including Certificates on Invoices, and Shipping Manifests, and for every *jurat* or verification on oath 0 20
For recording Conveyance or Certificate of Satisfaction of a Record 0 50
Furnishing Certificate of facts regarding the Record of a Vessel 1 00
Furnishing Certified Copies of the Record 0 50

In all cases where the Invoice or Entry does give them, there shall be charged for—

Weighing—1⅞c. per 112 lbs.

Gauging—Casks, 12c. each; Cases and Baskets, 4⅜c. each; Ale, Porter, &c., 1⅜c. per dozen bottles.

Measuring—Coal, 90c. per 100 bushels; Chalk, Brimstone, &c., 90c. per 100 bushels; Salt, 75c. per 100 bushels; Potatoes, Seeds, Grain, and all other measurable articles, 45c. per 100 bushels.

Measuring—Marble, Mahogany, Cedar-wood, &c., the actual expense incurred.

Marking—Spirits, Wines, &c., 2⅜c. per package; issuing Certificates (Spirits only), 3⅛c. per package—when requested by the importer.

NATURALIZATION.

In order for a free white person, born in a foreign country, to become a citizen of the United States, it is necessary that he should make a declaration under oath, at least two years before his admission, of his intention to become a citizen, and must renounce his allegiance to his own sovereign. This declaration must be made before—

1. Any state court, being a court of record, and having a seal and clerk, and common-law jurisdiction.
2. Before a circuit court of the United States.
3. Before a district court of the United States.
4. Before a clerk of either of these courts.

After he has been a resident of the United States for five years, and has made his declaration of intentions at least two years before, he may then be admitted to the rights of citizenship. In order for this, he must prove, by the oath of two citizens of the United States, that he has been a resident of the United States for five years, and one year within the state where the court is held.

He must also take an oath to support the constitution of the United States, and on oath renounce and abjure his native allegiance.

If he have been a minor, and shall have resided in the United States for three years next before his attaining his majority, he may be admitted without such declaration, on proving by two witnesses that he has resided five years in the United States, three years as a minor and two since he became of age, making the declaration of his intentions at the time of his admission, and declaring on oath and proving to the satisfaction of the court that for three years next preceding it had been his *bona-fide* intention to become a citizen.

The alien's country must, at the time of his admission, be at peace with the United States.

If an alien die after having made his declaration of intention and before his admission, his widow and children are citizens.

The minor children of any one duly naturalized, if dwelling in the United States, are citizens.

No. 114.—Form of Declaration of Intention.

I, John Doe, do declare, on oath, that it is *bona fide* my intention to become a citizen of the United States, and to renounce for ever all allegiance and fidelity to all and any foreign prince, potentate, state, and sovereignty whatever; and particularly to the *queen of Great Britain and Ireland*, of whom I was a subject.

JOHN DOE.

Sworn in open court, this *first* day of *October*, 1850.

Clerk's Certificate.

I, John Smith, clerk of the *district* court of the *United States*, do certify that the above is a true copy of the original declaration of intention of John Doe to become a citizen of the United States, remaining of record in my office.

In testimony whereof, I have hereunto subscribed my name, and affixed the seal of the said court, this *first* day of *October*, one thousand eight hundred and *fifty*.

(Seal of the court.) JOHN SMITH, *Clerk.*

12

No. 115.—Affidavit of one who arrived before he was Eighteen.

In the matter of JOHN DOE, on his Naturalization. }

JOHN DOE, being duly sworn, says, that for the continued term of five years last past he has resided within the United States, and that for one year last past he has resided within the state of *Michigan;* and at the time he so arrived in the United States he had not attained his eighteenth year; that it is bona fide his intention, and has been for the last three years, to become a citizen of the United States, and to renounce for ever all allegiance and fidelity to all and every foreign prince, potentate, state, and sovereignty whatever; and particularly to VICTORIA, *the queen of Great Britain and Ireland,* of whom he was a subject.

JOHN DOE.

Sworn in open court, the *tenth* day of *August,* 1850. } JOHN SMITH, *Clerk.*

No. 116.—Affidavit to prove the Intention of becoming a Citizen, to accompany the preceding Affidavit.

State of *Michigan,* County of *Wayne,* } to wit:

JOHN JONES, being duly sworn, says that he is a citizen of the United States; that he is well acquainted with the above-named JOHN DOE, and that the said JOHN DOE has resided within the territory of the United States for five years last past, and for one year last past in the state of *Michigan;* and that during such period he has behaved himself as a man of good moral character, attached to the principles of the constitution of the United States, and well disposed to the good order and happiness of the same; that for three years last past it has been bona fide the intention of the said JOHN DOE to become a citizen of the United States, and that at the time the said JOHN DOE arrived in the United States he had not attained his eighteenth year.

JOHN JONES.

Sworn to in open court, this *tenth* day of *August,* 1850. } JOHN SMITH, *Clerk.*

No. 117.—Proof of Residence, &c., to be made at the time of Admission.

State of *Indiana,* County of *Jefferson,* } to wit:

PETER SMITH and JOHN JONES, being duly sworn, say that they are both of them citizens of the United States of America; that they know JOHN DOE, and that he has resided within the territory and jurisdiction of the United States for five years last past; that during that time he has behaved as a man of good moral character, attached to the principles of the constitution of the United States, and well disposed to the good order and happiness of the same.

PETER SMITH,
JOHN JONES.

Sworn in open court, this *first* day of *November,* 1850, before me, GEORGE GOODMAN, *Judge.* }

No. 118.—Oath to support the Constitution of the United States, &c.

I, JOHN DOE, do solemnly swear that I will support the constitution of the United States of America, and that I do absolutely and entirely renounce and abjure all allegiance and fidelity to any foreign prince, potentate, state, or sovereignty whatever; and particularly to VICTORIA, *queen of the United Kingdom of Great Britain and Ireland*, of whom I was a subject.

JOHN DOE.

Sworn in open court, the *first* day of *November*, 1852,
before me, GEORGE GOODMAN, *Judge*.

No. 118.—Certificate of Citizenship.

United States of America,
State of *Indiana*, ss.
County of *Jefferson*,

Be it remembered, that on the *first* day of *November*, in the year of our Lord one thousand eight hundred and *fifty-three*, JOHN DOE appeared in the *circuit court* (the said court being a court of record, having common-law jurisdiction, and a clerk and seal), and applied to the said court to be admitted to become a citizen of the United States of America, pursuant to the provisions of the several acts of the Congress of the United States of America, for that purpose made and provided; and the said applicant having thereupon produced to the court such evidence, made such declaration and renunciation, and taken such oaths as are by the said acts required:

Thereupon, it was ordered by the said court, that the said applicant be admitted, and he was accordingly admitted by the said court, to be a citizen of the United States of America.

In testimony whereof, the seal of the said court is hereunto affixed, this *first* day of *November*, one thousand eight hundred and *fifty-three*, and in the *seventy-eighth* year of our Independence.

Per curiam, JOHN SMITH, *Clerk*.

(Seal of the court.)

PATENT LAWS AND REGULATIONS.

THE laws now in force relative to *patents* are those approved July 4, 1836 March 3, 1837, March 3, 1839, August 29, 1842, May 27, 1848, and March 3, 1849. The forms resting upon these are fixed, and can not, of course, be varied without the intervention of Congress; but rules, having their origin in the commissioner, can be revised or modified at his discretion.

For what Patents may be granted.—By the act of 1836, section 6, patents were granted for any new and useful art, machine, manufacture, or composition of matter, or any new and useful improvement on any art, machine, manufacture, or composition of matter, not known or used by others before the applicant's discovery or invention thereof, and not, at the time of his application for a patent, in public use, or on sale, with his consent or allowance, as the inventor or discoverer; but, by the act of the 3d of March, 1839, no patent is held to be invalid by reason of the purchase, sale, or use of the invention, prior to the application for a patent, except on proof of abandonment of such invention to the public, or that such purchase, sale, or public use, has been for more than two years prior to such application for a patent.

By the third section of the act of 1842, patents are also granted for new and original *designs*:—

1. For a manufacture, whether of metal or other material.
2. For the printing of woollen, silk, cotton, or other fabrics.
3. For busts, statues, or bas-reliefs, or composition in alto or basso relievo.
4. For any impression or ornament (whether complete in itself, or) to be placed on any article of manufacture in marble or other material.
5. For any new and original pattern, or print, or picture, to be either worked into or worked on, or printed or painted, or cast or otherwise fixed on, any article of manufacture.
6. For any new shape or configuration of any article of manufacture.

All such designs not being previously known or used by others.

To whom Patents may be granted.—Patents are granted to citizens of the United States; to aliens who shall have been resident in the United States one year next preceding, and shall have made oath of their intention to become citizens thereof; to one or more assignees of entire patent-rights; to administrators and executors, and to foreign inventors or discoverers: but the law makes no provision for granting to the latter patents for new and original *designs*.

In case of the decease of an inventor before he has obtained a patent for his invention, "the right of applying for and obtaining such patent shall devolve on the administrator or executor of such person, in trust for the heirs-at-law of the deceased, if he shall have died intestate; but if otherwise, then in trust for his devisees, in as full and ample manner, and under the same conditions, limitations, and restrictions, as the same was held, or might have been claimed or enjoyed, by such person in his or her lifetime; and when application for a patent shall be made by such legal representatives, the oath or affirmation shall be so varied as to be applicable to them."

Joint inventors are entitled to a joint patent, but neither can claim one separately.

Applications for Patents.—In presenting an application for a patent, much disappointment and delay will be avoided by attending to the following directions:* 1. The *petition* should be made to the *commissioner*, praying that a

* Of the propriety of making an application for a patent, the inventor or his agent must be the sole judge. The patent-office is open; the records and models may be consulted during office-hours; and the applicant can personally, or by attorney, satisfy himself of the expediency of filing his papers. Further than the facilities thus afforded, the office can yield no assistance, until the case is regularly before it in manner prescribed by law.

patent may be granted for the invention. 2. The *specification* should be filed, describing, as clearly and concisely as possible, the improvement made. 3. The *oath* or *affirmation* should be made to the originality of the invention. 4. *Drawings*, when the nature of the case admits of them, should accompany the application. 5. The *model* or *specimen*, as the case may be, clearly representing the improvement, should be deposited. 6. The *fee* required by law should be paid, and in manner hereafter pointed out.

All the papers and the fee in each application must be filed in the patent-office at the same time, whether they be delivered by the applicant or his agent, or forwarded by mail; and in those cases where the party or his agent is in Washington, then the model must be delivered at the same time. If the party or his agent is not on the spot, the model can be forwarded at their convenience. Not until these requirements are faithfully and minutely fulfilled, according to the instructions hereafter given, can any case receive the action of the office.

1. *The Petition.*—The inventor, having made a useful invention or discovery, must make application in writing to the commissioner, signifying his desire of obtaining an exclusive property therein, and praying that a patent may be granted therefor. The usual form is annexed. The petition must be signed by the applicant.

No. 120.—Form of Petition.

To the Commissioner of Patents:

The petition of John Fitch, of *Philadelphia*, in the county of *Philadelphia*, and State of *Pennsylvania*—

Respectfully represents, That your petititoner has invented a new and improved mode of *preventing steam-boilers from bursting*, which he verily believes has not been known or used prior to the invention thereof by your petitioner. He therefore prays that the letters-patent of the United States may be granted to him therefor, vesting in him and his legal representatives the exclusive right to the same, upon the terms and conditions expressed in the act of Congress in that case made and provided; he having paid thirty dollars into the treasury, and complied with the other provisions of the same act.

JOHN FITCH.

2. *The Specification.*—He must then deliver a written description of his invention or discovery, and of the manner and process of making, constructing, using, and compounding the same, in such full, clear, and exact terms, avoiding unnecessary prolixity, as to enable any person skilled in the art or science to which it appertains, or with which it is most clearly connected, to make, construct, compound, and use the same; and in case of any machine, he shall fully explain the principle, and the several modes in which he has contemplated the application of that principle or character by which it may be distinguished from other inventions; and shall particularly specify and point out the part, improvement, or combination, which he claims as his own invention or discovery.

It is important, in all cases, to have the specification describe the sections of the drawings, and refer by letters to the parts. The following is the form adopted by the office:—

No. 121.—Form of Specification.

To all whom it may concern: Be it known that I, John Fitch, of *Philadelphia*, in the county of *Philadelphia*, and state of *Pennsylvania*, have invented a new and improved mode of *preventing steam-boilers from bursting*; and I do hereby declare that the following is a full and exact description thereof—reference being had to the accompanying drawings and to the letters of reference marked thereon.

The nature of my invention consists in providing the upper part of a steam-boiler with an aperture in addition to that for the safety-valve; which aperture is to be closed by a plug or disk of alloy, which will fuse at any given degree of heat, and permit the steam to escape, should the safety-valve fail to perform its functions.

To enable others skilled in the art to make and use my invention, I will proceed to describe its construction and operation: I construct my steam-boiler in any of the known forms, and apply thereto gauge-cocks, a safety-valve, and the other appendages of such boilers; but, in order to obviate the danger arising from the adhesion of the safety-valve, and from other causes, I make a second opening in the top of the boiler, similar to that made for the safety-valve, as shown at A, in the accompanying drawing; and in this opening I insert a plug or disk of fusible alloy, securing it in its place by a metal ring and screws, or otherwise. This fusible metal I, in general, compose of a mixture of a lead, tin, and bismuth, in such proportions as will insure its melting at a given temperature, which must be that to which it is intended to limit the steam; and will, of course, vary with the pressure the boiler is intended to sustain. I surround the opening containing the fusible alloy by a tube B, intended to conduct off any steam which may be discharged therefrom. When the temperature of the steam, in such a boiler, rises to its assigned limit, the fusible alloy will melt, and allow the steam to escape freely, thereby securing it from all danger of explosion.

What I claim as my invention, and desire to secure by letters-patent, is, the application to steam-boilers of a fusible alloy, which will melt at a given temperature, and allow the steam to escape, as herein described; using for that purpose the aforesaid metallic compound, or any other substantially the same, and which will produce the intended effect. JOHN FITCH.

Witnesses, { JOHN SMITH,
JOHN JONES.

When the application is for a machine, the specification should commence thus:—

Be it known that I, JOHN FITCH, of *Philadelphia*, in the county of *Philadelphia*, and state of *Pennsylvania*, have invented a new and useful machine for— [*stating the use and the title of the machine; and if the application is for an improvement, it should read thus:* a new and useful improvement on a, or on the, machine, &c.]; and I do hereby declare that the following is a full, clear, and exact description of the construction and operation of the same; reference being had to the annexed drawings, making a part of this specification, in which figure 1 is a perspective view, figure 2 a longitudinal elevation, figure 3 a transverse section, &c. [thus describing all the sections of the drawings, and then referring to the parts by letters. Then follows the description of the construction and operation of the machine, and ending with the claim, which should express the nature and character of the invention, and identify the part or parts claimed separately or in combination. If the specification is for an improvement, the original invention should be disclaimed, and the claim confined to the improvement.]

3. *The Oath or Affirmation.*—"Every inventor, before he can receive a patent, must make oath or affirmation that he does verily believe that he is the original and first inventor or discoverer of the art, machine, manufacture, composition, or improvement, for which he solicits a patent; and that he does not know or believe that the same was ever before known or used; and also of what country he is a citizen." In every case the oath or affidavit must be made before a person having general powers to administer oaths. Justices of the peace have not, in all cases, this general power.

The oath required from applicants for patents may be taken when the applicant is not, for the time being, residing in the United States, before any minister plenipotentiary, chargé d'affaires, consul, or commercial agent holding commission under the government of the United States, or before any notary public of the foreign country in which such applicant may be.

If the applicant be an alien, and have resided one year in the United States next preceding the application, and have given legal notice of his intention to become a citizen of the United States, he must make oath to these facts before he can apply for a patent for the same fee as that paid by a citizen.

No. 122.—Form of Oath.

City and County of *Philadelphia*, } *ss.*
State of *Pennsylvania*, }

On this *first* day of *December*, one thousand eight hundred and *fifty*, before the subscriber, a *justice of the peace*, personally appeared the within-named JOHN FITCH, and made solemn oath [*or affirmation*] that he verily believes himself to be the original and first inventor of the mode herein described for *preventing steam-boilers from bursting*; and that he does not know or believe the same was ever before known or used; and that he is a citizen of the United States.

JOHN SMITH.

A foreigner should make oath of what country he is a citizen. An alien-resident should make oath that he has resided in the United States one year next preceding his application for letters-patent, and has made oath of his intention to become a citizen thereof.

4. *Drawings.*—The law requires that "the applicant for a patent shall accompany his application with drawings and written references, when the nature of the case admits of drawings." These drawings should, in general, be in perspective, and neatly executed; and such parts as can not be shown in perspective, must, if described, be represented in plans, sections, or details. Duplicates of them are required, as one must accompany the patent, and one must be kept on file in the office. But an examination, as to originality of invention, may be made on a single drawing. Duplicates are only required in case the patent issues.

They must be signed by the patentee, and attested by two witnesses, except when the specification describes the sections or figures, and refers to the parts by letters, in which case they are neither required to be signed nor accompanied by written references—the whole making one instrument. Drawings are absolutely necessary, when the case admits of them. They must be on separate sheets, distinct from the specification, and one at least must be made on stiff drawing paper.*

5. *The Model or Specimen.*—Every application must be accompanied by a model when the invention admits of one. It must be neatly and substantially made, of durable material, and if possible not over one cubic foot in contents. In case models are made of pine or other soft wood, they should be painted, stained, or varnished. The name of the inventor (and assignee, if assigned) must be printed or engraved upon, or fixed to it, in a durable manner.

When the invention is of a "composition of matter," the law requires that the application be accompanied with specimens of the ingredients, and of the composition of matter, sufficient in quantity for the purpose of experiment.

Models and specimens forwarded without a name can not be entered on record, and are therefore liable to be lost or mislaid.

Models, if deposited with any of the following agents, will be forwarded to the patent office, free of expense: The collector of the port of Portsmouth, New Hampshire; Portland, Maine; Burlington, Vermont; Providence, Rhode Island; Boston, Massachusetts; Hartford, Connecticut; New York; Philadelphia, Pennsylvania; Baltimore, Maryland; Richmond, Virginia; Charleston, South Carolina; Savannah, Georgia; New Orleans, Louisiana; Detroit, Michigan; Buffalo, New York; and Cleveland, Ohio: the surveyor at St. Louis, Missouri; Pittsburgh, Pennsylvania; Cincinnati, Ohio; and Louisville, Kentucky.

Agents must send models received by them by packet, when the same are forwarded at the expense of the office.†

* The patent-office does not make original drawings to accompany applications for patents. It furnishes copies of the same only after the patent is completed. Draughtsmen in the city of Washington are always ready to make drawings at the expense of the patentees.

† If applicants prefer to have their models transmitted by express instead of by packet, they must in all cases pay the expense of transportation. Neither models nor specimens must, under any circumstances, be sent by mail. The transmission of models by the agents extends to those for new applications as well as those restored in consequence of the destruction of the originals. Models of unpatented machines, specimens of compositions and

6. *Fees payable for a Patent.*—The fee payable on an application for a patent by a citizen of the United States, or by a foreigner who has resided in the United States one year next preceding the application, and has made oath of his intention to become a citizen, is *thirty dollars:* by a subject of Great Britain, *five hundred dollars:* by any other foreigner, *three hundred dollars.*

In case of a total assignment, before the patent issues, of his invention, by a foreigner to a citizen of the United States, the same fee is required as if the patent issued to the inventor himself. Instructions in regard to the manner of paying these fees may be found hereafter.

The above six pre-requsites having been complied with, the application is ready for examination. But the neglect of any one of them, or of the instructions relative thereto, will be sufficient to delay the action of the office until they have been satisfactorily fulfilled.

If the following questions can be answered affirmatively, before transmitting the papers, few applications will be returned for correction:—

1. Is the petition signed by the applicant, and addressed to the commissioner of patents?

2. Is the specification signed, and attested by two witnesses; and does it contain a specific claim?

3. Has the inventor made oath of his citizenship, and in accordance with the instructions and forms given above?

4. Are the drawings described and referred to in the specification? If not, are they signed before two subscribing witnesses, and accompanied by written references? Are duplicates sent?

5. Has the model (or specimen) been deposited, and is the name of the inventor and assignee, if the invention be assigned, durably affixed thereto?

6. Is the fee remitted, and in manner prescribed in instructions on fees?

Results of an Examination.—If a patent is issued, it is transmitted to the inventor or his agent. If to the latter, he must have filed a full power of attorney, authorizing him to receive it. In case an assignment be made of the entire patent right, the patent will be sent to the assignee or his attorney. In cases of rejection, such references are made in the official communication as, in the opinion of the office, justify its decision. If the applicant is satisfied with the grounds of rejection, he may withdraw his application; if, on the contrary, he still deems himself entitled to a patent, he can appeal from the decision of the commissioner, as prescribed by law.

Withdrawal.—When either an American or foreign application is rejected, and the applicant relinquishes his claim, and desires to avail himself of the provisions of the seventh section of the act of 1836, and the twelfth section of the act of 1837, he must petition the commissioner of patents, stating the abandonment of his application, in which case two thirds of the original fee will be returned. The model and papers are retained by the office; and if the latter have been withdrawn for correction, or for any other purpose, they must be returned to their files before a withdrawal of two thirds of the fee can be allowed. No money is, however, refunded on the withdrawal of an application, after an appeal has been taken from the decision of the commissioner; nor any part of the fees received on filing caveats, or applications for additional improvements, or for re-issues, or for extensions, or for designs.*

In withdrawing an application, the following forms may be followed:—

To the Commissioner of Patents:

Sir: I hereby withdraw my application for a patent for improvements in the *cotton-gin*, now in your office, and request that twenty dollars may be returned

of fabrics, and other manufactures, or works of art, will be received and arranged in the National Repository of the patent-office.

* As the law does not allow public moneys to be paid in bank-bills or by draft on banks, particular instructions should be given, by the person withdrawing, as to the manner in which the money shall be paid—that is, whether to his order at the patent-office, or remitted by mail, in gold, at his risk. Money in gold and silver only is receivable and payable at the patent-office.

to me agreeably to the provision of the act of Congress authorizing such withdrawal. ELI WHITNEY.

CABOTVILLE, *Mass., July* 16, 1850.

Received of the treasurer of the United States, per THOMAS EWBANK, commissioner of patents, twenty dollars, being the amount refunded on withdrawing my application for a patent for improvements in the *cotton-gin*.

ELI WHITNEY.

CABOTVILLE, *Mass., July* 16, 1850.

Appeal.—When a patent is refused by the commissioner, the applicant can have remedy by an "appeal to the chief-justice of the district court of the United States for the District of Columbia," by giving notice thereof to the commissioner, and filing in the patent-office, within such time as the commissioner shall appoint, his reasons of appeal, specially set forth in writing, and also paying into the patent-office, to the credit of the patent fund, the sum of twenty-five dollars.

Interfering Applications.—Whenever an application is presented for a patent which, in the opinion of the commissioner, would interfere with any other patent for which an application may be pending, or with any unexpired patent which shall have been granted, it shall be the duty of the commissioner to give notice thereof to such applicants, or patentees, as the case may be; and if either shall be dissatisfied with the decision of the commissioner on the question of priority of right or invention, on a hearing thereof he may appeal from such decision on like terms and conditions as are provided in the case of applications for inventions not new; and the like proceedings shall be had to determine which, or whether either, of the applicants is entitled to receive a patent as prayed for.

Additional Improvements.—"Whenever the original patentee shall be desirous of adding the description and specification of any new improvement of the original invention or discovery, which shall have been invented or discovered by him subsequent to the date of his patent, he may, like proceedings being had in all respects as in the case of original applications, and on the payment of fifteen dollars, as hereinafter mentioned, have the same annexed to the original description and specification; and the commissioner shall certify on the margin of such annexed description and specification, the time of its being annexed and recorded; and the same shall thereafter have the same effect in law, to all intents and purposes, as though it had been embraced in the original description and specification."

In all such cases, the claim in the original patent is subject to a re-examination: and if it shall appear that any part of the claim was not original at the time of granting the patent, a disclaimer of said part must be filed in the patent-office, or the specification of claims restricted, by having the patent re-issued before the improvement can be added. If the improvement can not be added, it may, if patentable, be secured by a separate patent, on the payment of the fee of thirty dollars. If the patent was granted before the 15th of December, 1836, a model and drawings of the invention as first patented, verified by oath, must be furnished, unless dispensed with by the commissioner.

No. 123.—Form for Addition of new Improvements.

To the Commissioner of Patents:

The petition of JOHN DOE, of the county of Berkely, and State of Virginia—

RESPECTFULLY REPRESENTS: That your petitioner did obtain letters-patent of the United States for an improvement in the *boilers of steam-engines*, which letters patent are dated on the *first* day of *March*, one thousand eight hundred and *forty-five*; that he has, since that date, made certain improvements on his said invention; and that he is desirous of adding the subjoined description of his said improvements to his original letters-patent, agreeably to the provisions of the act of Congress in that case made and provided; he having paid fifteen dollars into the treasury of the United States, and otherwise complied with the requirements of the said act. JOHN DOE.

Disclaimers.—The seventh section of the law of the 3d of March, 1837, provides "that whenever any patentee shall have, through inadvertence, accident, or mistake, made his specification of claim too broad, claiming more than that of which he was the original or first inventor, some material and substantial part of the thing patented being truly and justly his own, any such patentee, his administrators, executors, and assigns, whether of the whole or of a sectional interest therein, may make disclaimer of such parts of the thing patented as the disclaimant shall not claim to hold by virtue of the patent or assignment, stating therein the extent of his interest in such patent; which disclaimer shall be in writing, attested by one or more witnesses, and recorded in the patent-office, on payment by the person disclaiming, in manner as other patent duties are required by law to be paid, of the sum of ten dollars. And such disclaimer shall thereafter be taken and considered as part of the original specification, to the extent of the interest which shall be possessed in the patent or right secured thereby, by the disclaimant, and by those claiming by or under him, subsequent to the record thereof. But no such disclaimer shall affect any action pending at the time of its being filed, except so far as it may relate to the question of unreasonable neglect or delay in filing the same."

No. 124.—Form of Disclaimer.

To the Commissioner of Patents:

The petition of John Fitch, of *Philadelphia*, in the county of *Philadelphia*, and State of *Pennsylvania*—

Respectfully represents: That he has, by assignment, duly recorded in the patent office, become the owner of a right for the several states of *Massachusetts*, *Connecticut*, and *Rhode Island*, to certain improvements in the *steam-engine*, for which letters-patent of the United States were granted to John Jones, of *Boston*, in the state of *Massachusetts*, dated on the *first* day of *March*, one thousand eight hundred and *forty-eight*. That he has reason to believe that, through inadvertence and mistake, the claim made in the specification of said letters-patent is too broad, including that of which the said patentee was not the first inventor. Your petitioner, therefore, hereby enters his disclaimer to that part of the claim in the aforesaid specification which is in the following words, to wit: "I also claim the particular manner in which the piston of the above-described engine is constructed, so as to insure the close fitting of the packing thereof to the cylinder, as set forth;" which disclaimer is to operate to the extent of the interest in said letters patent vested in your petitioner, who has paid ten dollars into the treasury of the United States, agreeably to the requirements of the act of Congress in that case made and provided.

JOHN FITCH.

Witness: John Prince.

When the disclaimer is made by the original patentee, it must, of course, be so worded as to express that fact.

Re-issues.—When an applicant wishes to cancel an old patent, and to correct a mistake or error which has arisen from inadvertence, he should state this fact in his application, and expressly *surrender* the old patent, which must be transmitted to the patent-office before a new patent will be issued. And no improvement or alteration made subsequently to the filing of the application upon which the original patent was granted, can be introduced into a patent upon re-issue.

In a re-issue, the claim is subject to re-examination, and if it shall appear that any part was not original at the time of granting the patent, the re-issue will not be granted, unless said part be omitted, or a disclaimer filed in the patent-office. If nothing can be claimed, the re-issue can not be granted, nor the surrendered patent returned.

In case of the death of an inventor, or of any assignment of the original patent made by him, a similar right vests in his executors, administrators, or assigns.

On a surrender, several patents may be issued for distinct and separate parts of the invention, upon the payment of thirty dollars for each.

No. 125.—Form of Surrender of a Patent for Re-issue.

To the Commissioner of Patents:

The petition of SAMUEL MOREY, of *Philadelphia*, in the county of *Philadelphia*, and State of *Pennsylvania*—

RESPECTFULLY REPRESENTS: That he did obtain letters-patent of the United States for an improvement in the *boilers of steam-engines*, which letters-patent are dated on the *first* day of *March*, one thousand eight hundred and *forty-eight*. That he now believes that the same is inoperative and invalid, by reason of a defective specification, which defect has arisen from inadvertence and mistake. He therefore prays that he may be allowed to surrender, and he hereby does surrender the same, and request that new letters-patent may issue to him for the same invention, for the residue of the period for which the original patent was granted, under the amended specification herewith presented; he having paid fifteen dollars into the treasury of the United States, agreeably to the requirements of the act of Congress in that case made and provided.

SAMUEL MOREY.

Extensions.—The acts of 1836 and 1848 provide for the extension of a patent for seven years from the expiration of the fourteen years for which it was originally granted, upon certain conditions to be determined by the commissioner of patents. The questions which arise on each application for an extension are—

1. Is the invention *novel?* 2. Is it *useful?* 3. Is it *valuable* and *important* to the public? 4. Has the inventor been *adequately remunerated* for his time and expenses in originating and perfecting it? 5. Has he used due diligence in introducing his invention into general use?

The law now requiring that a notice of sixty days shall be given of each application for extension, it will be necessary for the applicant to file his petition, and pay the requisite fee, at least three months before his patent expires.

Designs.—In making an application to secure a design, the same course of proceedings is required as in applying for a regular patent. The petition, specification, and oath, executed as prescribed below, must be filed, and the specimen and duplicate drawings deposited. In case of rejection, no part of the fee is refunded on designs.

No. 126.—Form of Application for Patents for Designs.

To the Commissioner of Patents:

The petition of BENJAMIN WEST, of the city and county of *Philadelphia*, and State of *Pennsylvania*—

RESPECTFULLY REPRESENTS: That your petitioner has invented or produced *a new and original design for a composition in alto-relievo*, which he verily believes has not been known prior to the production thereof by your petitioner. He therefore prays that letters-patent of the United States may be granted to him therefor, vesting in him and his legal representatives the exclusive right to the same, upon the terms and conditions expressed in the act of Congress in that case made and provided; he having paid fifteen dollars into the treasury, and complied with the other provisions of the said act.

BENJAMIN WEST.

No. 127.—Form of Specification.

TO ALL WHOM IT MAY CONCERN: Be it known that I, BENJAMIN WEST, of the *city* of *Philadelphia*, in the county of *Philadelphia*, and state of *Pennsylvania*, have invented or produced a new and original design for *a composition in alto-relievo*, and I do hereby declare that the following is a full and exact description of the same. [*Here follows a description of the design, with reference to the specimen or drawing; the specification to conclude with declaring what the inventor claims, in terms characteristic of the design, &c.*]

BENJAMIN WEST.

Witnesses: { JOHN SMITH, JOHN JONES.

No. 128.—Form of Oath.

City and County of *Philadelphia*, } *ss.*
State of *Pennsylvania*, }

On this *first* day of *December*, one thousand eight hundred and *fifty*, before the subscriber, a *justice of the peace*, personally appeared the within-named BENJAMIN WEST, and made solemn oath [*or affirmation, as the case may be*] that he verily believes himself to be the original and first inventor or producer of the design for *a composition in alto-relievo*; and that he does not know or believe that the same was ever before known or used; and that he is a citizen of the United States.

PETER SMITH.

Foreign Patents.—A patent may be taken out by the inventor in a foreign country without affecting his right to a patent in the United States, provided the invention has not been introduced into public and common use in the United States prior to the application. In every such case the patent is limited to fourteen years from the date of the foreign letters-patent. The introducer, *as such*, of a new invention from a foreign country, is not entitled to letters-patent. If an alien neglects to put and continue on public sale the invention in the United States, on reasonable terms, for eighteen months, the patentee loses all benefit of the patent.

Caveats.—The act of 1836 provides that any citizen of the United States, or alien who has declared his intention to become a citizen, who shall have invented any new art, machine, or improvement thereof, and desires further time to improve the same, may file in the patent-office a *caveat*, setting forth the design thereof, with its distinguishing characteristic, until he shall have matured his invention; and such caveat shall be filed in the confidential archives of the office. The patent can take date from the time of filing the specification, if the patent is issued within six months of the date of filing. The applicant is entitled to notice of interfering applications. A full description of the invention is required. Caveat papers can not be withdrawn or altered after they have been filed, but additional papers relating to the invention can be added to them.

No. 129.—Form of Caveat.

To the Commissioner of Patents:

The petition of AMOS WHITTEMORE, of the City and County of *New York*, and State of *New York*—

RESPECTFULLY REPRESENTS: That he has made certain improvements in the *machine for making wool-cards*, and that he is now engaged in making experiments for the purpose of perfecting the same, preparatory to his applying for letters-patent therefor. He therefore prays that the subjoined description of his invention may be filed as a CAVEAT, in the confidential archives of the patent-office, agreeably to the provisions of the act of Congress in that case made and provided; he having paid twenty dollars into the treasury of the United States, and otherwise complied with the requirements of the said act.

AMOS WHITTEMORE.

NEW YORK, *July* 16, 1850.

Here should follow a description of the general principles of the invention, so far as it has been completed

The Duration of Patents, and the Penalty for illegally Stamping Articles.—The term for which a regular patent is granted is *fourteen years*; but it may, under certain circumstances, be extended for seven years. Patents for designs are granted for *seven years* only.

Stamping or affixing the name of any patentee on any article without authority so to do, or affixing the word *patent*, or *letters-patent*, or the stamp, mark, or device of any patentee, on any unpatented article, is forbidden under a penalty of not less than one hundred dollars.

Patentees or their assignees are required to affix the date of the patent on each article vended or offered for sale, under a like penalty—thus affording to the public notice of the duration of the patent. When the article is of such a nature that the name of the patentee can not be printed thereon, it should be affixed to the case or package containing it.

Assignments.—An inventor can assign his entire right before a patent is obtained, so as to enable the assignee to take out a patent in his own name; but the assignment must be first entered of record, and the application therefor must be duly made, and the specification signed and sworn to by the inventor. In the case of an assignment by a foreigner, the same fee will be required as if the patent issued to the inventor.

The assignment of a patent may be of the whole or of an undivided part, "by any instrument in writing." All assignments, and also the grant or conveyance of the use of the patent in any town, county, state, or specified district, must be recorded in the patent-office within three months from the date of the same. But assignments, if recorded after three months have expired, will be on record as notice to protect against subsequent purchasers. Grants and assignments, recorded prior to the 15th of December, 1836, must be recorded anew before they can be valid as evidence of any title.

In all cases in which the entire invention has been assigned before the issue of the patent, the correspondence should be in the name of the assignee, he being the party in interest. (The forms of assignment will be found on page 37.)

The Fees: how payable.—All fees must be paid in *specie*, and in advance, except those required for drawings and copies, the expense of which will be communicated on application for the same.

Every applicant, on presenting his petition or application, must pay into the treasury of the United States, or into the patent-office, or to any of the assistant-treasurers, treasurers of the mint and branch-mints, collectors and surveyors of customs, and receivers of public money, particularly named below, a deposite to the credit of the treasurer, as follows:—

If a citizen of the United States, as a patent-fee	$30 00
If a foreigner who has resided in the United States one year next preceding the application for a patent, and shall have made oath of his intention to become a citizen	30 00
If a subject of the sovereign of Great Britain	500 00
All other foreigners	300 00
On entering a caveat	20 00
On entering an application for an appeal from the decision of the Commissioner	25 00
On extending a patent beyond the fourteen years	40 00
For adding to a patent the specification of a subsequent improvement	15 00
In case of re-issues, for every additional patent	30 00
On surrender of an old patent, to be re-issued to correct a mistake of the patentee	15 00
On application for a design	15 00
For a disclaimer	10 00
For copies of patents, or any other paper on file, for each 100 words	10
On all assignments, &c., which shall not contain over 300 words	1 00
On all assignments, &c., containing more than 300 and not more than 1,000 words	2 00
On all assignments, &c., containing more than 1,000 words	3 00

For copies of drawings, a reasonable sum, in proportion to the time occupied in making the same.

In case of deposite made with the assistant-treasurers, or other persons authorized to receive public moneys, a *duplicate receipt* should be taken, stating by whom the payment was made, and for what object. The particular invention should be referred to, to enable the applicant to recover back the twenty dollars, in case of the withdrawal of the petition. The certificate of deposite may be made in the following form:—

No. 130.—Form of Certificate of Deposite.

Office of the *Collector of Boston*,
December 10, 1850.

The treasurer of the United States has credit at this office for *thirty* dollars, in specie, deposited by JOHN FITCH, of the *city* of *Philadelphia*, in the county of *Philadelphia*, and state of *Pennsylvania*, the same being for a patent [*or whatever the object may be*] for a *steam-boiler*. JOHN JONES.

Officers who are authorized to receive Patent-Fees on account of the Treasury of the United States, and to give Receipts or Certificates of Deposite therefor.— Assistant-treasurer of the United States at Boston, New York, Charleston, S. C., and St. Louis, Mo.: treasurer of the mint, Philadelphia, and of the branch mint, New Orleans, La.: surveyor and inspector, Pittsburgh, Pa.: Collector, Baltimore, Md.; Richmond, Va.; Norfolk, Va.; Buffalo Creek, N. Y.; Wilmington, N. C.; Savannah, Ga.; Mobile, Ala.: surveyor of the customs, Nashville, Tenn., and Cincinnati, Ohio: receiver of public moneys, Little Rock, Ark.; Jeffersonville, Ind.; Chicago, Ill.; Detroit, Mich.

Any person wishing to pay a patent or other fee, may deposite it with either of the officers above named, and forward the receipt or certificate to the patent-office, at Washington, as evidence thereof.

Money sent by mail is at the risk of the person sending the same; and all money sent from the office, by mail, is at the risk of the person requesting to have it transmitted in that way. In no case should money be sent enclosed with models.

GENERAL INFORMATION.

THE following suggestions, gathered from the circular of the commissioner of patents, are inserted for the benefit of those who may have business with the office:—

The patent-office can not act as counsellor for individuals, nor as an expounder of law, except in reference to questions arising within the office; and the extent of information that can be given in these cases is to forward a copy of patent-laws and the usual printed official circular.

Applications are examined and patents issued in the order in which the proper documents are completed, except in cases in which the claims so nearly resemble those undergoing examination as to render an interference probable—in which case they will be taken up and examined with the cases then under examination.

A decision deliberately made and affirmed by one commissioner, can not be disturbed by his successor. The only remedy is by appeal, in the manner prescribed by law.

The personal attendance of an applicant at the patent-office is unnecessary: the business can be done by correspondence or by attorney. The examiners will decide questions of novelty and patentability upon papers imperfectly prepared, if sufficiently perspicuous to be understood, *when such papers are prepared by the inventor himself.* But if an agent be employed, it is presumed that he is qualified for the business he has undertaken without calling on the office for instructions. No double correspondence can be sanctioned: when an inventor employs an agent, the office will correspond with either, *but not with both.*

All communications relating to official business should be addressed to the commissioner of patents—no other can receive attention. Correspondence with the examiners or other subordinates relating to patents is strictly prohibited.

"REQUEST.—Congress having authorized the collection and distribution of seeds through the patent-office, a transmission to Washington of any rare and useful seeds may confer a great benefit on the community, and will, so far as is practicable, be reciprocated by the commissioner. A history of the seed transmitted, together with the place of its production, is respectfully solicited."

PUBLIC LANDS—PRE-EMPTION.

THE right of pre-emption to the public lands of the United States is granted and defined by the act of Congress of September 4, 1841, and the amendatory or supplementary act of March 3, 1843. The regulations which we here present have been compiled from instructions issued from the general land-office to the registers and receivers, and will be found to contain all the information requisite to enable pre-emptors to avail themselves of the privileges of the acts.

The individual claiming the benefits of the act of 1841, as amended by the act of 1843, must be—

1. Either a citizen of the United States, or have filed his declaration of intention to become a citizen, at the time of the settlement on which his claim is based.

2. Either the head of a family, or a widow, or a single man over the age of twenty-one years.

3. An inhabitant of the tract sought to be entered, upon which in person he has made a settlement and erected a dwelling-house, and otherwise improved said tract since the 1st of June, 1840, and prior to the time when the land is applied for; which land must, at the date of the settlement, have had the Indian title extinguished, and been surveyed by the United States.

By the ninth section of the act of the 3d of March, 1843, the entry of a claim under the act of the 4th of September, 1841, may be made, although it may be for land not surveyed at the time of the settlement, where such settlement was made prior to the 4th of September, 1841, and after the extinguishment of the Indian title.

A person failing in any one of these requisites can have no claim by virtue of this act.

A person bringing himself within each of the above requirements by proof satisfactory to the register and receiver of the land-district in which the lands may lie, taken pursuant to the rules hereinafter prescribed, will, after having taken the affidavit required by the act, be entitled to enter, by legal subdivisions, any number of acres not exceeding one hundred and sixty, or a quarter-section, to include his residence, and he may avail himself of the same at any time prior to the day of the commencement of the public sale, including said tract where the land has not yet been proclaimed.

Where the land was subject to private entry at the date of the law, and a settlement shall thereafter be made upon such land, or where the land shall have become, or shall hereafter become, subject to private entry, and after that period a settlement shall be made, which the settler is desirous of securing under this act, such notice of his intention must be given within thirty days after the date of such settlement. Such notice, in all cases, must be a written one, describing the land settled upon, and declaring the intention of such person to claim the same under the provisions of this act. (See forms 131 and 132.) The proof, affidavit, and payment, must be made within twelve months after the date of such settlement.

Where the land has *not* been *offered at public sale*, and thus rendered subject to private entry, a similar "notice in writing" must be filed within *three* months after settlement (or sooner, if the land is proclaimed for sale); and the proof, payment, and affidavit of the claimant, must be made *before* the day fixed for the *commencement* of the public sale which shall include the tract claimed. (See form 133.)

A person who has filed, or shall hereafter file, according to law, a declaratory statement for a tract of land subject to private entry, may enter the same after the twelve months from the time of his settlement shall have expired, without filing any proof of his right as a pre-emptor, provided he is the first applicant, after that time, for the entry of the same at private sale.

The tracts liable to entry under these acts are some one of the following designations:—

1. A regular quarter-section, notwithstanding its quantity, may be a few acres more or less than one hundred and sixty; or a quarter-section, which, though fractional in quantity by the passage of a navigable stream through the same, is still bounded by regular sectional and quarter-sectional lines.

2. A fractional section, containing not over one hundred and sixty acres, or any tract being a detached or anomalous survey, made pursuant to law, and not exceeding said quantity.

3. Two adjoining half quarter-sections of the regular quarters mentioned in the first designation; or, two adjoining eighty-acre subdivisions of the irregular quarters found on the north and west sides of townships, where more than two such subdivisions exist, or the excess may render them necessary, provided in the latter case the aggregate quantity does not exceed one hundred and sixty acres.

4. Two half-quarter or eighty-acre subdivisions of a fractional or broken section, adjoining each other, the aggregate quantity not exceeding one hundred and sixty acres.

5. A regular half-quarter and an adjoining fractional section, or an adjoining half-quarter subdivision of a fractional section, the aggregate quantity not exceeding one hundred and sixty acres.

6. If the pre-emptor should not wish to enter the quantity of one hundred and sixty acres, he may enter a single half-quarter section, or an eighty-acre subdivision of a fractional section.

7. One or more adjoining forty-acre lots may be entered, the aggregate not exceeding one hundred and sixty acres.

8. A regular half-quarter, a half-quarter subdivision, or a fractional section, may each be taken with one or more forty-acre subdivisions lying adjoining, the aggregate not exceeding one hundred and sixty acres.

Forty-acre tracts or quarter-quarter sections, are subject to entry, selection, or location, precisely in the same manner that eighty-acre tracts, or half-quarter sections, have heretofore been.

Only one person on a quarter-section is protected by this law, and that is the one who made the *first settlement*, provided he shall have conformed to the other provisions of the law.

A person who has *once availed himself* of the provisions of this act, can not at any future period, or at any other land-office, acquire another right under it.

No person who is the proprietor of *three hundred and twenty acres* of land in any state or territory of the United States, is entitled to the benefits of this act.

No person who shall *quit* or *abandon his residence* on his *own land*, to reside on the public land in the *same state* or *territory*, is entitled to the benefits of this act; and satisfactory proof must be furnished that he has not done so.

Land is not properly, legally surveyed, until the surveys made by the deputies are approved by the surveyor-general; but in accordance with the spirit and intent of the law, and for the purpose of bringing the settler within its provisions, the land is to be construed as surveyed when the requisite lines are run on the field, and the corners established by the deputy-surveyor.

No assignments or *transfers* of pre-emption rights can be recognised. The patents must issue to the claimants, in whose names alone all entries must be made.

Sundry Descriptions of Land which are exempted from the Operations of this Act.—1. Lands included in any reservation by any treaty, law, or proclamation, of the president of the United States, and lands reserved for salines or for other purposes.

2. Lands reserved for the support of schools.

3. Lands acquired by either of the last two treaties with the Miami tribe of Indians in the state of Indiana, or which may be acquired of the Wyandot tribe of Indians in the state of Ohio, or other Indian reservation to which the title has

been or may be extinguished by the United States at any time during the operation of these acts.

4. Sections of land reserved to the United States, alternate to other sections granted to any of the states for the construction of any canal, railroad, or other public improvement.

5. Sections or fractions of sections included within the limits of any incorporated town.

6. Every portion of the public lands which has been selected as a site for a city or town.

7. Every parcel or lot of land actually settled and occupied for the purposes of trade, and not agriculture.

8. All lands on which are situated any known salines or mines.

Persons claiming the benefits of this act, are required to file duplicate affidavits such as the law requires, and to furnish proof by one or more disinterested witnesses of the facts necessary to establish the three requisites pointed out in the commencement of these instructions, and that referred to in a succeeding place, in relation to the claimant not having quit or abandoned his residence on his own land.

The witnesses are to be first duly sworn or affirmed to speak the truth and the whole truth, touching the subject of inquiry, by some officer competent to administer oaths and affirmations; and, if not too inconvenient by reason of distance of residence from the land-office of the district, or other good cause, must be examined by the register or receiver, and the testimony reduced to writing in their presence, and signed by each witness, and certified by the officer administering the oath or affirmation, who must also join in certifying as to the respectability and credit of each witness.

In case adverse claims shall be made to the same tract, each claimant will be notified of the time and place of taking testimony, and allowed the privilege of cross-examining the opposite witnesses, and of producing counter-proof, which will also be subject to cross-examination.

When, by reason of distance, sickness, or infirmity, the witnesses can not come before the register or receiver, these officers are authorized to receive their depositions, which must be, in all other respects, conformable to the within regulations.

The proof furnished to the register or receiver, in all cases, should consist of a simple detail of facts merely, and not of statements in broad or general terms, involving conclusions of law. It is the exclusive province of the register or receiver to determine the legal conclusions arising from the facts. For instance, a witness will not be permitted to state that a claimant is the "head of a family," &c., following the words of the law, but must set forth the facts on which he grounds such allegations; because such a mode of testifying substitutes the judgment of the witness for that of the register or receiver, and allows him not only to determine the facts, but the law. A witness may possibly conscientiously testify that a minor son, living with a widowed mother, was the head of the family; and, in another case, similar in point of fact, another witness, equally conscientious, might testify that the widowed mother was the head of the family. There can not be a uniform construction given to the law, if it is carelessly left to the opinion of every witness. Registers and receivers have therefore been instructed not to receive as testimony or proof a general statement, which embodies, in general terms, the conclusions of law, without stating the facts specifically.

The witnesses must state, if the pre-emptor be the "head of a family," the facts which constitute him such; whether a husband having a wife and children, or a widower, or an unmarried person under twenty-one years of age, having a family, either of relatives or others depending upon him, or hired persons, or slaves.

All the facts respecting the settlement in person, inhabitancy or personal residence, *the time of commencement*, the manner and extent of continuance, as well as those showing the apparent objects, should be stated.

It must be stated that the claimant made the settlement on the land in person; that he has erected a dwelling upon the land; that the claimant lived in it, and made it his home, &c. By this means, the register or receiver will be enabled to determine whether or not the requisites of the law have been complied with in any given case.

The *only* affidavit required of the claimant is that prescribed by the thirteenth section of the act of 1841. (See form 134.) This affidavit *must* be taken "before the *register* or *receiver* of the land-district in which the land is situated," before an entry is permitted, and must be of the same date with the certificate of entry. An affidavit *before any other person* will not justify the entry of the land. Duplicates thereof must be signed by the claimant.*

A claimant is bound to prove his right to, and enter, *all* the land embraced by his declaratory statement, if liable to the operations of the act. No transfer or assignment of his claims can be made by a claimant under the law of 1841. The law declares such "null and void."

The proof filed by *every* claimant must show the *time*† *of the commencement of the settlement.*

The second section of the act of March 3, 1843, provides for the rights of parties who shall have died before consummating their claims, by the filing, in due time, of all the papers essential to establish the same. If proof of such right shall be filed, and payment therefor be made by the *executor*, *administrator*, or *one of the heirs, during the period prescribed by the law upon which the claim is founded,* the entry may be made in the name of "*the heirs*" of the deceased claimant. A patent on such an entry will cause the title to inure to said heirs, as if their names had been specially mentioned. In cases of this kind, the affidavit required of the pre-emptor will be taken by the person so filing the proof; and should such person be one of the heirs, he or she should be of age and mind competent to appreciate the nature and obligation of an oath. (See form 135.)

The fourth section of the act of 1843 declares it unlawful for an individual, who has once filed a declaration for one tract of land, to file at any future time a second declaration for another tract. This has reference to those required, under the fifteenth section of the act of 1841, for land subject at the time of settlement to entry *at private sale.*

The fifth section requires that similar notices or declarations in writing should be filed by settlers, under the act of the 4th of September, 1841, on land *not subject to private entry.* These declarations are to be filed in the office of the register or receiver by every such settler within *three months after his settlement.*

By the sixth section, a claimant is authorized hereafter to file a declaration, under the law of the 4th of September, 1841, or to make an entry of a claim under it, although the time prescribed by the law, for the filing of such declaration, or the making of such entry, shall have expired, provided the claimant was prevented, by vacancy in either the receiver's or register's office, from performing said act or acts within such time, and shall perform the duties required by the law within the *same period* after the disability is removed, as he would have had if such vacancy had not occurred.

The only things required of a *purchaser* of public lands are, that he shall make an application in writing to the register for the tract desired to be entered, and pay to the receiver the purchase-money. He will find a blank application at any of the land-offices where such purchase may be desired to be made.

* The law provides that "if any person shall swear falsely in the premises, he or she shall be subject to all the pains and penalties of perjury, and shall forfeit the money which he or she may have paid for said land, and all right and title to the same; and any grant or conveyance which he or she may have made, except in the hands of *bona-fide* purchasers, for a valuable consideration, shall be null and void."

† This date is all important for the purpose of determining in *all cases* whether the settlement was made within the proper time, and whether the declaratory statement was filed in due season, and the entry made within the legal period after the settlement.

No. 131.—Form for Cases where the Land claimed *was subject to Private Entry prior to September 4, 1841.*

I, JOHN DOE, of the *town* of *Peoria*, in the county of *Peoria*, and state of *Illinois*, being [*the head of a family, or widow, or single man over the age of twenty-one years, as the case may be, and a citizen of the United States, or having filed my declaration to become a citizen as required by the naturalization laws, as the case may be*], have, since the *first* day of *June*, one thousand eight hundred and *forty*, to wit: on the *fifteenth* day of *January*, one thousand eight hundred and *fifty*, settled and improved the *northeast* quarter of sect. number *two*, in township number *four north*, of range number *eight east*, in the district of lands subject to sale at the land-office at *Chicago*, and containing *one hundred and sixty* acres, which land was subject to private entry at the passage of the act of the fourth of September, one thousand eight hundred and forty-one; and I do hereby declare my intention to claim the said tract of land as a pre-emption right under the provisions of said act of the fourth of September, one thousand eight hundred and forty-one.

Given under my hand, this *twentieth* day of *January*, one thousand eight hundred and *fifty*. JOHN DOE.

Signed in presence of JOHN SMITH.

No. 132.—For Cases where the Land claimed shall *have been rendered subject to Private Entry since September 4, 1841.*

I, JOHN DOE, of the *town* of *Galena*, in the county of *Jo Daviess*, and state of *Illinois*, being [*the head of a family, or widow, or single man over the age of twenty-one years, as the case may be, and a citizen of the United States, or having filed my declaration to become a citizen as required by the naturalization laws, as the case may be*], have, since the *first* day of *June*, one thousand eight hundred and *fifty*, settled the *southeast* quarter of section number *three*, in township number *five north*, of range *four east*, in the district of lands subject to sale at the land office of *Chicago*, and containing *one hundred and sixty* acres, which land has been rendered subject to private entry since the passage of the act of the fourth of September, one thousand eight hundred and forty-one, but prior to my settlement thereon; and I do hereby declare my intention to claim the said tract of land as a pre-emption right, under the provisions of said act of the fourth of September, one thousand eight hundred and forty-one.

Given under my hand, this *first* day of *July*, one thousand eight hundred and *fifty*. JOHN DOE.

Signed in presence of JOHN SMITH.

No. 133.—Declaratory Statement for Cases where *the Land is not subject to Private Entry.*

I, JOHN DOE, of the *city* of *Detroit*, in the county of *Wayne*, and state of *Michigan*, being, &c. [*as in Nos.* 131 *and* 132], have, on the *first* day of *October*, one thousand eight hundred and *fifty*, settled and improved the *northeast* quarter of section number *ten*, in township number *eight north*, of range number *six east*, in the district of lands subject to sale at the land-office at *Detroit*, and containing *one hundred and sixty* acres, which land has not yet been offered at public sale, and thus rendered subject to private entry; and I do hereby declare my intention to claim the said tract of land as a pre-emption right, under the provisions of said act of the fourth of September, one thousand eight hundred and forty-one.

Given under my hand, this *tenth* day of *October*, one thousand eight hundred and *fifty*.

JOHN DOE.

Signed in presence of JOHN SMITH.

No. 134.—Affidavit required of Pre-emption Claimant.

I, JOHN DOE, claiming the right of pre-emption under the provisions of the act of Congress, entitled "An act to appropriate the proceeds of the sale of the public lands, and to grant pre-emption rights," approved September 4, 1841, to the *northwest* quarter of section number *two*, of township number *six north*, of range number *two west*, subject to sale at *Chicago*, do solemnly swear [*or affirm, as the case may be*], that I have never had the benefit of any right of pre-emption under this act; that I am not the owner of three hundred and twenty acres of land in any state or territory of the United States, nor have I settled upon and improved said land to sell the same on speculation, but in good faith to appropriate it to my own exclusive use and benefit; and that I have not, directly or indirectly, made any agreement or contract, in any way or manner, with any person or persons whatsoever, by which the title which I may acquire from the government of the United States should enure, in whole or in part, to the benefit of any person except myself.

JOHN DOE.

I, JOHN SMITH, *register* [*or* JOHN JONES, *receiver*], of the land-office at *Chicago*, do hereby certify that the above affidavit was taken and subscribed before me, this *first* day of *November*, one thousand eight hundred and *fifty*.

JOHN SMITH, *Register*.
Or, JOHN JONES, *Receiver*.

No. 135.—Form of Affidavit to be filed in Cases, *under the Act of the 4th of September, 1841, where the Settler shall have died before proving up and entering his Claim.*

I JOHN DOE [*executor of the estate of* RICHARD ROE, *or administrator of the estate of* RICHARD ROE, *or one of the heirs of* RICHARD ROE, *aged forty years, as the case may be*], do solemnly swear [*or affirm, as the case may be*], that, to the best of my knowledge and belief, the said RICHARD ROE, who was a settler on the *north half of the northeast* quarter of section number *seven*, of township number *three north*, of range number *one east*, subject to sale at *Chicago*, has never had the benefit of any right of pre-emption, under the act entitled "An act to appropriate the proceeds of the sales of the public lands, and to grant pre-emption rights," approved September 4, 1841; that he was not, at the time of his death, the owner of three hundred and twenty acres of land in any state or territory of the United States; that he did not settle upon and improve the above tract of land on speculation, but in good faith to appropriate it to his own exclusive use and benefit; and that he has not, directly or indirectly, made any agreement or contract, in any way or manner, with any person or persons whatsoever, by which the title which he might have acquired from the government of the United States should enure, in whole or in part, to the benefit of any person except himself.

JOHN DOE, *Executor*,
[*Or administrator, or one of the heirs of* RICHARD ROE, *as the case may be*].

I, JOHN SMITH, *register* [*or* JOHN JONES, *receiver*] of the land-office at *Chicago*, do hereby certify that the above affidavit was taken and subscribed before me, this *fifth* day of *December*, one thousand eight hundred and *fifty*.

JOHN SMITH, *Register*.
Or JOHN JONES, *Receiver*.

MILITARY BOUNTY LAND-BILL.

On the 28th September, 1850, Congress passed an act granting bounty land to certain officers and soldiers who have been engaged in the military service of the United States, or to their widows or minor children. To enable the numerous class who are affected by the privileges of the law, to avail themselves of its benefits, we insert the law entire.

Be it enacted by the Senate and House of Representatives of the United States of America in Congress assembled, That each of the surviving, or the widow or minor children of deceased commissioned and non-commissioned officers, musicians, or privates, whether of regulars, volunteers, rangers, or militia, who performed military service in any regiment, company, or detachment, in the service of the United States, in the war with Great Britain, declared by the United States on the eighteenth day of June, eighteen hundred and twelve, or in any of the Indian wars since seventeen hundred and ninety, and each of the commissioned officers who was engaged in the military service of the United States in the late war with Mexico, shall be entitled to lands as follows: Those who engaged to serve twelve months, or during the war, and actually served nine months, shall receive one hundred and sixty acres; and those who engaged to serve six months, and actually served four months, shall receive eighty acres; and those who engaged to serve for any, or an indefinite period, and actually served one month, shall receive forty acres: *Provided*, That whenever any officer or soldier was honorably discharged in consequence of disability in the service before the expiration of his period of service, he shall receive the amount to which he would have been entitled if he had served the full period for which he had engaged to serve: *Provided*, The person so having been in service shall not receive said lands, or any part thereof, if it shall appear by the muster-rolls of his regiment or corps that he deserted, or was dishonorably discharged from service, or if he has received or is entitled to any military land bounty under any act of Congress heretofore passed.

SECT. 2. *And be it further enacted*, That the period during which any officer or soldier may have remained in captivity with the enemy shall be estimated and added to the period of his actual service, and the person so detained in captivity shall receive land under the provisions of this act in the same manner that he would be entitled in case he had entered the service for the whole term made up by the addition of the time of his captivity, and had served during such term.

SECT. 3. *And be it further enacted*, That each commissioned and non-commissioned officer, musician, and private, for whom provision is made by the first section hereof, shall receive a certificate or warrant from the department of the interior for the quantity of land to which he may be entitled, and which may be located by the warrantee, or his heirs-at-law, at any land-office of the United States, in one body, and in conformity to the legal subdivisions of the public lands, upon any of the public lands in such district then subject to private entry; and upon the return of such certificate or warrant, with evidence of the location thereof having been legally made, to the general land-office, a patent shall be issued therefor. In the event of the death of any commissioned or non-commissioned officer, musician, or private, prior or subsequent to the passage of this act, who shall have served as aforesaid, and who shall not have received bounty land for said services, a like certificate or warrant shall be issued in favor and enure to the benefit of his widow, who shall receive one hundred and sixty acres of land, in case her husband was killed in battle, but not to her heirs: *Provided*, She is unmarried at the date of her application: *Provided further*, That no land warrant issued under the provisions of this act shall be laid upon any land of the United States to which there shall be a pre-emption right, or upon which there shall be an actual settlement and cultivation, except with the consent of such settler, to be satisfactorily proven to the proper land-officer.

SECT. 4. *And be it further enacted*, That all sales, mortgages, letters of attorney, or other instruments of writing going to affect the title or claim to any warrant or certificate issued, or to be issued, or any land granted, or to be granted, under the provisions of this act, made or executed prior to the issue, shall be null and void to all intents and purposes whatsoever; nor shall such certificate or warrant, or the land obtained thereby, be in any wise affected by, or charged with, or subject to, the payment of any debt or claim incurred by such officer or soldier prior to the issuing of the patent: *Provided*, That the benefits of this act shall not accrue to any person who is a member of the present Congress: *Provided further*, That it shall be the duty of the commissioner of the general land-office, under such regulations as may be prescribed by the secretary of the interior, to cause to be located, free of expense, any warrant which the holder may transmit to the general land-office for that purpose, in such state and land-district as the said holder or warrantee may designate, and upon good farming land, so far as the same can be ascertained from the maps, plats, and field-notes of the surveyor, or from any other information in the possession of the local office; and upon the location being made, as aforesaid, the secretary shall cause a patent to be transmitted to such warrantee: *And provided further*, That no patent issued under this act shall be delivered upon any power of attorney or agreement dated before the passage of this act; and that all such powers of attorney or agreements be considered and treated as null and void.

Louisiana Homestead and other Exemptions.

In addition to the property now exempt from sale under execution, there shall be exempt from sale on execution, for debts hereafter contracted, the lot and building thereon, occupied as a residence, and bona fide owned by the debtor having a family, to the value of one thousand dollars. But no debtor shall be entitled to this exemption whose wife shall own in her own right and be in the actual enjoyment of property worth more than $1,000.

§ 2. To entitle any property to the exemption provided for in the preceding section, a full and accurate description thereof shall be recorded in the office of the recorder of mortgages of the parish in which said property is situated, in the "Homestead-Exemption Book;" but no property shall, by virtue of this act, be exempt from sale for non-payment of taxes or assessments levied pursuant to law, or for debt contracted for the purchase-money thereof, or prior to the recording of the description of said property as aforesaid.

§ 3. In addition to the homestead hereinbefore exempted from sale under execution, there shall be exempt by law, from seizure for rent and sale on execution, such household effects as may be necessary for housekeeping, owned by any person being a housekeeper, or having a family for which he or she provides, to the amount of two hundred and fifty dollars: Provided that such exemption shall not extend to execution issued on a demand for the purchase-money or any of the effects or things in this section specified and contained.

§ 4. In addition to the property and effects hereinbefore exempted from seizure, for rent and for sale under execution, there shall also be exempt by law, from seizure for rent and sale on execution, the books of the family library, the family portraits and pictures, the working tools and instruments of any mechanical trade, and the books, instruments, and apparatus of any lawful profession, which may be necessary for the exercise of such trade, or the practice of such profession, and by which any person gains a living for himself and family: Provided that such exemption shall not extend to any execution issued on a demand for the purchase-money of any of the articles or things in this section mentioned.

§ 5. In addition to the property and effects hereinbefore exempted from sale under execution, and from seizure for rent, there shall also be exempted by law, from seizure or attachment, or from being garnisheed, the wages of labor, and the compensation for professional and other services, which shall have been earned and due within at least thirty-one days preceding the issuing of any seizure, attachment, or garnishment, against a debtor, to any amount sufficient for the necessary support of any person having a family for which he or she provides: Provided, that such wages or compensation may in all cases be seized, attached, or garnisheed, for alimony furnished to the debtor or his family, and also for rent of the premises occupied by them at the time.

Whenever the widow or minor children of a deceased person shall be left in necessitous circumstances, and not possessed in their own right of property to the amount of one thousand dollars, the widow or the legal representative of the children shall be entitled to demand and receive from the succession of their deceased father or husband a sum which, added to the amount of property owned by them, or either of them, in their own right, will make up the sum of one thousand dollars; and which said amount shall be paid in preference to all other debts, except those for the vendor's privilege, and expenses incurred in selling the property. The surviving widow shall have and enjoy the usufruct of the money so received from her deceased husband's succession, during her widowhood; afterward to rest in and belong to the children or other descendants of said deceased.

Tennessee Homestead Exemption.

The homestead of every housekeeper or head of a family, residing in this state, to the value of five hundred dollars, consisting of a dwelling-house and out-buildings, and land appurtenant, occupied by such person as a homestead, shall be exempt from the debts of every such housekeeper, or head of a family, and from attachment and execution, in all cases where the contract shall be made or cause of action shall accrue after the first of January, 1853, except as hereinafter provided. Before any person shall be entitled to the benefits of this act, he or she shall first declare his or her intention of claiming the homestead, by having a declaration or notice of such intention signed, sealed, and witnessed, and duly registered in the register's office in the county in which such homestead may be situated; and the right to the protection against execution being levied on such homestead, shall be only from and after date of such registration.

When the real estate is levied upon, the homestead, occupied as such by the head of the family, shall be set apart out of the real estate levied upon, by three disinterested freeholders, and the remainder may be sold. If the homestead can not be divided, the whole may be sold, and five hundred dollars of the proceeds must be paid to the clerk of the court rendering the judgment, to be used only for the purchase of another homestead; the surplus from the sale to be applied to the payment of the execution. The widow of a housekeeper, and also in case of a divorce resulting from his misconduct, is entitled to the benefits of this exemption during her widowhood. The same applies to children during their minority.

The homestead can not be aliened or mortgaged except by the joint deed of husband and wife, if he be a married man, executed in the usual manner of conveyances, except for payment of the purchase-money agreed to be given therefor. The homestead is subject to sale for all state, county, or corporation taxes, legally assessed thereon. To be entitled to the benefit of this exemption, the person must permanently reside on the premises. The person to whom the homestead is set apart, must, within one year after the delivery of the certified description of the real estate set apart by the freeholders, have the same registered in the register's office of the county wherein such land may be, to obtain a valid title thereto.

Homestead-Exemption Law.

From and after the first day of January, A. D., 1852, the family homestead of the head of each family shall be exempt from attachment and levy or sale on execution on any judgment rendered on any cause of action accruing after the taking effect of this act: provided such homestead shall not exceed in value five hundred dollars. Such homestead shall not be assets in the hands of an administrator for the payment of debts, nor subject to the laws of distribution or devise, so long as the widow or minor children, or any or either of them, shall occupy the same; and no release or waiver of such exemption shall be valid unless made by deed executed by the husband and wife, with all the formalities required by law for the conveyance of real estate; or if the wife be dead, and there be minor children, by such deed executed by the husband, with the consent of the judge of probate for the county in which the land is, indorsed on said deed.

Such exemption shall extend to any interest which the debtor may own in such homestead, and to any interest in any building occupied by him as a homestead, standing on land not owned by him to an amount not exceeding five hundred dollars.

The sheriff executing any writ of execution, founded on any judgment such as is mentioned above, on application of the debtor or his wife, if such debtor shall have a family, and if the lands and tenements about to be levied on, or any part thereof, shall be the homestead or estate thereof, shall cause a homestead such as the debtor may select, not exceeding five hundred dollars in value, to be set off to the debtor in the manner following, to wit: he shall cause three appraisers to be appointed, one by the creditor, one by the debtor, and one by himself, who shall be discreet and disinterested men, residents in the county, and shall be sworn by a justice of the peace impartially to appraise and set off by metes and bounds a homestead of the estate of the debtor, such as he may select, not exceeding five hundred dollars in value; and the set-off and assignment so made as aforesaid by the appraisers shall be returned by the sheriff, along with the writ, for record in court; and if no complaint shall be made by either party, no further proceedings shall be had against the homestead: but the remainder of the debtor's land and tenements, if any more he shall have, shall be liable to levy or sale on execution in the same manner as heretofore provided by law; provided that upon good cause shown, the court out of which the writ issued may order a re-appraisement and re-assignment of the homestead, either by the same appraisers or others appointed by the court, and under such instructions as the court may give; and such appraisement shall be made and returned to said court as aforesaid.

When the homestead of any head of a family, being a debtor in execution, shall consist of a house, or a house and lot of land, which in the opinion of the appraisers can not be divided without injury and inconvenience, they shall make and sign an appraisal of the whole value thereof, and deliver the same to the officer having the execution, who shall deliver a copy thereof to the execution-debtor, or some member of his family of sufficient age to understand the nature thereof, with a notice thereof attached, that unless the execution-debtor shall pay to said officer the surplus over and above the five hundred dollars, within sixty days thereafter, said premises will be sold; and in case such surplus shall not be paid within the said sixty days it shall be lawful for the officer to advertise and sell the same at auction, by posting up notices of the time and place of sale, with a description of the premises, in two or more of the most public places in the town where the same is situate, and a like notice in the next adjoining town, thirty days prior to the sale; and out of the proceeds of such sale to pay the said execution-debtor, with the written consent of his wife, the sum of five hundred dollars; provided, however, if the wife of such debtor shall not consent to such payment, the sheriff or officer having such proceeds shall deposite said sum of five hundred dollars in some savings institution in this state, to the credit of said debtor and wife; and the same may be withdrawn therefrom only by the joint order of the husband and wife, or by the surviver in case one should decease; and the same shall be exempt from attachment and levy of execution for the term of one year from the time it shall be paid or deposited as aforesaid. And the said sheriff or officer shall apply the balance of said proceeds on the execution, or so much thereof as shall be necessary to satisfy the same; provided that no such sale shall be made unless a greater sum than five hundred dollars shall be bid therefor, in which case the officer shall return the execution for want of property, with a certificate thereon of his proceedings.

The provisions of this act shall not extend to any judgment rendered on any contract made before the taking effect of this act, or judgment rendered on any note or mortgage executed by the debtor and his wife, nor any claim for labor less than one hundred dollars, nor to impair the lien by mortgage of the vender for the purchase-money of the homestead in question, nor of any mechanic or other person, under any statute of this state, for any debt contracted for or in aid of the erection of the buildings, nor from the payment of taxes due thereon.

No conveyance or alienation by the husband of any property exempt and set off as aforesaid, shall be valid unless the wife join in the deed of conveyance; provided, however, that such husband may without the consent of his wife, mortgage such homestead, at the time of the purchase thereof, for the payment of the purchase-money.

The provisions of this act shall not be so construed as to affect any property fraudulently purchased by the debtor, when in insolvent circumstances.

New Hampshire, *approved* July 4, 1851.

MAINE.

NEW BRUNSWICK
St. Johns River
Woodstock
Houlton
Grand L.
Mars Hill
Ft. Fairfield
Aroostook R.
Green R.
Eagle L.
St. Johns R.
Allagash R.
Walloostook R.
Mt. Katahdin
Moosehead L.
Penobscot R.
Moose R.
Chaudiere R.
St. Marie
New Liverpool
Quebec
I. of Orleans
River St. Lawrence
Saguenay R.
Scale of Miles
70 Lon. West from Greenwich

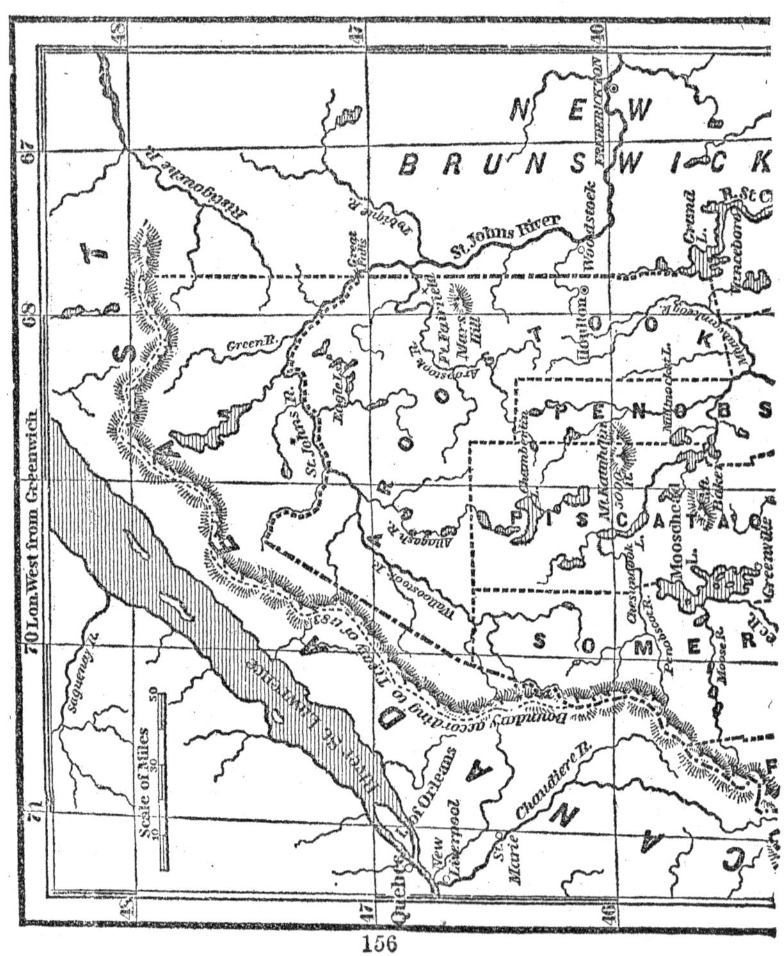

MAINE.

MAINE
NEW HAMPSHIRE
Lon. E. from Washington
Penobscot Bay
Casco Bay
Bangor
Belfast
Portsmouth

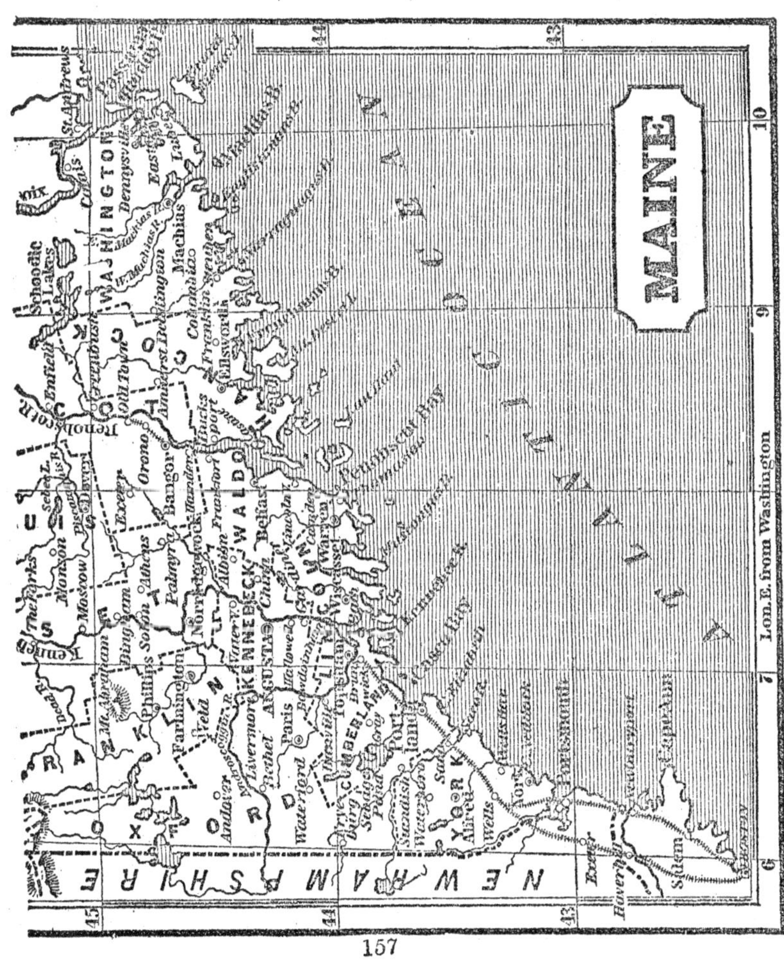

SPECIAL STATE LAWS.

MAINE.

Constitution adopted 1820.—Square Miles 32,628.—Population in 1850, 583,026.

Exemptions.

THERE is exempt from sale on execution the debtor's wearing-apparel, beds, bedsteads, bedding, and household utensils necessary for himself, his wife and children, provided that the beds and bedding so exempted shall not exceed one bed, bedstead, and necessary bedding, for every two persons, nor the other household furniture the value of fifty dollars; the tools of any debtor necessary for his trade or occupation; all bibles and schoolbooks in actual use in the family, and one copy of the statutes of the state; all cast-iron and sheet-iron stoves used exclusively for warming buildings; one cow, and one heifer till she shall become three years old; two swine, one of which shall not weigh more than one hundred pounds; and when he owns a cow, and a heifer more than three years old, or two swine, each weighing more than one hundred pounds, he may elect the cow, or the heifer, or either of the swine, to be exempt as aforesaid; ten sheep, and the wool that may be sheared from them, and thirty hundred weight of hay for the use of said cow, and two tons for the use of said sheep, and a sufficient quantity for said heifer according to its age; all produce of farms while standing and growing, until harvested, and corn and grain necessary and sufficient for the sustenance of the debtor and his family, not exceeding thirty bushels; one pew in any meetinghouse where he and his family statedly worship; all potatoes raised or purchased for the consumption of himself and family; all firewood conveyed to the debtor's house for the use of himself and family, not exceeding twelve cords; one boat, not exceeding two tons' burden, usually employed in fishing-business, belonging wholly to an inhabitant of this state; one plough, of the value of ten dollars; one cart, of the value of twenty-five dollars; one harrow, of the value of five dollars; and one cooking-stove, of the value of thirty-five dollars; and all anthracite and bituminous coal and charcoal conveyed to any person's house to be consumed in the family of such person, not exceeding five tons of anthracite and fifty bushels of bituminous; one pair of bulls, steers, or oxen, raised by the owner from his own cows, or purchased by him before the said bulls or steers were one year old, or by him at any time obtained by exchange of said bulls, steers, or oxen, for others of the same age, with a sufficient quantity of hay to keep the same through the winter season, provided that the owner began to raise or purchased said stock after the 24th day of April, 1839; one ox-yoke, with bows ring, and staple, value of three dollars; two chains value of three dollars; one ox sled value of ten dollars; one pair of oxen, steers, or bulls, purchased or obtained legally, the same as if raised; one or two horses, instead of oxen, not to exceed one hundred dollars in value; one barrel of flour, and ten dollars worth of lumber wood, or bark; also, any piece of land, not exceeding half an acre, appropriated by any number of individuals as a place of burial, constantly enclosed with a fence, and not used for the purposes of cultivation; a description of which, under the hands of individuals who appropriated the same, attested by two disinterested witnesses, shall have been recorded in the registry of deeds in the county or registry district where the land lies.

Homestead Exemption.

A LOT of land, dwelling-house and out-buildings thereon, or so much thereof as shall not exceed five hundred dollars in value—the property of a householder in actual possession thereof—exempted from any debt contracted after January 1st, 1850.

The widow and minor children of any person deceased who held property thus exempted, may continue to hold the exempted premises during the minority of such children, or while said widow remains unmarried; and the exempted property shall not be sold during such minority, or while such widow remains unmarried, for the payment of any debt contracted prior to January 1st, 1850.

Exemptions under this act shall not operate to defeat the liens of mechanics, as provided on the statutes

The head of any family, or any householder, wishing to avail himself of the benefits of this act, may file a certificate by him signed, declaring such wish, and describing the property, with the register of deeds, in the county where the same is situate; and upon receiving the fees now allowed for recording deeds, such register shall record the same in a book kept for that purpose: and so much of the property as does not exceed the value aforesaid, shall be for ever exempt from liability for any debt contracted by such householder after the date of the recording of the certificate; and the record in said register's office shall be *prima facie* evidence that the certificate purporting to be there recorded, was made, signed, and filed, as appears upon such record. And upon being recorded as aforesaid, the property as described in the first section of this act shall be exempted within the provisions thereof.

When property, exempted as aforesaid, is claimed by a creditor to be of greater value than five hundred dollars, it may be seized on execution, and the appraisers shall first set off such part of the property as the debtor may select, and if he neglects so to do, the officer may select for him to the value of five hundred dollars, by metes and bounds; and shall then appraise and set off to the creditor, in manner now prescribed by law, the remainder, or so much thereof as may be necessary to satisfy such execution; and the appraisers shall be sworn accordingly, and the officer shall make return of his doings thereon.

Mechanics' Lien.

ANY ship carpenter, calker, blacksmith, joiner, or other person, who shall perform labor or furnish materials for or on account of any vessel building or standing on the stocks, or under repairs after having been launched, shall have a lien on such vessel for his wages or materials, until four days after such vessel is launched or such repairs afterward have been completed; and may secure the same by an attachment on said vessel within that period, which shall have precedence of all other attachments.

In case any such creditor shall demand or claim more for his said services performed or materials furnished as aforesaid than is just and reasonable, the owner, agent, or contractor, may tender the full, fair, and just balance to such claimant, and such tender shall, if refused, absolutely discharge the lien on such vessel.

Any person who shall perform labor or furnish materials for erecting, altering, or repairing any house or other building or appurtenances, or furnish labor or materials for the above purposes by virtue of any contract with the owner thereof, shall have a lien, to secure the payment of the same, upon such house or building, and the lot of land on which the same stands, and upon the right of redeeming the same when under mortgage; and such lien shall continue in force for the space of ninety days from the time when such payment becomes due, notwithstanding the decease of any such debtor and the representation of his estate as insolvent. And the administrator or executor of any insolvent estate shall, upon citation, be holden to answer to any action brought upon a claim secured by such lien.

Such person may secure the benefit of such lien by an attachment of such house or building, land, or right of redemption, within the said ninety days; and such attachment shall have precedence of all other attachments not made under any such lien.

When the debtor shall tender to the creditor the sum justly due to him, as aforesaid, such lien shall cease. In case of the death of any person owing a debt secured by a lien in the manner above contemplated, within the ninety days mentioned therein, and before the commencement of the action mentioned above, then a further time of sixty days from and after an appointment of an administrator or executor, and notice thereof given, shall be allowed in which to commence said action, and such lien shall continue in force during said sixty days.

When any lot or parcel of land, or any mill-privilege, may be leased for the purpose of having a house, shop, mill, or other building, erected or placed thereon, and rent is reserved in the lease, all the buildings erected as aforesaid, together with all the interest which the lessee before had or may have in the premises, by force of such lease, shall remain liable to be attached by any such lessor or his assignee, to secure the rent due on such lease, notwithstanding any previous transfer of property by the lessee, provided such attachment be made within six months from the time such rent becomes due.

Every person in whose name any merchandise shall be shipped, shall be deemed the true owner thereof, so far as to entitle the consignee of such merchandise to a lien thereon for any moneys advanced or negotiable security given by such consignee to and for the use of the person in whose name such shipment shall have been made, and for any money or negotiable security received by the person in whose name the shipment shall have been made, to and for the use of any such consignee.

Any person who is entitled to receive annual compensation for damages sustained to his land by the overflowing of a milldam, shall have a lien therefor from the time of the institution of the original complaint, on the mill and milldam, with the appurtenances, and the land under and adjoining the same, and used therewith, provided that it shall not extend to any sum due more than three years before the commencement of the action.

If the demandant in a writ of entry shall claim an estate for life only in the premises, and if he shall pay any sum allowed to the tenant for improvements, he or his executors or administrators, at the termination of his estate, shall be entitled to receive of the remainder man, or reversioner the value of such improvements as they then exist, and shall have a lien therefor, and he may keep possession thereof accordingly till the same be paid.

Chattel Mortgages.

No mortgage of personal property, made since the twenty-fourth day of April, one thousand eight hundred and thirty-nine, or that shall be made hereafter, where the debt thereby secured amounts to more than the sum of thirty dollars, shall be valid against any other persons than the parties thereto, unless possession of the mortgaged property be delivered to and retained by the mortgagee, or unless the mortgage has been or shall be recorded by the clerk of the town where the morgager resides; and if such mortgagee resides in any unincorporated place, the mortgage shall be recorded in that incorporated town which may be nearest to the place where such mortgager resides.

Personal property mortgaged may be redeemed by the lawful claimant at any time within sixty days after breach of condition, unless the property has been sold, in pursuance of the contract of the parties, or on execution for debt of mortgager.

Upon tender of lawful amount, if the property is not returned, the party entitled to redeem may replevin.

Law regulating Contracts.

No action shall be brought and maintained in any of the following cases:—

1. To charge an executor or administrator, upon any special promise, to answer damages out of his own estate: 2. To charge any person, upon any special promise, to answer for the debt, default, or misdoings, of another: 3. To charge any person upon an agreement made in consideration of marriage: 4. Upon any contract for the sale of lands, tenements, or hereditaments, or of any interest in or concerning them: 5. Upon any agreement that is not to be performed within one year from the making thereof; unless the promise, contract, or agreement, upon which such action shall be brought, or some memorandum or note thereof, shall be in writing, and be signed by the party to be charged therewith, or by some person thereunto lawfully authorized.

The consideration for the agreement need not be expressed in the writing.

No action shall be brought to charge any person, upon or by reason of any representation or assurance made concerning the character, conduct, credit, ability, trade, or dealings, of any other person, unless such representation or assurance shall be made in writing, and signed by the party to be charged thereby, or by some person thereunto by him lawfully authorized.

No contract for the sale of any goods, wares, or merchandise, for the price of thirty dollars or more, shall be allowed to be good, unless the purchaser shall accept part of the goods so sold, and actually receive the same, or give something in earnest to bind the bargain, or in part payment, or some note or memorandum in writing, of the said bargain, be made and signed by the party to be charged, or by his agent, thereunto by him lawfully authorized.

Limitation of Actions.

The following actions shall be commenced within six years next after the cause of action shall accrue, and not afterward, namely:—

1. All actions of debt, founded upon any contract or liability, not under seal, except such as are brought upon a judgment or decree of some court of record of the United States, or of this, or some other of the United States, or of some justice of the peace in this state. 2. All actions upon judgments rendered in any court, not being a court of record, except justices of the peace in this state. 3. All actions for arrears of rent. 4. All actions of assumpsit, or upon the case, founded on any contract or liability, express or implied. 5. All actions for waste, and all actions of trespass on land, and all actions of trespass, except those of trespass for assault, battery, and false imprisonment. 6. All actions of replevin, and other actions for taking, detaining, or injuring goods or chattels. 7. All other actions on the case, except actions for slanderous words and for libels.

All actions against a sheriff, except for the escape of prisoners committed on execution, for the negligence or misconduct of his deputies, shall be commenced within four years next after the cause of action shall accrue.

All actions of assault and battery and for false imprisonment, and all actions for slanderous words and for libels, shall be commenced within two years next after the cause of action shall accrue.

All actions for the escape of prisoners committed on execution shall be commenced within one year next after the cause of action shall accrue.

No *scire facias* shall be served on bail, unless within one year next after judgment rendered against the principal.

All actions against an endorser of a writ must be commenced within one year next after judgment entered in the original action.

None of the foregoing provisions shall apply to any action brought upon a promissory note which is signed in the presence of an attesting witness, nor to an action brought upon any bills, notes, or other evidences of debt, issued by any bank.

In all actions of debt or assumpsit brought to recover the balance due upon a mutual and open account, the cause of action shall be deemed to have accrued at the time of the last item proved in such account.

If any person entitled to bring any of the before-mentioned actions, shall, at the time when the cause of action accrues, be a minor, a married woman, insane, imprisoned, or without the limits of the United States, such person may bring the actions within the times respectively limited, after the disability shall be removed.

All personal actions on any contract not limited by any of the foregoing sections, or any other law of the state, shall be brought within twenty years after the accruing of the cause of action.

When a writ shall fail of a sufficient service or return, by any unavoidable accident, or by the default or negligence of any officer to whom it was delivered or directed; or when such writ shall be abated, or the action otherwise avoided and defeated, for any matter of form, or by the death of either party; or if a judgment for the plaintiff shall be reversed on a writ of error, in such case the plaintiff may commence a new action on the same demand within six months after the abatement or determination of the original suit, or reversal of judgment in the same; and if the cause of action by law survives, his executor or administrator, in case of his death, may commence such new action within said six months.

No action shall be maintained against any person as surety in a replevin bond, unless the writ be served on him within one year after the final judgment in the action of replevin.

In suits by aliens, the time of continuance of war between the United States and the country of which such alien is the subject is not deemed a part of the time limited for the commencement of any of the before-mentioned actions.

In actions of debt or upon the case founded upon any contract, no acknowledgment or promise shall be allowed as evidence of a new or continuing contract, whereby to take any case out of the operations of the provisions of [these limitations], or to deprive any party of the benefit thereof, unless such acknowledgment or promise be an express one, and made or contained in some writing signed by the party chargeable thereby.

If there are two or more joint contractors, such acknowledgment or promise, made or signed by one or more, shall not deprive the other joint-promissor of the benefit of the limitation.

If, at the time when any cause of action mentioned in this act shall accrue against any person, he shall be out of the state, the action may be commenced within the time herein limited therefor, after such person shall come into the state; and if, after any cause of action shall have accrued, the person against whom it shall have accrued shall be absent from and reside without the state, time of his absence shall not be taken as any part of the time limited for the commencement of the action.

REAL ACTIONS AND RIGHTS OF ENTRY.—No person shall commence any real or mixed action for the recovery of lands, or make an entry thereon, unless within twenty years after the right to make such entry, or bring such action, first accrued, or within twenty years after he or those under or from whom he claims, and shall have been seized or possessed of the premises, except as hereinafter provided.

If such right or title first accrued to an ancestor or predecessor of the person who brings the action or makes the entry, or to any other person from, by, or under whom he claims, the said twenty years shall be computed from the time when the right or title so first accrued to such ancestor, predecessor, or other person.

If any minister, or other sole corporation, shall be disseized, any of his successors may enter upon the premises, or may bring an action for the recovery of them at any time within five years after the death, resignation, or removal of the person disseized, notwithstanding the twenty years after the disseizin shall have expired.

If, at the time when such right of entry or of action upon or for any lands shall first accrue, the person entitled to such entry or action shall be within the age of twenty-one years, or a married woman, insane, imprisoned, or absent from the United States, such person, or any one claiming from, by, or under him, may make the entry or bring the action at any time within ten years after such disability shall be removed, notwithstanding the twenty years before limited in that behalf shall have expired.

No real or mixed actions for the recovery of lands shall be commenced by or on behalf of the state, unless within twenty years from and after the day on which this act shall become a law, or within twenty years next after the time of the accruing of the title to the state.

No person shall acquire any right or privilege of way, air, or light, or any other easement, from, in, upon, or over the land of another, by the adverse use and enjoyment thereof, unless such use shall have been continued uninterrupted for twenty years.

No action for the recovery of any estate, sold under license by an executor, administrator, or guardian, shall be maintained by any heir, or other person claiming under the deceased testator or intestate, unless it be commenced within five years next after the sale.

No real or mixed action for the recovery of any lands in this state shall be commenced or maintained against any person in possession of such lands, where such person or those under whom he claims have been in actual possession for more than forty years, and claiming to hold the same in his or their own right—and which possession shall have been adverse, open, peaceable, notorious, and exclusive.

Collection of Debts.

ARREST.—No person shall be arrested on mesne process on any suit brought on any contract, express or implied, or brought on any judgment founded on such contract, except as provided in the following section:—

Any person, whether a resident within this state or not, may be arrested and held to bail, or committed to prison on mesne process on any contract, expressed or implied, when the sum demanded amounts to ten dollars, or on a judgment founded on contract, when the debt originally recovered and still remaining due is ten dollars or more, exclusive of interest on such judgment, when he is about to depart and reside beyond the limits of this state, with property or means exceeding the amount required for his own immediate support, provided that the creditor, his agent or attorney, shall make oath before a justice of the peace, to be certified by such justice on the said process, that he he has reason to believe, and does believe, that such debtor is about to depart and reside, and to take with him property or means as aforesaid, and that the demand in the said process, or the principal part thereof, amounting to at least ten dollars, is due to him.

In all actions not founded on contract, or on a judgment on such contract, the original writ or process shall run against the body of the defendant, and he may be thereon arrested and imprisoned, or he may give bail.

ATTACHMENT.—All goods and chattels may be attached and held as security to satisfy the judgment for damages and costs, which the plaintiff may recover, except such as from their nature and situation have been considered as exempted from attachment according to the principles of the common law, as adopted and practised in this state, and such as are exempt from levy or sale on execution.

All real estate which is liable to be taken in execution may be attached on mesne process, and held as security for the purposes aforesaid.

Deeds.

IT is necessary that they be sealed with a seal in this state, but there need be only one attesting witness, nor need the wife of the grantor be separately examined. They should be acknowledged and immediately recorded.

ACKNOWLEDGMENT.—The acknowledgment may be made before any justice of the peace in this state, or any justice of the peace, magistrate, or notary public, within the United States, or any commissioner appointed for that purpose by the governor of this state, or before any minister or consul of the United States or notary public in any foreign country.

Form of Acknowledgment.

State of Maine,
County of *Lincoln*, } *ss.* *Bath, January* 14, 1851.

Before me then personally appeared JOHN DOE *and* SUSAN *his wife*, in the foregoing instrument named, and acknowledged that they did sign and seal the same as their free act and deed.

JOHN JONES, *Justice of the Peace.*

Rights of Married Women.

ANY married woman may become seized or possessed of any property, real or personal, by direct bequest, demise, gift, purchase, or distribution, in her own name and as of her own property; provided it shall be made to appear by such married woman, in any issue touching the validity of her title, that the same does not in any way come from the husband after coverture.

Hereafter, when any woman possessed of property, real or personal, shall marry, such property shall continue to her, notwithstanding her coverture; and she shall have, hold, and possess the same, as her separate property, exempt from any liability for the debts or contracts of her husband.

Any married woman possessing property by virtue of this act, may release to the husband the right of control of such property, and he may receive and dispose of the income thereof, so long as the same shall be appropriated for the mutual benefit of the parties.

Any married woman who is seized and possessed of property, real or personal, as provided for above, may commence, prosecute, or defend, any suit in law or equity, as if she were unmarried, or jointly with her husband, but the person of such married woman is free from arrest. In case of the decease of such married woman intestate, her property, real and personal, shall descend to her heirs—but any married woman may by will divide or bequeath any property belonging to her.

Rate of Interest.

THE legal rate of interest is six per cent. If more be agreed to be taken, only legal interest can be recovered. Usurious interest paid may be recovered *back*.

Wills.

In this state a will must be in writing, signed by the testator, or by some person in his presence and by his express direction, and shall be attested and subscribed in his presence by three credible witnesses.

Form of Attestation answering for every State of the Union.

Signed, sealed, published, and declared, by the said JOHN DOE, as and for his last will and testament, in the presence of us, who, at the request of the said JOHN DOE, and in his presence and in the presence of each other, have hereunto subscribed our names and respective places of residence as witnesses.

JOHN SMITH, Boston,
JOHN JONES, Boston,
DUNN BROWN, Roxbury.

NEW HAMPSHIRE.

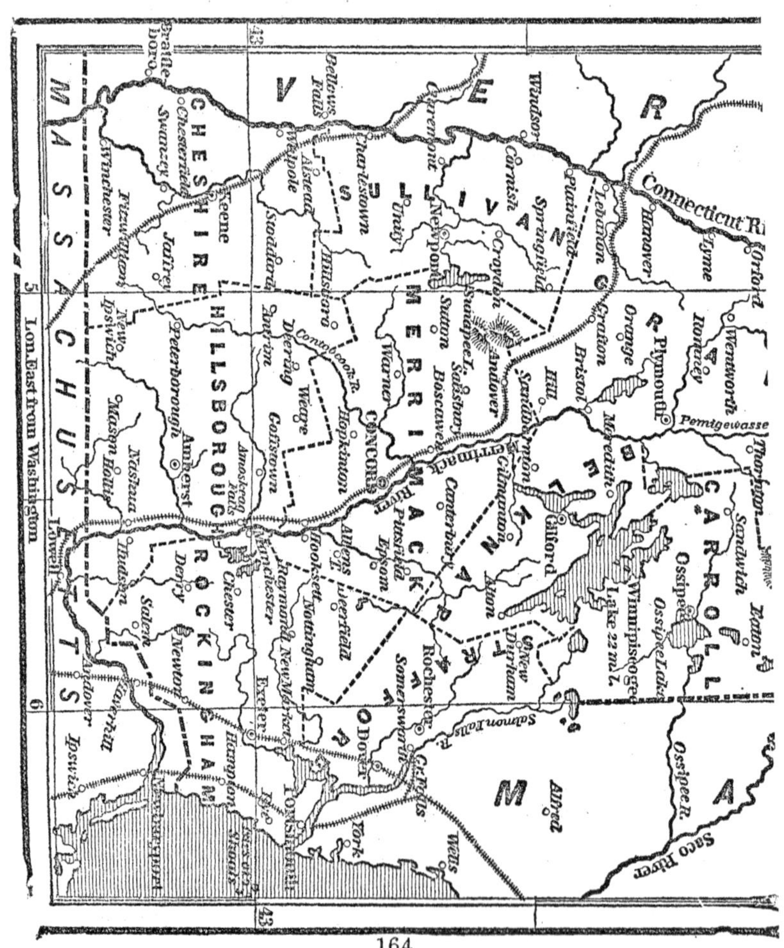

NEW HAMPSHIRE.

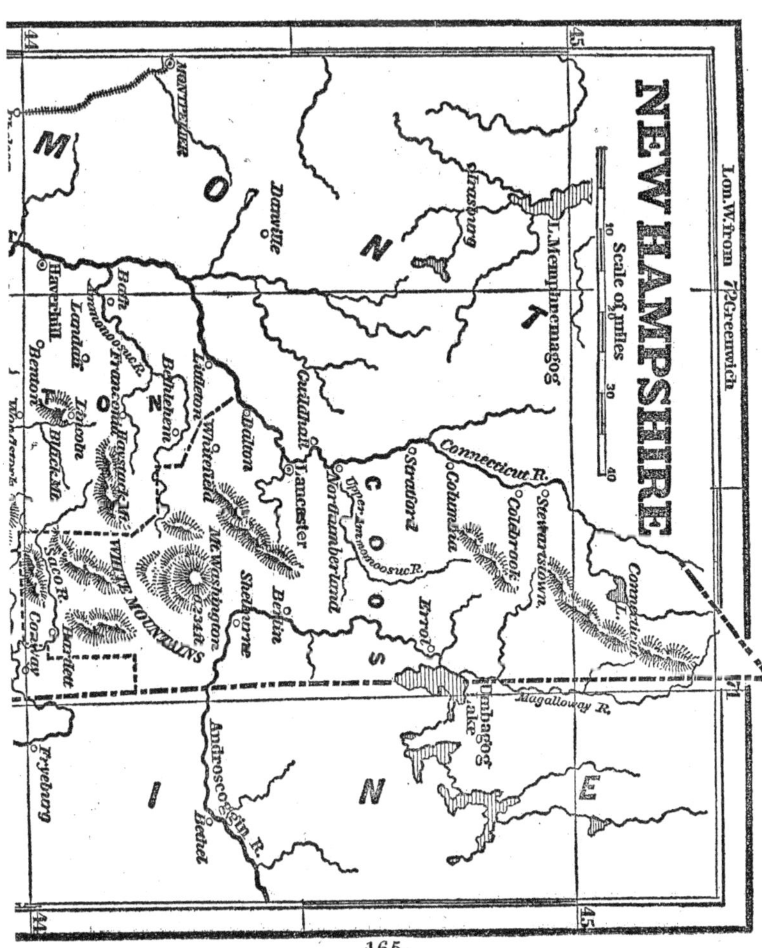

NEW HAMPSHIRE.

Constitution adopted 1792.—Square Miles 9411.—Population in 1850, 317,997.

Exemptions.

THERE is exempt from sale on execution wearing apparel necessary for the use of the debtor and his family, comfortable beds, bedsteads, and bedding, necessary for the debtor, his wife and children, household furniture to the value of twenty dollars; the bibles and schoolbooks in use in the family, one cow, and one and a half tons of hay, tools of his occupation to the value of twenty dollars; six sheep and the fleeces of the same, one cooking stove and the necessary furniture belonging to the same, provisions and fuel to the value of twenty dollars, the uniform, arms and equipments of every officer and private in the militia, his interest in one pew in any meetinghouse in which he or his family usually worship, and his interest in one lot or right of burial in any cemetery. (See page 155.)

Mechanics' Lien.

IF any person shall perform any labor or furnish any materials toward building, repairing, fitting or furnishing any vessel, payment for which is due, he shall have a lien therefor on such vessel for the space of four days after the vessel is completed. Such lien may be secured by attachment of the vessel within said four days, and such attachment shall have precedence of all other attachments and claims, except the lien for mariners' wages.

If any person under any written contract, shall furnish any labor or materials for erecting, repairing, or altering, any building, he shall have a lien therefor upon such house or building and upon the interest of the person for whom such labor and materials are furnished, in the lot of land on which it stands, for the space of thirty days after the payment of said labor or materials shall become due by said contract. Such lien shall not attach unless such contract is made in writing, expressing the terms thereof fully, and a true copy of the same left with the town-clerk of the town in which such house or building is situate.

Such lien may be secured within the thirty days aforesaid, by an attachment of such building and land, and such attachment shall have precedence of all attachments made where no such lien exists, after the filing of such contract with the town-clerk.

If the land on which such building is situate, or to be erected, is under mortgage or attachment at the time of filing the copy of the contract as aforesaid, such prior mortgagee, or attaching creditor shall be preferred to the extent of the value of the land and building at that time.

If two or more persons having such lien upon the same property, shall secure the same by attachment, they shall severally hold according to the priority of their several liens.

If the owner of such land or building shall have failed to perform his part of any such contract, by reason whereof the other party shall without his default, have been prevented from completing such contract, the latter shall have a lien on such building and land for such sum as is his due for what he has done.

Any lien aforesaid may be discharged at any time by the payment or tender of the amount due, together with the costs of any attachment made to secure the same.

These provisions shall not be in force in any town, unless adopted by such town at some meeting called for that purpose.

Limitation of Actions.

No action for the recovery of any real estate shall be maintained, unless such action is brought within twenty years after the right first accrued to the plaintiff, or to any person under whom he claims, to commence an action for the recovery thereof.

If the person first entitled to maintain an action for the recovery of such real estate was within the age of twenty-one years, a married woman, or insane, at the time such right accrued, such action may be commenced within five years after such disability is removed.

Actions for words, and for assault, battery, wounding, or imprisonment, shall be brought within two years after the cause of action accrued, and not afterward.

All other personal actions shall be brought within six years after the cause of action accrued, and not afterward.

Actions of debt founded upon any judgment or recognizance, or upon any contract under seal, may be brought within twenty years after the cause of action accrued, and not afterward.

Actions upon notes secured by mortgage, may be brought so long as the plaintiff is entitled to commence any action upon the mortgage.

Writs of error may be commenced within three years after judgment, rendered, and not afterward.

Any infant, married woman, or insane person, may commence either of the personal actions aforesaid, within two years after such disability is removed.

If the defendant, at the time the cause of action accrued, or afterward, was absent from or residing out of the state, the time of such absence shall be excluded in the computation of the several times before limited for the commencement of personal actions.

If judgment shall be rendered against the plaintiff in any action commenced within the times before limited, or upon any writ of error brought thereon, he may commence a new action thereon within one year thereafter, in case his right of action is not barred by such judgment.

Collection of Debts.

Arrest.—No female shall be arrested or imprisoned upon any writ in any action founded on contract.

No person shall be liable to arrest on mesne process in any real action or actions of ejectment.

No person shall be arrested or imprisoned on any writ in any action founded on a contract unless the debt or damage for the recovery of which such action may be brought, exclusive of all the costs, shall exceed the sum of thirteen dollars and thirty-three cents.

No person shall be arrested upon any writ or execution founded on a contract made after the first day of March, eighteen hundred and forty-one, unless the plaintiff or some person in his behalf shall make an affidavit before a justice, on the back of such writ, that in his belief the defendant is justly indebted to him in a certain sum exceeding thirteen dollars and thirty-three cents, and that he conceals his property so that no attachment or levy can be made, or there is good reason to believe he is about to leave the state, to avoid the payment of his debts.

If any person shall be committed to prison by the officer or his bail, or upon surrender by his bail, he shall, unless he shall be bailed before the judgment, be held in prison until the expiration of thirty days after the rendition of such judgment for the plaintiff as execution may issue upon, unless sooner legally discharged.

Attachment.—All property, real and personal, which is liable to be taken in execution, may be attached and held as security for the judgment the plaintiff may recover.

Chattel Mortgages.

POSSESSION of the mortgaged property must be delivered to, and retained by the mortgagee, or the mortgage must be recorded in the office of the clerk of the town in which the mortgager resides at the time of making the same.

Each mortgager and mortgagee, shall make and subscribe an affidavit in substance as follows:—

We severally swear that the foregoing mortgage is made for the purpose of securing the debt specified in the condition thereof, and for no other purpose whatever, and that said debt was not created for the purpose of enabling the mortgager to execute said mortgage, but is a just debt, honestly due and owing from the mortgager to the mortgagee.

Every such affidavit with the certificate of the justice who administered the oath shall be made upon or appended to such mortgage, and recorded therewith.

No mortgager of personal property, shall sell or pledge any such property, by him mortgaged, without the consent of the mortgagee in writing, upon the back of the mortgage, and on the margin of the record thereof, in the office where such mortgage is recorded.

No mortgager shall execute any second or subsequent mortgage of personal property, while the same is subject to a previously existing mortgage given by such mortgager, unless the fact of the existence of such previous mortgage is set forth in the subsequent mortgage.

If any mortgager shall be guilty of any offence specified in the two preceding paragraphs, he shall be punished by fine, equal to double the value of the property so wrongfully sold, pledged, or mortgaged, one half to the use of the party injured, and the other half to the use of the county.

Law Regulating Contracts.

No action shall be maintained upon any contract for the sale of lands, unless the agreement upon which such action shall be brought or some memorandum thereof is in writing, and signed by the parties to be charged therewith, or by some other person thereunto lawfully authorized by writing.

No action shall be brought in the following cases:—

1. To charge any executor or administrator upon any special promise to answer damages out of his own estate;

2. To charge any person upon any special promise to answer for the debt, default, or miscarriage of another person,

3. To charge any person upon an agreement made upon consideration of marriage;

4. To charge any person upon any agreement that is not to be performed within one year from the time of making it;

Unless such promise or agreement or some memorandum or note thereof is in writing and signed by the party to be charged therewith, or by some person thereunto by him lawfully authorized.

No action shall be brought upon any contract for the sale of any goods, wares or merchandise, for the price of thirty-three dollars, or upward, and no such contract shall be valid unless the buyer shall accept part of the property so sold and actually receive the same, or give something in earnest to bind the bargain, or in part payment, or unless some note or memorandum in writing of the said bargain be made and signed by the parties to be charged by such contract or their agents thereunto lawfully authorized.

Deeds.

EVERY deed or other conveyance of real estate shall be signed and sealed by the party granting the same, attested by two or more witnesses, acknowledged by such grantor before a justice of the peace, notary public, or commissioner, or before a minister or consul of the United States in a foreign country, and recorded at length in the registry of deeds in the county in which such lands lie. A SEAL should be used. The wife need not be separately examined.

Form of acknowledgment the same as in Maine.

Rights of Married Women.

WHENEVER any married woman shall be entitled to hold property in her own right and to her separate use, she may make contracts, may sue and be sued in her own name and may dispose of said property, by will or otherwise, as if she were sole and unmarried; and if she shall decease intestate, her husband shall be excluded from any share in her said estate, and such estate shall be administered and inherited in the same manner as if she were sole and unmarried.

Any married woman of full age may join with her husband in any conveyance of real estate, and any married woman may join with her husband in release of dower, although she is not of full age.

Any married woman, of the age of 21 years or upward, and of sane mind, who may be seized in her own right of any real estate in this state, shall have power to give, devise, and dispose of, the same by will in writing, which will, when signed and sealed by the devisor, and duly attested and subscribed by three credible witnesses thereto, in her presence, and executed with the formalities now required by law in other cases, shall be proved and allowed by the courts of probate in this state, and shall be effectual in distributing the estate devised according to the intention of the devisor; provided, that any such will shall in no case affect injuriously the rights acquired by the husband in any estate so devised, by virtue of the marriage contract.

DOWER.—The widow of every person deceased shall be entitled to her dower in the real estate of which her husband was seized during coverture.

Rate of Interest.

THE legal rate is six per cent, and if more be taken, the party forfeits three times the amount unlawfully taken.

Wills.

WILLS should be in writing, signed and SEALED by the testator or by some person in his presence, and by his express direction, and attested and subscribed in his presence by three or more credible witnesses.

For form of attestation, see page 163.

VERMONT.

VERMONT
Scale of Miles
10
20
30
Connecticut River
MASSACHUSETTS
BENNINGTON
WINDHAM
WINDSOR
RUTLAND
Bennington
Pownal
Wilmington
Brattleboro
Halifax
Guilford
Vernon
Wardsboro
Fayetteville
Newfane
Townsend
Stratton
Manchester
Arlington
Cambridge
Dorset
Pawlet
Wells
Poultney
Castleton
Benson
Sudbury
Brandon
Pittsford
Rutland
Clarendon
Wallingford
Danby
Peru
Andover
Chester
Rockingham
Bellows Falls
Weathersfield
Cavendish
Plymouth
Killington
Stockbridge
Barnard
Woodstock
Hartland
Hartford
Norwich
Windsor
Cornish
Hanover
Newport
Keene
Concord
Plymouth
Merrimack R.
White R.
Lon. E. from Washington

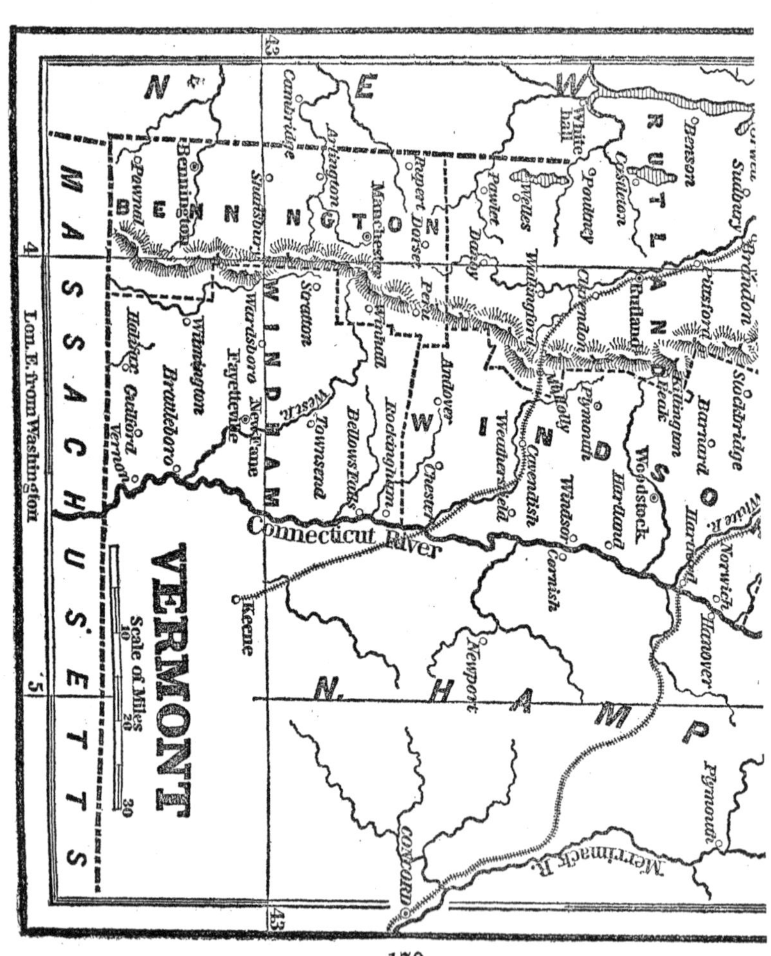

VERMONT.

Lon. West from Greenwich
CANADA
LOWER
NEW YORK
NEW HAMPSHIRE
LAKE CHAMPLAIN
FRANKLIN
ORLEANS
LAMOILLE
CHITTENDEN
ADDISON
WASHINGTON
ORANGE
CALEDONIA
ESSEX
MONTPELIER
Burlington
St. Albans
Middlebury
Vergennes
Platts burg
Connecticut River
Onion R.
Lamoille River
Missisque R.
Hyde Park
Danville
Guildhall
Chelsea
Montgomery
Derby
Troy
Canaan
Lemington
Bloomfield
Brunswick
Concord
Waterford
Barnet
Peacham
Lyndon
Hardwick
Craftsbury
Johnston
Bakersfield
Fletcher
Fairfax
Cambridge
Westford
Essex
Jericho
Waterbury
Morristown
Barre
Northfield
Warren
Williamstown
Brookfield
Randolph
Rochester
Hancock
Lincoln
New Haven
Monkton
Charlotte
Shelburne
Shoreham
Bridport
Goshen
Topsham
Newbury
Bradford
Haverhill
Fairlee
Strafford
Berkshire
Highgate
Lowell
Irasburg
Barton
Sutton
44
45
72
73

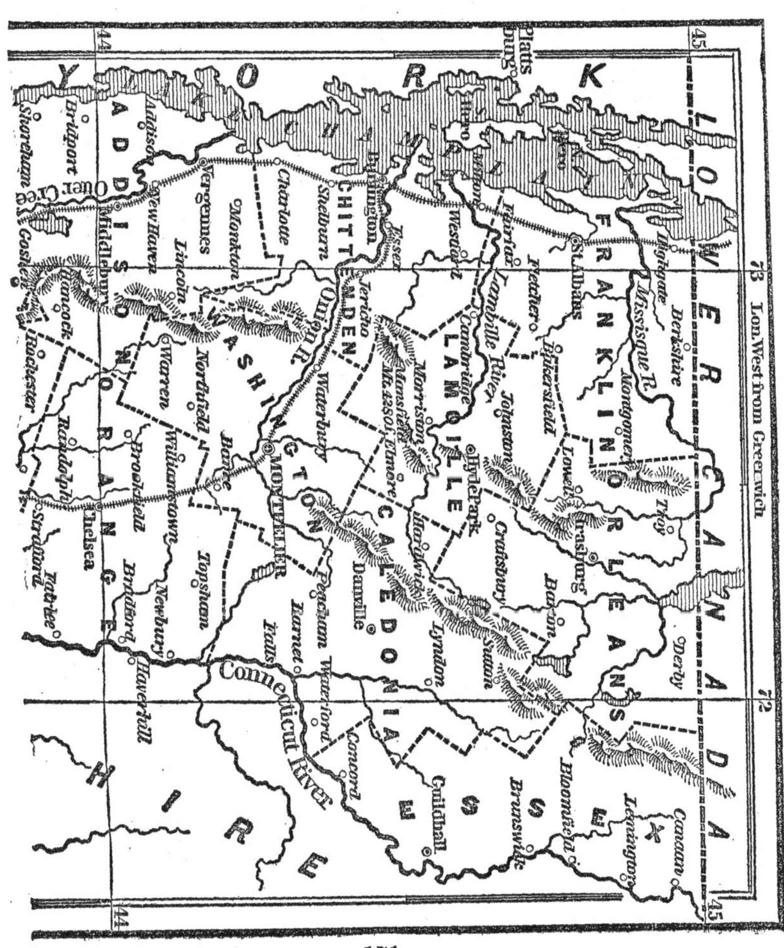

VERMONT.

Constitution adopted 1793.—Square Miles, 10,212.—Population in 1850, 313,451.

Exemptions.

THERE is exempted from sale on execution such suitable apparel, bedding, tools, arms, and articles of household furniture, as may be necessary for upholding life; one cow; the best swine, or the meat of one swine; ten sheep, and one year's product of said sheep in wool, yarn, or cloth; forage sufficient for keeping not exceeding ten sheep and one cow through one winter; ten cords of firewood; five bushels of grain; twenty bushels of potatoes; such military arms and accoutrements as the debtor is required by law to furnish; and all growing crops: also the bibles and other books used in the family; and five bushels of grain in addition, and three swarms of bees and hives, together with their produce in honey, and 200 pounds of sugar.

Homestead-Exemption Law.

THE homestead of every housekeeper or head of a family, residing in this state, to the value of five hundred dollars, such homestead consisting of a dwelling-house, out-buildings, and lands appurtenant, occupied by such person as a homestead, and the yearly products thereof, shall be exempt from attachment and execution, in all cases where the contract shall be made or the cause of action shall accrue after the first day of December, one thousand eight hundred and fifty, except as hereinafter provided.

Whenever the real estate of such housekeeper or head of a family shall be levied upon by virtue of any execution, such portion thereof as may be occupied by him as a homestead, and as he may then elect to regard as such, to the value of five hundred dollars, in case such person is entitled to hold the same exempt from said execution, shall be set out to him by the appraisers on said execution, upon their oaths, and the remainder only shall be set off to the creditor therein, and such homestead shall be set out in the same manner as is now provided by law for the setting off of lands on execution.

If any such housekeeper or head of a family shall decease, leaving a widow, his homestead, of the value aforesaid, shall wholly pass to his widow, and children if any there be, in due course of descent, without being subject to the payment of the debts of the deceased, unless made specially chargeable thereon, or for taxes assessed thereon.

Such homestead shall not be alienated or mortgaged by the owner thereof, if a married man, except by the joint deed of such husband and wife, executed and acknowledged in the manner provided for the conveyance of the lands of married women: Provided, however, that such husband may, without the consent of his wife, mortgage such homestead, at the time of the purchase thereof, for the payment of the purchase-money.

Such homestead shall be subject to attachment and execution upon any contract that may be made, and for all matters and causes of action which may accrue, previous to or at the time of the purchase of such homestead, and shall be subject to sale for non-payment of taxes assessed thereon; and the time when the deed to the owner of such homestead shall be left in the town-clerk's office, for record, shall be deemed the time of the purchase thereof for the purpose mentioned in this act.

Mechanics' Lien.

ANY person who shall perform any labor or furnish materials in this state for or toward the building, repairing, fitting, or furnishing any ship, vessel, or steamboat, shall have a lien on the same for his wages and materials so furnished until four days after the ship, vessel, or steamboat, shall be completed, and may secure the same by attachment, which shall have precedence of all other attachments and claims.

Before such lien shall attach or be in force, such person shall have a just and legal claim for his services performed or materials furnished, and shall demand payment of the same of the owner, agent, contractor, or person, in whose care such ship, vessel, or steamboat, may be; and in case such person, having a lien as aforesaid, shall demand more than is due to him, such owner, agent, contractor, or person in whose care such ship, vessel, or steamboat, may be, may tender or pay to such person the just and full amount due him for his labor or materials furnished as aforesaid, and fully and absolutely discharge such lien.

When any contract or agreement shall hereafter be made in writing for erecting, repairing, or altering any house or other building in this state, or for furnishing labor or materials for the purposes aforesaid, the person proceeding in pursuance of such contract or agreement shall have a lien to secure the payment of the same, upon such house or building and the lot of land on which the same stands, and the lien hereby created shall continue in force for the space of three months from the time when payment shall become due for the work, labor, or materials, furnished as aforesaid.

Law regulating Contracts.

No action, in law or equity, shall be brought in any of the following cases:—

1. To charge an executor or administrator upon any special promise, to answer damages out of his own estate; or—

2. To charge any person, upon any special promise, to answer for the debt, default, or misdoings, of another; or—

3. To charge any person, upon any agreement made upon consideration of marriage; or—

4. Upon any contract for the sale of lands, tenements, or hereditaments, or of any interest in or concerning them; or—

5. Upon any agreement that is not to be performed within one year from the making thereof: unless the promise, contract, or agreement, upon which such action shall be brought, or some memorandum or note thereof, shall be in writing, and signed by the party to be charged therewith, or by some person thereunto by him lawfully authorized; and if the contract or agreement relate to the sale of real estate or any interest therein, such authority shall be conferred in writing.

No contract for the sale of any goods, wares, or merchandise, for the price of fourty dollars or more, shall be good or valid, unless the purchaser shall accept and receive part of the goods so sold, or shall give something in earnest to bind the bargain, or in part payment, or unless some note or memorandum of the bargain be made in writing, and signed by the party to be charged thereby, or by some person thereunto by him lawfully authorized.

No action shall be brought to charge any person, upon or by reason of any representation or assurance made concerning the character, conduct, credit, ability, trade, or dealings, of any other person, unless such representation or assurance be made in writing, and signed by the party to be charged thereby, or by some person thereunto by him lawfully authorized.

No mortgage of any machinery used in any factory, shop, or mill, hereafter made, shall be valid against any other person than the parties thereto, unless possession of the mortgaged machinery be delivered to and retained by the mortgagee.

Limitation of Actions.

No action for the recovery of any lands, or for the recovery of the possession thereof, shall be maintained, unless such action is commenced within fifteen years next after the cause of action first accrued to the plaintiff, or those under whom he claims.

No person having right or title of entry into houses or lands shall thereinto enter but within fifteen years next after such right of entry shall accrue.

The following actions shall be commenced within six years next after the cause of action accrued, and not after:—

1. All actions of debt founded upon any contract, obligation, or liability, not under seal, excepting such as are brought upon the judgment or decree of some court of record of the United States, or of this or some other state.
2. All actions upon judgments rendered in any court, not being a court of record.
3. All actions of debt for arrearages of rent.
4. All actions of account, assumpsit, or on the case, founded on any contract or liability, express or implied.
5. All actions of trespass upon land.
6. All actions of replevin, and all other actions for taking, detaining, or injuring goods or chattels.
7. All other actions on the case, except actions for slanderous words and for libels.

All actions for assault and battery and for false imprisonment shall be commenced within three years next after the cause of action shall accrue, and not afterward.

All actions for slanderous words and for libels shall be commenced within two years next after the cause of action shall accrue, and not afterward.

All actions against sheriffs, for the misconduct or negligence of their deputies, shall be commenced within four years next after the cause of action shall accrue, and not afterward.

None of the foregoing provisions shall apply to any action brought upon a promissory note which is signed in the presence of an attesting witness, but the action in such case shall be commenced within fourteen years next after the cause of action shall accrue thereon, and not afterward.

All actions of debt or *scire facias* on judgment shall be brought within eight years next after the rendition of such judgment; and all actions of debt on SPECIALTIES within eight years after the cause of action accrued.

All actions of covenant other than the covenants of warranty and seisin, contained in deeds of conveyance of lands, shall be brought within eight years after the cause of action accrued, and not afterward.

All actions of covenant brought on any covenant of warranty contained in any deed of conveyance of land shall be brought within eight years next after there shall have been a final decision against the title of the covenanter in such deed, and all actions of covenant brought on any covenant of seisin contained in any such deed, shall be brought within fifteen years next after the cause of action shall accrue, and not afterward.

When any person shall be disabled to prosecute an action in the courts of this state by reason of his being an alien subject, or citizen of any country at war with the United States, the time of the continuance of such war shall not be deemed any part of the respective periods herein limited for the commencement of any of the actions before mentioned.

If, at the time when any cause of action of a personal nature, mentioned in this act, shall accrue against any person, he shall be out of the state, the action may be commenced within the time herein limited therefor, after such person shall come into the state; and if, after any cause of action shall have accrued, and before the statute has run, the person against whom it has accrued shall be absent from and reside out of the state, and shall not have known property within this state which could be attached, the time of his absence shall not be taken as any part of the time limited for the commencement of the action.

If, in any action duly commenced within the time limited and allowed therefor, the writ fail of a sufficient service or return, by any unavoidable accident, or by any default or neglect of the officer to whom it is committed, or if the writ shall be abated, or the action otherwise defeated or avoided by the death of any party thereto, or for any matter of form; or if, after verdict for the plaintiff, the judgment shall be arrested; or if a judgment for the plaintiff shall be reversed on a writ of error or on execution, the plaintiff may commence a new action for the same cause at any time within one year after the abatement or other determination of the original suit, or after the reversal of the judgment thereon, and if the cause of action survive, his executor or administrator may, in case of his death, commence such new action within the said one year, or within one year after letters shall have been granted.

Whenever the commencement of any suit shall be stayed by an injunction of any court of equity, the time during which such injunction shall be in force shall not be deemed any portion of the time limited for the commencement of such suit.

If any person, entitled to bring any action in this act specified, shall, at the time when the cause of action accrues, be a minor, or a married woman, insane, or imprisoned, such person may bring the said action within the times respectively limited after the disability shall be removed.

None of the provisions of this act shall apply to suits brought to enforce payment on bills, notes, or other evidences of debt, issued by moneyed corporations.

All the provisions of this act shall apply to the case of a debt or contract alleged by way of setoff, and the time of limitation of such debt shall be computed in like manner as if an action had been commenced therefor at the time when the plaintiff's action was commenced.

If one of two or more joint contractors make such written promise or acknowledgment, it shall not affect the other joint contractors.

Collection of Debts.

ARREST.—No female shall be arrested or imprisoned by virtue of any mesne process which shall issue in an action founded on contract, nor by virtue of any execution which shall issue on a judgment recovered in any such action.

No person, who is a resident citizen of this state, shall be arrested or imprisoned by virtue of any mesne process which shall issue in an action founded on a contract, express or implied, made or entered into after the first day of January, in the year one thousand eight hundred and thirty-nine, nor by virtue of an execution issued on a judgment recovered in an action founded on any such contract; provided, that if the plaintiff, his agent, or attorney, praying out a writ on any contract made after the first day of January, 1839, shall file with the authority issuing such writ an affidavit stating that he has good reason to believe and does believe that the defendant is about to abscond or remove from the state and has secreted about his person or elsewhere, money or other property, to an amount exceeding twenty dollars, or sufficient to satisfy the demand upon which he is to be arrested, such writ may issue as an attachment against, and be served upon the body of the defendant.

ATTACHMENT.—The ordinary mode of process in civil causes shall be by writ of summons or attachment.

Writs of attachment may issue against the goods, chattels, or estate of the defendant, and for want thereof against his body.

Deeds.

All deeds and other conveyances of lands or of any estate or interest therein shall be signed and sealed by the party granting the same, and signed by two or more witnesses, and acknowledged by the grantor, before a justice of the peace, and recorded at length in the clerk's office of the town in which such lands lie. Town-clerks, notaries public, and masters in chancery, have the same power to take acknowledgments as justices of the peace, by act of 1850.

If such lands lie in a town in which there is no town-clerk, the conveyance shall be recorded by the clerk of the county in which such lands lie.

Every deed by husband and wife shall contain an acknowledgment by the wife, made apart from her husband, before a judge of the supreme court, or a judge of the county court, or some justice of the peace, that she executed such conveyance freely and without any fear or compulsion of her husband, a certificate of which acknowledgment so taken shall be endorsed on the deed by the authority taking the same, and recorded at large with the deed; and every such deed, not so acknowledged and recorded, shall be void as against the wife.

All deeds and other conveyances, and powers of attorney for the conveyance of lands, the acknowledgment or proof of which shall have been or hereafter shall be taken without this state, if certified agreeably to the laws of the state, province, or kingdom, in which it was taken, shall be as valid as though the same were taken before some proper officer or court within this state; and the proof of the same may be taken and the same acknowledged with like effect before any justice of the peace, magistrate, or notary public, within the United States or in any foreign country, or before any commissioner appointed for that purpose by the governor of this state, or before any minister, chargé des affaires, or consul, of the United States, in any foreign country; and the acknowledgment of a deed by a *femme covert* (married woman), in the form required by this act, may be taken by either of said persons.

No deed or other conveyance of any lands, or of any estate or interest therein made, by virtue of a power of attorney, shall be of any effect or admissible in evidence, unless such power of attorney shall have been signed, sealed, and acknowledged and recorded in the office where such deed shall have been recorded. A seal must be used.

Form of Acknowledgment.

State of Vermont,
Windsor County, *ss.* } *Windsor, January, 14th*, 1851.

Then personally appeared John Doe *and* Susan Doe, *wife of said* John Doe, and *severally* acknowledged the foregoing instrument, by *them* signed and sealed, to be *their* free act and deed; *and the said* Susan Doe, *being by me examined apart from her husband, acknowledged that she executed the said deed freely and without any fear or compulsion of her husband.*

Before me, JOHN JONES, *Justice of the Peace.*

Rights of Married Women.

It shall be lawful for any married woman, by herself and in her name, or in the name of any third person, with his assent as her trustee, to cause to be insured for her sole use, the life of her husband for any definite period or for the term of his natural life, and in case of her surviving her husband, the sum or net amount of the insurance becoming due and payable by the terms of the insurance, shall be payable to her and for her own use, free from the claims of the representatives of her husband or of any of his creditors; but such exemptions shall not apply when the amount of premium annually paid shall exceed three hundred dollars.

In case of the death of the wife before the decease of her husband, the amount of the insurance may be made payable, after death, to her children, for their use, and to their guardian if under age.

It shall be lawful for any unmarried woman by herself and in her own name, or in the name of any third person as her trustee, to cause to be insured for her sole use, the life of her father or brother for any definite period, or during his natural life; and in case of her surviving such person, she shall be entitled to receive the amount of the net insurance in the same manner as in case of married women.

DOWER.—The widow of any deceased person shall be entitled to dower, or the use, during her natural life, of one third of the real estate of which her husband died seized in his own right, unless she shall be barred.

The widow may be barred of her dower in all the lands of her husband in the following ways:—

1. When a jointure shall have been settled on such widow by her husband or other person, or some pecuniary provision shall have been made for her, before her marriage, with or without her agreement or consent; or after her marriage, with her consent, to have effect after the death of her husband, and expressed to be in lieu and discharge of her dower.

2. When her husband, by his last will and testament, shall have made provision for such widow, which, it shall appear to the probate court, was intended to be in lieu of dower.

3. When the husband shall die, leaving no children or representatives of children, and the widow shall thereby be entitled to one half of the estate of her husband.

Yet she may elect to waive all these provisions, and to take her dower instead, and notify the court, within eight months after the will is proved, or letters of administration are granted, of her election, in writing.

Rate of Interest.

THE rate of interest is fixed at six per cent.; and interest paid beyond that rate may be recovered back, with costs.

Wills.

WILLS must be in writing, and signed by the testator, or by some other person in his presence and by his express direction, and attested and subscribed by three or more credible witnesses in the presence of the testator AND OF EACH OTHER.

MASSACHUSETTS.

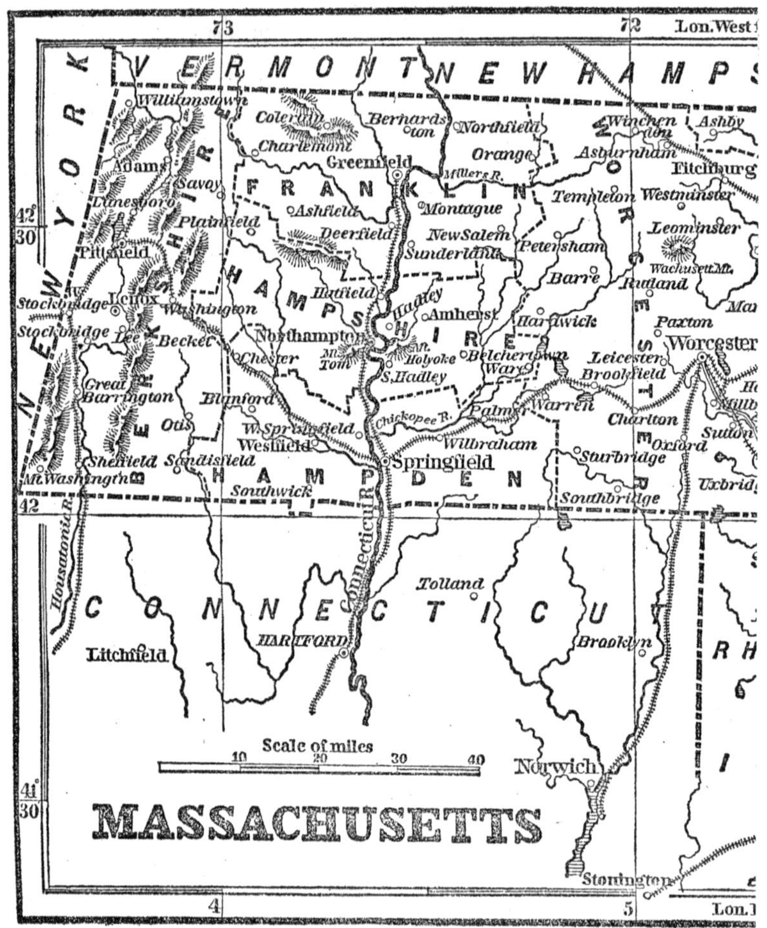

MASSACHUSETTS.

MASSACHUSETTS.

Constitution adopted 1821—Square Miles 7,500—Population in 1850, 993,715.

Exemptions.

THERE is exempt from sale on execution in this state the necessary wearing-apparel of the debtor and of his wife and children; one bedstead, bed, and the necessary bedding, for every two persons of the family; one iron stove, used for warming the dwelling-house, and fuel not exceeding the value of ten dollars, procured and designed for the use of the family; other household furniture, necessary for the debtor and his family, not exceeding fifty dollars in value; the bibles and schoolbooks used in the family; one cow, six sheep, one swine, and two tons of hay, the six sheep not to exceed thirty dollars in value; the tools and implements of the debtor necessary for carrying on his trade or business, not exceeding fifty dollars in value; the uniform of an officer or private in the militia, and the arms and accoutrements required by law to be kept by him; and rights of burial and tombs, while in use as repositories for the dead; also ammunition and provisions necessary and intended for the use of a family, not exceeding in value fifty dollars.

Mechanics' Lien.

EVERY person who shall, by contract with the owner of any piece of land, furnish labor or materials for erecting or repairing any building or the appurtenances of any building on such land, shall have a lien upon the whole piece of land for the amount due to him for such labor or materials—if the contract is made in writing, and signed by the owner of the land, or by some person duly authorized by him, and recorded in the registry of deeds for the county where the land lies.

The lien shall be dissolved at the expiration of six months after the time when the money due by the contract, or the last instalment thereof, shall become payable, unless a suit for enforcing the lien shall have been commenced within the said six months.

Whenever a debt is contracted for labor performed or materials used in the construction or repair of, or for provisions and stores or other articles furnished for or on account of, any ship or vessel within this commonwealth, such debt shall be a lien upon such ship or vessel, her tackle, apparel, and furniture, and shall be preferred to all other liens thereon, except mariners' wages.

When the ship or vessel shall depart from the port at which she was when such debt was contracted, to some other port within this commonwealth, every such debt shall cease to be a lien at the expiration of twenty days after the day of such departure; and in all cases such lien shall cease immediately after the vessel shall have arrived in any port out of this commonwealth: provided, nothing in this act shall alter or in any way affect the lien as now existing on foreign ships and vessels.

LIEN FOR DAMAGES BY OVERFLOWING.—All persons entitled to receive damages for the overflowing of their lands, by reason of the erection or maintenance of a milldam, shall have a lien therefor from the time of the institution of the original complaint, on the mill, milldam, and their appurtenances, and the land under and adjoining the same and used therewith, for any sum not due more than three years before the commencement of an action therefor.

When any mill, owned by several persons as joint tenants or tenants in common, or the dam or appurtenances of such mill, shall need to be repaired or rebuilt in whole or in part, and the proprietors shall not all agree to join in repairing or rebuilding the same, the greater part in interest, of the proprietors, at a meeting duly notified and held, may take measures to cause the mill, dam, or appurtenances thereof, to be repaired or rebuilt, as they shall judge most for the interest of all concerned, and at the expense of the whole in proportion of their respective interests. The proprietors who shall advance the money so expended, shall have a lien therefor on the rents and profits of the mill, and may retain so much thereof, as belongs to any proprietor who is indebted to them for such advance, to be applied to the payment of his debt.

MECHANICS' AND LABORERS' LIEN.—Any person who shall actually perform labor in erecting, altering, or repairing, any building, by virtue of any contract with the owner thereof, or other person who has contracted with such owner for erecting, altering, or repairing, such building, or for the purchase of the land for the purpose of erecting and building thereon, shall have a lien to secure the payment of the wages due or owing him for such labor, by him *personally* so performed upon such building, and the lot of land on which the same stands, and upon the right of redeeming the same when under mortgage.

Such lien shall be dissolved unless, within sixty days after such labor is performed, there be filed in the office of the registry of deeds for the county where the land lies, a certificate, containing a just and true account of the demand justly due to him, after all just credits given, which is to be a lien upon such land and buildings, and a true description of the property, or so near as to identify the property to which the lien is intended to apply, with the name of the owner or contractor, or both, if known, which shall in all cases be subscribed and sworn to by the person seeking the lien, or some credible person in his behalf, which certificate shall be recorded by the register of deeds.

Unless a suit for enforcing the lien shall have been commenced within seventy days after the time when such labor is performed, such lien shall be dissolved.

Such lien may be enforced by petition to the court of common pleas for the county where the land lies.

When any debt secured by such lien shall be fully paid, the creditor shall, at the expense of the debtor, enter on the margin of the registry where said certificate is recorded, a discharge of his said lien, or shall execute a deed of release thereof, in like manner as is provided in relation to the release of mortgages after the payment thereof.

Homestead-Exemption Law.

IN addition to the property now exempted by law from sale or levy on execution, there shall be exempted the lot and buildings thereon, occupied as a residence, and owned by the debtor, or any such buildings owned by the debtor on land not his own, but of which he shall be in the rightful possession, by lease or otherwise, he being a householder and having a family, to the value of five hundred dollars. And no release or waiver of such exemption shall be valid in law unless by deed for good consideration, acknowledged and recorded as in the case of conveyances of real estate.

Such exemption shall continue after the death of such householder, for the benefit of the widow and family of the deceased party, some one of them continuing to occupy such homestead, until the youngest child become twenty-one years of age, and until the death of the widow.

To entitle any property to such exemption, it shall be set forth in the deed of purchase that it is designed to be held as a homestead, under this act, or if already purchased, the said design shall be declared by writing, duly sealed and acknowledged, and recorded in the registry of deeds of the county wherein the land lies.

No property shall, by virtue of this act, be exempted from levy for taxes, or for a debt contracted for the purchase thereof, or for any debt contracted before such deed or writing as aforesaid shall have been recorded according to law; nor shall buildings on land not owned by the debtor, be exempted from levy for the ground-rent of the lot of land whereon such buildings are situated.

Such exemption shall not be deemed to defeat or otherwise affect any mortgage, or other incumbrance or lien existing by virtue of any deed, attachment, policy of insurance, or otherwise.

No conveyance by the husband, of any property exempted as aforesaid, shall be valid in law, unless the wife join in the deed of conveyance.

If any judgment-creditor shall require an execution to be levied on property claimed by the debtor to be exempted from levy under this act, and the officer holding such execution shall be of opinion that the premises are of greater value than five hundred dollars, then appraisers shall be appointed to appraise the premises in the same manner as is provided by law for the levy of executions on real estate. And if in their judgment the premises be of greater value than five hundred dollars, and can be divided without injury to the parties, the said appraisers shall set off to the judgment-debtor so much of the said premises, including the dwelling-house, as shall appear to them to be of the value of five hundred dollars, and the residue of the property shall be dealt with as other real estate not exempted by law from levy on execution; but if, in the judgment of the appraisers, the said property can not be conveniently so divided, they shall make and deliver to the said officer their appraisal of the value of said premises, and the said sheriff, or his deputy, shall deliver a copy thereof to the judgment-debtor, or other lawful occupant of said homestead. And it shall be the right of such judgment-debtor or other lawful occupant of the said premises, to pay on such execution the excess of the value of the said premises above the sum of five hundred dollars, and to continue to hold the said homestead as provided by this act; but in case the judgment-debtor shall not make such payment within sixty days, then the judgment-creditor may require the premises to be sold by such sheriff or his deputy, at public sale, after duly advertising the same, and out of the proceeds of said sale to pay to the debtor the sum of five hundred dollars, to be exempted from liability for his debts for one year thereafter, and to apply the balance to such execution: *Provided*, that unless a greater sum than five hundred dollars shall be bid for the said premises, they shall not be sold, and the execution may be returned unsatisfied, for want of property to satisfy the same.

Chattel Mortgages.

No mortgage of personal property hereafter made shall be valid against any other person than the parties thereto, unless possession of the mortgaged property be delivered to and retained by the mortgagee, or unless the mortgage be recorded by the clerk of the town where the mortgager resides, and by the clerk of the town in which he principally transacts his business, or follows his trade or calling.

Sixty days' written notice of intention to foreclose a breach of the condition, must be given to the mortgager or person in possession of the property, and a copy of the same notice must be recorded in the clerk's office where the mortgage is recorded.

Law Regulating Contracts.

No action shall be brought in any of the following cases:—

1. To charge an executor, administrator, or assignee, in insolvency, upon any special promise, to answer damages out of his own estate; 2. To charge any person, upon any special promise, to answer for the debt, default, or misdoing of another; 3. To charge any person upon an agreement made in consideration of marriage; 4. Upon any contract for the sale of lands, tenements, or hereditaments, or of any interest in or concerning them; 5. Upon any agreement that is not to be performed within one year from the making thereof; unless the promise, contract, or agreement, upon which such action shall be brought, or some memorandum or note thereof, shall be in writing, and signed by the party to be charged therewith, or by some person thereunto by him lawfully authorized. The consideration for such promise need not be expressed in the writing.

No action shall be brought to charge any person, upon or by reason of any representation or assurance made concerning the character, conduct, credit, ability, trade, or dealings of any other person, unless the same be made in writing, and signed by the party to be charged thereby, or by some person thereunto by him lawfully authorized.

No contract for the sale of any goods, wares, or merchandise, for the price of fifty dollars or more, shall be good or valid, unless the purchaser shall accept and receive part of the goods so sold, or give something in earnest to bind the bargain, or in part payment, or unless some note or memorandum in writing of the bargain be made and signed by the party to be charged thereby, or by some person thereunto by him lawfully authorized.

All contracts, written or oral, for the sale or transfer of any certificate or other evidence of debt due, by or from the United States, or any separate state, or of any stocks, or of any share or interest in the stock of any bank, or of any company, city, or village, incorporated under any law of the United States, or of any individual state, shall be absolutely void, unless the party or parties contracting to sell or transfer the same, shall at the time of making such contract, be the owner or assignee thereof, or shall be duly authorized, by some person who is the owner or assignee, or by the legally authorized agent of such owner or assignee, to sell or transfer the said certificate or other evidence of debt, share or interest, so contracted for.

Limitation of Actions.

The following actions shall be commenced within six years next after the cause of action shall accrue, and not afterward:—

1. All actions of debt, founded upon any contract or liability not under seal, except such as are brought upon the judgment or decree of some court of record of the United States, or of this or some other of the United States; 2. All actions upon judgments rendered in any court, not being a court of record; 3. All actions for arrears of rent; 4. All actions of assumpsit, or upon the case, founded in any contract or liability, express or implied; 5. All actions for waste, and for trespass on land; 6. All actions of replevin, and all other actions for taking, detaining, or injuring, goods or chattels; 7. All other actions on the case, except actions for slanderous words and for libels.

All actions for assault and battery, false imprisonment, slanderous words and libels, shall be commenced within two years next after the cause of action shall accrue.

All actions against sheriffs, for the negligence or misconduct of their deputies, shall be commenced within four years next after the cause of action shall accrue.

None of the foregoing provisions shall apply to any action brought on a promissory note which is signed in the presence of an attesting witness, provided the action be brought by the original payee or his executor or administrator, nor to an action brought upon any bills, notes, or other evidences of debt, issued by any bank.

In all actions of debt and assumpsit brought to recover the balance due upon a mutual and open account, the cause of action shall be deemed to have accrued at the time of the last item proved in such account.

If any person, entitled to bring any of the actions before mentioned in this act, shall be, at the time when the cause of action accrues, a minor, a married woman, insane, imprisoned, or absent from the United States, such person may bring them within the times respectively limited, after the disability shall be removed.

All personal actions on any contract not limited by the foregoing sections, or by any other law of the state, shall be brought within twenty years after the cause of action accrues.

In the case of an alien, the time during which his country is at war with the United States will not be computed.

In case the defendant is out of the state, the time of such absence is not to be computed.

No acknowledgment or promise shall be evidence of a new or continuing contract, whereby to take any case out of the operation of the provisions of this act, unless made or contained in some writing signed by the party to be chargeable thereby.

If one of several debtors make such promise, it shall not deprive his co-contractor of the benefit of the provisions of this act.

No one shall commence an action for the recovery of lands, or make entry thereupon, unless within twenty years after the right to make such entry or bring such action first accrued, or within twenty years after he or those from, by, or under whom he claims, shall have been seized or possessed of the premises.

If any person entitled to such entry or action, shall be, at the time when such right of entry or of action first accrues, a minor, a married woman, insane, imprisoned, or absent from the United States, such person or any one claiming from, by, or under him, may make the entry or bring the action at any time within ten years after such disability shall be removed.

If any minister or other sole corporation shall be disseized, any of his successors may enter upon the premises, or may bring an action for the recovery thereof, at any time within five years after the death, resignation, or removal, of the person so disseized, notwithstanding the twenty years after such disseizin shall have expired.

No executor, administrator, or administrator *de bonis non*, who has given legal notice of his appointment to that trust, shall be held to answer to the suit of any creditor of the deceased, unless commenced within four years from the time of his giving bond, provided however if new assets are found, such action may be commenced within one year after the creditor shall have notice of the receipt of such new assets, but not more than four years after the same shall be actually received.

Actions against the sureties in any bond, given by the guardian of minors, insane persons, idiots, spendthrifts, must be commenced within four years from the time when the guardian shall be discharged.

Collection of Debts.

ARREST.—No person shall be arrested or held to bail for any debt or demand arising on any contract made after July fourth, one thousand eight hundred and thirty-four, unless the plaintiff or some person in his behalf shall make oath before some justice of the peace that the plaintiff has a demand against the defendant upon the cause of action stated in the writ, which the deponent believes to be justly due, and upon which he expects the plaintiff will recover ten dollars or upward, and that the deponent has reasonable cause to believe that the defendant is about to depart beyond the jurisdiction of the court to which the writ is returnable, and not to return until after judgment may probably be recovered on said suit, so that he can not be arrested on the first execution, if any, which may issue in such suit.

ATTACHMENT.—All real estates that are liable to be taken in execution may be attached upon the original writ in any action in which any debt or damages are recoverable, and held as security to satisfy such judgment as the plaintiff may recover.

All goods and chattels that are liable to be taken in execution, may be attached and held as security as aforesaid, except such as from their nature or situation have been considered as exempted from attachment according to the principles of the common law as adopted and practised in this state.

Deeds.

CONVEYANCES of land, or of any estate, or interest therein, may be made by deed, executed by any person having authority to convey the same, or by his attorney, and acknowledged and recorded as directed in this act, without any other act or ceremony whatsoever.

The acknowledgment of deeds shall be by the grantor or one of them, or by the attorney executing the same.

The acknowledgment may be made before any justice of the peace in this state, or before any justice of the peace, magistrate, or notary public, within the United States or in any foreign country, or before any commissioner appointed for that purpose by the governor of this commonwealth, or before any minister or consul of the United States in any foreign country.

A certificate of the acknowledgment of the deed, under the hand of the officer taking the same, shall be endorsed upon the deed or annexed thereto; and such deed and certificate may be recorded at length in the registry of deeds for the county where the lands lie, and no deed shall be recorded without such certificate.

In this state a seal is necessary. The wife of a grantor need not be separately examined; it is sufficient to bar her dower, if she join with her husband in the conveyance. (The form of acknowledgment is the same as in Maine.)

Rights of Married Women.

ANY person capable in law of making a deed or will may convey, devise, or bequeath to any married woman, any property or estate to be held by her without the intervention of a trustee, to her sole and separate use, free from the interference or control of her husband. Such conveyance, devise, or bequest, may be of an absolute estate, of an estate for life, or of a less estate, with any lawful limitations, after the termination of the estate so vested in such woman.

Any grant or conveyance made as is above provided shall within ninety days from the delivery thereof, be recorded in the registry of deeds for the county in which the husband shall reside at the time of such delivery, or, if he be not a resident of this commonwealth, for the county in which the grantor shall then reside; and if such record be not made, any creditor of the husband may attach or seize on execution any of the property so conveyed, in like manner and with the same effect as if this act had not been passed. Nothing in this act shall be so construed to empower any husband to convey any of his property to his wife in other manner or with any other effect than if the same had not been passed.

None of the property to be holden by any married woman, by virtue of the provisions of this act shall be used or employed for the purposes of trade or commerce; but the same shall be invested in real estate, in stocks of the United States, in state stock, in corporation stock, in personal securities, or in furniture in the actual use and occupation of such woman.

Any policy of insurance made by any insurance company on the life of any person, expressed to be for the benefit of a married woman, whether the same be effected by herself or by her husband, or by any other person on her behalf, shall enure to her separate use and benefit and that of her children, if any, independently of her husband and of his creditors and representatives, and also independently of any other person effecting the same in her behalf, his creditors and representatives; and a trustee or trustees may be appointed by any court authorized to appoint trustees, to hold and manage the interest of any married woman in any such policy, or the proceeds thereof.

Married women of the age of twenty-one years and of sound mind, may devise and dispose of any property held in her own right, and separate from that of her husband, with the husband's assent thereto, endorsed thereon in writing, and may revoke such will at her pleasure without the husband's consent; but if all the devises or bequests in such will are to the husband, or for his benefit solely, his assent is not necessary.

DOWER.—Every woman shall be entitled to her dower at common law in the lands of her husband, to be assigned to her after his decease, unless she is lawfully barred thereof.

A married woman may bar her right of dower in any estate conveyed by her husband, by joining with him in the deed conveying the same, and releasing her claim to dower, or by releasing the same by a subsequent deed executed jointly with her husband, or with his guardian: also by a jointure of freehold estate in lands for the life of the wife at least, and to take effect in possession or profit immediately on the death of her husband; and also by a provision in the will of her husband in lieu of dower, at her election within six months after probate of the will.

Rate of Interest.

THE legal rate is six per cent. When the defence of usury is established, the defendant shall recover his full costs, and the plaintiff shall forfeit threefold the amount of the interest unlawfully reserved or taken. The party paying usurious interest may recover back threefold the amount of the unlawful interest so paid.

Wills.

WILLS must be in writing, and signed by the testator, or by some other person in his presence and by his express direction, and attested and subscribed in the presence of the testator by three or more competent witnesses.

RHODE ISLAND.

Constitution adopted, 1842.—Square Miles, 1,340.—Population in 1850, 147,543.

Exemptions.

THE household furniture and family stores of a housekeeper shall not be liable to attachment on any warrant of distress, or on any writ, original or judicial: *provided*, the whole, including beds and bedding, do not exceed in value the sum of two hundred dollars. Neither shall the necessary wearing-apparel of such housekeeper and his family, nor one cow; nor one hog; nor his working tools necessary for his usual occupation; *provided*, the said tools do not exceed in value the sum of fifty dollars; neither shall the working tools, not exceeding in value the sum of fifty dollars, nor the necessary wearing-apparel of any debtor, be liable to distress or attachment.

Mechanics' Lien.

WHENEVER any building, canal, turnpike, railroad, or other improvement, shall be constructed, erected, or repaired, by contract with, or at the request of the owner thereof, such owner being at the time the owner of the land on which the same then is, such building, canal, turnpike, railroad, or other improvement, together with the said land is hereby made liable, and shall stand pledged for all the work done in the construction, erection, or reparation thereof, which have been furnished by any person who had contracted or been requested as aforesaid, to construct, erect, or repair the same, before any other lien which shall originate subsequent to the commencement of such erection, construction, or reparation, on such land.

When such construction or reparation is done by contract, with, or at the request of any lessee or tenant, the interest and title of such lessee and tenant in the improvement and the land on which the same is located, shall stand pledged for all the work done and materials used and furnished, but not the interest of the landlord unless his written consent is first obtained assenting to such construction, erection, or reparation, and acknowledging his estate to be also holden for the payment thereof.

So also the buildings and improvements and the estate in the land of one who is the owner of less than a freehold in the land, shall be pledged for the work done and materials furnished, but not the estate of the owner in fee of the land, unless his written consent is first obtained assenting to such construction, erection, or reparation, and acknowledging his estate to be also holden for the payment thereof.

If the work be done under a written contract, then the lien shall be lost unless legal process be commenced for enforcing the same within four months from the time that any payment on such contract shall become due, if such payment shall not then be made.

No person doing work or furnishing materials without written contract, shall have any lien unless he shall commence legal process for enforcing the same within six months from the time of commencing such work, or of commencing the delivery of materials if payment for the same shall not then be made.

No person doing work at the request of any person who had entered into a contract, whether in writing or not, shall have any lien unless he shall within thirty days after commencing the work, give notice in writing to the person against whose estate or title he claims a lien, that he has commenced the work and that he will claim the benefit of the lien created by this act. But this lien will be lost unless such person shall, within four months from time of giving such notice, commence legal process to enforce such lien.

The commencement of legal process to enforce such lien shall be the lodging the account or demand for which the lien is claimed, in the office of the clerk of the town or towns in which the improvement is situate, with notice to what building, &c., and land, and to what or whose estate therein the account or demand refers.

Twenty days before the term of the court of common pleas, in the county or counties in which the building, &c., shall lie, which shall be holden not less than twenty days next after the commencement of legal process aforesaid, the person so commencing the same shall file his petition in the clerk's office of said court, setting forth the particulars of his demand, describing particularly the building, &c., and land, and praying that the lien may be enforced against the same, and that the same be sold to satisfy the said demand, and all other demands for which it is liable.

RHODE ISLAND.

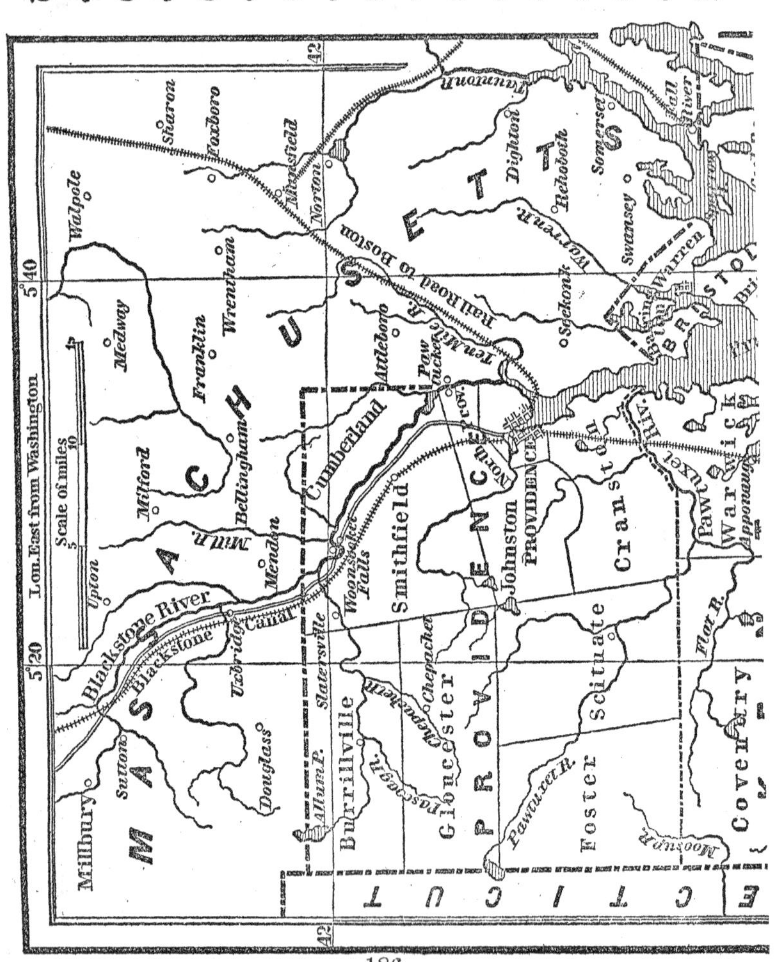

RHODE ISLAND.

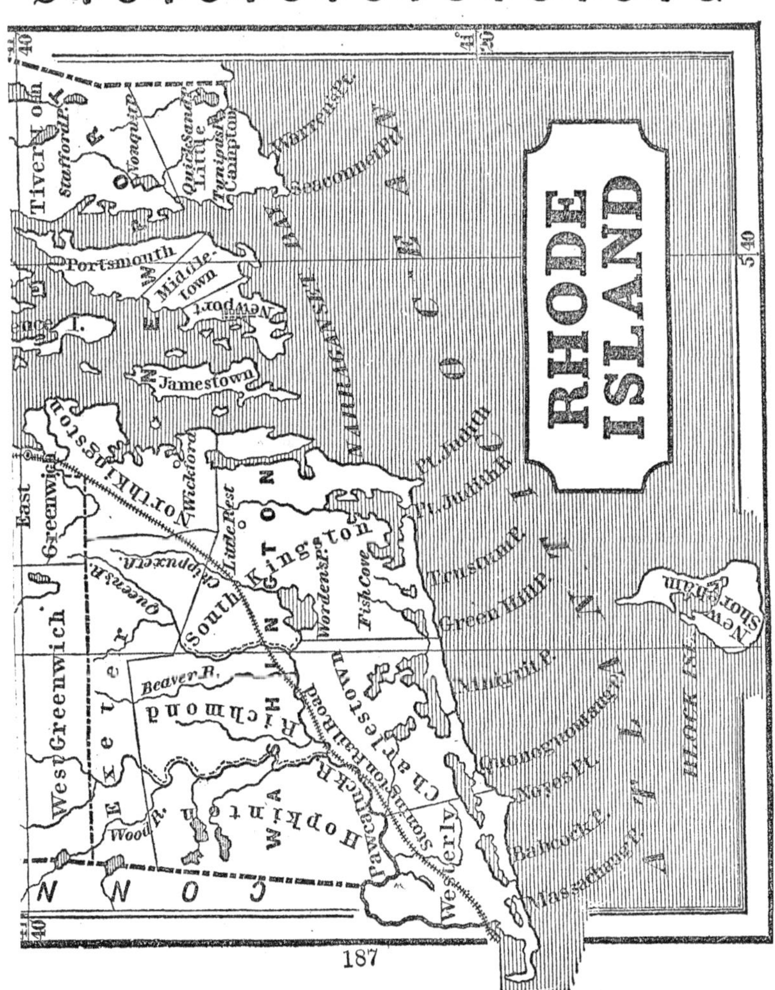

Chattel Mortgages.

No mortgage of personal property, hereafter made, shall be valid against any other person than the parties thereto, unless possession of the mortgaged property be delivered to, and retained by the mortgagee, or unless the said mortgage be recorded in the office of the clerk of the town where the mortgager shall reside at the time of making the same.

Law regulating Contracts.

No action shall be brought whereby to charge any executor or administrator upon his special promise to answer any debt or damage out of his own estate, or whereby to charge the defendant on his special promise to answer for the debt, default, or miscarriage of another person, or to charge any person upon any agreement made upon consideration of marriage, or upon any contract for the sale of lands, tenements, or hereditaments, or the making of any lease thereof for a longer term than one year, or upon any agreement which is not to be performed within the space of one year from the making thereof, unless the promise or agreement upon which such action shall be brought or some note or memorandum thereof shall be in writing and signed by the party to be charged therewith, or by some other person by him thereunto lawfully authorized.

Limitation of Actions.

All actions of trespass, detinue or replevin: all actions of account, and upon the case, except on such accounts as concern trade or merchandise between merchant and merchant, their factors or servants; all actions of debt founded on any contract, without speciality; all actions of debt for arrearages of rent; actions of debt for other causes, and all actions of covenant, shall be commenced and sued within the time hereinafter directed, namely:—

The said actions upon the case, except actions for slander, and the said actions of account, and the said actions for debt, founded upon any contract without speciality, or brought for arrearages of rent, and all actions of detinue or replevin, shall be commenced within six years after the cause of the said actions; the said actions of trespass, and trespass and ejectment, within four years next after the cause of such action; and actions upon the case for words, within two years next after the words spoken; all actions of debt other than those before specified, and all actions of covenant, within twenty years next after the cause of said actions.

If any person, against whom there shall exist any of the causes of action, aforesaid, be without the limits of this state or shall go out before the action is barred, and shall not have or leave property or estate therein that can be attached, the person entitled to such action may commence the same within the time before limited after such person's return into the state.

If any person at the time any such action shall accrue to him, shall be a minor, *femme covert*, non compos mentis, imprisoned, or beyond the limits of the United States, such person may bring the same within such time as is hereinbefore limited, after such impediment is removed.

Collection of Debts.

Arrest and Attachment.—In this state there is no exemption from arrest, except in the case of a female. By the revised laws it is provided that every original writ issued against a female founded on a contract not under seal shall be a writ of summons and not of arrest, that no execution shall issue against the body of any female on any judgment founded on contract not under seal, where the debt or damages recovered do not exceed the sum of fifty dollars; but she may be arrested, if the instrument be under seal, for any sum.

It is also provided that wherever a writ authorizing an arrest shall be delivered to an officer for service, he shall use his best endeavors to arrest the body of the defendant, but if such officer can not find the body of the defendant within his precinct, he shall attach his goods and chattels to the value commanded in the writ; and that when he shall attach any goods or chattels on original writ, he shall keep the same in his hands as security to satisfy such judgment as the plaintiff may recover.

Deeds.

No estate of inheritance or freehold, or for a term exceeding one year in lands or tenements, shall be conveyed from one to another by deed unless the same be in writing signed, sealed, and delivered by the party making the same, and acknowledged before a senator, judge, justice of the peace, public notary, or town-clerk, by the party or parties who shall have sealed or delivered it, and recorded or lodged to be recorded in the office of the town-clerk of the town where the said lands or tenements lie.

Any conveyance of lands within this state, or any instrument relating thereto, executed without the limits of this state and within the United States, may be acknowledged before any judge, justice of peace, mayor, or public notary, in the state where the same is executed; and if without the limits of the United States, before any embsssador, minister, charge de affaires, recognised consul, vice-consul, or commercial agent of the United States, in the country in which such deed or instrument is executed.

A married woman may bar her right of dower in any estate conveyed by her husband, by joining with him in the deed conveying the same, and therein releasing her claim to dower or by releasing the same by subsequent deed jointly with her husband, or by joining in a deed given by a guardian of her husband.

The wife acknowledging a deed shall be examined privily and apart from her husband; and shall declare to the officer taking such acknowledgment that the deed or instrument shown and explained to her by such magistrate is her voluntary act, and that she doth not wish to retract the same.

Form of Acknowledgment.

State of Rhode Island, }
County of *Providence*, } To wit.

On this *sixteenth* day of *April*, one thousand eight hundred and *fifty-one*, before me, personally appeared JOHN DOE, *and* SUSAN DOE *his wife*, and severally acknowledged the foregoing instrument to be *their* free and voluntary act and deed; *and the said* SUSAN, *on a private examination, separate and apart from her husband, declared to me, that the foregoing instrument, then by me shown and explained to her, is her free and voluntary act and deed, and that she doth not wish to retract the same.*

JOHN JONES, *(seal)*
Justice of the Peace.

It is requisite that a seal be use in this state.

Rights of Married Women.

THE real estate, chattels real, household furniture, plate, jewels stock, or shares in the capital stock of any incorporated company of this state, or debts secured by mortgage on property within this state, which are the property of any woman before marriage, or which may become the property of any woman after marriage, shall be, and are hereby so far secured to her sole and separate use that the same and the rents, profits, and income thereof, shall not be liable to be attached or in any way taken for the debts of her husband, either before or after his death.

Any policy of insurance made by any insured company, on the life of any person, expressed to be for the benefit of a married woman, whether the same be effected by herself or by her husband, or by any other person ou her behalf, shall enure to her separate use and benefit and that of her children, if any, independently of her husband and of his creditors and representatives, and also independently of any other person effecting the same on her behalf, his creditors and representatives, and a trustee or trustees may be appointed by any court authorized to appoint trustees, to hold and manage the interest of any married woman in any such policy or the proceeds thereof. *Provided, however*, that the provisions of this act shall not apply to any policy upon which the amount of annual premium shall exceed the sum of three hundred dollars.

DOWER.—The widow of any person shall be endowed of one full and equal third part of all the lands, tenements, and hereditaments, whereof her husband or any other to his use, was seized of an estate of inheritance at any time during the intermarriage.

Rate of Interest.

THE legal rate of interest is six per cent. In an action brought upon a usurious contract, the plaintiff can recover the principal, with legal interest and costs of suit.

Wills.

WILLS must be in writing, signed by the testator or by some person in his presence, and by his express direction, and attested and subscribed in the presence of the testator, by three or more competent witnesses.

CONNECTICUT.

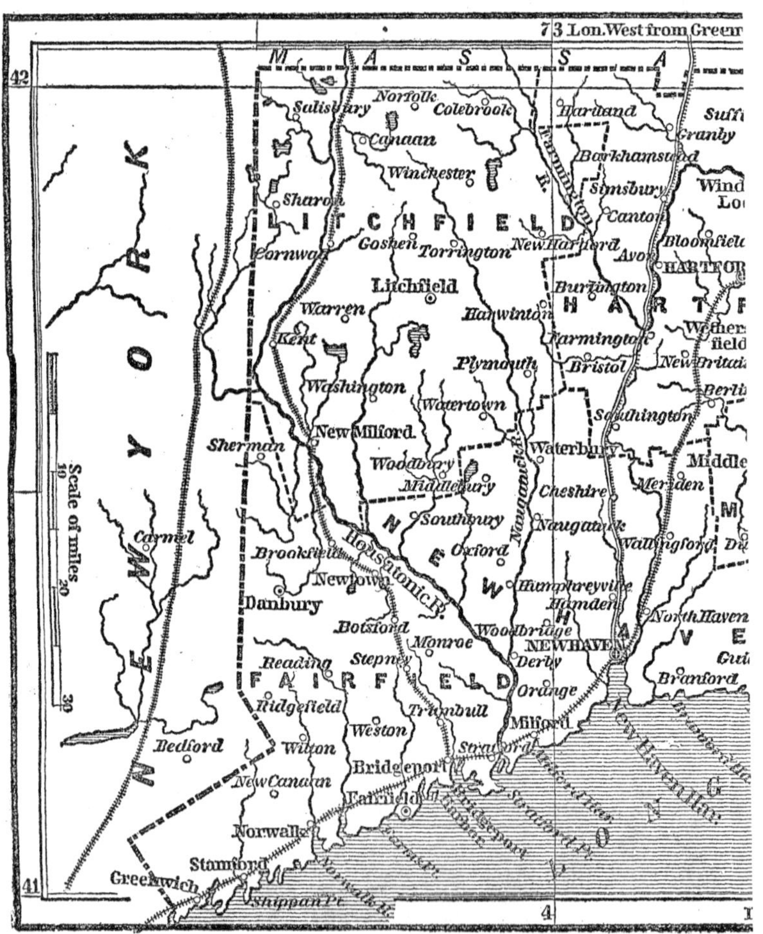

CONNECTICUT.

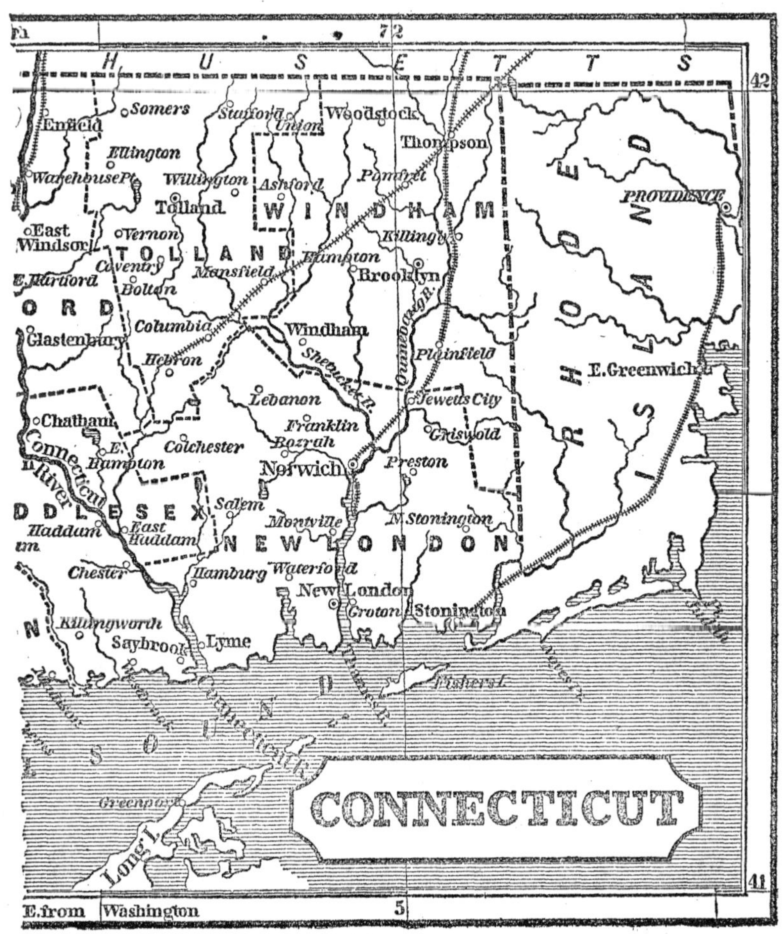

CONNECTICUT.

Constitution adopted 1818.—Square Miles 4,764.—Population in 1850, 371,982.

Exemptions.

THERE is exempt from sale on execution the necessary apparel, bedding and household furniture necessary for supporting life; arms, military equipments; implements of the debtor's trade; one cow; sheep not exceeding ten; two swine, and the pork produced from two swine, or two swine, and two hundred pounds of pork, being the property of one person; charcoal not exceeding twenty-five bushels; any quantity of coal, other than charcoal, not exceeding two tons; wheat-flour, not exceeding two hundred pounds weight; wood, not exceeding two cords; hay, not exceeding two tons; beef, not exceeding two hundred pounds; fish, not exceeding two hundred pounds; potatoes or turnips, not exceeding five bushels of each; Indian corn or rye, not exceeding ten bushels of each, and the meal or flour manufactured therefrom; wool or flax, not exceeding twenty pounds weight of each, or the yarn or cloth made therefrom; one stove, and the pipe belonging thereto, being the property of any one person having a wife or family; the horse, saddle, and bridle, of any practising physician or surgeon, of a value not exceeding one hundred dollars; and one pew, being the property of any person or persons having a family, who ordinarily occupy the same.

Mechanics' Lien.

EVERY dwelling-house or other building with the land on which the same may stand, shall be subject to the payment of all sums exceeding two hundred dollars, due from the proprietor to the contractor for any work done or materials found, in erecting, constructing, or repairing such building, and the same shall be a lien thereon, and shall take precedence of any other lien or incumbrance which originated subsequent to the commencement of such building or repairs.

Any sub-contractor or joint sub-contractors, having a legal claim for labor or materials to the amount of fifty dollars or more, and the contract between the sub-contractor and the original contractor, be in writing, shall also have a like lien.

Such lien continues only sixty days after the building is finished, or the contractor has ceased to labor thereon, unless he lodge with the town-clerk of the town in which such building is situate a certificate in writing, describing the premises and the amount claimed as a lien thereon, the same being first subscribed and sworn to as to the amount justly due, so near as the same can be ascertained, which certificate shall be recorded by the town-clerk with deeds of land.

Chattel Mortgages.

WHEN any one mortgages machinery, engines, or implements in any factory, or household furniture in a dwelling-house, or hay in a building, together with the realty on which the same are situate, and particularly describes the personal property so mortgaged in the instrument of mortgage, it shall be as effectual to hold the personal as if it were a part of the real estate, although the mortgager retain possession.

If he shall mortgage the said personal property, situated as aforesaid, without mortgaging the real, and shall execute, acknowledge, and record it in all respects as a mortgage of lands, it shall be valid, though the mortgager retain the possession.

Law regulating Contracts.

No suit shall be brought upon any contract or agreement whereby to charge any executor or administrator upon any special promise to answer damages out of his own estate; or whereby to charge the defendant upon any special promise to answer for the debt, default, or miscarriage of another person; or to charge any person upon any agreement made upon consideration of marriage; or upon any contract for the sale of lands, tenements, or hereditaments, or any interest in or concerning them; or upon any agreement that is not to be performed within the space of one year from the making thereof; unless the contract or agreement, or some memorandum or note thereof, shall be made in writing and signed by the party to be charged therewith, or by some other person thereunto by him lawfully authorized.

No contract for the sale of any goods, wares, or merchandise, for the price of thirty-five dollars or upward, shall be allowed to be good, unless the buyer shall accept part of the goods so sold, and actually receive the same, or give something in earnest to bind the bargain, or in part payment, or unless some note or memorandum in writing, of the said bargain, shall be made and signed by the parties to be charged by such contract, or by their agents, thereunto lawfully authorized.

Limitation of Actions.

Entry upon lands must be made within fifteen years after the right accrued, and no such entry shall be sufficient unless an action be brought within one year thereafter.

No action shall be brought on any bond, or writing obligatory, contract under seal, or promissory note not negotiable, but within seventeen years after right accrued. Those legally incapable at the time such right accrued, may bring the same at any time within four years after becoming legally capable.

Actions of account, debt on book, on simple contract, assumpsit founded upon implied contract or upon any contract in writing not under seal, except promissory notes not negotiable, must be brought within six years. Those not capable may bring it within three years after becoming capable.

Actions of trespass on the case must be brought within six years.

Actions upon an express contract not in writing, of trespass, and actions upon the case for words, must be brought within three years.

The time when the defendant is out of the state is excluded from the computation.

Collection of Debts.

Arrest.—No execution issued in an action founded on contract merely, express or implied, shall be levied on the body of a debtor, except in actions founded upon promises to marry, on misconduct or neglect in any office or professional employment, or in actions instituted against a public officer, trustee, or any person acting in a fiduciary capacity, to recover moneys collected or received by him.

Whenever any person shall be guilty of fraud in contracting a debt, or shall conceal, remove, withhold, assign, or convey away, his estate, moneys, goods, chattels, or choses in actions with intent to prevent the same from being taken by legal process, or shall refuse to pay any debt admitted by him, or established by a valid judgment, while having moneys or estate not exempt from execution, sufficient to discharge the same, concealed or withheld by him so that the same can not be taken by legal process, or shall refuse to disclose his rights of actions, with intent to prevent the same from being taken by foreign attachment, any creditor aggrieved thereby may institute an action on the case, against such person, setting forth his debt in the declaration, and also setting forth particularly such fraudulent act, or acts, and have process of attachment and execution against the body of the defendant, to be proceeded with in all respects as in other actions of tort.

Attachment.—Attachments may be granted against the goods and chattels of the defendant, and for want thereof, against his lands, or against his person when not exempt from imprisonment on the execution of the suit.

Deeds.

All grants, bargains, and mortgages of land, shall be in writing, subscribed by the grantor, and attested by two witnesses.

They shall be acknowledged by the grantor or grantors to be his or their free act and deed, before a justice of the peace or notary public, or before a judge of the supreme or district court or the United States, or of the supreme or superior court, or court of common pleas, or county court, of any individual state, or before the commissioner of the school fund, or before a commissioner or other officer having power to take acknowledgments of deeds, or before a county surveyor when the land lies in his county, and when deeds are executed by an attorney duly authorized, his acknowledgment will be sufficient.

When the grantor resides in any foreign state or country, they may be acknowledged to be his or their free act or deed, before any United States consul, resident in such foreign state or country, or before any notary public, or justice of the peace, in such foreign state or country.

They must be recorded at length by the register or town-clerk of the town where such lands are; and where deeds are executed by a power of attorney, such power of attorney shall be recorded with the deed.

It is requisite that a SEAL be used in this state. The wife need not be privately examined apart from her husband.

Form of acknowledgment same as in Maine.

Rights of Married Women.

The interest of a married man in the real estate of his wife, belonging to her at the time of their intermarriage, or which she may have acquired by devise or inheritance during coverture, shall not be liable to be taken by execution against him, during the life of the wife, or the life or lives of children the issue of such marriage.

All real estate acquired during coverture by the personal services of the wife, and all personal property acquired by or accruing to her during the abandonment of her husband, or while living apart from him by reason of his abuse or habitual intemperance, is her sole and separate estate.

When the real estate of a married woman is sold, and the avails invested in her name or for her benefit, the same is construed in equity to be her separate estate, and is not liable for the debts of her husband.

All personal estate which shall hereafter accrue, *during* coverture, to any married man, in right of his wife, by virtue of bequest to her, or distribution to her, as heir at law, and all property derived from the sale or investment thereof, shall vest in him in trust for the use of his wife; and at his decease, if undisposed of, vests in the wife, or her devisees, legatees, or heirs at law.

Husband is entitled to the rents and profits of said estate, but such rents and profits cannot be taken for his debts—except debts contracted for the support of the wife and her children after such estate has vested in him as aforesaid.

No sale or transfer of such estate by the husband is valid unless by consent of the wife, or if she be dead the consent of those in whom her estate shall have vested—and they must join with the husband in the conveyance thereof.

Courts of probate may call husband to account and remove him from being trustee and appoint a trustee in his place.

An insurance on the life of any person, expressed to be for the benefit of a married woman, will enure to her separate use and benefit, independent of her husband and his creditors and representatives, provided the annual premium shall not exceed one hundred and fifty dollars, unless paid from the private property of the wife.

Whenever any married woman shall earn wages by her own labor, payment of the same may be made to her, and when made shall be valid in law as though made to her husband; and no debt for the wages of a married woman, earned as aforesaid, shall be liable to be taken by virtue of any process against her husband.

Payment to a married woman of any money deposited by her, either before or after marriage, shall be valid, and her receipt shall have the same effect as that of her husband; not to affect right of husband's creditor to levy.

DOWER.—The widow shall have right of dower in one third part of the real estate of which her husband died possessed in his own right, to be to her during her natural life.

Rate of Interest.

The legal rate of interest is six per cent. In usurious contracts the principal can be recovered without the interest. Persons guilty of taking usury forfeit the whole of the interest—one half to him who shall prosecute to effect, one half to state treasury.

Wills.

All wills shall be in writing, subscribed by the testator, and attested by three witnesses all of them subscribing in his presence.

NEW YORK.

Constitution adopted, 1846.—Square Miles, 46,085.—Population in 1850, 3,090,018.

Exemptions.

THERE is exempt from execution, when owned by any person being a householder, the following property: all spinning-wheels, weaving-looms, and stoves, kept for use in any dwelling-house; the family Bible, family pictures, and schoolbooks used in the family, and a family library not exceeding in value fifty dollars; church-pew; ten sheep, and three fleeces, and the yarn or cloth manufactured from the same; one cow, two swine, and necessary food for them; all necessary pork, beef, fish, flour, and vegetables, actually provided for family use, and necessary fuel for the use of the family for sixty days; all necessary wearing-apparel, beds, bedsteads, and bedding, for such person and his family; arms and accoutrements required by law to be kept; necessary cooking-utensils; one table, six chairs, six knives and forks, six plates, six teacups and saucers, one sugar-dish, one milkpot, one teapot, and six spoons; one crane and appendages, one pair of andirons, and a shovel and tongs; the tools and implements of any mechanic necessary to the carrying on of his trade, not exceeding twenty-five dollars in value. IN ADDITION to the foregoing, there is exempt necessary household furniture, and working tools and team, owned by any person being a householder, or having a family for which he provides, to the value of one hundred and fifty dollars: this exemption not to exist if the demand be for the purchase-money of such furniture, tools, team, &c. See page 205.

Wills.

EVERY last will and testament of real or personal property, or both, shall be executed and attested in the following manner:—

1. It shall be subscribed by the testator at the end of the will.
2. Such subscription shall be made by the testator, in the presence of each of the attesting witnesses, or shall be acknowledged by him to have been so made, to each of the attesting witnesses.
3. The testator, at the time of making such subscription, or at the time of acknowledging the same, shall declare the instrument so subscribed to be his last will and testament.
4. There shall be at least two attesting witnesses, each of whom shall sign his name as a witness, at the end of the will, at the request of the testator.

The witnesses to any will shall write opposite to their names their respective places of residence:* whoever shall neglect to do so, shall forfeit fifty dollars, to be recovered by any person interested in the property devised or bequeathed, who will sue for the same.

* If residing in a city, the street and number of the house should also be given.

NEW YORK.

LAKE HURON
L. SIMCOE
CANADA WEST
Kingston
Port Hope
Windsor
Toronto
LAKE ONTARIO
195 m. long, 45 wide, 550 ft. deep.
Oswego
Niagara
Falls of Niagara
London
Sherbrooke
Victoria
Port Colborne
LAKE ERIE
250 m. long, 45 wide, 120 ft. deep.
ORLEANS
NIAGARA
Albion
Rochester
MONROE
WAYNE
Lyons
Lockport
Batavia
Buffalo
GENESEE
Attica
Geneseo
Canandaigua
Geneva
ONTARIO
SENECA
Colden
Warsaw
WYOMING
LIVINGSTON
Penn Yan
YATES
Ovid
Cayuga
ERIE
Collins
Crooked L.
Cortland
Dunkirk
ALLEGHANY
Angelica
Bath
TOMPKINS
Ithaca
Mayville
CATTARAUGUS
Ellicottville
Havanna
CHAUTAUQUE
STEUBEN
CHEMUNG
TIOGA
Owego
Jamestown
Erie
Olean
Independence
Corning
Elmira
Warren
Smethport
Coudersport
Towanda
Athens
Allegheny R.
OHIO
PENNSYLVANIA
Williamsport
Susquehanna
NEW YORK
10 30 50 70 Miles
Lon. West from Washington
East from

NEW YORK.

CANADA EAST
R. St. Lawrence
Ogdensburg
Canton
ST. LAWRENCE
Malone
FRANKLIN
CLINTON
Plattsburg
Mt. Lyon
Keeseville
Port Kent
Elizabeth
Mt. Marcy
ESSEX
Ticonderoga
Watertown
Sackets Harbor
LEWIS
Martinsburg
Pulaski
Camden
ONEIDA
Rome
HAMILTON
Lake Pleasant
WARREN
L. George
Caldwell
Sandy Hill
Salem
WASHINGTON
LAKE CHAMPLAIN
FULTON
Johnstown
Ballston Spa
Herkimer
Morrisville
MONTGOMERY
Cooperstown
OTSEGO
CHENANGO
Norwich
Butternuts
Oxford
Troy
RENSSELAER
ALBANY
SCHOHARIE
Schoharie
Knox
Westerlo
Harpersfield
Kinderhook
Delhi
DELAWARE
GREENE
Catskill
Hudson
COLUMBIA
Binghamton
BROOME
Deposit
ULSTER
Kingston
SULLIVAN
Monticello
Poughkeepsie
DUTCHESS
Newburg
ORANGE
Goshen
PUTNAM
WESTCHESTER
ROCKLAND CO.
Sing Sing
White Plains
N. JERSEY
Morristown
Delaware R.
Montrose
Carbondale
Wilkesbarre
Washington
RICHMOND CO.
QUEENS
SUFFOLK
River Head
LONG ISLAND
L. ISLAND SOUND
Hempstead
St. Albans
Hyde Park
Burlington
MONTPELIER
Middlebury
Haverhill
Rutland
VERMONT
N. HAMPSHIRE
Newport
CONCORD
Keene
Greenfield
Lancaster
Pittsfield
MASSACHUSETTS
Worcester
Sheffield
Springfield
Litchfield
HARTFORD
CONNECTICUT
Norwich
NEW HAVEN
RHODE I.

Mechanics' Lien.

§ 1 ANY person who shall hereafter, by virtue of any contract with the owner thereof, or his agent, or any person who in pursuance of an agreement with any such contractor, shall, in conformity with the terms of the contract with such owner or agent, perform any labor or furnish materials in building, altering, or repairing any house or other building in the several cities in this state (except the city of New York), and in the villages of Syracuse, Williamsburgh, Geneva, Oswego, Auburn, and Canandaigua, shall have a lien for the value of such labor and materials, upon such house or building and appurtenances, and upon the lot of land on which the same stand, to the extent of the right, title, and interest, at that time existing of such owner, in the manner and to the extent hereinafter provided; but the aggregate of all the liens authorized by this act to be created, for the labor performed and materials furnished, shall not exceed the price stipulated in the contract with such owner or his agent to be paid therefor.

§ 2. The person performing such labor or furnishing such materials shall cause to be drawn up specifications of the work by him contracted to be perfermed or materials to be furnished, and stating the price or prices agreed to be paid therefor, and shall file them, or if there be a contract in writing, a true copy thereof in the office of the clerk of the county in which the city or village may be situated, and serve a notice thereof personally on such owner, or his said agent, within twenty days after the making such contract, or after commencing such labor, or the furnishing of said materials. Time extended to 30 days in Buffalo.

§ 3. The lien so created by this act shall take effect from the time of such filing and such service of said notice, and shall continue in full force for the space of one year thereafter.

§ 4. Any owner and any contractor or laborer, or any person furnishing materials in pursuance of any contract made by such contractor with such owner, or his said agent therefor, may, after such labor has been performed or materials furnished, enforce or bring to close such lien, by serving or causing a notice to be served personally on such owner or his agent, contractor or laborer, or person furnishing materials, requiring him to appear in the court of common pleas of the county, or in a justice's court of the city or village in the county in which such building is situated, either in person or by attorney, at a time certain on some day to be specified in such notice, not less than twenty days from the service thereof, and submit to an accounting and settlement in such court of the amount due or claimed to be due under such contract, for the labor thus performed, or the materials thus furnished.

§ 5. At the time of, or within ten days after the service of such notice, a bill of particulars of the amount claimed to be due shall be served personally on such owner, and accompanying the same shall be a notice to produce a bill of particulars of any offset which may claimed to the same within ten days thereafter, which shall be served in like manner.

§ 9. Any person performing such labor or furnishing such materials, in pursuance of any agreement made by him with the original contractor with such owner or his said agent, who shall have done the acts prescribed by the second section of this act, to create a lien therefor, shall have a lien for only such labor as shall be performed and for only such materials as shall be furnished subsequently thereto.

§ 10. Any such person, within thirty days after such labor has been performed or such materials have been furnished, and claiming to have a lien therefor, shall produce and deliver to the owner or his agent a statement in writing, signed by himself and the said contractor, specifying how much is due to such person for such labor done or materials furnished; or, in default of so doing, shall take the necessary proceedings against such contractor to procure an accounting and settlement of the amount due or owing for such labor or materials. The amount so ascertained to be due shall be paid by the owner, and the same shall be deemed to be a payment by the owner on the contract made with such owner or his agent.

The above provisions are extended to the town of Kingston, in the county of Ulster.
The same provisions are extended to Richmond county, except that the bill of particulars and of offset required by the fifth section may be served at the time or within fifteen days after the service of such notice.

By act of 1851, provision is made for a lien in Westchester, Putnam, and Ulster counties.

LIEN FOR THE CITY OF NEW YORK.

ANY person who shall hereafter, by virtue of any contract with the owner thereof, or his agent, or any person who, in pursuance of an agreement with any such contractor, shall, in conformity with the terms of such contract, perform any labor or furnish materials in building, altering, or repairing, any house or other building, or appurtenances to any house or other building, in the city of New York, shall, upon filing the notice prescribed in the sixth paragraph, have a lien for the value of such labor and materials upon such house or building and appurtenances, and upon the lot of land upon which the same stand, to the extent of the right, title, and interest, at that time existing, of such owner, in the manner and to the extent hereinafter provided; but such owner shall not be obliged to pay for, or on account of such house, other building, or other appurtenances, in consideration of all the liens authorized by this act to be created, any greater sum or amount than the price stipulated and agreed to be paid therefor in and by such contract.

Any person furnishing such materials or performing such labor, in pursuance of a written contract with such owner or his agent, shall produce such contract, or the best evidence thereof in his possession, the validity of which shall be established in evidence before the court in which he may bring his suit to recover the value of his lien, and shall recover no more than the price stipulated to be paid to him in such contract.

Any person performing such labor or furnishing such materials, without a written contract with such owner or his agent, shall produce evidence as mentioned in the preceding paragraph, to establish the value of such labor or materials, and that the same were used by the said owner or his agent, or the original contractor in the erection, alteration, or repairing, of such building.

Any contractor or laborer, or any person furnishing materials in pursuance of any contract made by such contractor with such owner or his said agent therefor, may, after such labor has been performed or materials furnished, enforce or bring to a close such lien, by serving or causing a notice to be served personally on such owner or his agent, contractor, or laborer or person furnishing materials, requiring him to appear in the court of common pleas, or, provided the amount claimed do not exceed one hundred dollars, in a justice's court of the judicial district in which such building is situated, or in the marine court of said city and county of New York, either in person or by attorney, at a time certain upon some day to be specified in such notice, not less than twenty days from the service thereof, and submit to an accounting and settlement in such court, of the amount due or claimed to be due for the labor thus performed, or the materials thus furnished.

At the time, or within fifteen days after the service of such notice, a bill of particulars of the amount claimed to be due shall be served personally on such owner, or his legal representatives, and also a bill of particulars of any offset which may be claimed to the same shall be served in like manner upon the laborer, contractor, or person furnishing materials, as the case may be.

Within six months after the performance of such labor or the furnishing of such materials, the contractor, sub-contractor, laborer or person furnishing materials shall serve a notice in writing upon the county clerk, specifying the amount of the claim, and the person against whom the claim is made, the name of the owner of the building, and the situation of the building, by its street and number, if the number be known.

In case said owner shall not appear at the time and place specified in the notice given, in pursuance of the requirements of the fourth and fifth paragraphs, then, on filing with the county clerk, or with the clerk of the marine court, or with the justice, an affidavit of the service of such notice, and of the default of the owner to appear, a writ of inquiry may be issued to the sheriff of said city and county, to assess the amount of such claim, or the amount of such claim may be assessed by the court of common pleas, justice's court, or the marine court, as the case may be; and upon the return of the writ of inquiry, or the assessment by the court, judgment shall be entered upon the same, and execution shall issue for the enforcement of said claim so adjudicated and established, in the same manner as in cases upon other judgments in such courts.

On the appearance of both parties in pursuance of the above requirement, issue shall be joined upon the claims made, and notice of set-off served, and the same may be noticed for trial and put upon the calendar of said court by either party, and shall be governed, tried, and the judgment thereon enforced, in all respects in the same manner as upon issues joined and judgments rendered in all other civil actions for the recovery of moneys in said court.

The judgment obtained may be filed by the successful party with the county clerk, who shall record the name of the court, amount of judgment if for claimant, or where the judgment is against the claimant, the word, " discharged" shall be entered against it.

The lien may be discharged as follows: 1. By filing a certificate of the claimant or his successors in interest, acknowledged or proved in the same manner as the satisfaction of a mortgage, stating that the lien is discharged: or—2. By the deposite with the clerk of a sum of money equal to the amount claimed, which money shall thereupon be held subject to the lien: or—3. By an entry of the clerk made in the book of liens, after one year has elapsed since the filing of the claim, stating that no notice has been given to him of legal steps to enforce the lien: or—4. By an affidavit of service of a notice from the owner to the claimant, requiring him to commence an action for the enforcement of his lien, on or before a certain hour or day specified in said notice, and the lapse of thirty days thereafter, without any affidavit from the claimant being filed of the service of the notice required in the fourth paragraph: or—5. By satisfaction of the lien, upon an action for the enforcement thereof.

Every lien created under the first paragraph of this act, shall continue until the expiration of one year from the creation thereof, and until judgment rendered in any proceedings for the enforcement thereof.

LIEN ON SHIPS.

WHENEVER a debt, amounting to fifty dollars or upward, shall be contracted by the master, owner, agent, or consignee, of any ship or vessel within this state, for either of the following purposes—1. On account of any work done or materials furnished in this state, for or toward the building, repairing, fitting, furnishing, or equipping, such ship or vessel; 2. For such provisions and stores furnished within this state as may be fit and proper for the use of such vessel at the time when the same were furnished; 3. On account of the wharfage and the expense of keeping such vessel in port, including the expense incurred in employing persons to watch her—such debt shall be a lien upon such ship or vessel, her tackle, apparel, and furniture, and shall be preferred to all other liens thereon, except mariners' wages.

When the ship or vessel shall depart from the port at which she was when such debt was contracted, to some other port within this state, every such debt shall cease to be a lien at the expiration of twelve days after the day of such departure; and in all cases such lien shall cease immediately after the vessel shall have left the state.

Whenever any ship or vessel shall have been run down or run afoul of by any other ship or vessel, through the negligence or wilful misconduct of those navigating such other ship or vessel, and shall thereby have sustained damage to the extent of fifty dollars or upward, the owner of said ship or vessel so sustaining damage shall have a lien upon the ship or vessel causing such damage in manner aforesaid, her tackle, apparel, and furniture, to the extent of such damage. The lien shall cease unless a warrant to enforce the same be issued within twenty days after the damage shall be done.

Chattel Mortgages.

EVERY mortgage of personal property which shall not be accompanied with an immediate delivery, and be followed by an actual and continued change of possession of the things mortgaged, is absolutely void as against the creditors of the mortgager and subsequent mortgagees and purchasers in good faith, unless the mortgage, or a true copy thereof, shall be filed in the several towns and cities of the state where the mortgager, if a resident of the state, resides; if he be not a resident, then in the city or town where the property mortgaged shall be at the time of the execution of the mortgage. In the city of New York they must be filed in the register's office; in the several towns in which the county clerk's office is kept, in the county clerk's office; in other towns, in the town clerk's office.

Law Regulating Contracts.

EVERY contract for the leasing for a longer period than one year, or for the sale of any lands, or any interest in lands, shall be void, unless the contract, or some note or memorandum thereof, expressing the consideration, be in writing, and be subscribed by the party by whom the lease or sale is to be made, or subscribed by the agent of such party lawfully authorized.

In the following cases, every agreement shall be void, unless such agreement, or some note or memorandum thereof, expressing the consideration, be in writing, and subscribed by the party to be charged therewith: 1. Every agreement that, by its terms, is not to be performed within one year from the making thereof. 2. Every special promise to answer for the debt, default, or miscarriage, of another person. 3. Every agreement, promise, or undertaking, made upon consideration of marriage, except mutual promises to marry.

Every contract for the sale of any goods, chattels, or things in action, for the price of fifty dollars or more, shall be void, unless—1. A note or memorandum of such conduct be made in writing, and be subscribed by the parties to be charged thereby: or—2. Unless the buyer shall accept and receive part of such goods, or the evidences, or some of them, of such things in action: or—3. Unless the buyer shall, at the time, pay some part of the purchase-money.

Whenever goods shall be sold at public auction, and the auctioneer shall, at the time of sale, enter in a sale-book a memorandum specifying the nature and price of the property sold, the terms of the sale, the name of the purchaser, and the name of the person on whose account the sale is made, such memorandum shall be deemed a note of the contract of sale, within the meaning of the last section.

Limitation of Actions.

No action for the recovery of real property, or for the recovery of the possession thereof, shall be maintained, unless it appear that the plaintiff, his ancestor, predecessor, or grantor, was seized or possessed of the premises in question, within twenty years before the commencement of such action.

No entry upon real estate shall be deemed sufficient, or valid as a claim, unless an action be commenced thereupon within one year after the making of such entry, and within twenty years from the time when the right to make such entry descended or accrued.

An action upon a judgment or decree of any court of the United States, or of any state or territory within the United States, or an action upon a sealed instrument, shall be commenced within twenty years.

The following actions shall be commenced within six years:—

1. An action upon a contract, obligation, or liability, express or implied, excepting those mentioned in the previous section.

2. An action upon a liability created by statute, other than a penalty or forfeiture.

3. An action for trespass upon real property.

4. An action for taking, detaining, or injuring any goods or chattels, including actions for the specific recovery of personal property.

5. An action for criminal conversation, or for any other injury to the person or rights of another, not arising on contract, and not hereinafter enumerated.

6. An action for relief, on the ground of fraud; in cases which heretofore were solely cognisable by the court of chancery; the cause of action in such case not to be deemed to have accrued, until the discovery by the aggrieved party, of the facts constituting the fraud.

An action against a sheriff, coroner, or constable, upon a liability incurred by the doing of an act in his official capacity, and in virtue of his office, or by the omission of an official duty, including the non-payment of money collected upon an execution, shall be commenced within three years; but this section shall not apply to an action for an escape.

An action for libel, slander, assault, battery, or false imprisonment, or an action upon a statute, for a forfeiture or penalty to the people of this state, shall be commenced within two years.

In an action brought to recover a balance due upon a mutual, open, and current account, where there have been reciprocal demands between the parties, the cause of action shall be deemed to have accrued from the time of the last item proved in the account on either side.

Collection of Debts.

ARREST.—No person shall be arrested in a civil action except as prescribed by this act.

The defendant may be arrested, as hereinafter prescribed, in the following cases:—

1. In an action for the recovery of damages, on a cause of action not arising out of contract, where the defendant is not a resident of the state, or is about to remove therefrom, or where the action is for an injury to person or character, or for injuring or for wrongfully taking, detaining, or converting property.

2. In an action for a fine or penalty, or on a promise to marry, or for money received, or property embezzled or fraudulently misapplied, by a public officer or by an attorney, solicitor, or counsellor, or by an officer or agent of a corporation or banking association, in the course of his employment as such, or by any factor, agent, broker, or other person in a fiduciary capacity, or for any misconduct or neglect in office, or in a professional employment.

3. In an action to recover the possession of personal property unjustly detained, where the property or any part thereof has been concealed, removed, or disposed of, so that it can not be found or taken by the sheriff.

4. When the defendant has been guilty of a fraud, in contracting the debt, or incurring the obligation for which the action is brought, or in concealing or disposing of the property, for the taking, detention, or conversion of which, the action is brought.

5. When the defendant has removed or disposed of his property, or is about to do so, with intent to defraud his creditors.

But no female shall be arrested in any action, except for a wilful injury to person, character, or property.

Before making the order, the judge shall require a written undertaking on the part of the plaintiff, with or without sureties, to the effect that if the defendant recover judgment, the plaintiff will pay all costs that may be awarded to the defendant, and all damages which he may sustain by reason of the arrest, not exceeding the sum specified in the undertaking, which shall be at least one hundred dollars.

ATTACHMENT.—In an action for the recovery of money, against a corporation created by or under the laws of any other state government or country, or against a defendant who is not a resident of this state, or against a defendant who has absconded or concealed himself as hereinafter mentioned, the plaintiff, at the time of issuing the summons, or at any time afterward, may have the property of such defendant attached, in the manner hereinafter prescribed, as a security for the satisfaction of such judgment as the plaintiff may recover.

The warrant may be issued whenever it shall appear by affidavit that a cause of action exists against such defendant, specifying the amount of the claim, and the grounds thereof, and that the defendant is either a foreign corporation, or not a resident of this state, or has departed therefrom with intent to defraud his creditors, or to avoid the service of a summons, or keeps himself concealed therein with the like intent.

Before issuing the warrant, the judge shall require a written undertaking on the part of the plaintiff, with sufficient surety, to the effect that if the defendant recover judgment, the plaintiff will pay all costs that may be awarded to the defendant, and all damages which he may sustain, by reason of the attachment, not exceeding the sum specified in the undertaking, which shall be at least two hundred and fifty dollars.

The warrant shall be directed to the sheriff of any county in which property of such defendant may be, and shall require him to attach and safely keep all the property of such defendant within his county. Several warrants may be issued at the same time to the sheriffs of different counties.

Deeds.

EVERY grant in fee or of a freehold estate shall be subscribed and sealed by the person from whom the estate or interest conveyed is intended to pass, or his lawful agent; and if not duly acknowledged previous to its delivery, according to the provisions [below], its execution and delivery shall be attested by at least one witness; or if not so attested, it shall not take effect as against a purchaser or incumbrancer, until so acknowledged.

Every conveyance of real estate within this state, hereafter made, shall be recorded in the office of the clerk of the county where such real estate shall be situated; and every such conveyance not so recorded shall be void as against any subsequent purchaser, in good faith and for a valuable consideration of the same real estate, or any portion thereof, whose conveyance shall be first duly recorded.

To entitle any conveyance, hereafter made, to be recorded by any county clerk, it shall be acknowledged by the party or parties executing the same, or shall be proved by a subscribing witness thereto, before any one of the following officers:—

If acknowledged or proved within this state, justices of the supreme court, judges of county courts, mayors and recorders of cities, commissioners of deeds in cities, justices of the peace in the several towns of this state; but no county judge or commissioner of deeds for a city, nor justice of the peace for a county, shall take any such proof or acknowledgment out of the city or county for which he was appointed:

If acknowledged or proved out of this state, and within the United States, the chief justice and associate justices of the supreme court of the United States, district judges of the United States, the judges or justices of the supreme, supe-

tion, or circuit court, of any state or territory within the United States, and the chief judge or any associate judge of the circuit court of the United States in the District of Columbia; but no proof or acknowledgment, taken by any such officer, shall entitle a conveyance to be recorded, unless taken within some place or territory to which the jurisdiction of the court to which he belongs extends:

In foreign countries, before any consul of the United States resident in any foreign port or country, duly certified under their hand and seal of office.

The proof or acknowledgment of any deed, when made by any person residing out of this state, and within any other state or territory of the United States, may be made before any officer of such state or territory, authorized by the laws thereof to take the proof and acknowledgment of deeds; provided that no such acknowledgment shall be valid unless the officer taking the same shall know or have satisfactory evidence that the person making such acknowledgment is the individual described in, and who executed the said deed.

There shall be subjoined to the certificate of proof or acknowledgment, signed by such officer, a certificate under the name and official seal of the clerk or register of the county in which such officer resides, specifying that such officer was, at the time of taking such proof or acknowledgment, duly authorized to take the same, and that such clerk or register is well acquainted with the handwriting of such officer, and verily believes that the signature to said certificate of proof and acknowledgment is genuine.

No acknowledgment of any conveyance having been executed shall be taken by any officer, unless the officer taking the same shall know or have satisfactory evidence that the person making such acknowledgment is the individual described in and who executed such conveyance.

The acknowledgment of a married woman residing within this state, to a conveyance purporting to be executed by her, shall not be taken, unless, in addition to the requisites contained in the preceding section, she acknowledge, on a private examination, apart from her husband, that she executed such conveyance freely, and without any fear or compulsion of her husband.

When any married woman, not residing in this state, shall join with her husband in any conveyance of any real estate situate within this state, the conveyance shall have the same effect as if she were sole; and the acknowledgment or proof of the execution of such conveyance by her may be the same as if she were sole.

Form of Acknowledgment.

State of New York, }
County of *Kings*, } to wit:

On this *first* day of *October*, one thousand eight hundred and *fifty*, before me personally came JOHN DOE *and* SUSAN *his wife*, to me known to be the individuals described in and who executed the foregoing *conveyance*, and acknowledged that they executed the same [*and the said* SUSAN, *on a private examination, separate and apart from her husband, acknowledged that she executed the same freely, and without any fear or compulsion of her said husband*].

JOHN JONES, *Justice of the Peace.*

Where there is no wife, the parts referring to her may be omitted.

Form of Certificate of Proof by the subscribing Witness.

State of New York, }
County of *Kings*, } to wit:

On this *first* day of *October*, one thousand eight hundred and *fifty*, before me personally came JOHN SMITH, subscribing witness to the foregoing *conveyance*, to me known, who being by me duly sworn, did depose and say, that he resides in the *town* of *Bushwick*, in said county; that he knew JOHN DOE, the individual described in and who executed the said *conveyance*; that he was present, and did see the said JOHN DOE sign, seal, and deliver the same, as and for his act and deed; and that the said JOHN DOE then acknowledged the execution thereof, whereupon the said JOHN SMITH became the subscribing witness thereto.

JOHN JONES, *Justice of the Peace.*

Rights of Married Women.

THE real and personal property of any female who may hereafter marry, and which she shall own at the time of marriage, and the rents, issues, and profits thereof, shall not be subject to the disposal of her husband, nor be liable for his debts, and shall continue her sole and separate property, as if she were a single female.

Any married female may take, by inheritance, or by gift, grant, devise, or bequest, from any person other than her husband, and hold to her sole and separate use, and convey and devise real and personal property, and any interest or estate therein, and the rents, issues, and profits thereof, in the same manner and with like effect as if she were unmarried, and the same shall not be subject to the disposal of her husband, nor be liable for his debts.

Any person who may hold, or may hereafter hold, as trustee for any married woman, any real or personal estate, or other property, under any deed of conveyance or otherwise, on the written request of such married woman, accompanied by a certificate of a justice of the supreme court, that he has examined the condition and situation of the property, and made due inquiry into the capacity of such married woman to manage and control the same, may convey to such married woman, by deed or otherwise, all or any portion of such property, or the rents, issues, or profits thereof, for her sole and separate use and benefit.

All contracts made between persons in contemplation of marriage shall remain in full force after such marriage takes place.

It shall be lawful for any married woman, by herself and in her name, or in the name of any third person, with his assent, as her trustee, to cause to be insured, for her sole use, the life of her husband for any definite period, or for the term of his natural life; and in case of her surviving her husband, the sum or net amount of the insurance becoming due and payable, by the terms of the insurance, shall be payable to her, to and for her own use, free from the claims of the representatives of her husband or of any of his creditors; but such exemption shall not apply where the amount of premium annually paid shall exceed three hundred dollars.

In case of the death of the wife before the decease of her husband, the amount of the insurance may be made payable, after her death, to her children, for their use, and to their guardian if under age.

Every married woman, being a resident of this state, who shall receive a patent for her own invention, pursuant to the laws of the United States, may hold and enjoy the same, and all the proceeds, benefits, and profits thereof and of such invention, to her own separate use, free and independent of her husband and his creditors, and may transfer and dispose thereof, and in every respect perform all acts in relation thereto, in the same manner as if she were unmarried; but this act shall not authorize such married woman to contract any pecuniary obligations to be discharged at any future time.

When any deposite shall be made in any savings bank or institution, by any female, being or hereafter becoming a married woman, in her own name, it shall be lawful for the trustees or officers of such bank or institution to pay such depositor such sum or sums as may be due such female, and the receipt or acquittance of such depositor shall be a sufficient legal discharge to the said corporation therefor.

DOWER.—A widow shall be endowed with the third part of all the lands whereof her husband was seized, of an estate of inheritance, at any time during the marriage.

Rate of Interest.

THE legal rate is seven per cent. All contracts, whereby a higher rate is reserved, are void. Corporations can not set up the defence of usury.

Homestead-Exemption Law.

In addition to the property now exempt by law from sale under execution, there shall be exempt by law from sale on execution for debts hereafter contracted, the lot and buildings thereon, occupied as a residence and owned by the debtor, being a householder and having a family, to the value of one thousand dollars. Such exemption shall continue after the death of such householder, for the benefit of the widow and family, some or one of them continuing to occupy such homestead until the youngest child become twenty-one years of age, and until the death of the widow. And no release or waiver of such exemption shall be valid unless the same shall be in writing, subscribed by such householder, and acknowledged in the same manner as conveyances of real estate are by law required to be acknowledged.

To entitle any property to such exemption, the conveyance of the same shall show that it is designed to be held as a homestead under this act, or if already purchased, or the conveyance does not show such design, a notice that the same is designed to be so held shall be executed and acknowledged by the person owning the said property, which shall contain a full description thereof, and shall be recorded in the office of the clerk of the county in which the said property is situate, in a book to be provided for that purpose, and known as the "Homestead-Exemption Book." But no property shall, by virtue of this act, be exempt from sale for non-payment of taxes or assessments, or for a debt contracted for the purchase thereof, or prior to the recording of the aforesaid deed or notice.

If, in the opinion of the sheriff holding an execution against such householder, the premises claimed by him or her as exempt, are worth more than one thousand dollars, he shall summon six qualified jurors of his county, who shall upon oath, to be administered to them by such sheriff, appraise said premises, and if, in the opinion of the jury, the property may be divided without injury to the interests of the parties, they shall set off so much of said premises, including the dwelling house, as, in their opinion, shall be worth one thousand dollars, and the residue of said premises may be advertised and sold by such sheriff.

In case the value of the premises shall, in the opinion of the jury, be more than one thousand dollars, and can not be divided as is provided for in the last section, they shall make and sign an appraisal of the value thereof, and deliver the same to the sheriff, who shall deliver a copy thereof to the execution debtor, or to some of his family, of suitable age to understand the nature thereof, with a notice thereof attached, that unless the execution debtor shall pay to said sheriff the surplus over and above one thousand dollars within sixty days thereafter, that such premises will be sold.

In case such surplus shall not be paid within the said sixty days, it shall be lawful for the sheriff to advertise and sell the said premises, and out of the proceeds of such sale to pay to such execution debtor the said sum of one thousand dollars, which shall be exempt from execution for one year thereafter, and apply the balance on such execution; provided, that no sale shall be made unless a greater sum than one thousand dollars shall be bid therefor, in which case the sheriff may return the execution for want of property.

The costs and expenses or selling off such homestead, as provided herein, shall be charged and included in the sheriff's bill of costs upon the said execution.

This act shall take effect on the first day of January, one thousand eight hundred and fifty-one.

NEW JERSEY.

Delaware River
Philadelphia
Camden
Woodbury
Salem
Bridgeton
Millville
Mt. Holly
Cape May
Long Beach
Island Beach
Longitude East from Washington

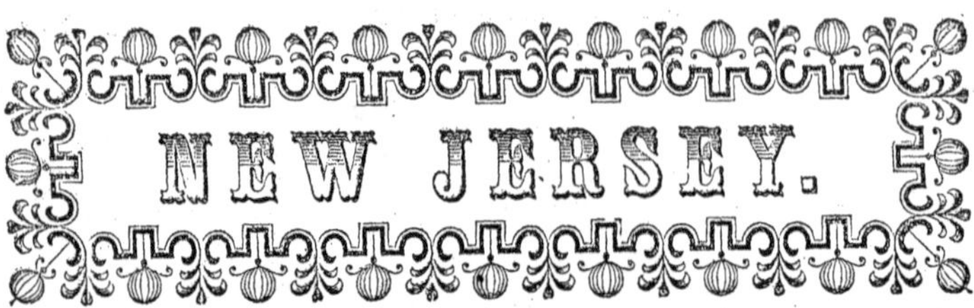

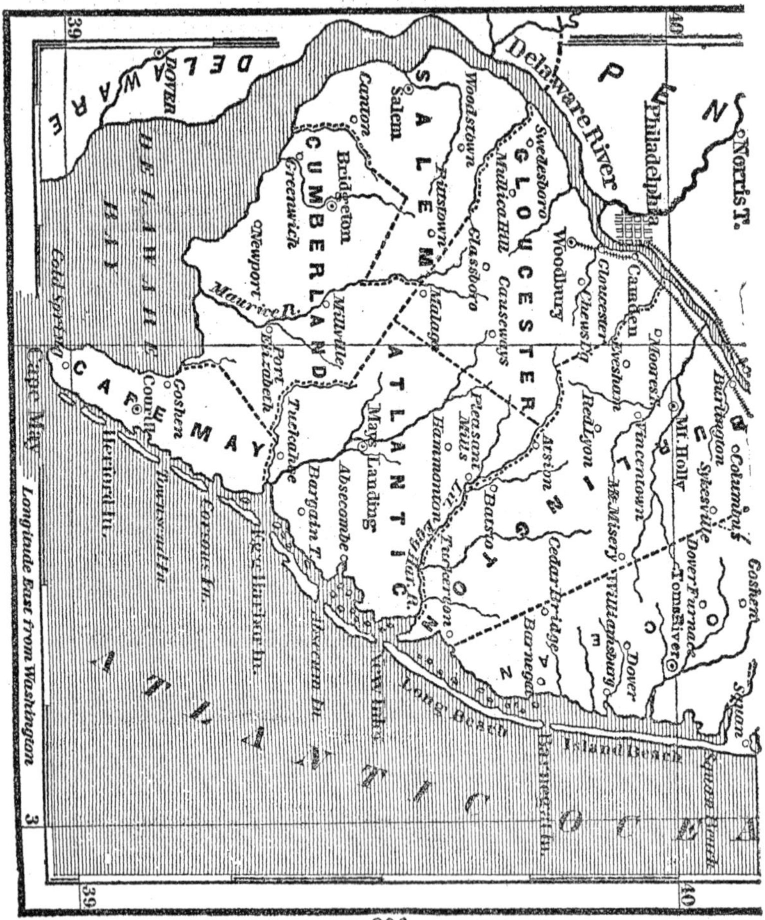

NEW JERSEY.

NEW JERSEY
Scale of Miles
5 10 15 20
Delaware River
Hudson River
Stroudsburg
Easton
Richmond
Belvidere
Phillipsburg
Mansfield
Johnsonburg
Columbia
Hope
Newton
Sparta
La Fayette
Hamburg
Montague
Deckertown
Carpenter Pt.
Edenton
Monroe
Haverstraw
Ramapo
Pompton
Powerville
Paterson
Morristown
Dover
Parsippany
Andover
Stanhope
Flemington
Clinton
Somerville
Ringoes
Harlingen
Princeton
Lambertville
Sergeantsville
Doylestown
Allentown
TRENTON
Hightstown
Cranberry
Freehold
Howell
Middletown
Shrewsbury
Long Branch
New Brunswick
Perth Amboy
Elizabeth T.
Newark
Orange
Rahway
Jersey C.
Hackensack
Brooklyn
Staten I.
Warren
Bound Brook
Chatham
Mendham
Lawrenceville
Georgia
Clinton
SUSSEX
WARREN
MORRIS
HUNTERDON
SOMERSET
MIDDLESEX
MONMOUTH
BERGEN
ESSEX
PENNSYLVANIA
NEW YORK
LONG I.
41
2
3

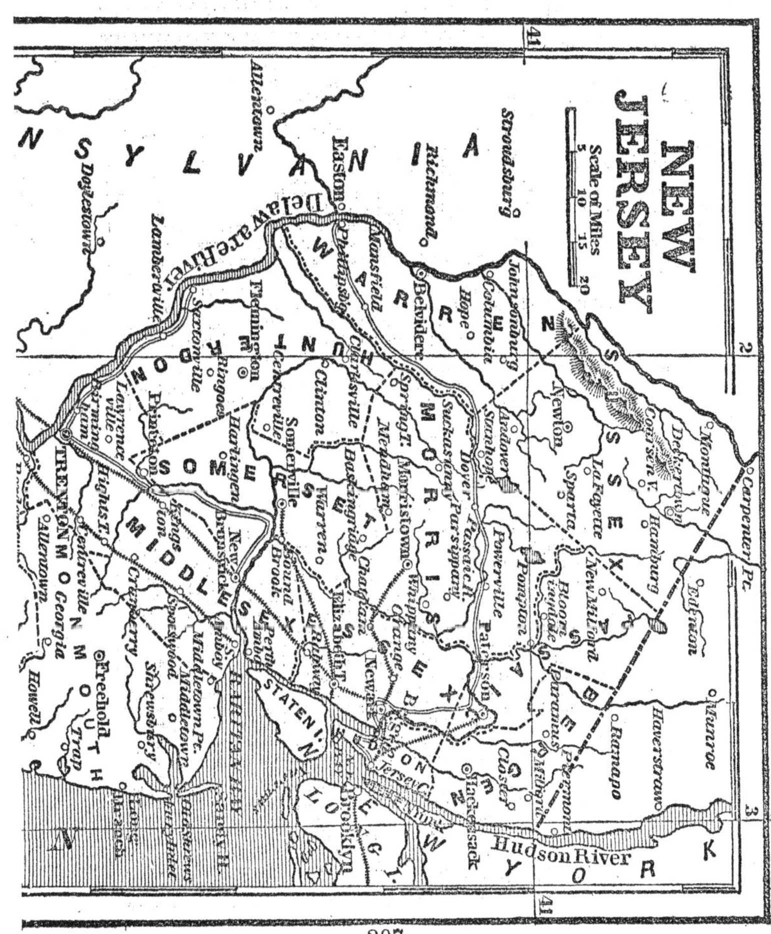

NEW JERSEY.

Constitution adopted 1844—Square Miles 8,320—Population in 1850, 488,673.

Exemptions.

THE following articles being the property of any one having a family is exempt from levy and sale on execution. One cow; one bed and bedding; one cradle; one stove; one half cord of firewood; one half ton of stone coal; one spinning-wheel; one table; six chairs; one hog; one hundred weight of flour; one iron cooking pot; one dozen knives and forks; one dozen plates; one dozen spoons; one half dozen bowls; two pails; one barrel; one coffee-pot; one tub; one frying-pan; the necessary tools of a tradesman, not exceeding in value ten dollars; and all necessary wearing apparel.

The above exemptions apply to contracts made previous to March 18, 1851; after that date, household goods, chattels, and tradesmen's tools, to the value of $200, and all wearing apparel, the property of any debtor having a family residing in this state, shall be reserved, as well after as before the death of the debtor, for the use of the family against all creditors, and shall not be liable to be seized or taken by virtue of any execution or civil process whatever, issued out of any court in this state (except the same be issued in cases of taxation) on any contract made after the passage of this act.

This act does not protect from sale under any execution or process any goods, chattels, or property, for the purchase whereof the debt or demand for which the judgment on which the execution or process was issued shall have been contracted.

If an officer can not find sufficient other property to satisfy an execution, then a judge of common pleas is to appoint three disinterested persons to appraise the goods, without reference to what they might bring at vendue, when, if they amount to more than $200, the debtor is allowed to select such as he may choose to this amount, and the balance to be sold. The plaintiff must have five days notice of time and place of appraisement.

A widow of a deceased debtor, or his administrator, may select the same amount under similar provisions.

Mechanics' Lien.

ALL and every dwelling-house or other building hereafter constructed and erected within this state, shall be subject to the payment of the debt contracted for, or by reason of any work done, or materials found and provided by any person or persons employed, or furnishing materials for or in erecting and constructing such house, or other building; but if such house or other building should not sell for a sum of money sufficient to pay all the demands for work and materials over and above any prior claim on mortgage or judgment against any land owner, on the land on which such building or buildings may be erected, then the same shall be averaged, and each of the creditors paid a sum proportional to their several demands; *provided*, no such debt shall remain a lien on said buildings longer than two years from the commencement of the building thereof, unless the claim be filed within six months after performing the work or furnishing the materials, in the office of the clerk of the court of common pleas of the county where such building may be erected, and an action for the recovery of the same may be instituted within one year after such work done or materials found; and all claim for work and materials must be filed within one year from the time the work was done or materials furnished.

When any master-workman refuses to pay any journeyman employed by him, such journeyman shall give to the owner of the house notice of such refusal in writing, and the amount due and demanded; then said owner shall be authorized to retain the amount due such journeyman, out of the amount due such master-workman, and pay the same to the journeyman. Any person who shall hereafter, by virtue of any contract with the owner, perform any labor, or furnish materials in building, altering, or repairing, any building, shall have a lien for the value of such labor and materials, upon such building, and upon the lot of land on which the same stands, to the extent of the title, at the time existing of such owner, but the aggregate of the liens not to exceed the contract price.

The person performing such labor or furnishing such materials, shall cause to be drawn up specifications of the work by him contracted to be performed, or materials to be furnished, and stating the price or prices agreed to be paid therefor, and shall file them, or if there be a contract, a true copy thereof, if the same be in writing, in the office of the clerk of the county in which the lien is created, and serve a notice thereof, personally, on such owner, or his agent, within fifteen days after the making of such contract, or after commencing such labor or furnishing the said materials. The lien so created shall take effect from such filing and service of the notice, and shall continue in force for six months after the completion of the building.

A lien given by this act, extends to all mills and manufactories within the county of Mercer, for all debts contracted by the owners thereof, or by any other person, with their consent in writing, for machinery or fixtures furnished for said mill or manufactory, or work done or materials furnished for or about the erecting, constructing, or repairing machinery in the same.

Law Regulating Contracts.

No leases, estates, or interests, or term or terms of year or years, or any uncertain interest of, in, to, or out of, any messuages, lands, tenements, or hereditaments, shall, at any time hereafter, be assigned, granted, or surrendered, unless it be by deed or note in writing, signed by the party so assigning, granting, or surrendering the same, or his, her, or their agent or agents, thereunto lawfully authorized by writing, or by act and operation of law.

No action shall be brought, whereby to charge any executor, or administrator, upon any special promise to answer damages out of his own estate; or whereby to charge the defendant upon any special promise to answer for the debt, default, or miscarriages of another person; or to charge any person upon any agreement made upon consideration of marriage; or upon any contract or sale of lands, tenements, or hereditaments, or any interest in or concerning them; or upon any agreement that is not to be performed within the space of one year from the making thereof; unless the agreement upon which such action is brought, or some memorandum or note thereof, shall be in writing and signed by the party to be charged therewith, or some other person thereunto, by him or her lawfully authorized.

No contract for the sale of any goods, wares, and merchandise, for the price of thirty dollars or upward, shall be allowed to be good, except the buyer shall accept part of the goods so sold, and actually receive the same, or give something in earnest to bind the bargain, or in part payment, or that some note or memorandum in writing of the said bargain be made and signed by the parties, to be charged by such contract, or their agents thereunto lawfully authorized.

Limitation of Actions.

All actions of trespass, quare clausum fregit, trespass, detinue, trover and replevin, for taking away of goods and chattels, all actions of debt, founded upon any lending or contract without speciality, or for arrearages of rent due on a parol demise, and all actions of account and upon the case, except actions for slander, and except also such actions as concern the trade or merchandise between merchants, their factors, agents, and servants, shall be commenced within six years next after the cause of action accrued.

Actions of trespass for assault, menace, battery, wounding, and imprisonment, or any of them within four years.

Every action upon the case for words, within two years next after the words spoken.

Minors, married women, and insane persons, may bring these actions within the times limited respectively after their disability is removed.

Actions of debt, or covenant for rent, or arrearages of rent, founded upon any lease under seal, and actions of debt upon any single or penal bill for the payment of money only, or upon any obligation with condition for the payment of money only, or upon any award under the hands and seals of arbitrators for the payment of money only, shall be brought within sixteen years; but time of infancy, marriage, or insanity, not to be computed.

Time of defendant's absence from the state not to be computed.

Entry upon lands must be made, and action brought to recover the possession of lands must be done, within twenty years.

Collection of Debts.

ARREST.—It shall not be lawful to arrest or imprison the person of any female, by virtue of any mesne process or process of execution in any civil action.

Any person arrested and held in custody in any civil action upon mesne process or process of execution, or upon an attachment for not performing an award, or surrendered in discharge of bail, shall be discharged from arrest or custody by such officer, if he make out and deliver to the officer making the arrest, or in whose custody he may be, a true and perfect inventory, under oath or affirmation, of all his goods and chattels, rights, credits, lands, tenements, hereditaments, and real estate, and give bond to the plaintiff with sufficient security, being a freeholder or freeholders resident in the county, in double the sum for which he is arrested, conditioned that he will appear before the next court of common pleas, to be holden in the county where such arrest is made, and petition such court for the benefit of the insolvent laws, &c. And in case of forfeiture by breach of condition, the plaintiff may bring an action thereon, and recover debt, damages, and costs, due from the person arrested, and for which the arrest was made.

ATTACHMENT.—If any creditor shall make oath or affirmation before any judge of any of the courts of record of this state, or justice of the peace of any county in the same, that he verily believes that his debtor absconds from his creditors, and is not, to his knowledge or belief, resident in this state at the time, then an attachment shall issue against the rights and credits, moneys and effects, goods and chattels, lands and tenements of such debtor, wheresoever they may be found.

And the writ shall bind the property and estate of the defendant, from the time of executing the same.

And all conveyances of the property attached, made by the defendant pending the attachment, shall be void as against the plaintiff, and the creditors shall become parties to the attachment.

Deeds.

IF any deed, or conveyance of lands, tenements, or hereditaments, lying and being in this state, heretofore made and executed, and not already acknowledged or proved according to law, or hereafter to be made and executed, shall be acknowledged by the party or parties who shall have executed it, the officer having first made known the contents thereof to the person making such acknowledgment, and being also satisfied that such person is the grantor mentioned in said deed, of all which the said officer shall make his certificate, or if it be proved by one or more of the subscribing witnesses to it, that such party or parties signed, sealed, and delivered the same as his, her, or their voluntary act and deed, before the chancellor of this state, or one of the justices of the supreme court of this state, or one of the masters in chancery, or one of the judges of any of the courts of common pleas of this state, and if a certificate of such acknowledgment or proof, shall be written upon or under the said deed or conveyance, and be signed by the person before whom it was made, then every such deed or conveyance, so acknowledged, or proved and certified, shall be received as evidence in any court of this state.

Acknowledgment or proof may be made before a judge of the court of common pleas for any county, whether the lands are situate in said county, or elsewhere in the state.

After deeds have been thus acknowledged, or proved and certified, they may be recorded in the office of the clerk of the court of common pleas, of the county in which such lands are situate.

No estate of a *femme covert*, in any lands, tenements, or hereditaments, lying and being in this state, shall hereafter pass by her deed or conveyance without a previous acknowledgment made by her on a private examination, apart from her husband, before one of the officers aforesaid, that she signed, sealed, and delivered the same as her voluntary act and deed, freely without any fear, threats, or compulsion, of her husband, and a certificate thereof, written on or under the said deed or conveyance, and signed by the officer before whom it was made: and further, that every deed or conveyance so executed and acknowledged by a *femme covert*, and certified as aforesaid, shall release and bar her right of dower, and be good and effectual to convey the lands, tenements, hereditaments, thereby intended to be conveyed: *provided*, that this clause shall not be construed to enable any *femme covert*, under the age of twenty-one years, to convey lands, tenements, hereditaments, or any right of dower, interest, or estate therein.

If the grantor reside in some other of the United States, or territory, or District of Columbia, such acknowledgment or proof may be made before the chief justice of the United States, or an associate justice of the supreme court of the United States, or district judge of the same, or any judge or justice of the supreme or superior court of any state in the Union, or territory thereof, or in the District of Columbia, or judge of any district or circuit court, or chancellor, of any of the United States, or before any mayor, or any other chief magistrate of any city in such state, district, or territory, duly certified under the seal of such city, or before a judge of any court of common pleas, of the state, district, or territory, in which such party or witnesses may be; *provided*, that where the acknowledgment or proof is made before a judge of a court of common pleas, in such state, district, or territory, a certificate under the great seal of the state, or under the seal of the county court in which it is made that he is such officer, shall be deemed sufficient evidence of his authority for that purpose, and be annexed to, and recorded with such deed, acknowledgment, or proof.

When made by a party residing in a foreign state, kingdom, nation, or colony, if made before any court of law, or mayor, or other chief magistrate of any city, borough, or corporation, of the said foreign kingdom, &c., certified by the said court, mayor, or chief magistrate, in the manner such acts are usually authenticated by them or him, it shall be as valid as if made before a justice of the supreme court of this state.

The above two sections comprehend acknowledgments of deeds or conveyances made by married women residing out of this state in any part of the Union, or in a foreign country.

Form of Acknowledgment.

State of New Jersey,
County of *Essex*, } *ss.*
Town of *Rahway*,

On this *first* day of *October*, one thousand eight hundred and *fifty*, before me personally came JOHN DOE *and* SUSAN *his wife*, to me known to be the persons described in and who executed the foregoing *conveyance*; and, having first made known to them the contents thereof, they acknowledged that they executed the same, *and the said* SUSAN, *on a private examination, apart from her husband, acknowledged that she signed, sealed, and delivered the same as her voluntary act and deed, freely, and without any fear, threats, or compulsion of her husband.*

JOHN JONES,
Justice of the Supreme Court.

Where there is no wife, the part referring to her should be omitted.

Deeds should be SEALED; a scrawl with the pen has been held valid in place of a seal.

Rights of Married Women.

IT shall be lawful for any married woman, by herself, and in her name, or in the name of any third person, with his assent, as her trustee, to cause to be insured, for her sole use, the life of her husband for any definite period, or for the term of his natural life; and in case of her surviving her husband, the sum or net amount of the insurance becoming due and payable by the terms of the insurance shall be payable to her, to and for her own use, free from the claims of the representatives of her husband or his creditors; but such exemption shall not apply where the amount of premium annually paid shall exceed one hundred dollars.

In case of the death of the wife before the decease of the husband, the amount of the insurance may be made payable, after the death, to her children, for their use, and their guardian, if under age.

DOWER.—The widow, whether alien or not, of any person, shall be endowed, for the term of her natural life, of the one full and equal third part of all the lands, tenements, and other real estate, whereof her husband, or any other to his use, was seized of an estate of inheritance at any time during the coverture, to which she shall not have relinquished her right of dower, by deed executed and acknowledged in the manner prescribed by law for that purpose.

Rate of Interest.

THE legal rate of interest is six per cent., and contracts for a higher rate are void. Persons taking a higher rate shall forfeit the whole value of the subject-matter of the contract—one half to the state, one half to the prosecutor.

By act of 1852, the legal rate is seven per cent in Jersey City and Hoboken.

Wills.

ALL last wills and testaments of persons dying after March 7, 1850, shall be in writing, and shall be signed, or acknowledged to have been signed, by the testator, and declared to be his or her last will, in the presence of at least two credible witnesses present at the same time, who shall subscribe their names thereto as witnesses in the presence of the testator; and no will or testament of personal estate, made after this act shall take effect, by a person within the age of twenty-one years, shall be good or effectual in law.

Homestead Exemption.

§1. In addition to the property now exempt from sale under execution, there shall be exempt by law from sale or execution for debts hereafter contracted, the lot and buildings thereon occupied as a residence and owned by the debtor, being a householder and having a family, to the value of one thousand dollars; such exemption shall continue after the death of such householder for the benefit of the widow and family, some or one of them continuing to occupy such homestead, until the youngest child shall become twenty-one years of age, and until the death of the widow; and no release or waiver of such exemption shall be valid.

A notice of the design to hold the property as a homestead must be executed and recorded with the clerk of the county where the property is situated, and published once a week for six weeks in a newspaper published in the county, or in the newspaper published nearest the same; but no property shall by virtue of this act be exempt from sale, for non-payment of taxes or assessments, or for any labor done thereon, or materials furnished therefor, or for a debt contracted for the purchase thereof, or prior to the recording of the aforesaid deed of notice.

The act provides for the sale or division of the homestead on execution, when its value exceeds one thousand dollars, by six appraisers.

7. *And be it enacted*, That in case any lot and buildings have been declared according to the provisions of this act, a homestead, it shall be reserved as such for the use of the family, and shall not be sold, aliened, or encumbered by the owner thereof, nor leased for a longer term than one year; and any such sale, alienation, encumbrance, or leasing, shall be void, unless the same be made with the full consent of the wife or husband of said owner (if he or she have any), by deed duly acknowledged, and unless the consideration paid for the same be its full, fair value, and the same, or one thousand dollars thereof shall be actually invested in the purchase of other lands and buildings, declared to be a homestead in the manner herein provided, and the title of such purchaser shall not be good until such purchase-money is so invested, and also except in cases where such householder has removed out of the state; nor shall any homestead be rented out or leased for any time without the consent of the wife of the owner.

Approved, March 17, 1852.

PENNSYLVANIA.

Constitution adopted 1838.—Square Miles 46,000.—Population in 1850, 2,311,204.

Exemptions.

By a law that took effect July 4th, 1849, it was enacted that, in lieu of the property then exempt by law from levy and sale on execution, issued upon any judgment obtained upon contract and distress for rent, property to the value of three hundred dollars ($300) exclusive of all wearing apparel of the defendant and his family, and all bibles and school-books in use in the family (which shall remain exempt as heretofore), and no more, owned by or in the possession of any debtor, shall be exempt from levy and sale on execution or distress for rent.

Mechanics' Lien.

EVERY building erected within the counties of Allegany, Armstrong, Beaver, Bedford, Berks, Bucks, Butler, Cambria, Centre, Chester, Clearfield, Columbia, Crawford, Cumberland, Dauphin, Delaware, Erie, Franklin, Huntingdon, Indiana, Juniata, Lancaster, Lebanon, Luzerne, Lycoming, Mercer, Mifflin, Montgomery, Northumberland, Perry, Philadelphia, Schuylkill, Somerset, Susquehannah, Tioga, Union, Venango, Warren, Washington, York, and the boroughs of Easton, Lehigh, Bradford, Monroe, Greene, Clinton, Carion, M'Kean, Wayne, Fayette, Potter, Jefferson, and Northampton, shall be subject to a lien for the payment of all debts contracted for work done, or materials furnished for the same; extending also to the ground necessary for the ordinary and usual purposes of the building.

This lien shall be preferred to every other lien attaching subsequent to the commencement of such building.

A statement of the demand must be filed in the office of the prothonotary of the court of common pleas of the county where the building is situate.

Unless such statement be filed, lien shall not continue for more than six months.

Lien expires at the end of five years from the day of filing the statement, unless renewed by *scire facias*.

The furnishers of labor and materials, in many of the counties, have a lien for six months after the work is done or the material furnished. This lien may be extended to five years by filing the claim in the proper office, and by proper legal process until satisfied.

PENNSYLVANIA.

PENNSYLVANIA.

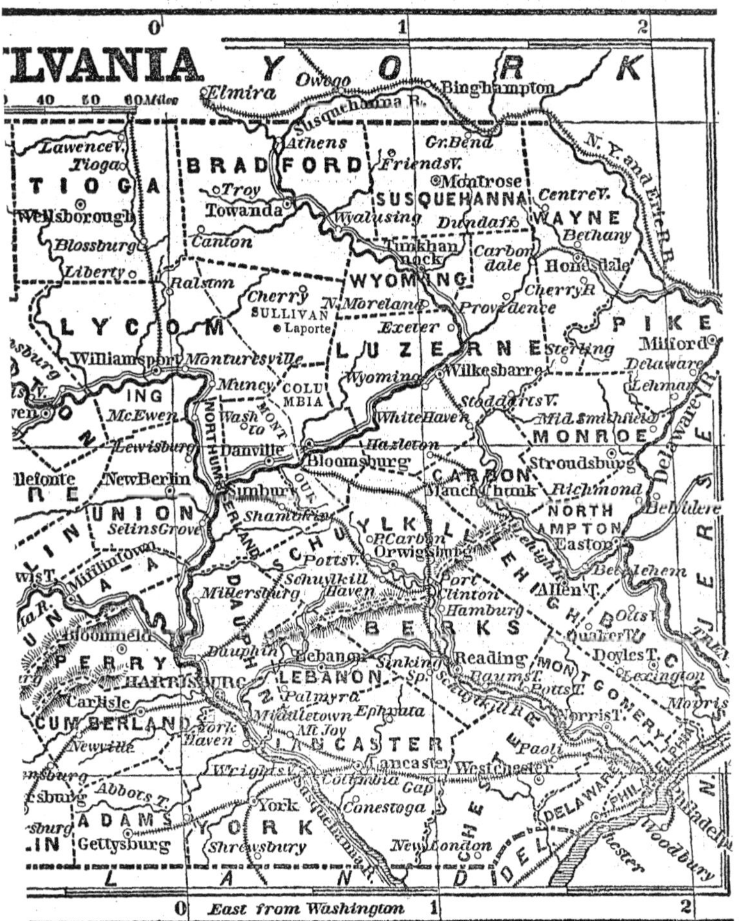

Law regulating Contracts.

ALL leases, and estates, and interests in lands, except leases for three years, must be in writing, and signed by the parties so making or creating the same, or their agents thereunto lawfully authorized by writing, or they will have the effect of leases at will only.

All the other regulations are the same as in CONNECTICUT, page 193.

Limitation of Actions.

ENTRY can not be made into lands after twenty-one years after the right accrued, nor any suit brought to recover possession.

Infants, married women, and persons imprisoned, have ten years after their disability is removed.

All actions upon the case, other than for slander; actions of account (other than such accounts as concern the trade of merchandise between merchants, their factors and servants); actions of debt founded upon any lending or contract without specialty; for arrearages of rent, except the proprietaries' quit-rents; actions of detinue and replevin for goods and chattle; actions of trespass, *quare clausum fregit*, must be brought within six years after the cause of action accrued.

Actions of trespass, of assault, menace, battery, wounding, imprisonment, or any of them, must be brought within two years. Actions upon the case for words, within one year next after words spoken.

Infants, married women, persons imprisoned or out of the United States, may bring the above actions within the times respectively limited after their disability is removed.

Collection of Debts.

ARREST.—Arrest is abolished, except in proceeding as for contempt to enforce civil remedies; action for fines or penalties, or on promises to marry; on moneys collected by any public officer, or for any misconduct or neglect in office or in any professional employment.

But yet, in other cases, if the party is about to remove any of his property out of the jurisdiction of the court in which such suit is brought, with intent to defraud his creditors, or has property which he fraudulently conceals, or has rights in action or some interest in any public or corporate stock, money, or evidence of debt, which he unjustly refuses to apply to the payment of any judgment which shall have been rendered against him; or has assigned, removed, or disposed of, or is about to dispose of, any of his property, with the intent to defraud his creditors; or has fraudulently contracted the debt or incurred the obligation respecting which suit is brought, he may be arrested.

ATTACHMENT.—Property of defendant may be attached when he is about to remove any of it from the county with intent to defraud his creditors, or has assigned, disposed of, or secreted, or is about to assign, dispose of, or secrete, any of it, with the like fraudulent intent; and also if the debtor, being an inhabitant of the state, shall have absconded from the place of his usual abode, or shall have remained absent from this commonwealth, or shall have confined himself in his own house, or concealed himself elsewhere, with design to defraud his creditors and, if not an inhabitant, shall confine or conceal himself within the county, with intent to avoid the service of process, and to defraud his creditors.

Deeds.

All deeds and conveyances of lands, tenements, or hereditaments, shall be acknowledged by one of the grantors, or proved by one of the subscribing witnesses, before one of the judges of the supreme court, or alderman of a city, or before a justice of the peace, or one of the justices of the court of common pleas, of the county where the lands lie, and shall be recorded in the office for recording of deeds in the county where such lands lie, within six months after the execution of such deeds.

Acknowledgment by husband and wife must be made before one of the judges of the supreme court, or alderman of a city, or a justice of the peace, or justice of the county court of common pleas, of and for the county where such lands lie, who shall examine the wife separate and apart from her husband, and shall read or otherwise make known the full contents of such deed or conveyance to the said wife; and if, upon such separate examination, she shall declare that she did, voluntarily and of her own free will and accord, seal, and as her act and deed deliver, the said deed or conveyance, without any coercion or compulsion of her said husband, the conveyance shall be valid.

The mayor and recorder of Philadelphia may take proof and acknowledgment of deeds; and, in other states, commissioners of deeds appointed by the governor of Pennsylvania. A scrawl of the pen is recognised as a seal. Two witnesses are necessary.

Form of Acknowledgment.

Commonwealth of Pennsylvania, } ss.
County of *Philadelphia.* }

Be it remembered that on this *tenth* day of *April*, A. D. one thousand eight hundred and fifty-*one*, before me the subscriber, *a justice of the peace of* —— [or, *judge of*, *&c.*, or *one of the aldermen of the city of* ——] personally appeared John Doe, the grantor in the foregoing indenture, deed, or conveyance, named and in due form of law acknowledged the said indenture to be his act and deed, and desired that the same as such, might be recorded according to law. In testimony whereof I have hereunto set my hand and seal the day and year last abovenamed. JOHN JONES, *(seal.)*

Justice of the Peace, or *Judge*, or *Alderman*, as the case may be.

The Form when the Wife joins with the Husband.

Com. of Penn., county of *Berks, ss.* Be it remembered that on this *tenth* day of *May*, A. D., 185–, before me the subscriber, *a justice &c.* [or *judge*, or *alderman*, as above] of the county aforesaid, personally appeared John Roe and Susan Roe his wife, grantors in the above indenture, deed, or conveyance, named, and in due form of law severally acknowledged the foregoing indenture, deed, or conveyance, to be their act and deed, and desired that the same, as such, might be recorded according to law. She, the said Susan Roe being of full age, separate and apart from her said husband, by me thereon privately examined, and the full contents thereof being by me first made known to her, did declare and say, that she did, voluntarily, and of her own free will and accord, sign, seal, and as her own act and deed, deliver the foregoing indenture, deed, or conveyance, without any coercion or compulsion of her said husband.

In testimony, &c. JOHN JONES, *Justice, &c. (Seal.)*

Rights of Married Women.

Every species and description of property, whether consisting of real, personal, or mixed, which may be owned by or belong to any single woman, shall continue to be the property of such woman as fully after her marriage as before; and all such property, of whatever name or kind, which shall accrue to any married woman during coverture by will, descent, deed of conveyance, or otherwise, shall be owned, used, and enjoyed, by such married woman, as her own separate property; and the said property, whether owned by her before marriage, or which shall accrue to her afterward, shall not be subject to levy and execution for the debts or liabilities of her husband, nor shall such property be sold, conveyed, mortgaged, transferred, or in any manner encumbered, by her husband, without her written consent, first had and obtained, and duly acknowledged before one of the judges of the courts of common pleas of this commonwealth, that such consent was not the result of coercion on the part of her said husband, but that the same was voluntarily given and of her own free will: provided that her said husband shall not be liable for the debts of the wife contracted before marriage; provided that nothing in this act shall be construed to protect the property of any such married woman from liability for debts contracted by herself, or in her name by any person authorized so to do, or from levy and execution on any judgment that may be recovered against a husband for the wrongs of the wife, and in such cases execution shall be first had against the property of the wife.

Any married woman may dispose, by her last will and testament, of her separate property, real, personal, or mixed, whether the same accrues to her before or during coverture: provided that said last will and testament be executed in the presence of two or more witnesses, neither of whom shall be her husband.

In all cases where debts may be contracted for necessaries for the support and maintenance of the family of any married woman, it shall be lawful for the creditor in such case to institute suit against the husband and wife for the price of such necessaries, and, after obtaining a judgment, have an execution against the husband alone; and if no property of the said husband be found, the officer executing the said writ shall so return, and thereupon an *alias* execution may be issued, which may be levied upon and satisfied out of the separate property of the wife, secured to her under the provisions of the first section of this act: provided that judgment shall not be rendered against the wife in such joint action unless it shall have been proved that the debt sued for in such action was contracted by the wife, or incurred for articles necessary for the support of the family of the said husband and wife.

Rate of Interest.

THE legal rate of interest is six per cent. Usurious interest can not be recovered; and if paid, may be recovered back, but usury does not render the entire contract void.

When any railroad or canal company has borrowed money, and given a bond or other evidence of indebtedness in a larger sum than the amount actually received, such transactions shall not be deemed usurious.

Wills.

WILLS must be in writing; and, unless the person making the same shall be prevented by the extremity of his last sickness, shall be signed by him at the end thereof, or by some person in his presence and by his express direction, and in all cases shall be proved by the oaths or affirmations of two or more competent witnesses.

DELAWARE.

Constitution adopted, 1831.—Square Miles, 2,100.—Population in 1850, 91,407.

Law regulating Contracts.

ALL promises and assumptions whereby any person shall undertake to answer or pay for the default, debt, or miscarriage, of another, any sum under forty shillings, being proved by the oath or affirmation of the person or persons to whom such promise and assumption shall be made, are hereby declared to be good and available in law to charge the party or parties making such promise or assumption.

No action shall be brought whereby to charge any executor or administrator, upon any special promise, to answer damages out of his own estate; or whereby to charge any defendant, upon any special promise, to answer for the debt, default, or miscarriage, of another person, of the value of forty shillings, and not exceeding ten pounds, unless such promise and assumption shall be proved by the oath or affirmation of one credible witness, or some memorandum or note in writing shall be signed by the party to be charged therewith.

No action shall be brought whereby to charge any person or persons upon any agreement made upon considerations of marriage, or upon any contract or sale of lands, tenements, or hereditaments, or any interest in or concerning them, or upon any agreement that is not to be performed within the space of one year from the making thereof; or to charge any person or persons whereby to answer for the debt, default, or miscarriage, of another, in any sum of the value of ten pounds and upward, unless the same shall be reduced to writing, or some memorandum or note thereof shall be signed by the party or parties to be charged therewith, or some other person thereunto by him or them lawfully authorized, except for goods, wares, and merchandise, sold and delivered, and other items which be and are properly chargeable in an account,* in which case the oath or affirmation of the plaintiff, together with a book regularly and fairly kept, shall be allowed in all cases to be given in evidence, in order to charge the defendant or defendants with the sum or sums therein contained.

Limitation of Actions.

ACTIONS for recovery of lands must be brought and entry made within twenty years next after the right of action accrued.

Infants, married women, non compos-mentis, or a prisoner, may within ten years next after the removal of their disability.

No action of trespass, replevin, detinue, debt not founded upon a record or specialty, of account, of assumpsit, upon the case, shall be brought after the expiration of three years from the accruing of the cause of action.

In case of mutual and running account, limitation not to begin while the account continues open and current.

* Items of cash are not properly chargeable in account. Smith vs. M'Beath; Kent's Com. Pleas, Nov. term, 1814.

DELAWARE.

DELAWARE
Scale of Miles
5
10
15
20
DELAWARE RIVER
PENNSYLVANIA
NEW JERSEY
Woodbury
Millville
Maurice R.
Bridgeton
Newport
Salem
Chester
Centreville
Brandywine
Wilmington
Newport
New Castle
Christiana
Hamburg
Red Lion
Kennet Square
Red Clay Cr.
Milltown
Stanton
White Clay Cr.
Newark
Glasgow
Williamsburg
Big Elk Cr.
Elkton
Frenchtown
Elk River
Oxford
Port Penn
Cantwell
Middle T.
Fieldsboro
Warwick
Frederick
Bridge T.
Chester R.
Blackbird
Smyrna
Kenton
Leipsic
Jones R.
DOVER
Bombay Hook
Bombay H. I.

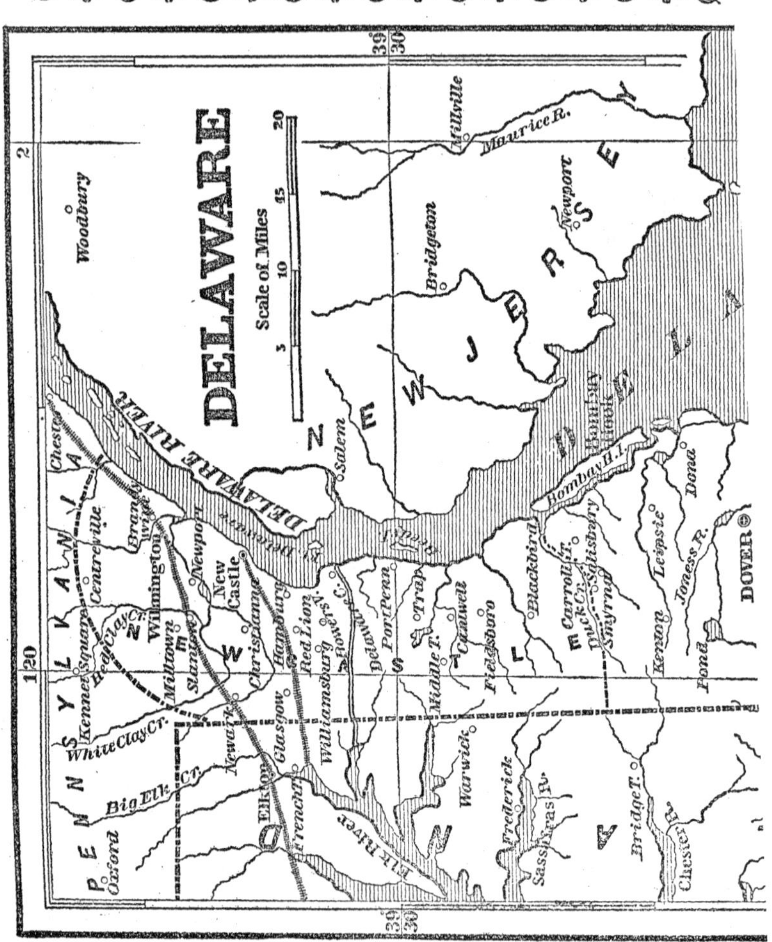

DELAWARE.

KENT
SUSSEX
DELAWARE BAY
MARYLAND
Cape May
C. Henlopen
Pilottown
Rehoboth Bay
Indian River
Kitts Hammock
Camden
Willow Grove
George T.
Canterbury
Frederica
Berrytown
Lewisville or Sand T.
Milford
Mispillion Cr.
Guinea T.
Teatown
Fleatown
Milton
Georgetown
Millsborough
Washington
Dogsborough
Frankford
Cypress Swamp
St. Johnstown
Bridgeville
Concord
Laurel
Middleford
Seaford
Nanticoke R.
Whiteleysburg
Marshy Hope Cr.
Denton
Federalsburg
Beartown
Choptank Cr.
Choptank R.
Tuckahoe Cr.
Hillsborough
Vienna
39
38 30
20 Longitude East from Washington

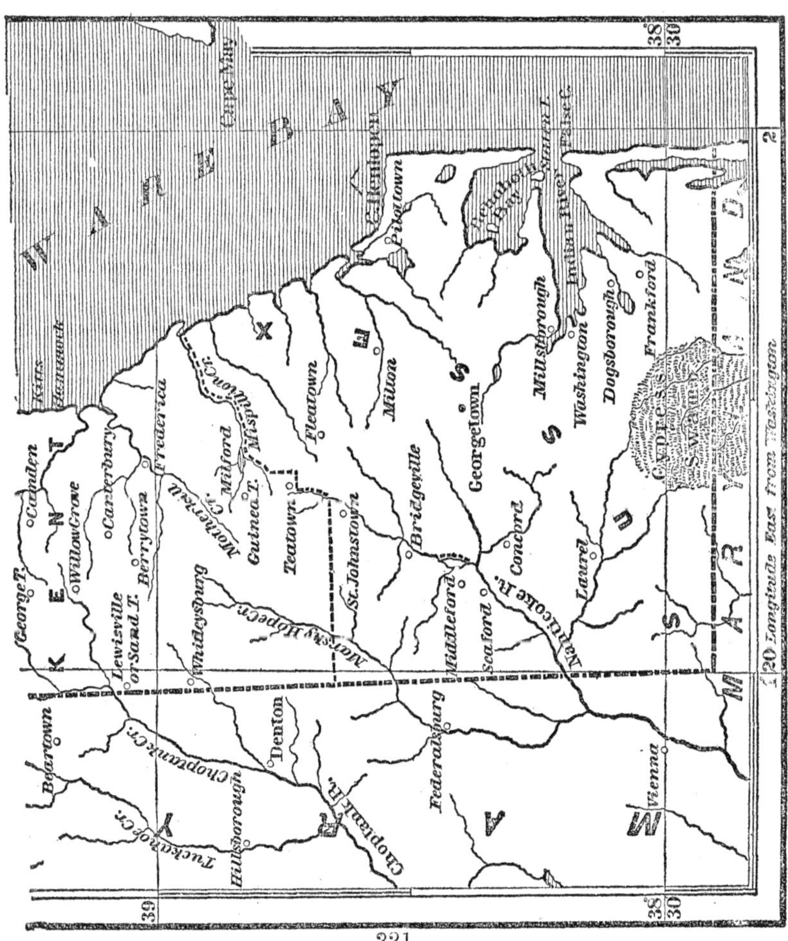

When the action arises from a promissory note, bill of exchange, or an acknowledgment under the hand of the party, of a subsisting demand, the action may be commenced at any time within six years.

Those under the disability of infancy, coverture, or incompetency of mind, to have three years after the removal of such incompetency.

The time the defendant is out of the state, to be deducted; and in every such case, one year after his return to be allowed, when the cause of action arises in this state.

Exemptions.

THE following goods and chattels, the property of the white citizens of this state, are exempt from execution process, and distress for rent, to wit: the necessary wearing apparel of the debtor, and of his wife and children, one bedstead, bed, and the necessary bedding for every two persons of the family, one iron stove used for warming the dwelling house, and fuel not exceeding the value of five dollars, procured and designed for the use of the family; the bibles, and school-books, used in the family; one cow, one swine and one ton of hay; the library and tools or implements of the debtor necessary for carrying on his profession, trade or business, not exceeding fifty dollars in value; rights of burial and tombs while in use as repositories for the dead; other household furniture necessary for the debtor and his family not exceeding twenty-five dollars in value; *Provided*, that the value of the whole of the articles thus exempted shall not exceed one hundred dollars, and provided further, that if the debtor shall not at the time of the execution of the said process, be in possession of all, or any of the above specified articles, then any other property which he shall have in his possession amounting in value to one hundred dollars, shall be exempt as aforesaid, except in every case for taxes due in either of the counties of this state, or in the city of Wilmington, which said articles and the value thereof shall be ascertained by two substantial citizens of the county whereof the debtor is an inhabitant, to be appointed and to be sworn or affirmed faithfully and justly to fulfil the duties of said appointment by any justice of the peace, constable, or sheriff of the said county.

This act shall not in any wise invalidate debts or contracts made previous to the fourth day of July, A. D. one thousand eight hundred and fifty-one, and that all acts and parts of acts inconsistent herewith, be and the same are hereby repealed.

Collection of Debts.

ARREST.—No free white citizen may be arrested, except upon oath that the defendant is justly indebted in a sum exceeding five dollars, and verily believes that defendant has secreted, conveyed away, assigned, settled, or disposed of, either money, goods, chattels, stocks, securities for money, or other real or personal estate, of the value of more than twenty-five dollars, with intent to defraud his creditors, and specify and set forth the supposed fraudulent transactions.

ATTACHMENT.—Attachment may issue against a residenter in this government, upon an affidavit that the defendant is justly indebted to the plaintiff in the sum of forty shillings, and absconded from the place of his usual abode, or is gone out of the government, with intent to deceive or defraud his creditors, as it is believed.

The above is called "*domestic attachment.*" There is another writ which is known as a "*foreign attachment,*" and which issues against a non-resident upon the oath of the plaintiff, or of some credible person for him, that the defendant resides out of the state, and is justly indebted to him in the sum of fifty dollars and upward.

Deeds.

DEEDS may be acknowledged in any county by any party to the same, in the superior court or before the chancellor or any judge of the said court, or before two justices of the peace for the same county, or before a notary public.

Deeds of a married woman, to which her husband is also a party, shall be valid if she, upon private examination apart from her husband, acknowledges that she executed said deed willingly, without compulsion or threats, or fear of her husband's displeasure. Such private examination may be taken in any county before the chancellor, any judge, or two justices of the peace for the same county, or before a notary public.

Such acknowledgment to be certified under the hand and seal of the clerk of the court in which, or under the hand of the chancellor, judge, or justices of the peace, or under the hand and notarial seal of the notary, before whom, it is taken, in a certificate endorsed upon or annexed to the deed.

If the party be out of the state, the acknowledgment, or private examination, may be made before the judge of any district court of the United States, or before the chancellor or any judge of a court of record in any state, territory, or country, or before the mayor or chief officer of any city or borough, and certified under the hand of such chancellor, judge, mayor, or officer, and the seal of his court, city, or borough, by certificate endorsed upon, or annexed to the deed; or such acknowledgment and examination may be made before any commissioner duly authorized by the governor of this state, and certified under his hand and seal.

Deeds must be recorded in the office for recording deeds in the county where the lands lie.

There should be two witnesses. A scrawl of the pen may be used for a seal.

The form of acknowledgment is the same as in PENNSYLVANIA, by *adding* "or fear of her husband's displeasure."

Rate of Interest.

THE legal rate is six per cent. Whoever exacts more, is liable to forfeit the whole debt—one half to the state, and one half to the prosecutor.

Wills.

WILLS must be in writing, and signed by the testator, or by some other person subscribing the testator's name, in his presence and by his express direction, and attested and subscribed by two competent witnesses, in the presence of the testator.

MARYLAND.

PENNSYLVANIA
VIRGINIA
Smithfield
Mt. Pleasant
Shelbyport
Jonasville
Frostburg
Westport
Glade
Yoxhiogen R.
Cumberland
Old T.
Potomac River
Pratts
Hancock T.
Wereffordsburg
Martinsburg
Williamsport
Boonsboro
Sharpsburg
Harpers Ferry
Hagars T.
Emmets
Creeg T.
Leesburg
Matilda
Simpsonville
Bladensburg
Rock Cr.
WASHINGTON COUNTY
WASHINGTON
George Town
ALEXANDRIA CO.
Four Mile Run
Eastern Br.
Alexandria
DISTRICT OF COLUMBIA
Reference
1 Capitol
2 Presidents House
1 2 3 Miles
39
38
Longitude West from W

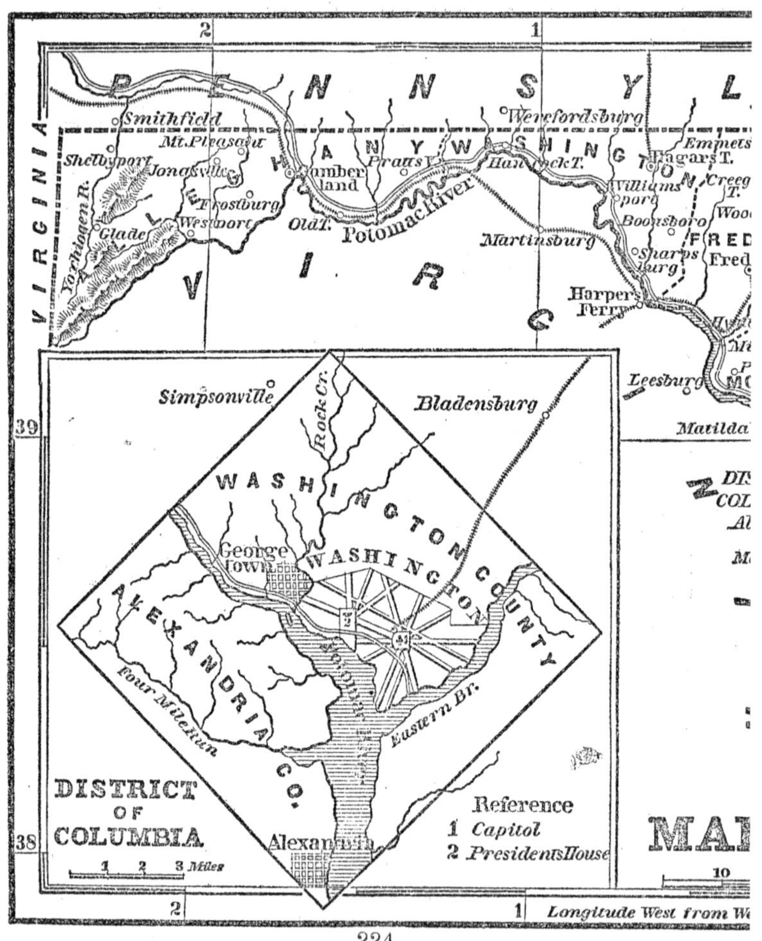

MARYLAND.

NEW JERSEY
Susquehanna R.
Delaware R.
Chester
Wilmington
Shrewsbury
Manchester
Taney T.
CARROLL
Westminster
Hereford
Wiersburg
HARFORD
Bellair
Havre de Grace
Port Deposit
Elk T.
Bohemia
Abingdon
BALTIMORE
Towson T.
Owings Mills
Lisbon
Baltimore
Ellicotts Mills
Elkridge
Savage
George T.
Bridge T.
Smyrna
Chester T.
KENT
DOVER
Indian L.
Centrev.
Greensboro
ANNAPOLIS
PRINCE GEORGES
WASHINGTON
U. Marlboro
Nottingham
Piscataway
Denton
Easton
TALBOT
CAROLINE
Georgetown
Federalsburg
New Market
Concord
L. Marlboro
CALVERT
Washington
Bryantown
CHARLES
Pt. Tobacco
Pr. Frederick
Cambridge
Church Cr.
DORCHESTER
Vienna
Bucktown
Newport
ST. MARY
Leonard T.
Quantico
St. Martins
Salisbury
WORCESTER
Nanticoke R.
Newtown
Princess Ann
Snow Hill
SOMERSET
Kingston
Potomac River
LAND
30
40
50 Miles
38

MARYLAND.

Constitution adopted, 1851. Square Miles, 13,959.—Population in 1850, 582,922.

Exemptions.

No real estate hereafter acquired by marriage shall be liable to execution during the life of the wife, for debts due from the husband.

Corn for necessary maintenance, bedding, gun, axe, pot. and laborers' necessary tools, and such like household implements, and ammunition, for subsistence, are also exempt.

Slaves of the wife (acquired either before or after marriage), and also her earnings not exceeding one thousand dollars, may be held for her own use, and exempted from liability for her husband's debts.

Mechanics' Lien.

MECHANICS' liens have been enacted for all the counties on the western shore of the Chesapeake bay, except St. Mary's, Montgomery, and Charles, and for Cecil county on the eastern shore, but they have been altered so often, and the several enactments are so conflicting, that it is impossible to give a reliable abstract of what is required to make them available.

Chattel Mortgages.

CHATTEL mortgages must be in writing, and acknowledged before a justice of the county where the mortgager resides, and the affidavit of the mortgagee or grantee sworn to before the judge, or justice or justices, must be endorsed thereon that the consideration as therein set forth is true and *bona fide*, and be recorded within twenty days in the records of the county. Where the amount conveyed is over two hundred dollars they must be stamped (fee $1.00) which must be receipted for on the deed.

Limitation of Actions.

ACTIONS of trespass *quare clausum fregit*, trespass, detinue, sur-trover, replevin for taking away goods or chattels, account, contract, debt, book-debt, or upon the case, other than such accounts as concern the trade or merchandise between merchants, their factors and servants, non-residents, debt for lending, contract without speciality, and debt for arrearages of rent, must be brought within three years.

Actions on the case for words, trespass of assault, battery, wounding, and imprisonment, must be brought within one year.

Actions on administration and testamentary bonds shall be commenced within twelve years after the framing such bonds.

No speciality can be pleadable after the principal debtor and creditor have both been dead twelve years, or the debt is above twelve years standing.

No person absenting himself from the state, or removing from county to county, after any debt contracted, so that his creditors can not with certainty find his person or effects, shall have any benefit of such limitations. No person absent at the time the cause of action accrues shall have any benefit of the law.

Infants, married women, persons non-compos-mentis, imprisoned, or beyond seas, have the same time after their disability is removed.

Collection of Debts.

ATTACHMENT.—Any person, having obtained a judgment, may take out an attachment against the lands, tenements, goods, chattels, and credits, of the defendant.

Any creditor, making affidavit that the debtor is indebted to him in a certain sum named, and producing the evidences thereof or accounts, and that he doth know or is credibly informed, and verily believes, that the debtor is not a citizen of this state, and doth not reside therein, or that the debtor is actually run away or fled from justice, or removed from his place of abode, with intent to injure and defraud his creditors, an attachment may issue against the lands, tenements, goods, chattels, and credits, of the debtor. No person can be imprisoned for debt.

Deeds.

DEEDS may be acknowledged before any chief or associate judge of a district for lands within the district, or any two justices of the peace within their county.

The officer taking the acknowledgment must be satisfied of the identity of the person making it, and return a certificate thereof.

They may be acknowledged out of the state before any judge of the United States court, or any judge of a court of record, certified by the judge taking the acknowledgment, under his hand; and the clerk of the court shall certify, under his hand and the seal of the court, that the person taking the acknowledgment is a judge of said court, duly commissioned and qualified, at the time of taking the acknowledgment.

In the case of a married women, her estate will not be conveyed, nor her dower barred, unless the officer taking the acknowledgment shall examine her, out of the presence and hearing of her husband, whether she doth execute and acknowledge the same freely and voluntarily, and without being induced to do so by fear or threats of or ill usage by her husband, or by fear of his displeasure; and unless the *femme covert* shall sign and seal such deed before such officer, out of the presence and hearing of her husband, and certificate be made upon or annexed to the deed, under his or their hands, of such private examination, execution, and acknowledgment

Consuls and vice-consuls of the United States, duly appointed and recognised, may take acknowledgments of persons being in their consulates, and make certificate under their official seals.

There must be two witnesses to a deed, and a scrawl of the pen may be used as a seal. Deeds must be stamped.

Form of Acknowledgment.

State of Maryland,
Prince George's Co. } sct:

Be it remembered and it is hereby certified, that on this *first* day of *May*, in the year eighteen hundred and *fifty-one*, before the subscribers, *two justices of the peace*, of the state of Maryland, in and for *Prince George's* county aforesaid, personally appeared JOHN DOE and SUSAN DOE *his wife*, they being known to us [*or* "they being satisfactorily proven by oral testimony under oath, received by us," *as the case may be*], to be the persons who are named and described as, and professing to be, the parties to the foregoing deed or indenture, and do severally acknowledge the said indenture or instrument of writing, to be the their respective act and deed; *the said* SUSAN DOE *signed and sealed said indenture before us, out of the presence and hearing of her husband: and the said* SUSAN DOE *being by us examined, out of the presence and hearing of her said husband, "whether she doth execute and acknowledge the same, freely and voluntarily, and without being induced to do so by fear or threats of or ill-usage by her husband, or by fear of his displeasure," declareth and saith, that she doth.* In testimony whereof, we hereunto subscribe our names, on the day and year aforesaid.

(Seals.) JOHN JONES, *Justice of the Peace.*
JAMES SMITH, *Justice of the Peace.*

Rate of Interest.

THE legal rate is six per cent. In contracts, where more is taken, only the excess of interest over the legal rate is void.

Wills.

WILLS shall be in writing, and signed by the party making them, or by some other person in his presence and by his express directions, and shall be attested and subscribed, in the presence of the testator, by three or four credible witnesses.

A wife may make a will and give all her property on any part thereof, to her husband on any one other person, with the consent of the husband subscribed to said will. Provided the wife shall have been privately examined by witnesses to said will, apart and out of the presence and hearing of her husband &c. (in the same manner as provided in deeds), and provided also said will be made sixty days before death of the testatrix.

VIRGINIA.

Wheeling
NORTHERN PART OF VIRGINIA
OHIO
PENNSYLVANIA
Wellsburg
BROOKE
HANCOCK
Wheeling
Ohio Riv.
MARSHALL
Elizabeth T.
MONONGAHELA
Morgan T.
Kingwood
PRESTON
New Martins
WETZEL
Fairmount
Middlebourne
TYLER
MARION
Marietta
Ohio River
Harrisville
Parkersburg
WOOD
West Union
DODDRIDGE
HARRISON
Clarksburg
TAYLOR
BARBOUR
Philippa
Weston
LEWIS
Elizabeth
Kanawha R.
De Kalb
WIRT
Gallipolis
Point Pleasant
Ripley
JACKSON
MASON
GILMER
Beverly
Cheat R.
PUTNAM
C.H.
Sutton
BRAXTON
RANDOLPH
Burlington
Guyandotte
Barbourville
Charleston
Elk R.
KANAWHA
Summersville
NICHOLAS
POCAHONTAS
Huntersville
CABELL
WAYNE
Big Sandy R.
Trout Hill
Ballardsville
Coal R.
Fayette V.
FAYETTE
GREENBRIER
BATH
BOONE
LOGAN
Lewisburg
Covington
Lexington
Berkley
RALEIGH
MONROE
Union
Guyandotte R.
WYOMING
Princeton
MERCER
BOTTETOURT
Fincastle
ROANOKE
Salem
Liberty
BEDFORD
MONTGOMERY
KENTUCKY
TAZEWELL
GILES
Parisburg
Jeffersonville
RUSSELL
WYTHE
PULASKI
Christiansburg
Newbern
FLOYD
Rocky Mount
FRANKLIN
Clinch R.
Lebanon
Wytheville
SMYTH
Marion
Jacksonville
SCOTT
Jonesville
Estillville
WASHINGTON
Greensville
GRAYSON
CARROLL
Hillsville
Taylorsville
PATRICK
HENRY
Martinsville
PITTSYLVANIA
Competition
Danville
TENNESSEE
NORTH C
Longitude West

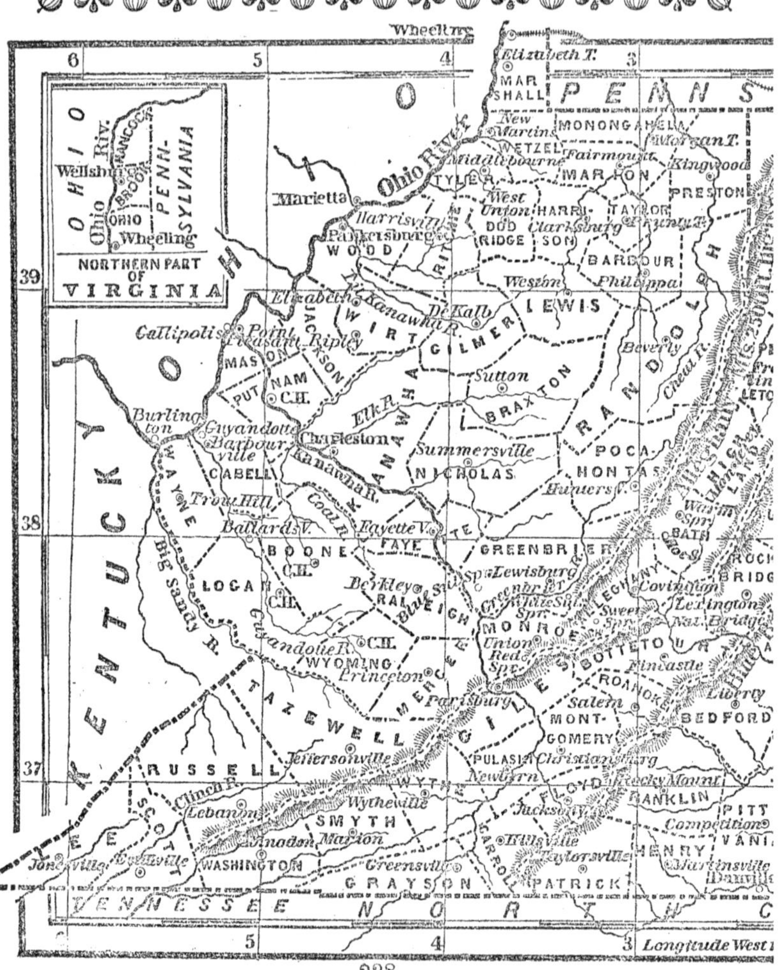

VIRGINIA.

VIRGINIA
Scale of Miles
10 30 50
Baltimore
Harpers Ferry
ANNAPOLIS
WASHINGTON
Alexandria
Mt.Vernon
Port Tobacco
Potomac Riv.
Denton
DOVER
DELAWARE
Princess Anne
HAMPSHIRE
Romney
Martinsburg
MORGAN
Winchester
FRED ERICK
CLARKE
Charlestown
Leesburg
LOUDON
FAIRFAX
C.H.
Front Royal
Woodstock
SHENAN DOAH
ROCKINGHAM
Harrisonburg
Warrenton
Fairfax
CUL-PEPPER
Madison
Fredericksb'g
STAF-FORD
KING GEORGE
SPOTSYL-VANIA
ORANGE
GREENE
Virginia University
Charlottesv.
LOUISA
HANOVER
CAROLINE
Bowling Green
WESTMORELD
RICHMOND
Tappahannock
KING WILLIAM
KING & QUEEN
MIDDLESEX
LANCASTER
ESSEX
NELSON
Lovingston
Palmyra
FLUVANA
GOOCHLAND
James R.
BUCKING HAM
Maysville
POWHATAN
Scottsville
HENRICO
RICHMOND
NEW KENT
CHESTERFIELD
CHARLES CITY
JAMES CITY
York R.
Lynchburg
Concord
AMHERST
APPOMATTOX
PRINCE EDWARD
AMELIA
Petersburg
PRINCE GEORGE
NOTTOWAY
DINWIDDIE
SURRY
Smithfield
LUNENBURG
Marysville
Lewistown
BRUNSWICK
Lawrenceville
HALIFAX
Banister
Boydton
MECKLENBURG
Dan R.
Hicksford
SUSSEX
Jerusalem
SOUTHAMPTON
ISLE OF WIGHT
Portsmouth
NORFOLK
NANSEMOND
Suffolk
PRINCESS ANNE
ACCOMAC
NORTHAMPTON
Roanoke R.
AMPBELL
39
38
37
2
1
0
1
rom 2 Washington

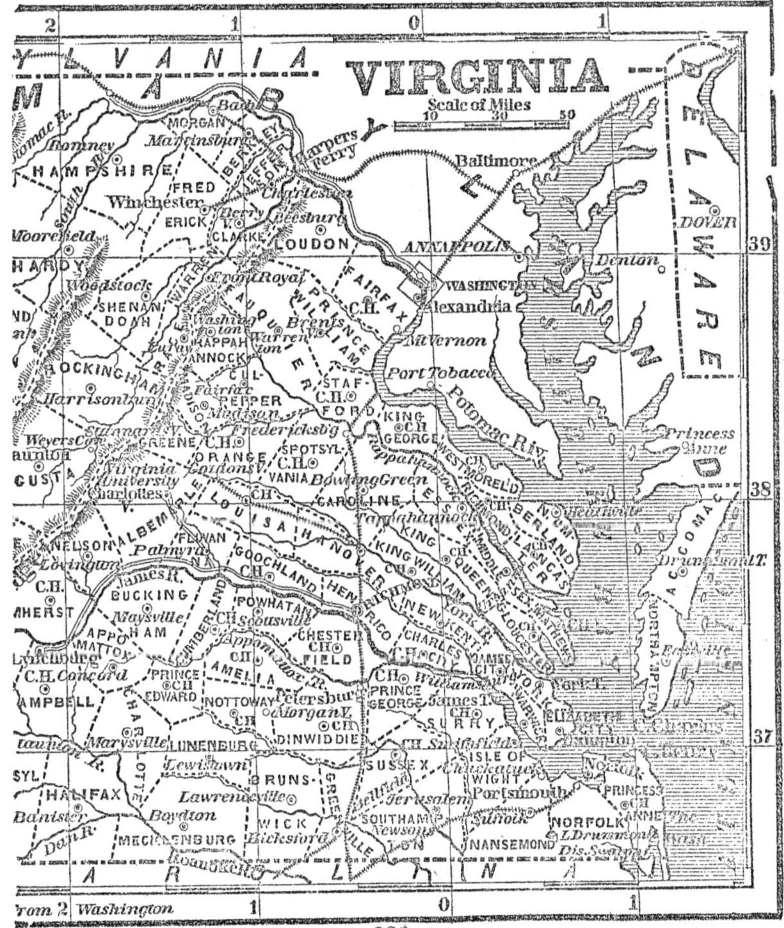

VIRGINIA.

Constitution adopted 1851.—Square Miles, 61,352.—Population in 1850, 1,421,081.

Exemptions.

No growing crop of any kind, not severed, shall be liable to distress or levy, except Indian corn, which may be taken at any time after the fifteenth of October in any year.

In case of a husband or parent, there shall be exempted from such distress or levy the following articles, or so much or so many thereof as the party may have: One cow; one bedstead, with a bed and necessary bedding for the same; six chairs, one table, six knives and six forks, six plates, two dishes, two basins, one pot, one oven, six pieces of wood or earthen ware, one loom and its appurtenances, one spinning-wheel, one pair of cards, and one axe; five barrels of corn; five bushels of wheat, or one barrel of flour; two hundred pounds of bacon or pork, and five dollars in value of forage or hay. Slaves shall not be distrained or levied upon, without the debtor's consent, where there are other goods and chattels of such debtor sufficient for the purpose, and which it is in his power to take.

Mechanics' Lien.

If a person, owning or having an interest in land in a city or town, shall, by a writing signed by him, contract with another to pay him money for erecting or repairing any building or the appurtenances of any building on such land, there shall be a lien for such money on the whole interest of the said person in such land, from the time that the said writing is duly admitted to record in the county or corporation wherein the said land lies.

But the said lien shall not be in force more than six months from the time when the money or the last instalment of the money to be paid under such contract shall become payable, unless a suit in equity to enforce the lien shall have been commenced within the said six months. If, in such suit, the lien be established, the court shall order a sale of such interest in the said land, to satisfy the money which ought to be paid under such contract.

Law regulating Contracts.

No action shall be brought—

1. To charge any person, upon or by reason of any representation or assurance concerning the character, conduct, credit, ability, trade, or dealings of another, to the intent or purpose that such other may obtain thereby credit, money, or goods; or—

2. To charge any person, upon a promise made after full age, to pay a debt contracted during infancy; or upon a ratification, after full age, of a promise or simple contract made during infancy; or—

3. To charge a personal representative, upon a promise, to answer any debt or damages out of his own estate; or—

4. To charge any person upon a promise, to answer for the debt, default, or misdoings, of another; or—

5. Upon any agreement made upon consideration of marriage; or—

6. Upon any contract for the sale of real estate, or the lease thereof, for more than a year; or—

7. Upon any agreement that is not to be performed within a year—

Unless the promise, contract, agreement, representation, assurance, or ratification, or some memorandum or note thereof, be in writing, and signed by the party to be charged thereby, or his agent; but the consideration need not be set forth or expressed therein.

Limitation of Actions.

No person shall make an entry upon, or bring an action to recover any land, but within fifteen years next after the time at which the right to make such entry or to bring such action shall have first accrued to himself or to some person through whom he claims.

An infant, married woman, and an insane person, have ten years after the removal of such disability, provided the disability shall not enable the person to bring such action or make such entry after the lapse of thirty years from the time when the right first accrued.

Every action to recover money which is founded upon an award, or on any contract other than a judgment or recognisance, shall be brought within the following number of years after the right shall have first accrued, viz.:—

If the case be upon an indemnifying bond taken under any statute, or upon a bond of an executor, administrator, guardian, curator, committee, sheriff or sergeant, deputy sheriff or sergeant, clerk or deputy-clerk, or any other fiduciary or public officer, within ten years.

If it be upon any other contract by writing under seal, within twenty years.

If it be upon an award, or be upon a contract by writing, signed by the party to be charged thereby, or by his agent, but not under seal, within five years.

And if it be upon any other contract, within five years, unless it be an action for any articles charged in any store account, in which case the action may be brought within two years; or an action by one partner against his copartner for a settlement of the partnership accounts, or upon accounts concerning the trade of merchandise between merchants, their factors or servants, where the action of account would lie; in either of which cases the action may be brought until the expiration of five years from a cessation of the dealings in which they are interested together, but not after.

Every personal action, for which no limitation is otherwise prescribed, shall be brought within five years.

Every action upon a judgment or decree rendered in any other state or country shall be barred, if, by the laws of such state or country, such action would there be barred. And whether so barred or not, no action can be brought on such judgment against a resident for the ten years last past, which was rendered more than ten years before the commencement of the action.

Collection of Debts.

Attachment.—When any suit is instituted for any debt, or for damages for breach of any contract, on affidavit, stating the amount and justice of the claim, that there is present cause of action therefor, that the defendant or one of the defendants is not a resident of this state, and that the affiant believes he has estate or debts due him within the county or corporation in which the suit is, or that he is sued with a defendant residing therein, the plaintiff may forthwith sue out of the clerk's office an attachment against the estate of the non-resident defendant for the amount so stated.

Imprisonment for debt does not exist.

Deeds.

A SCROLL, affixed by way of seal, is as valid as a seal.

Any deed of trust, mortgage, or other writing, made by a husband or parent to give a lien on property which is exempt from distress or levy, shall be void as to such property.

Every deed of gift, of trust, or mortgage, conveying real estate or goods and chattels, shall be void as to creditors and subsequent purchasers for valuable consideration, without notice, until and except from the time that it is duly admitted to record in the county or corporation wherein the property may be.

The husband is entitled to courtesy and the wife to dower in a trust estate.

When a husband and wife have signed a writing purporting to convey or transfer any estate, real or personal, she may appear before a court authorized to admit such writing to record, or before the clerk thereof in his office; and if, on being examined privily and apart from her husband, by one of the justices of the court, or by the clerk, and having such writing fully explained to her, she acknowledge the same to be her act, and declare that she had executed it willingly, and does not wish to retract it, such privy examination, acknowledgment, and declaration, shall be thereupon recorded in such court or in the clerk's office, or she may appear before two justices who shall be present together, or a notary public within the United States, or a commissioner appointed within the same by the governor of this state; and such justices, or notary, or commissioner, may so examine her, and if, after such explanation, she make such acknowledgment and declaration, shall certify the same on or annexed to the said writing to the following effect, viz.:—

Form of Acknowledgment.

State of *New York*,
County of *Monroe*, } to wit:

I, JOHN JONES, a *notary public* for the county of *Monroe*, in the state of *New York*, do certify that SUSAN DOE, the wife of JOHN DOE, whose names are signed to the writing above, bearing date on the *tenth* day of *November*, one thousand eight hundred and *fifty*, personally appeared before me, in the county aforesaid, and being examined by me privily and apart from her husband, and having the writing aforesaid fully explained to her, she, the said SUSAN DOE, acknowledged the said writing to be her act, and declared that she had willingly executed the same, and does not wish to retract it.

Given under my hand, this *twenty-fifth* day of *November*, one thousand eight hundred and *fifty*.

JOHN JONES, *Notary Public.*

Other acknowledgments may be made in the state before the court or the clerk of the court, in his office, where the same is to be recorded. If made elsewhere in the United States, then before a justice or notary public, who must write on or annex to the deed a certificate to the following effect:—

State of *New Hampshire*,
County of *Cheshire*, } to wit:

I, JOHN JONES, a *justice of the peace* for the county aforesaid, in the state of *New Hampshire*, do certify that JOHN DOE, whose name is signed to the writing above, bearing date on the *tenth* day of *November*, one thousand eight hundred and *fifty*, has acknowledged the same before me, in my county aforesaid.

Given under my hand, this *thirtieth* day of *November*, one thousand eight hundred and *fifty*.

JOHN JONES, *Justice of the Peace.*

One witness is sufficient to a deed.

Rights of Married Women.

DOWER.—A widow shall be endowed of one third part of all the real estate whereof her husband, or any other to his use, was at any time during the coverture seized of an estate of inheritance, unless her right of dower shall have been lawfully barred or relinquished.

In addition to dower, she is entitled to one third of the personal estate, after the payment of debts and charges, taking in slaves an estate for life only. If the marriage be without issue, she is entitled absolutely to the slaves and other personal property so remaining, which were derived from her, and was preserved in kind; and again, if the marriage be without issue, and the deceased husband was without issue by any former marriage, she is entitled to one half of the residue, qualified in respect to slaves as before.

If provision be made for her in her husband's will she may renounce it at any time within one year from the probate, and entitle herself thereby to her legal rights.

Rate of Interest.

THE legal rate is six per cent. All usurious contracts are void, with the penalty of forfeiture of twice the amount of the debt.

On protested bills payable out of Virginia, and within the United States, the damages are three per centum on the principal, and ten per centum when the bills are payable out of the United States—the bills in either case being drawn or endorsed within the state.

Wills.

THESE should be in writing, and signed by the testator, or by some other person in his presence and by his direction, in such manner as to make it manifest that the name is intended as a signature; and, moreover, unless it be wholly written by the testator, the signature shall be made or the will acknowledged by him in the presence of at least two competent witnesses, present at the same time, and such witnesses shall subscribe the will in the presence of the testator, but no form of attestation shall be necessary.

NORTH CAROLINA.

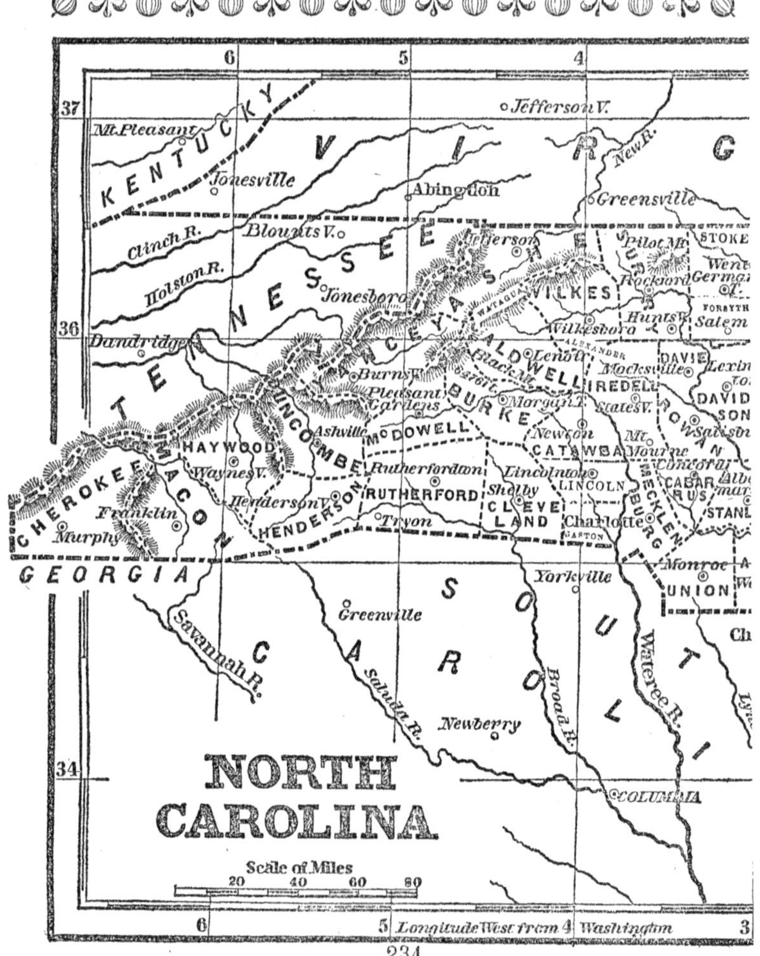

NORTH CAROLINA.

NORTH CAROLINA.

Constitution adopted, 1835.—Square Miles, 43,800.—Population in 1850, 868,870.

Exemptions.

THERE is exempted from sale on execution in this state, wearing-apparel; working-tools, and arms for muster; one bed and furniture; one wheel and cards, and one loom; one bible and testament; one hymn-book; one prayer-book; and all necessary school-books, the property of the defendant.

There is also exempt from seizure under execution the following property of every housekeeper, to wit: one cow and calf; ten bushels of corn or wheat; fifty pounds of bacon, beef, or pork, or one barrel of fish; all necessary farming-tools for one laborer; one bed, bedstead, and covering, for every two members of the family, and such other property as three disinterested freeholders, upon application made to some justice of the peace for the county in which the applicant resides, shall lay off and assign; such other property not to exceed in value the snm of fifty dollars at cash valuation

Chattel Mortgages.

No mortgage of any estate, whether real or personal, shall be good and available in law against creditors or purchasers for a valuable consideration, unless the same shall have been proved and registered within six months after the execution of such mortgage.

No deed of trust, or mortgage for real or personal estate, shall be valid at law to pass any property as against creditors or purchasers, for a valuable consideration from the donor, bargainer, or mortgager, but from the registration of such deed of trust or mortgage, in the county where the land lies, or in case of chattels, where the donor, bargainer, or mortgager, resides; or, in case the donor, bargainer, or mortgager, shall reside out of the state, then in the county where the said chattels or some of them are situate.

Law regulating Contracts.

ALL contracts to sell or convey any lands, tenements, or hereditaments, or interest in or concerning them, or any slave or slaves, shall be void unless such contract or some memorandum or note thereof, shall be put in writing, signed by the party to be charged therewith, or by some other person by him thereunto lawfully authorized, except leases not exceeding the term of three years.

No action shall be brought whereby to charge any executor or administrator upon a special promise to answer damages out of his own estate, or to charge the defendant upon any special promise to answer for the debt, default, or miscarriage of another person, unless the agreement upon which such action shall be brought, or some memorandum or note thereof, shall be in writing, and signed by the party to be charged therewith, or by some person thereunto by him lawfully authorized.

Limitation of Actions.

PERSONS having a right to lands must make claim within seven years next after the right accrued, except minors, married women, and persons insane, who may have three years after the removal of their disability, and persons beyond seas eight years after their right accrued.

All actions of account rendered, upon the case, of debt for arrearages of rent, of debt upon simple contract, of detinue, replevin, and trespass, either for goods and chattels, or *quare clausum fregit*, within three years.

Trespass, of assault and battery, wounding, imprisonment, within one year.

Actions upon the case for words, within six months after the words spoken.

Infants, married women, insane, and persons beyond sea, have the same periods after the removal of their disability.

Collection of Debts.

ATTACHMENT.—Upon any complaint being made on oath to any of the judges of the supreme or superior courts, or to any justice of any of the county courts, by any person, his attorney, agent, or factor, that any person [indebted to him] hath removed or is removing out of the county privately, or so absents or conceals himself, that the ordinary process of law can not be served on such debtor, and further swears to the amount of his debt or demand to the best of his knowledge and belief, an attachment may issue against the estate of such debtor, wherever the same may be found. An attachment may also issue in favor of a resident of this state against the estate of a non-resident.

By act of 1850, clerks of the county and superior courts may issue attachments returnable to their respective courts, and take bonds and administer oaths in cases of such attachments.

Deeds.

DEEDS must be acknowledged by the grantor before one of the judges of the supreme court, or of the superior court, or in the court of the county where the land lies, and registered by the public register of the county where the land lies, within two years from the date of the deed.

Residents in any of the other states, or in the territories, or in the District of Columbia, may acknowledge them before some one of the judges of supreme jurisdiction, or of the superior courts of law, or circuit courts of law of superior jurisdiction within said state, territory, or district, and an attestation of such acknowledgment endorsed or affixed to the deed by the judges, and a certificate of the governor of the state or territory, or if in the District of Columbia, a certificate of the secretary of state of the United States, that the judge before whom said acknowledgment was taken, was at the time of making the same one of the judges of the courts of supreme jurisdiction, or of the supreme courts of law, or circuit courts of law of superior jurisdiction within said state, territory, or district, shall also be affixed, or before any commissioner appointed by the governor of the state, and certified by him as by law required.

Conveyances by husband and wife must be by them personally acknowledged before one of the judges of the supreme or superior courts, or in the court of the county where the land lies, the wife being first privily examined by such judge, whether she doth voluntarily assent thereto.

A scrawl of the pen may be used instead of a seal.

Rights of Married Women.

WHENEVER a marriage shall take place, all the lands or real estate owned by the *femme coverte* at the time of the marriage, and all lands or real estate which she may subsequently acquire, by will, devise, inheritance, or otherwise, shall not be subject to be sold or leased by the husband for the term of his own life, or any less term of years, except by and with the consent of his wife first had and obtained, to be ascertained and effectuated by privy examination, according to the rules now required by law for the sale of lands by deed belonging to *femme covertes*. And further, that no interest of the husband whatever, in such lands or real estate, shall be subject to sale to satisfy any execution obtained against him, and all such sales are declared to be null and void both at law and in equity.

DOWER.—The widow is endowed of one third part of all the lands, tenements, and hereditaments, of which her husband died seized and possessed.

The dower of a widow shall not be subject to the payment of debts due from the estate or her husband, during the term of her life.

Rate of Interest.

THE legal rate is six per cent. All contracts whereby a higher rate is reserved are void, and the party exacting it is liable to forfeit double the amount of the debt, one half to the state, one half to the prosecutor.

Wills.

THE will must be written in the testator's lifetime, and signed by him or by some other person in his presence and by his direction, and subscribed in his presence by two witnesses, no one of whom shall be interested in the devise. Or, if found among his papers must be in his own handwriting, and his name subscribed thereto, or inscribed in some part thereof, and the handwriting generally known by his acquaintances, and proved by three witnesses to be every part in the testator's own handwriting.

No will in writing whereby personal estate is bequeathed, shall be sufficient to convey or give the same, unless such will be executed with the same formalities as are required in the execution of wills of real estate; provided, nevertheless, that the provisions of this act shall not be construed to affect nuncupative wills. No will in writing, made after 1846, which shall not be sufficient to convey or give personal estate, shall be good as to any real estate therein devised.

SOUTH CAROLINA.

SOUTH CAROLINA.

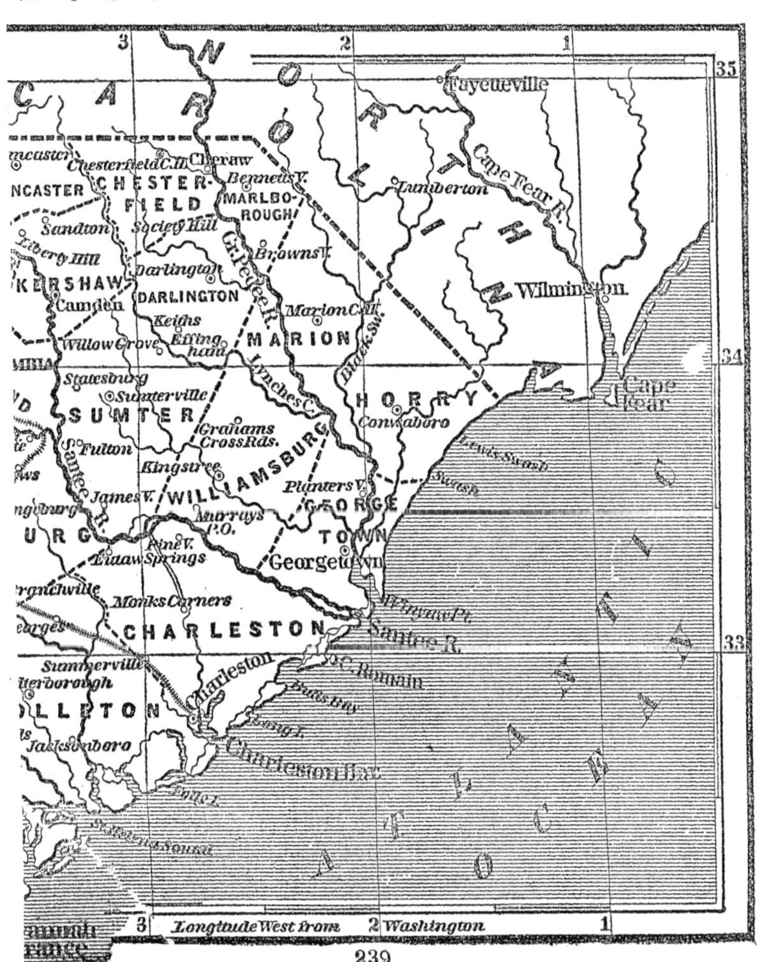

SOUTH CAROLINA.

Constitution adopted, 1790.—Square Miles, 25,200.—Population in 1850, 668,457.

Household and Homestead Exemptions.

THERE is in this state exempted from levy and sale on execution the following articles, namely: to each family two beds and necessary bedding; two bedsteads; one spinning-wheel, and two pairs of cards; one loom, and one cow and calf; if a farmer, the necessary farming utensils; if a mechanic, the tools of his trade; the ordinary cooking utensils, and ten dollars' worth of provisions.

Be it enacted, &c., That the following property, in addition to that now exempted by law, to wit: to each family the dwelling-house, and houses appurtenant thereto, together with fifty acres of land, and also one horse, and twenty-five dollars' worth of provisions, be and the same are hereby exempted from levy and sale, under fieri facias and assignment under mesne or final process: *Provided*, that the said exemption shall not include, or extend to, any property within the limits of any city or town corporate of this state. And *provided* further, that the value of the said real estate shall not exceed the sum of five hundred dollars.

That in all cases, where the landed property of the debtor shall exceed fifty acres, three commissioners shall be appointed by the clerk of the court, upon the application of either the plaintiff or defendant in the execution, whose duty it shall be to lay off to the debtor fifty acres of land, including the homestead, which shall always be done most favorably and beneficially for the family for whose benefit the provision is made; the remainder of whose land may be liable as in other cases.

And if the said fifty acres including the homestead, so laid off, shall exceed in value, by the estimate of the said commissioners, or a majority of them, the sum of five hundred dollars; then, and in all such cases, the said commissioners shall proceed to lay off such quantity less than fifty acres, as hereinbefore provided, the value of which shall not exceed the said sum of five hundred dollars, the remainder of which may be sold as in other cases.

That the said commissioners shall make a full return, under their hands and seals, of their proceedings in the premises, together with a plat or some other concise description of the lands laid off by them, to the clerk of the court, and shall be entitled to receive a compensation for their services, not exceeding one dollar each per day, to be paid by the defendant; and the clerk of the court shall keep a suitable book, in which the appointment of the commissioners, together with their return and all other proceedings in the case, shall be recorded; for which services, the said clerk shall be entitled to receive in like manner, from the defendant, the sum of three dollars.

That this act shall take effect, from and after the first day of March, 1852, in relation to all debts thereafter contracted.

Mechanics' Lien.

EVERY master mechanic, handicraftsman, and artificer, who shall erect, improve, or repair any building, shall have a lien thereon for the amount justly due him therefor.

A memorandum, in nature of a contract, must be signed in presence of one or more witnesses, by the parties to such contract and the proprietor of the premises or his lawful agent, containing a particular account of the work to be done, the materials to be furnished, and a general description of the premises, and recorded in the office of the register of mesne conveyances for the district in which such buildings are.

The lien shall be in no case for a greater sum than the just value which such building or improvement shall give to the land.

The lien to commence from the recording of the contract, and to continue only for three years. This not to impair any prior lien.

Chattel Mortgages.

No mortgage of personal property shall be valid so as to affect the rights of subsequent creditors or purchasers, for a valuable consideration, without notice, unless the same shall be recorded in the office of the register of mesne conveyances for the district where the mortgager resides. If he reside without the state, then where the property mortgaged is located at the time the mortgage is executed, within sixty days; and if the property consists of one or more slaves, then also in the office of the secretary of state, within sixty days. In the districts of Charleston and Richland, they shall be recorded in the office of the secretary of state only.

Law regulating Contracts.

PROMISES by executors or administrators to bind their own estate; by any one to pay the debt of another, or in consideration of marriage, or for any interest in lands, except leases not exceeding three years, or that are not to be performed within one year from the making thereof, are void, unless the agreement or some memorandum thereof be put in writing, and signed by the party to be charged or some one lawfully authorized.

Limitation of Actions.

ALL titles to lands or possessions for seven years shall be good against all claims whatsoever. Persons beyond seas allowed three years.

Any person may prosecute his right to land within ten years; persons beyond seas, married women, and persons imprisoned, have seven years; minors have five years after their majority.

In actions to try titles to land, if the plaintiff or claimant discontinue, or suffer a nonsuit verdict or judgment against him, or in any other way let the first action fall, he may bring a second action within two years; otherwise he is barred. The second action is final.

Actions of trespass *quare clausum fregit*, trespass, detinue, trover, replevin, debt, covenant, and case, must be brought within four years.

Actions of trespass of assault and battery, and imprisonment, must be brought within one year.

Actions of slander must be brought within six months.

Collection of Debts.

ATTACHMENT.—Attachment may issue against the property, real and personal, of a non-resident debtor, or a debtor who absconds, or who is removing out of the district, or who conceals himself so that process can not be served upon him.

ARREST.—A debtor, about to abscond before the maturity of the debt, may be held to bail.

A debtor may be held to bail in any case where the debt exceeds thirty dollars and sixty-two cts., upon affidavit of the fact being annexed to the writ or process.

Deeds.

ACKNOWLEDGMENTS of deeds by the grantor on proof of their execution by one of the subscribing witnesses may be made before any magistrate. Conveyances should be immediately recorded in the office of the register of mesne conveyances of the district where the land lies. In Charleston district there is a special register; in all the other districts the clerk of the court acts as register.

They may be acknowledged, out of the state, before commissioners appointed, by the governor for that purpose.

A scrawl of the pen may be used for a seal. The conveyance must be attested by two witnesses.

The wife may release her dower, if she be of lawful age, in the premises conveyed by her husband, by going before any judge of the court of common pleas or magistrate for the district in which she may reside or the land may be and acknowledge before him, upon a private and separate examination, that she did freely and voluntarily, without any compulsion, dread, or fear, of any person whomsoever, renounce and release her dower to the grantor, his heirs and assigns, in the premises mentioned in such deed.

A certificate, under the hand of the woman and the hand and seal of the magistrate, shall be endorsed upon such release, and recorded in the office of mesne conveyances, or office of the clerk of the county court in the district or county where the land lies.

Form of Acknowledgment by a Single Man.

The State of South Carolina, }
Charleston District. }

I, JOHN JONES, one of the *judges of the court of common pleas*, do hereby certify that JOHN DOE did this day appear before me and acknowledge that he did sign, seal, and deliver, the within conveyance unto the within-named JAMES SMITH, as his free act and deed.

Given under my hand and seal, this *thirtieth* day of *April*, Anno Domini one thousand eight hundred and *fifty-one*. JOHN JONES (*Seal.*)

Form by Statute for Release of Dower.

The State of South Carolina, }
Charleston District. }

I, JOHN JONES, one of the *judges of the court of common pleas*, do hereby certify unto all whom it may concern, that SUSAN DOE, the wife of the within-named JOHN DOE, did this day appear before me, and upon being privately and separately examined by me, did declare that she does freely, voluntarily, and without any compulsion, dread, or fear, of any person or persons whomsoever, renounce, release, and for ever relinquish unto the within-named DUNN BROWN, his heirs and assigns, all her interest and estate, and also all her right and claim of dower, of, in, or to, all and singular the premises within-mentioned and released.

Given under my hand and seal, this *thirtieth* day of *April*, Anno Domini one thousand eight hundred and *fifty-one*. SUSAN DOE.

(*Seal.*) JOHN JONES, *Judge.*

Form for Renunciation of Inheritance.

The State of South Carolina, }
Charleston District. }

I, JOHN JONES, one of the *judges of the court of common pleas*, do hereby certify unto all whom it may concern, that SUSAN DOE, the wife of the within named JOHN DOE, did this day appear before me, and upon being privately and separately examined by me, did declare that she did actually join her said husband in executing the within release, and that the same was positively and bonafide executed, at least *seven* days before this her examination, and that she did then, and still does at this time, freely, voluntarily, and without any manner of compulsion, dread, or fear, of any person or persons whomsoever, renounce, release, and for ever relinquish, unto the within-named JAMES SMITH, his heirs and assigns, all her estate, interest, and inheritance, in all and singular the premises within mentioned and released.

Given under my hand and seal, this *thirtieth* day of *April*, Anno Domini one thousand eight hundred and *fifty-one*. SUSAN DOE.

(*Seal.*) JOHN JONES, *Judge.*

Rights of Married Women.

THE common law in regard to the rights of married women prevails in this state, except that marriage-settlement deeds must be recorded in the office of the secretary of state, and register of mesne conveyance within three months after their execution.

Rate of Interest.

THE legal rate is seven per cent. The party reserving more, forfeits the entire interest, and must pay the costs.

Wills.

WILLS must be in writing, signed by the testator, or some person in his presence and by his express direction, and attested and subscribed in the presence of the testator by three or more competent witnesses.

For form of attestation, see page 163.

GEORGIA.

Constitution adopted 1798.—Square Miles 61,500.—Population in 1850, 877,897.

Exemptions.

THERE are exempt from attachment and sale on execution, two beds and bedding, common bedsteads, a spinning-wheel, and two pairs of cards; a loom, common tools of the debtor's trade, and ordinary cooking-utensils; thirty dollars' worth of provisions, and the family Bible; a cow and calf; one horse or mule, the value of which shall not exceed fifty dollars; also ten head of hogs: and the same privileges are extended to all widows and their families, during their widowhood.

Homestead-Exemption Law.

EVERY white citizen of this state, male or female, being the head of a family may own, free from levy and sale by virtue of any judgment, order, or decree, of any court of law or equity in this state, founded on any contracts made after the first day of May, one thousand eight hundred and forty-two, or any process emanating upon the same, twenty acres of land, and the additional sum of five acres for each of his or her children under the age of fifteen: *Provided*, that the same, or any part thereof, be not the site of any city, town, or village, or of any cotton or wool factory, saw or grist mill, or of any other machinery propelled by water or steam.

The twenty acres thus exempted shall include the dwelling-house and improvements of the original tract, provided the value of such dwelling-house and improvements shall not exceed $200—extended to cities, towns, and villages.

From and after the passage of this act (December 22, 1843), the amount of fifty acres of land to the head of each family is exempt from levy and sale by virtue of any judgment, order, or decree, of any court of law or equity in this state, founded on any contracts made after the first day of January, one thousand eight hundred and forty-four, except the same shall be for the purchase-money of said land, for the payment of which said land shall be bound.

The same property is likewise exempt from attachment.

Mechanics' Lien.

EVERY mason or carpenter, building or repairing any house, shall have a lien on the same, if he, within three months from the time the same is completed, cause to be recorded in the clerk's office of the county where such building may be, his claim thereon.

Within twelve months from the time his debt is due, he must institute a suit to enforce his lien.

All persons, employed in any capacity whatever, on all steamboats and other water-craft engaged in the navigation of the Chattahooche, Altamaha, Ocmulgee, Savannah, and Flint rivers, also those who furnish wood and provisions to said steamboats and water-craft, shall have an exclusive lien on the same for their debt, if they prosecute the collection within twelve months after it is due.

GEORGIA.

GEORGIA
Scale of miles
TENNESSEE
SOUTH CAROLINA
Knoxville
Athens
Chattanooga
Greenville
Newberry
Yorkville
Hamburg
Augusta
Savannah R.
Saluda R.
Tennessee R.

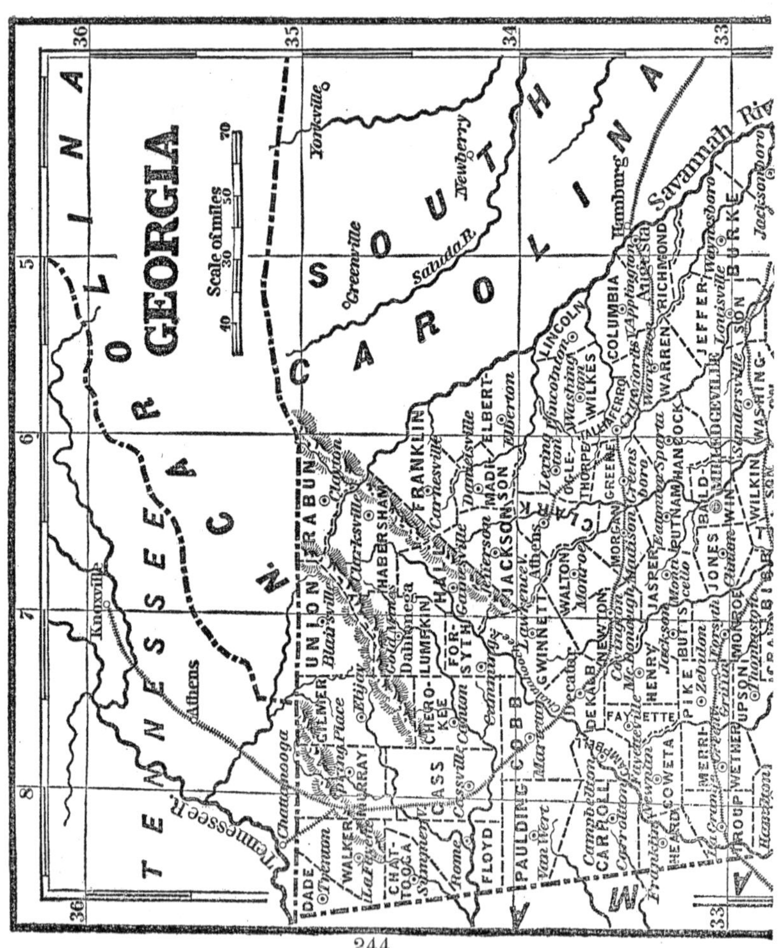

GEORGIA.

ATLANTIC OCEAN
St. Johns R.
FLORIDA
G. OF MEXICO
ALABAMA
Chattahoochee R.
Appalachicola R.
Okefinokee Swamp
Suwanee R.
St. Marys R.
Oconee R.
Ocmulgee R.
Alatamaha R.
Ogeechee R.
SCRIVEN
EFFINGHAM
CHATHAM
Savannah
BULLOCH
Statesboro
Springfield
BRYAN
LIBERTY
Hinesville
MC.INTOSH
Darien
GLYNN
Brunswick
St. Simons I.
Cumberland I.
Amelia I.
WAYNE
C.H.
CAMDEN
Jefferson
St. Marys
EMANUEL
Swainsboro
TATNALL
Reidsville
MONTGOMERY
Mt. Vernon
APPLING
Holmesville
TELFAIR
Jacksonville
LAURENS
Dublin
PULASKI
Hawkinsville
WARE
Waresboro
IRWIN
Irwinville
LOWNDES
Troupsville
THOMAS
Thomasville
DECATUR
Bainbridge
BAKER
Newton
EARLY
Blakely
RANDOLPH
Cuthbert
STEWART
Lumpkin
SUMPTER
Americus
LEE
Starkville
DOOLY
Vienna
HOUSTON
Perry
MACON
MARION
Tazewell
MUSCOGEE
Columbus
TALBOT
Talbotton
HARRIS
Macon
Marion
Irwinton
Lancaster
Monticello
TALLAHASSEE
St. Marks
Appalachee Bay
Appalachicola
Lon. West from Washington
32
31
30
5
7
8

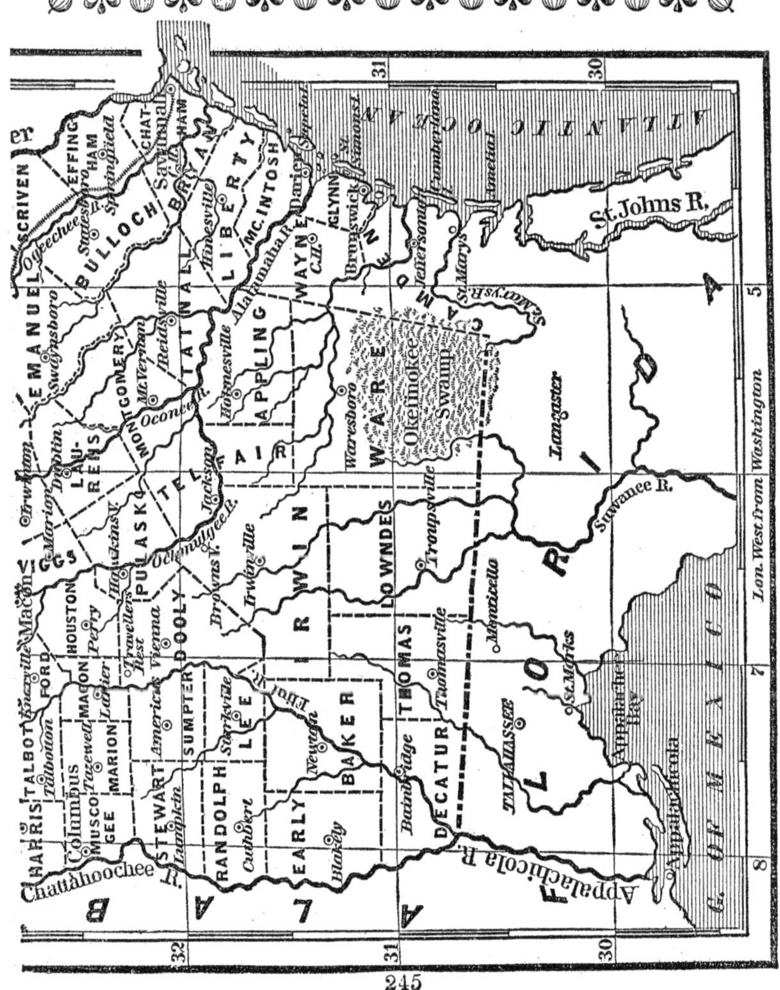

When the sum exceeds thirty dollars, they may make affidavit of the sum due before any judge of the superior court, or justice of tl e inferior court in the county where the craft lies, and judgment may be entered thereon, and execution issue immediately.

If the sum be thirty dollars or under, then the same proceeding may be had before a justice of the peace.

Provision is made for proceedings when the claim is contested.

The same lien and expeditious proceedings are allowed to persons employed in steam saw-mills, to those furnishing timber or firewood, provisions or supplies therefor.

Also millwrights and builders of gold-machines in this state are entitled to the same lien, and the same method of enforcing it.

Chattel Mortgages.

These must be proved by the affidavit of the subscribing witness, and recorded in the clerk's office of the superior court of the county in which the mortgager resided at the time of the execution of the mortgage, within three months from the date thereof.

Law regulating Contracts.

No action shall be brought whereby to charge any executor, or administrator, upon any special promise, to answer damages out of his own estate; or whereby to charge the defendant, upon any special promise, to answer for the debt, default, or miscarriage, of another person; or to charge any person, upon any agreement made upon consideration of marriage; or upon any contract or sale of lands, tenements, or hereditaments, or any interest in or concerning them; or upon any agreement that is not to be performed within the space of one year from the making thereof; unless the agreement upon which such action shall be brought, or some memorandum or note thereof, shall be in writing, and signed by the party to be charged therewith, or some other person thereunto by him lawfully authorized.

No contract for the sale of any goods, wares, and merchandises, for the price of ten pounds sterling or upward, shall be allowed to be good, except the buyer shall accept part of the goods so sold, and actually receive the same, or give something in earnest to bind the bargain or in part payment, or that some note or memorandum in writing of the said bargain be made and signed by the parties to be charged by such contract, or their agents thereunto lawfully authorized.

Limitation of Actions.

Actions for the recovery of land must be brought within seven years.

Infants, married women, persons insane, imprisoned, and beyond seas, have three years after the removal of such disability.

Actions upon the case, other than for slander, actions for account, for trespass, debt, detinue, and replevin, for goods and [chattels] cattle, and trespass *quare clausum fregit*, within four years.

Actions of trespass of assault, battery, wounding, and imprisonment, within two years.

Actions upon the case for words, within six months after the words spoken.

Infants, married women, persons insane, imprisoned, and beyond seas, have the same times after their disability is removed.

Notes and instruments in writing, not under seal, within six years. Instruments under seal, within twenty years; actions on open account, within four years.

Actions on foreign judgments in five years.

Collection of Debts.

ATTACHMENT.—In case of non-residence, or where both debtor and creditor reside without the limits of the state, the creditor may attach the real and personal property of the debtor in the state.

When a debt is not due, and the debtor is removing or about to remove without the limits of the state, and oath is made by the creditor, his agent, or attorney, of the amount due or to become due, and that the debtor is removing or about to remove out of the state, an attachment may issue against his property.

In all cases pending a suit, if the defendant place himself in such a circumstance as would, by the laws of the state, authorize an attachment, one may issue.

ARREST.—Any person imprisoned or arrested for debt, who shall make it appear to the court that he is insolvent, and shall deliver a schedule of his real and personal estate, debts, credits, and effects, and shall take the poor debtor's or insolvent's oath, shall obtain a discharge from imprisonment; and every debtor so discharged shall not be liable to be imprisoned on execution for any debt contracted before his discharge with any creditor having notice of his application for such discharge, nor shall he be arrested or held to bail in mesne process for any debt or contract entered into prior to his discharge.

Married women and widows are not liable to arrest for debt.

Deeds.

DEEDS must be executed under hand and seal (scroll), in the presence of two or more witnesses, and acknowledged or proved before a justice of the peace, or the chief justice, or one of the assistant justices, or clerk of the superior court, and registered by the clerk of the court in the county where such lands lie, within twelve months from the date of such deed. Seven years undisturbed possession gives good title to land.

Deeds must be attested or proved before the clerk of the superior court, to be admitted to record. Deeds made out of the state may be admitted to record on affidavit of one of the subscribing witnesses before an officer in this state as in other cases. The wife joining must acknowledge and agree, before the chief justice, or any justice of the peace, or other officer, authorized to take the acknowledgment, on private examination, that she did, of her own free will and accord, subscribe, seal, and deliver the said deed, with an intention thereby to renounce, give up, and for ever quit-claim to her right of dower and thirds, of, into, and to, the lands or tenements therein mentioned.

Consuls and vice-consuls of the United States, duly appointed and recognised, may take such acknowledgment of persons being within their consulates, and certify the same under their official seals.

Form of Acknowledgment.

State of Georgia,
County of *Crawford*, } to wit:

On this *first* day of *October*, one thousand eight hundred and *fifty*, before me personally came JOHN DOE *and* SUSAN *his wife*, to me known to be the persons described in, and who executed the foregoing *conveyance*, and severally acknowledged that they executed the same; *and the said* SUSAN, *on private examination, acknowledged and agreed that she did, of her own free will and accord, subscribe, seal, and deliver the said deed, with an intention thereby to renounce, give up, and for ever quit-claim, her right of dower and thirds, and all her other interest of, into, and to, the lands or tenements therein mentioned.*

JOHN JONES, *Justice of the Peace.*

Rights of Married Women.

DOWER.—The wife must make application for her dower within seven years from the time of her husband's death.

All conveyances of lands and tenements made by the husband alone during coverture shall convey the entire premises (except such lands as the husband is seized of by his intermarriage with his wife), any law, usage, custom, or rule of court, to the contrary notwithstanding; *Provided*, that nothing herein contained shall deprive the widow of her right to dower in all lands of which her husband may have died seized and possessed.

Rate of Interest.

THE legal rate is seven per cent. If more be reserved, the party loses the entire interest.

Wills.

THESE must be in writing, signed by the testator or some person in his presence and by his express direction, and attested and subscribed, in the presence of the testator, by three competent witnesses if to pass real estate, or two if personal property.

TEXAS—(SEE PAGE 271).

Rights of Married Women.

ALL property, real and personal, owned or claimed by married women, or which may be owned or claimed at the time of marriage by any woman, or which she may acquire by gift, devise, or descent, shall be registered.

A schedule thereof shall be made out, particularly describing the same and acknowledged by her that the property described therein is her separate property, and recorded in the county or counties where it really lies, and if there be personal property, then also in the county where she resides.

Property so recorded can not be recovered by the creditors of the husband.

She has also a community of acquits, or joins with the husband in all property acquired during coverture, except that acquired by devise, gift, or descent. The community property may be sold by the husband alone and is liable for his debts.

DOWER.—The widow is entitled to the use of one third of the real estate for her life.

Rate of Interest.

THE legal rate of interest where no rate is specified, is eight per cent. Parties may agree upon any rate as high as twelve per cent. Where more is reserved no interest can be recovered.

Wills.

No parent can deprive his descendants by will of more than one fourth of his or her property.

Wills must be in writing, signed by the testator or by some other person in his presence and by his direction; and moreover, if not wholly written by himself, be attested by two or more credible witnesses above the age of fourteen years, subscribing their names in h presence.

FLORIDA.

Constitution adopted 1845.—Square Miles 59,268.—Population in 1850, 87,387.

Exemptions.

THE necessary wearing-apparel and bedding of every person, and the necessary wearing apparel, bedding, and kitchen furniture of every family, shall be exempt from execution, attachment, and distress. The following property may be claimed as exempt from execution, attachment, and distress, except for violation of the criminal laws: the horse, saddle, and bridle, or the horse, saddle, vehicle, and harness, of every clergyman, not exceeding in value one hundred dollars.

The horse, saddle, and bridle, medicine, and professional books, and instruments, of every surgeon, midwife, or physician, not exceeding in value one hundred dollars: one set of working-tools, or instruments of every mechanic, artist, dentist, artisan, or tradesman, not exceeding in value one hundred dollars.

The horse and gun not exceeding in value one hundred dollars, belonging to every farmer who is in actual cultivation of five or more acres of land within the state;

Every actual housekeeper with a family, may claim as exempt, such portion of his property as may be necessary to the support of himself and family, not to exceed in value one hundred dollars; thereby waiving claim to all right to other exemption of property; provided, in every case, the defendant is not moving out of the state, nor resides beyond the limits thereof, nor is removing his property beyond the limits of the same, nor is secreting or fraudulently disposing of his property for the purpose of avoiding the payment of his just debts; and, provided also the defendant shall make affidavit that he hath made a fair, full, and complete statement of all his property, in trust or otherwise, of all moneys, debts, and demands, due or to become due, which statement shall be signed by him and with the affidavit accompanying the return of the process.

Every farmer seized and possessed of forty acres of land, in his or her own right in fee simple, and shall actually have in cultivation at least ten acres of the same, shall hold the same free and exempt from execution, attachment, or distress, except for a violation of the criminal law, or for fines or taxes; provided, the land and improvements do not exceed in value two hundred dollars.

Also the boat and gun of every fisherman, pilot, or resident upon any island or coast, or any bay, harbor, or inlet of the state, and the boat and flat of any ferryman, when in either case the same shall not exceed in value two hundred dollars.

Every owner of a dwelling-house in a city, town, or village, provided he shall actually reside in said house, and provided also the same shall not exceed in value three hundred dollars, shall hold the same free from execution, attachment, or distress, except for violation of the criminal laws, or for fines or taxes.—Passed January 22, 1851.

Mechanics' Lien.

MASTER-BUILDERS and mechanics of every denomination, in the state of Florida, contracting and engaging to put up and erect buildings of every description, or engaging to perform jobs of work on any such buildings, shall have a lien on all such buildings as they may put up or erect or work upon, until the compensation for services shall be fully paid and satisfied, to the amount agreed upon between the contracting parties.

They shall enforce the lien only in the following cases, viz.: 1. Where the contract shall be reduced to writing and signed by the parties making the same. 2. Where

FLORIDA.

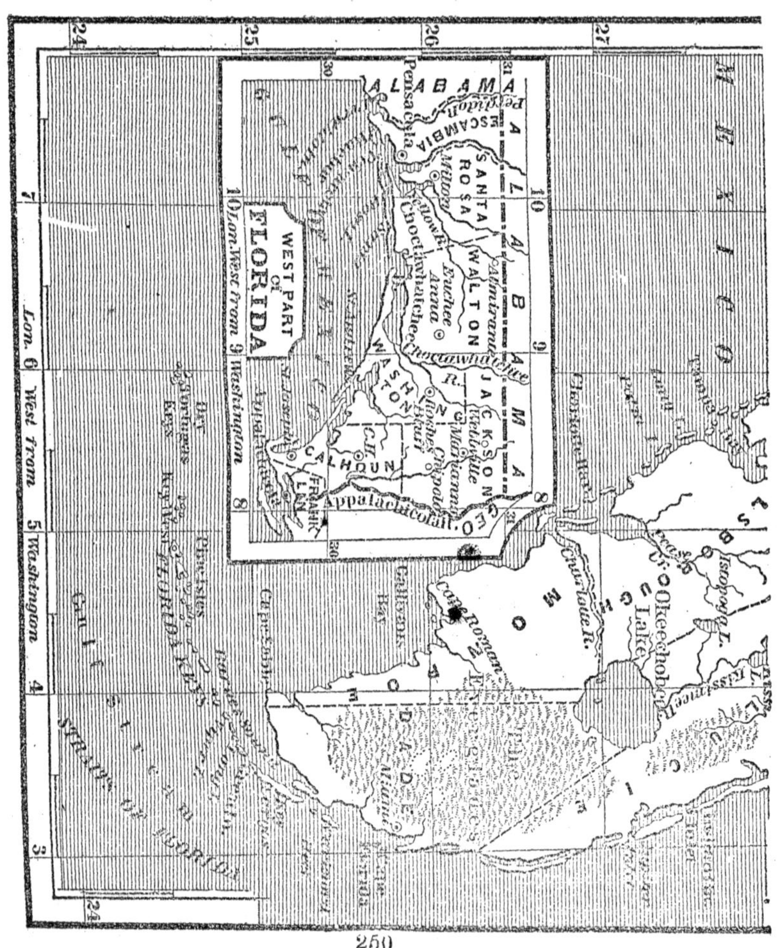

FLORIDA.

FLORIDA
Scale of Miles
10 30 50 70
Appatachicola Riv.
GADSDEN
Quincy
FRANKLIN
LEON
TALLAHASSEE
JEFFERSON
WAKULLA
Monticello
Madison
Appalachee Bay
St. Georges I.
HAMILTON
Jasper
COLUMBIA
Alligator
ALACHUA
Newnansville
Micanopy
LEVY
DUVAL
NASSAU
ST. JOHNS
St. Marys R.
Jacksonville
St. Augustine
Volusia
BENTON
Withlacoochee R.
Tampa
Waresboro
Brunswick
Darien
Holmesville
Altamaha Riv.
Savannah
Cape Canaveral
Indian R.

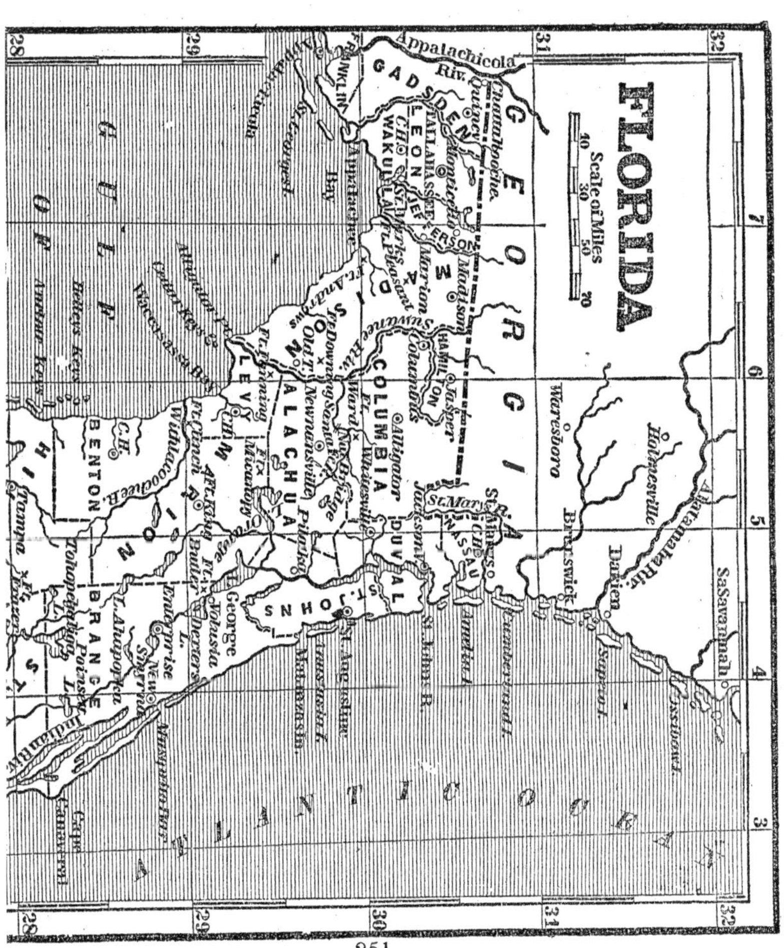

the amount shall be liquidated between the contracting parties, and a net balance be struck between the persons contracting to perform as aforesaid, or provide materials.

All contracts entered into, liquidated or net balance struck, shall be recorded in the clerk's office of the circuit court, for the county where such contract shall be required to be executed, within thirty days after their execution.

Artisans, builders, and mechanics, and those who furnish materials for buildings under contract with the proprietor thereof, and all sub-contractors, shall have a lien for such material furnished, and for work and labor done on houses and other edifices, by them hereafter erected in whole or in part, each one for his own work and materials furnished.

Every person wishing to avail himself of the benefits of this act, except sub-contractors, must file with the clerk of the circuit court of the county in which the building to be charged is situate, and within six months after the materials have been furnished or the work and labor performed, a just and true account of the demand due him after all credits, and verify it by his own oath or that of some other person, and also file at the same time a correct description of the property to be charged with said lien.

Every sub-contractor shall give notice in writing to the proprietor, of his intention to furnish materials or perform labor on the building, and the probable value thereof, and if afterward (the proprietor or his agent not objecting), materials are furnished or work done, the sub-contractor shall settle with the contractor in writing, the same signed by the contractor, and certified by him to be just, shall be left with the owner or proprietor, or his agent, and within ten days from the time the materials are furnished or work done, the sub-contractor shall file with the clerk of the circuit court of the county in which the building is situate, a copy of such settlement which shall be a lien on the building; and he must also file a correct description of the property to be charged with the lien.

The land upon which any building shall be erected, together with a convenient space around the same not exceeding five hundred square feet, clear of the building, shall also be subject to the above liens.

Ship-chandlers, storekeepers, and all dealers, mechanics, and workmen, shall have a lien on any ship, vessel, steamboat, or other water craft, for all stores, provisions, rigging, or other materials, or labor or services of any kind furnished or rendered to, or for the use of such vessel, &c.; which lien shall have a preference over all others; the lien to cease if not enforced within twenty days after the same accrued.

Chattel Mortgages.

THESE must be acknowledged and recorded in the county where the mortgaged property shall be at the time of the execution of the mortgage.

Law Regulating Contracts.

No action shall be brought whereby to charge any executor or administrator, upon any special promise, to answer damages out of his own estate; or whereby to charge the defendant, upon any special promise, to answer for the debt, default, or miscarriage, of another person; to charge any person, upon any agreement made upon consideration of marriage; or upon any contract for sale of lands, tenements, or hereditaments, or any uncertain interest in or concerning them, or for any hire thereof, for a longer term than one year; or upon any agreement that is not to be performed within the space of one year from the making thereof; unless the agreement upon which such action shall be brought, or some memorandum or note thereof, shall be in writing, and signed by the party to be charged therewith, or some other person thereunto by him lawfully authorized.

No contract for the sale of any personal property, or goods, wares, and merchandises, shall be allowed to be good, except the buyer shall accept part of the goods so sold, and actually receive the same, or give something in earnest to bind the bargain or in part payment, or that some note or memorandum in writing of the said bargain be made and signed by the parties to be charged by such contract, or their agents thereunto lawfully authorized.

Limitation of Actions.

Actions for the recovery of real property must be brought within seven years. In case of disability, of infancy, &c., within four years after the removal of such disability. In case of death during disability, then within three years thereafter.—Act of Jan. 1848.

All actions upon the case, other than for slander, of account, for trespass, debt, detinue and replevin for goods and chattels, and the said actions of trespass *quare clausum fregit*, must be brought within five years next after the cause of action accrued.

Actions of assault, battery, wounding, and imprisonment, within three years.

Actions upon the case for words within one year. Actions founded upon any account for goods sold and delivered, or for any article charged in any book-account, must be brought within two years from the delivery of the goods: if the creditors or the debtors die within such two years, then the further time of two years.

Infants, married women, persons insane, imprisoned, beyond seas, or out of the country, have the same periods respectively after the removal of their disability.

Actions of account, as concern merchandise between merchant and merchant, actions of debt on speciality, actions of covenant, are not regulated by statute, but governed by the English law prior to 1776.

In suits against administrators on open account, it is the duty of the court to expunge every item due five years before the death of the party.

No action can be brought on, or *scire facias* to revive a judgment against an administrator or executor after five years from the time such administrator or executor qualified.

If any person, by absconding, concealing himself, or otherwise, prevents his creditor from bringing suit within the time above specified, the statute may not be pleaded by such person in bar of any suit brought against him.

Collection of Debts.

Attachment.—Attachment may issue upon an affidavit that there is a debt due or to become due within nine months, and that the debtor is actually removing out of the state, or resides beyond the limits, or absconds, or conceals himself, so that ordinary process can not be served upon him, or is removing his property beyond the limits of the state, or secreting or fraudulently disposing of the same for the purpose of avoiding the payment of his just debts.

Imprisonment for debt does not exist.

Deeds.

Conveyances must be made by deed in writing, sealed and delivered in the presence of at least two witnesses. They must be acknowledged before the officer authorized by law to record the same, or before some judicial officer of this state. The officer taking the acknowledgment shall know or have satisfactory proof that the person making such acknowledgment is the individual described in and who executed the deed.

If the acknowledgment is made out of the state, then before the commissioner appointed for that purpose.

Dower in any lands, tenements, or hereditaments, in this state, may be extinguished by the wife making herself a party to the conveyance for the purpose of relinquishing the same, or she may by a separate relinquishment under her hand and seal, executed in the presence of two witnesses, renounce her right of dower, and in no other way whatever; provided, such relinquishment or renunciation shall not in either case be valid against or binding upon the wife executing the same or any person or persons claiming through or under her, unless it be accompanied by an acknowledgment under the hand and seal of the wife taken and made, separately and apart from her husband, before some judicial officer of this state, when it shall have been made therein, that the said relinquishment and renunciation of dower is made freely and voluntarily, and without any compulsion, constraint, apprehension, or fear, of or from the husband of the party making the said relinquishment.

Conveyances to be admitted to record must be acknowledged by the party making it, or proved by one of the subscribing witnesses. They must be recorded by the recording officer in the county where the lands lie.

Rights of Married Women.

WHEN any female, a citizen of this state, shall marry, or when any female shall marry a citizen of this state, the female being seized or possessed of real or personal property, her title to the same shall continue separate, independent, and beyond the control of her husband, notwithstanding her coverture, and shall not be taken in execution for his debts.

Married women may hereafter become seized or possessed of real and personal property during coverture, by bequest, demise, gift, purchase, or distribution.

The husband and wife shall join in all sales, transfers, and conveyances of the property of the wife, and the real estate of the wife shall only be conveyed by the joint deed of the husband and wife, duly attested, authenticated, and admitted to record.

The husband shall not be held or deemed liable to pay the debts of his wife contracted prior to any marriage hereafter (1845) to be solemnized in this state; but the property of the wife shall be subject to such debt.

If married women die in this state possessed of real and personal property, or of either species of property, the husband shall take the same interest in her said property, and no other, which a child would take and inherit; and if the wife should die without children, then the surviving husband shall be entitled to administration, and to all her property, both real and personal.

All the property, real and personal, which shall belong to the wife at the time of her marriage, or which she may acquire in any of the modes hereinbefore mentioned, shall be inventoried and recorded in the circuit court, or clerk's office of the county in which such property is situate, within six months after such marriage, or after said property shall be acquired by her at the peril of becoming liable for her husband's debts; but any omission to make such inventory and record shall confer no rights upon her husband.

DOWER.—A widow is entitled to a life estate in one third of her husband s real estate. In his personal estate, if there be no child or only one child, the widow takes one half of it absolutely. If more than one child she takes one third absolutely, except in slaves in which she takes a life estate. A widow may elect to take dower or a child's part, if she takes dower she has only a life estate in the real property; if she takes a child's part she has a fee-simple title to real property and absolute title to personal property including slaves.

Rate of Interest.

THE rate of interest is eight per cent. by agreement; if no rate be specified, then six per cent. Usury is punishable by indictment and loss of entire interest.

Wills.

WILLS must be in writing, signed by the testator or by some other person in his presence, and by his express directions, and shall be attested and subscribed in the presence of the testator by THREE or more witnesses.

ALABAMA.

Constitution adopted, 1819.—Square Miles, 50,722.—Population in 1850, 771,650.

Exemptions.

THERE are exempt from levy and sale on execution two beds and furniture; three cows and calves; one work-horse, mule, or pair of oxen; twenty head of hogs; twenty head of sheep: 500 weight of meat; 100 bushels of corn; all the meal that may at any time be on hand: two ploughs, two sets plough-gears; one table, one pot, one oven, two water-vessels, one dozen cups and saucers, one set of knives and forks, one dozen plates, one coffee-pot, two dishes; two pairs of cotton cards; one churn; three chairs; two spinning-wheels; two axes, two hoes; one horse or ox cart; one gun; all books and family portraits, and all tools or implements of trade. Goods and chattels lying on leasehold property can not be taken without first tendering the landlord the amount due him for rent, not more than for one year.

Homestead-Exemption Law.

FORTY acres of land, when not within the corporate limits of any town or city, and not exceeding in value four hundred dollars, is exempt from execution.

Limitation of Actions.

ACTIONS of trespass, detinue, trover, replevin for taking goods and chattels, actions of debt founded upon contract or lending not a specialty, for arrearages of rent, on a parol demise, of account, and upon the case (except between merchants concerning the trade of merchandise), must be commenced within six years.

Actions upon any lease under seal, or any sealed instrument for the payment of money, within sixteen years.

Trespass for assault, menace, battery, wounding, and imprisonment, within two years.

Actions on the case for words, within one year.

Judgment in any court of record may be revised by *scire facias*, or action of debt, within twenty years.

The right of entry upon lands is limited to twenty years after the accrual of such right. (Possession for twenty years, under claim of title, creates a presumption of a grant.)

Real, possessory, ancestral, mixed, and other actions for lands, are limited to thirty years.

Actions of forcible entry and detainer are barred by three years' adverse possession.

Actions on open account, except between merchants, are limited to three years.

Writs of error to the supreme court of the state are limited to three years.

Wills may be contested by bill in chancery within five years from the time of probate.

The time of absence from the state is not computed.

Infants, married women, persons insane or imprisoned, have the same periods respectively after the removal of their disability.

The law regulatiug contracts is the same as in GEORGIA (page 246).

Collection of Debts.

ATTACHMENT.—Upon an affidavit that the debtor absconds, secretes himself, or resides out of the limits of the state, or is about to remove out of the state, so that process can not be served upon him, or is about to remove his property out of the state, whereby the plaintiff may lose his debt or be compelled to sue for it in another state, or that the debtor has fraudulently disposed of, or is about fraudulently disposing of, his property; or that he has money, property, or effects, liable to satisfy his debts, which he fraudulently withholds; and stating the amount due, and that attachment is not sought for the purpose of vexing or harassing the debtor, and upon the plaintiff's executing bond to the defendant in double the amount sworn to be due, an attachment may issue against his property, real and personal. Attachments, ancillary to suits pending, may be sued out on the same grounds as original attachments.

Judgments are usually obtained at the second term of the court after the institution of suit, and create a lien on real estate, throughout the state, from the date of rendition.

Executions bind personal property, in any county within the state, upon their delivery to the sheriff thereof.

One year is the shortest time in which money can be collected by law.

ARREST.—A person can be arrested for debt only when the plaintiff makes affidavit that the debtor is about to abscond, or has or is about fraudulently to convey his property, or has money or effects which he fraudulently withholds, or that the debt was contracted by fraud. But the debtor may discharge himself from arrest by making oath that the ground upon which he is arrested is untrue, and that he has nothing with which to pay the debt; or

ALABAMA.

ALABAMA
GULF OF MEXICO
FLORIDA
MISS
Longitude West 11 10 from Washington 9
30
31
32
MOBILE
Mobile
Mobile Riv.
MOBILE B.
Mobile Pt.
Cedar Pt.
WASHINGTON
St. Stephens
CLARKE
Macon
Gosport
Barryton
BALDWIN
Blakeley
Tensaw
Stockton
Perdido R.
Perdido B.
Pensacola
Pensacola B.
Escambia R.
Santa Rosa B.
Choctawhatchee B.
MONROE
Monroeville
Alabama R.
CONECUH
Sparta
Brooklyn
WILCOX
Bethel
Barbour's V.
MARENGO
Linden
Tuscahoma
Tombigbee
DALLAS
Cahawba
LOWNDES
Lowndes port
Haynesville
BUTLER
Starlington
Greenville
Kirkville
COVINGTON
Montezuma
MONTGOMERY
Hickory Grove
PIKE
Troy
Monticello
COFFEE
Choctawhatchee R.
Wellburn
DALE
Clay Bank
BARBOUR
Clayton
Irwinton
HENRY
Abbeville
Columbia
Woodville
MACON
Tuskegee
Aberfoil
RUSSELL
Glenville
Crockett's V.
10 20 30 40 50 60 Miles

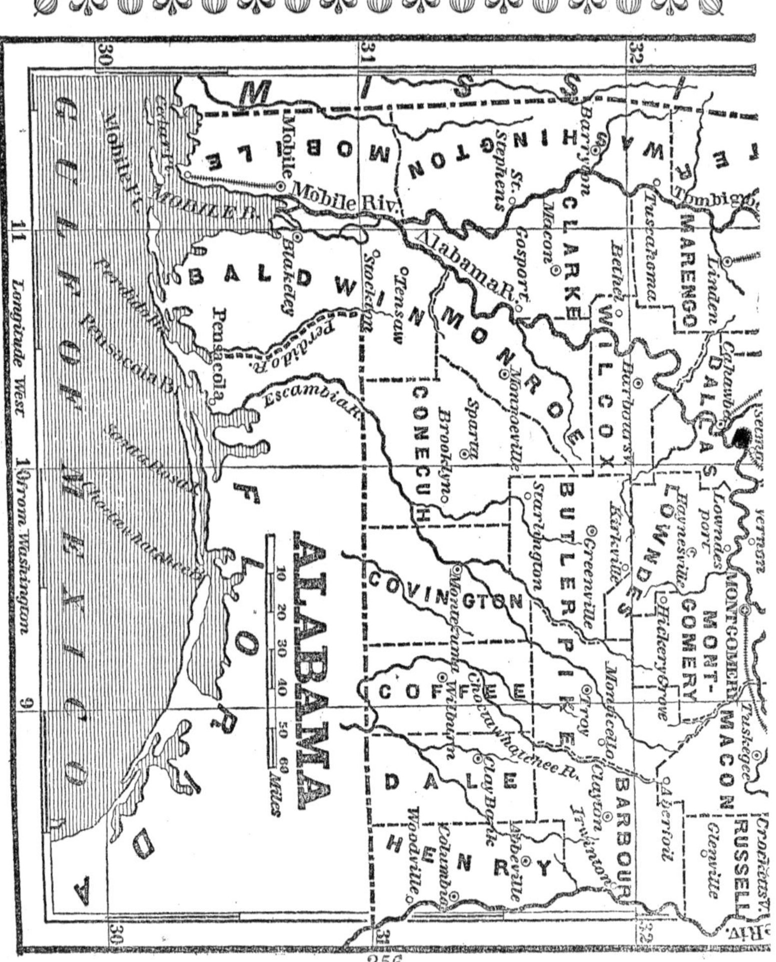

ALABAMA.

LAUDERDALE
LIMESTONE
MADISON
JACKSON
FRANKLIN
LAWRENCE
MORGAN
MARSHALL
DE KALB
CHEROKEE
BENTON
ST. CLAIR
BLOUNT
WALKER
MARION
FAYETTE
PICKENS
TUSCALOOSA
JEFFERSON
SHELBY
TALLADEGA
RANDOLPH
CHAMBERS
COOSA
BIBB
PERRY
GREENE

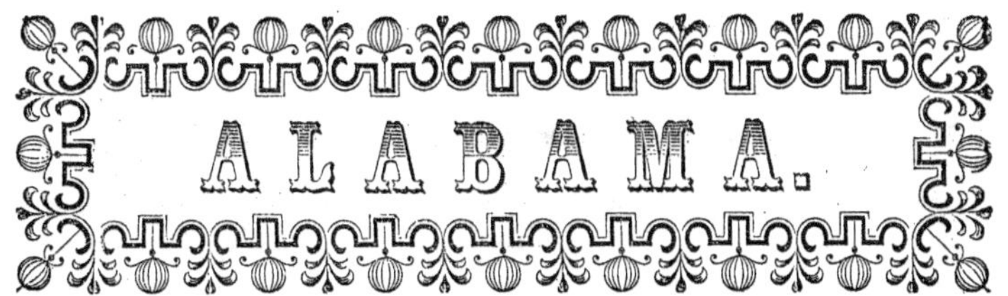

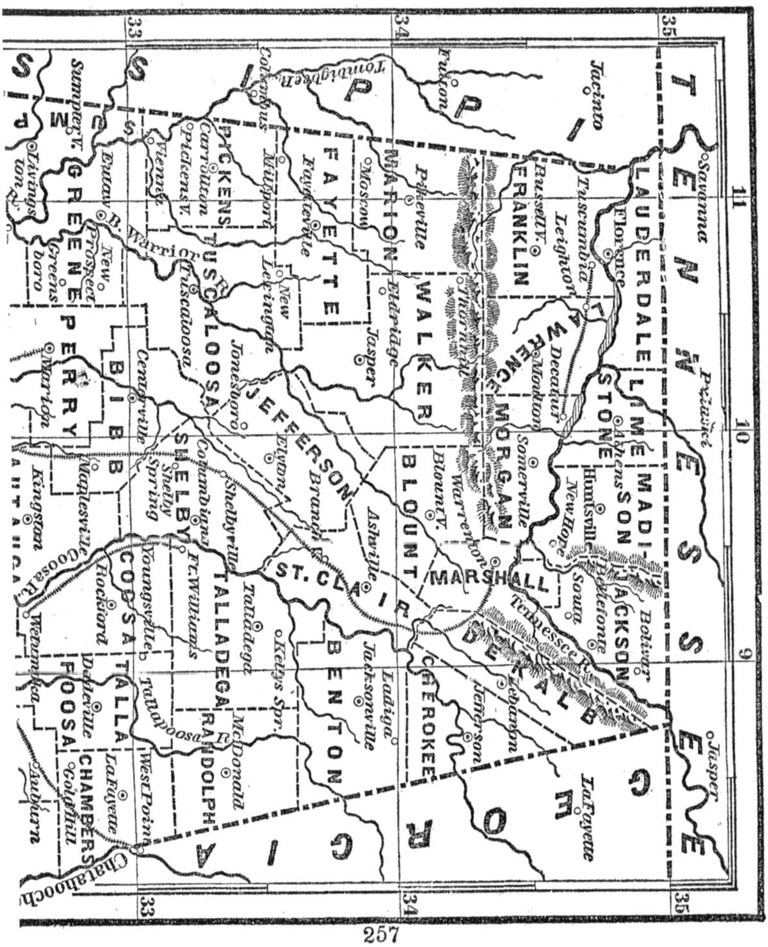

by rendering a schedule of all his property of every kind, and making oath that he has not property to the amount of twenty dollars, except that rendered in the schedule, and such property as is exempt by law from execution, and that he has not disposed of any property to secure the same to his own use, or to defraud his creditors.

The plaintiff may controvert the truth of the oath of the debtor.

A person convicted of rendering a false or fraudulent schedule, is liable to imprisonment for one year.

Deeds.

No witness is necessary where the maker of the deed acknowledges the same before the officer, and a scrawl of the pen may be used instead of a seal. Instruments importing on their face to be sealed shall be deemed sealed instruments, whether the scrawl be added or not. Deeds must be acknowledged or proved according to law before they can be properly recorded. They may be acknowledged before a judge of the county court, clerks of the circuit court of the several counties, and any notary public in any county for which he is commissioned, and any justice of the peace.

The wife of the grantor, joining with him in the deed, need not necessarily be privately examined. All conveyances should be immediately recorded, and in this state they must be recorded within six months, or they will be void against a subsequent *bonafide* purchaser or mortgagee without notice.

When a married woman joins her husband in the execution of a deed in the presence of two or more witnesses, or acknowledges the execution of the deed before a competent officer, the same operates as an absolute bar to her right of dower in the land conveyed, and in such case no private examination is necessary.

Form of Acknowledgment of Deed from John Jones and his Wife Mary Jones to John Brown.

The State of Alabama, } ss.
Montgomery County, }

Be it remembered, that the above-named JOHN JONES appeared personally before me, JOHN SMITH, *judge of the probate court of said county,* and acknowledged that he signed, sealed, and delivered, the foregoing deed, on the day and year therein mentioned, to the aforesaid JOHN BROWN; *and also appeared personally before me,* MARY JONES, *wife of the said* JOHN JONES, *who, being examined privately and apart from her said husband, acknowledged that she signed, sealed, and delivered the said deed, freely and of her own accord, and without any fear, threats, or compulsion, of her said husband.*

Given under my hand and seal, this *second* day of *April*, in the year of our Lord one thousand eight hundred and *fifty-one.* JOHN SMITH *(seal.),*
Judge of the Probate Court, M. C.

Rights of Married Women.

ALL the property which a woman has at the time of her marriage, and all that she acquires thereafter, is esteemed in law as her separate estate, notwithstanding her coverture, and the husband acquires no right to the property by marriage. The property vests in the husband as trustee of the wife, the husband controlling the property, without liability to account to the wife for the proceeds. The property can not be taken by legal process for the husband's debts. The husband and wife are jointly liable and suable at law for all necessary family supplies.

DOWER.—The widow (if no provision is made for her by will) is entitled to one third part of the real estate of which her husband died seized, and to which she has not relinquished the right of dower, and to one half of the personal property if there be no children, or if there be but one child; if there be more than one child, and less than five, she is entitled to a child's part; if there be five children or more, she is entitled to one fifth part in absolute right. She shall be endowed of one half of her husband's estate when he dies leaving no lineal descendants, unless the estate is insolvent.

The widow may dissent from or waive provision in a will, and claim her dower, at any time within one year after the probate of the will. The widow may retain the dwelling-house, plantation, &c., free of rent, until her dower is assigned her.

Rate of Interest.

THE legal rate of interest is eight per cent. In usurious contracts, the principal, without any interest, may be recovered. Persons taking usurious interest are liable to an action, *qui tam*, for the whole amount. The party borrowing the money may be a witness to prove the usury.

Wills.

EVERY person twenty-one years of age, and of sound mind, may dispose of lands by will. Wills must be signed by the testator, or by some one in his presence and at his request, and attested by three or more witnesses. Nuncupative wills may be established when the testator in his last illness calls on persons to take notice that such is his will.

MISSISSIPPI.

Constitution adopted, 1832.—Square Miles, 47,151.—Population in 1850, 600,000.

Exemptions.

THERE is exempted in this state from levy and sale on execution, the agricultural implements of a farmer necessary for one male laborer; the tools of a mechanic necessary for carrying on his trade; the books of a student necessary for the completion of his education; the wearing apparel of each and every person; one bed and bedding; one plough horse, provided the value thereof do not exceed one hundred dollars; and one cow and calf of every housekeeper, and the arms and accoutrements of each person of the enrolled militia of the state.

Goods on leasehold premises are not liable to execution until the rent in arrear, not to exceed one year, is tendered.

Mechanics' Lien.

MECHANICS have a lien on buildings for their labor done and materials furnished, provided the contract be reduced to writing and signed by the parties thereto, and recorded in the clerk's office of the court of probates of the county where such building is situate: or if there be no contract, that each person possessing a lien commence a suit within six months after the date of said written contract, or the commencement of said building, provided that the contractor or mechanic perform his work according to contract.

Chattel Mortgages.

MORTGAGES of chattels must be acknowledged and recorded in the court of the county where the property is situate; and if removed to another county, must be recorded in that county within twelve months after such removal.

Law regulating Contracts.

No action shall be brought whereby to charge any executor or administrator, upon any special promise, to answer any debt or damages out of his own estate; or whereby to charge the defendant, upon any special promise, to answer for the debt, default, or miscarriage, of another person; or to charge any person upon any agreement made upon consideration of marriage; or upon any contract for the sale of lands, tenements, or hereditaments, or the making any lease thereof for a longer term than one year; or upon any agreement which is not to be performed within the space of one year from the making thereof, unless the promise or agreement upon which such action shall be brought, or some memorandum or note thereof, shall be in writing, and signed by the party to be charged therewith, or some other person by him or her thereunto lawfully authorized.

MISSISSIPPI.

MISSISSIPPI.

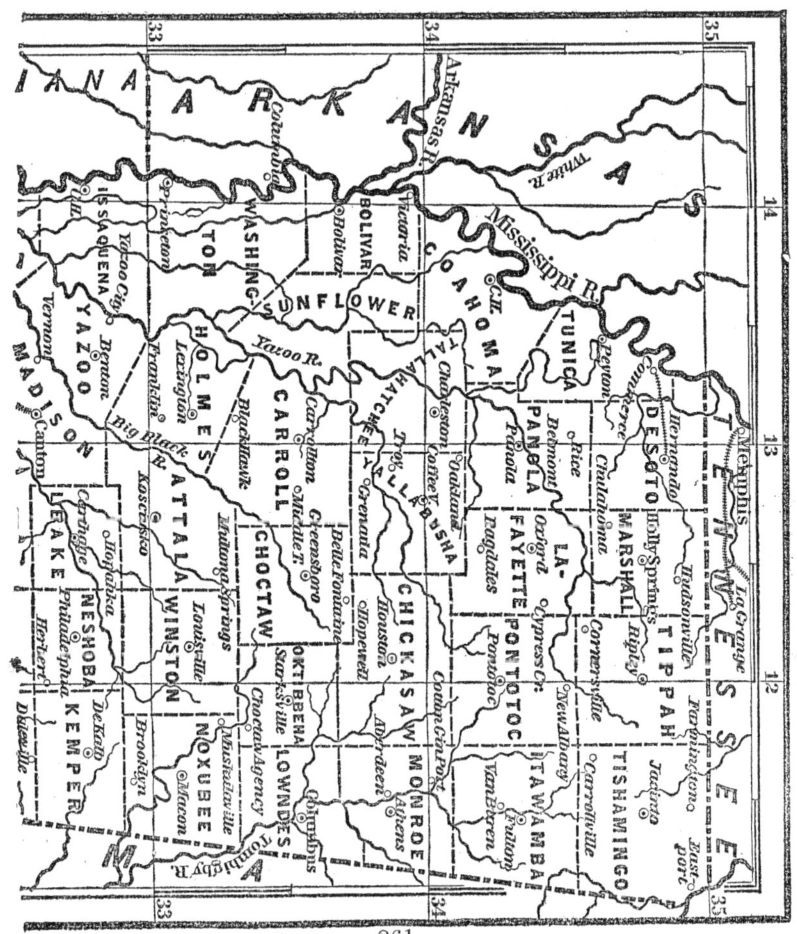

Limitation of Actions.

REAL and mixed actions must be brought within twenty years after the cause of action accrues.

All actions of trespass *quare clausum fregit*, of trespass, detinue, trover, and replevin, for taking away goods and chattels; all actions of debt founded upon any lending or contract without specialty, or for arrearages of rent due on a parol demise; all actions of account and upon the case, except actions for slander and such as concern the trade of merchandise between merchant and merchant, their factors and agents, must be commenced and sued within six years next after the cause of action has accrued.

Minors, *femme coverts*, and persons non-compos-mentis, at the time any cause of action may accrue, shall have the period of the limitation to institute suit, after the removal of their disability.

The time during which any person liable to a cause of action may be out of the state, is not reckoned a part of the limitation.

All actions founded upon any contract for goods, wares, or merchandise, sold and delivered, or for any article charged in any store account, must be commenced and prosecuted within two years after the accruing of such cause of action.

Every action of debt or covenant, for rent or arrearages of rent, founded upon any lease under seal, and every action of debt on a bill, obligation, and award, for the payment of money, must be commenced and sued within sixteen years next after the cause of action has accrued.

Judgments of any court of record may be revived by *scire facias*, or action of debt thereon, at any period within twenty years from the date of the judgment.

Collection of Debts.

ATTACHMENT.—If any creditor shall make complaint, on oath or affirmation, to any judge of the supreme court, or justice of the peace of any county, that his debtor has removed or is removing out of the state, or so absconds or privily conceals himself that process can not be served on him, and state the amount of his demand, an attachment shall be granted.

A bond must be given by the plaintiff to secure the payment of costs and dam ages that the defendant may recover against him.

Arrest for debt is abolished.

Deeds.

IT is necessary, to the due execution of a deed, that a SEAL be used, and that it be attested by two subscribing witnesses.

A deed must be acknowledged by the party or parties who shall have executed it, or proved by one or more of the subscribing witnesses, that such party or parties signed, sealed, and delivered the same, as his, her, or their voluntary act and deed, before a judge of the supreme court of this state, or a justice of the county court, justice of the peace, and notaries public, of that county in which the lands or some part thereof are situate, and a certificate of such acknowledgment written upon or under the said deed, and signed by the officer before whom it was made, and recorded with the clerk of the county court where the land is situate.

A married woman must acknowledge, on a private examination, apart from her husband, that she signed, sealed, and delivered the same, as her voluntary act and deed, freely, without any fear, threats, or compulsion, of her husband; and a certificate thereof must be written on or under the deed.

In other parts of the Union, acknowledgment must be made before and certified by the chief justice of the United States, or an associate justice of the supreme court of the United States, or a district judge of the same, or any judge or justice of the supreme or superior court of any state or territory in the Union.

In a foreign country, they may be acknowledged before any court of law, mayor or other chief magistrate of any city, borough, or corporation, of the said foreign country, certified as such acts are usually, and authenticated by him or them.

Form of Acknowledgment.

State of Mississippi, }
Claiborne County, } *ss.*

Personally appeared before me, JOHN JONES, *judge of the supreme court*, the above named JOHN DOE, who acknowledged that he signed, sealed, and delivered the foregoing deed, on the day and year therein mentioned, as his voluntary act and deed.

Given under my hand and seal, this *tenth* day of *December*, A. D. one thousand eight hundred and *fifty*.

(Seal.) JOHN JONES, *Judge of the Supreme Court.*

Rights of Married Women.

A MARRIED woman may become seized or possessed of property, real or personal, by direct bequest, gift, or purchase, or distribution, in her own name, and as of her own property, provided the same does not come from her husband after marriage.

The slaves owned before marriage, and their natural increase, continue her separate property, exempt from any liability for the debts or contracts of her husband; also those she may acquire by conveyance, gift, inheritance, distribution, or otherwise, after marriage, and their natural increase.

DOWER.—The widow is entitled for life to one third of all the lands, tenements, and hereditaments, of which her husband died seized and possessed, or had before conveyed, whereof said widow had not relinquished her right of dower as provided for by law.

Rate of Interest.

THE rate of interest is eight per cent. for the *bona fide* use of money; six per cent. upon other contracts. The penalty for usury is the loss of the entire interest.

Wills.

WILLS should be in writing, subscribed by the testator, and attested by three credible witnesses. If the will is wholly written by the testator, and subscribed by him, it need not be attested by any witness.

LOUISIANA.

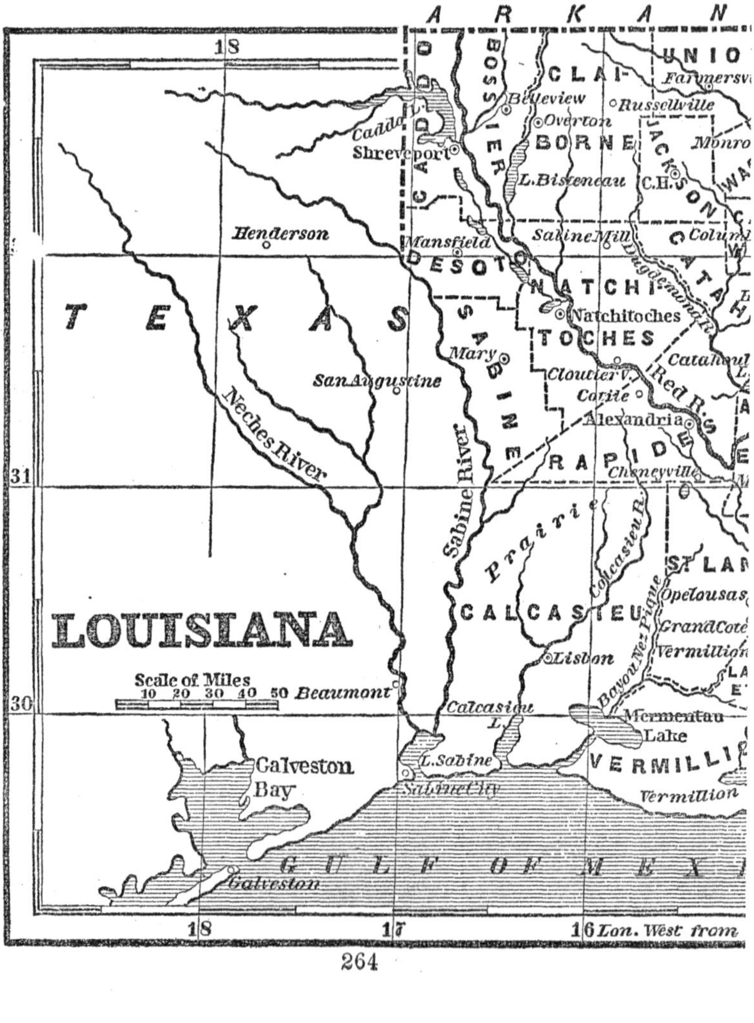

ARKAN
UNIO
Farmersv
CLAI-
BORNE
Belleview
Russellville
Overton
BOSSIER
CADDO
Caddo L.
Shreveport
L.Bisteneau
JACKSON
C.H.
Monro
Henderson
Mansfield
DESOTO
Sabine Mill
NATCHI-
TOCHES
Natchitoches
Dugdemona R.
CATAH
Catahoul
TEXAS
SABINE
Mary
San Augustine
Cloutier V.
Cotile
Alexandria
Red R.
Neches River
Sabine River
RAPIDE
Cheneyville
Prairie
Calcasieu R.
ST LAN
Opelousas
Grand Coté
Vermillion
CALCASIEU
Bayou Nez Pique
LOUISIANA
Lisbon
Scale of Miles
10 20 30 40 50
Beaumont
Calcasieu L.
Mermentau Lake
VERMILLI
Vermillion
L. Sabine
Sabine City
Galveston Bay
GULF OF MEX
Galveston
18
17
16
31
30
Lon. West from

LOUISIANA.

MORE HOUSE
C.H.
Providence
CARROLL
MADISON
Vicksburg
JACKSON
FRANK LIN
Winnsboro
Richmond
TENSAS
St. Joseph
Port Gibson
MISSISSIPPI
Tensas R.
CONCORDIA
Vidalia
Natchez
Mississippi R.
Pearl R.
Columbia
Woodville
Leaf R.
Pascagoula R.
ALABAMA
WEST FELICIANA
St. Francis V.
Jackson
Clinton
E. FELICIANA
ST. HELENA
Greensburg
WASHINGTON
Franklinton
POINT COUPEE
E. BATON ROUGE
BATON ROUGE
ST. TAMMANY
Covington
W. BATON ROUGE
LIVINGSTON
Springfield
Mississippi C.
IBERVILLE
Lake Pontchartrain
ST. MARTINS
St. Martins V.
ASCENSION
Donaldsonville
ST. JAMES
ASSUMPTION
Napoleon
ST. CHARLES
JEFFERSON
ST. BERNARD
Chandeleur Islands
ST. MARYS
Franklin
Thibodeaux V.
LA FOURCHE INTERIOR
PLAQUEMINE
Bay de la Riviere aux Chenes
Houma
TERRE BONNE
Mouths of the Mississippi
Washington
14
13
12
32
31
30

LOUISIANA.

Constitution adopted, 1845.—Square Miles, 46,431.—Population in 1850 500,762.

Exemptions.

THE sheriff can not seize the linen and clothes belonging to the debtor or his wife, nor his bed, nor those of his family, nor his arms and military accoutrements, nor the tools and instruments necessary for the exercise of the trade or profession by which he gains a living. Nor can he seize the agricultural implements and working-cattle, separately from the land to which they are attached; nor the rights of personal servitude, of use and habitation; of usufruct to the estate of a minor child, the income of dotal property. *See page* 154.

Mechanics' Lien.

THE undertaker [contractor] has a privilege [lien] for the payment of his labor, on the building or other work which he may have constructed. Workmen employed immediately by the owner in the construction or repair of any building, have the same privilege. Workmen and persons furnishing materials, who have contracted with the undertaker, have no action against the owner who has paid him. If the undertaker be not paid, they may cause the moneys due him to be seized, and they are of right subrogated to his privilege.

The payments which the proprietor may have made in anticipation to the undertaker, are considered, with regard to workmen and to those who furnish materials, as not having been made, and do not prevent them from exercising the right granted them by the preceding article.

No agreement or undertaking for work exceeding five hundred dollars, which has not been reduced to writing, and registered with the recorder of mortgages, shall enjoy the privilege above granted. For those not amounting to five hundred dollars, this formality is dispensed with: but the privilege granted to them is limited to six months, reckoning from the day when the work is completed. Workmen employed in the construction or repair of ships or boats enjoy the privilege established above, without being bound to reduce their contracts to writing, whatever may be their amount; but this privilege ceases if they have allowed the ship or boat to depart without exercising their right.

Architects, contractors, masons, and other workmen; those who have supplied the owner with materials for the construction or repair of his buildings or other works; those who have contracted, in the manner provided by the police regulations, to make or put in repair the levees, bridges, canals, and roads, of a proprietor, preserve their privileges only in so far as they have recorded with the register of mortgages the act containing the bargains they have made, or the amount or acknowledgment of what is due to them, in all cases where the amount of the account or acknowledgment exceeds the sum of five hundred dollars.

Limitation of Actions.

IMMOVEABLES [real estate] are prescribed for by [limited to] ten years when the possessor has been in good faith, and held by a just title during that time. The same species of property is prescribed for by thirty years, without any title on the part of the possessor, or whether he be in good faith or not. The property of slaves is acquired in five years, where the possessor has a title, and holds in good faith. To acquire the property of immoveables and slaves, the following conditions must concur: 1. Good faith on the part of the possessor. 2. A title which shall be legal and sufficient to transfer the property. 3. Possession during the time required by law, which possession must be accompanied by the incidents hereafter required. 4. And finally, an object, which may be acquired by prescription.

If a person has possessed in good faith and by a just title, as proprietor, a moveable [personal] thing, during three successive years without interruption, he shall acquire the property of it by prescription, unless the thing were stolen or lost.

The actions of masters and instructors in the arts and sciences, for lessons which they give by the month; inn-keepers and such others, on account of lodging and board; retailers of provisions and liquors; workmen, laborers, and servants, for the payment of their wages; for the payment of the freight of vessels, the wages of the officers, sailors, and others of the crew; for the supply of wood and other things necessary for the construction, equipment, and provisioning of vessels—are prescribed by one year.

The actions for injurious words, verbal or written; for damages caused by slaves or animals; that which a possessor may institute, to have himself maintained or restored to his possession, when he has been disturbed or evicted; for the delivery of merchandise or other effects shipped on board of vessels; for damage sustained by merchandise on board of ships, or which may have happened by ships running foul of each other—are prescribed by one year.

The action for arrearages of rent-charge, annuities, and alimony, or of the hire of moveables or immoveables; for the payment of money lent; for the salaries of overseers, clerks, secretaries, and teachers of the sciences, for lessons by the year or quarter; of physicians, surgeons, and apothecaries, for visits, operations, and medicines—are prescribed by three years.

Actions on bills of exchange, notes payable to order or bearer, except bank-notes; those on all effects negotiable or transferable by endorsement or delivery—are prescribed by five years.

All actions for immoveable property, or for an entire estate, as a succession, are prescribed by thirty years.

Collection of Debts.

Arrest.—Since March 28, 1840, no person can be arrested after judgment has been obtained, in order to compel payment thereof. But the debtor may be arrested before judgment, upon an affidavit that he is about to leave the state permanently, without leaving in it sufficient property to satisfy the judgment which the creditor expects to obtain.

Women, married or single, can not be arrested, nor can non-residents.

Attachment.—A creditor may obtain an attachment of the property of his debtor in the following cases: 1. Where such debtor is about leaving permanently the state, without there being a possibility of obtaining or executing judgment against him previous to his departure, or where such debtor has already left the state, never again to return. 2. When such debtor resides out of the state. 3. When he conceals himself, to avoid being cited. It may also be attached in the hands of third persons, in order to secure the payment of a debt, whether the amount be liquidated or not, provided the term of payment have arrived, and the creditor, his agent or attorney in fact, who prays for the attachment, state expressly and positively the amount which he claims. An obligation must be given in favor of the defendant for a sum exceeding one half that which he claimed, with the surety of one good and solvent person, residing within the jurisdiction of the court to which the petition is presented, as a security for the payment of such damages as such defendant may recover against him, in case it should be decided that the attachment was wrongfully obtained.

If a creditor know or suspect that a third person has in his possession property belonging to his debtor, or that he is indebted to such debtor, he may make such a person a party to the suit, by having him cited, to declare on oath what property belonging to the defendant he has in his possession, or in what sum he is indebted to such defendant, even when the term of payment has not yet arrived.

Deeds.

These may be recorded with a notary public, without any proof or authentication. They are termed acts of sale, and are of two kinds, private acts and authentic acts. Private acts are those merely under the hands of the parties. Authentic acts are those where the parties appear before a notary public, who reduces the contract to writing, and signs it, as well as the parties, in the presence of two free male witnesses, who must be fourteen years of age.

Rights of Married Women.

The debts of both husband and wife, contracted before marriage, are chargeable only on their separate and individual property.

The property which the husband or the wife owns before marriage, or that comes to either by gift, bequest, or inheritance, after marriage, remains the distinct and individual property of the party to whom it belongs. As to all other property, they are partners, unless she elects to the contrary.

The wife, even when she is separate in estate from her husband, can not alienate, grant, mortgage, or acquire, either by gratuitous or encumbered title, unless her husband concurs in the act, or yields his consent in writing.

The wife may make her last will without the authority of her husband.

The surviving wife has the usufruct of the portion coming to her children, until she marries again.

Rate of Interest.

The legal rate is five per cent.; but parties may agree on any sum as high as eight per cent. Bank interest is six per cent. The penalty for usurious contracts is a forfeiture of the entire interest.

(For WILLS, see Arkansas, page 277.)

TEXAS.

30
28
26
24
COMANCHE
INDIANS
Tosojunova R.
F
Saline L.
Ojo del Muerto
San Diego
Roblero
Brazito
La Rancheria
La Salinera
Passo del Norte
Pasigono R.
Organo Mountains
Rio Grande Del Norte
Rio Pacos or Puerco R.
Colorado R.
32
30
28
M
E
X
I
C
O
Ojo Caliente
Presidio del Norte
S. Vincente
B E X
Rio Grande Del Norte
Presid io Rio Grande
Mier
TEXAS
NORTHERN PART
INDIAN TERRITORY
Arkansas River
Cimarron R.
COMANCHE
INDIANS
Rio Grande
Taos
Canada
Santa Fe
Albuquerque
Belen
Socorro
Canadian R.
Red River
INDIAN TER
29
25
37
35
27
23
TEXAS
Scale of Miles
20 40 60 80 100
Lon. West from Washington

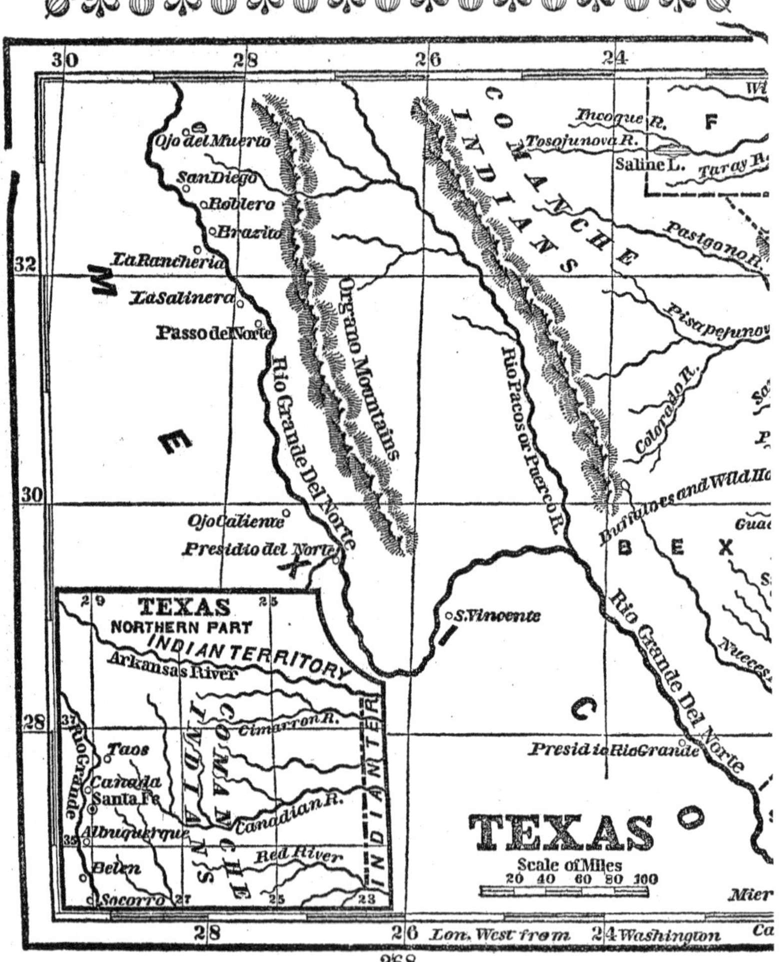

TEXAS.

INDIAN TERRITORY
ARKANSAS
LOUISIANA
ROBERTSON
NACOGDOCHES
HOUSTON
MILAM
TRAVIS
AUSTIN
BASTROP
FAYETTE
WASHINGTON
BRAZOS
MONTGOMERY
LIBERTY
JASPER
JEFFERSON
SABINE
SHELBY
RUSK
HARRISON
LAMAR
RED RIVER
BOWIE
HARRIS
AUSTIN
COLORADO
FORT BEND
BRAZORIA
GALVESTON
MATAGORDA
JACKSON
VICTORIA
GONZALES
GOLIAD
REFUGIO
SAN PATRICIO
Bonham
Paris
Clarksv.
Boston
Attach'd to Lamar
Attach'd to R.River
Attach'd to Bowie
Shreveport
Marshall
Henderson
Natchitoches
Ft.Houston
Shelby V.
S.Augustine
Milam
Alexandria
S.Nacogdoches
Crocket
Franklin
Nashville
Booneville
Washington
Jasper
Swartwout
Montgomery
Liberty
Beaumont
Lisbon
Lake Mermentau
Houston
San Jacinto
Sabine
La Grange
Bastrop
Columbus
Egypt
Gonzales
Victoria
Texana
Matagorda
Goliad
Refugio
Corpus Christi
S.Gertrudas C.
Olmos C.
Salt Lake
Padre Island
Ft.Polk
Ft. Brown
Reinosa
Matamoras
Brazos River
Colorado River
Trinity River
Red River
Sabine River
Navasota R.
Nueces R.
San Antonio R.
Galveston
Galveston B.
Matagorda B.
Matagorda I.
St. Joseph's I.
Corpus Christi B.
GULF OF MEXICO
16
18
22
28
30
32

TEXAS.

Constitution adopted, 1845.—Square Miles, 250,000.—Population in 1850, 187,403

Exemptions.

THERE is exempt from levy and sale on execution, household and kitchen furniture, not exceeding two hundred dollars in value; implements of husbandry not exceeding fifty dollars in value; the tools, apparatus, and books, appertaining to the trade or profession of any citizen; five milch cows; one yoke of oxen, or one horse; twenty hogs; and provisions for one year.

Homestead-Exemption Law.

THE homestead of a family not to exceed two hundred acres of land (not included in a town or city) or any town or city lot or lots, in value not to exceed two thousand dollars, shall not be subject to forced sale for any debts hereafter contracted; nor shall the owner, if a married man, be at liberty to alienate the same, unless by the consent of his wife, in such manner as the legislature may hereafter point out.

Mechanics' Lien.

MECHANICS contracting in writing to erect buildings, shall have a lien in the nature of a mortgage on all buildings they may erect or work upon, and also on the parcel or lot of land on which they are erected, until the price for services and materials found shall be fully paid. The contract shall be recorded in the office of the clerk of the county where such building shall be erected, within the space of thirty days after the contract is made.

Every person doing any work or furnishing any kind of materials toward the erection or finishing of any building erected under a contract in writing, between the owner and builder or other person whose demand therefor has not been paid, may deliver to the owner of such building an attested account of the amount and value of the work and labor or materials, and thereupon such owner shall retain out of his subsequent payment the amount of such work and labor or materials, for the benefit of the person so performing or furnishing the same. This does not apply to incorporated cities.

Chattel Mortgages.

IF any conveyance of goods and chattels or slaves be not on consideration deemed valuable in law, it shall be taken to be fraudulent, unless the same be by will duly proved and recorded, or by an instrument in writing acknowledged or proved by two or more witnesses and recorded the same as deeds of real estate, or unless possession shall really and bona fide remain with the donee. Mortgages on personal property must be recorded in the county where the mortgager lives.

Law regulating Contracts.

No action shall be brought whereby to charge any executor or administrator, upon any special promise, to answer any debt or damages out of his own estate; or whereby to charge the defendant, upon any special promise, to answer for the debt, default, or miscarriage, of another person; or to charge any person, upon any agreement made upon consideration of marriage; or upon any contract for the sale of lands, slaves, tenements, or hereditaments; or making any lease thereof, for a longer term than one year; or upon any agreement that is not to be performed within one year from the making thereof; unless the promise or agreement upon which such action shall be brought, or some memorandum thereof, shall be in writing, and signed by the party to be charged therewith, or some person thereunto by him lawfully authorized.

Limitation of Actions.

ACTIONS of trespass for injury to property, of trover and conversion, for taking away the goods and chattels of another, actions upon open account (except those that concern the trade of merchandise between merchants, their factors, and agents), must be brought within two years.

Actions of debt upon contract in writing within four years.

Actions upon an account for goods, wares, and merchandise sold or delivered, or articles charged in a store account, within two years.

Actions for assault and battery, slander, and libel, within one year.

Real actions in three, five, or ten years, according to the grade of title.

Minors, married women, persons insane or imprisoned, have the same periods respectively after the removal of their disability.

An acknowledgment to take a claim out of the statute of limitation must be in writing, and signed by the party to be charged thereby.

Collection of Debts.

ARREST.—The constitution provides that no person shall ever be imprisoned for debt.

ATTACHMENT.—When a summons to answer to any civil suit shall be returned by the sheriff that the defendant is not to be found in his county, the plaintiff may sue out a writ of attachment to be levied on the property of such defendant.

The judges and clerks of the district courts, and justices of the peace may issue original attachments, returnable to their respective courts upon the party applying for the same, his agent or attorney, making an affidavit in writing stating that the defendant is justly indebted to plaintiff and the amount of the demand, also that the defendant is not a resident of this state or that he is about to remove out of this state, or that he secretes himself so that the ordinary process of law can not be served on him, or that he is about to remove his property beyond this state, and that thereby the plaintiff will probably lose the debt, and that the attachment is not sued out for the purpose of injuring the defendant. A bond must at the same time be given, with two or more good and sufficient sureties, payable to the defendant in double the amount sworn to be due, conditioned that the plaintiff will prosecute his suit to effect and pay such damages as shall be adjudged against him for wrongfully suing out such attachment.

SEQUESTRATION.—Writs of sequestration may issue, 1. When a married woman sues for a divorce and makes oath that she fears her husband will waste her separate property, or their common property, or the fruits or revenue produced by either, or remove the same out of the limits of this state during the pendency of the suit; 2. When a person sues for the title or possession of a slave, or other moveable property or chattels of any description, and makes oath that he fears the defendant or person in possession thereof, will injure or ill treat such slave, or waste such moveable property or chattels, or remove the same out of the limits of this state during the pendency of the suit; 3. When a person sues for the foreclosure of a mortgage, or the enforcement of a lien upon a slave, or moveable property of any description, and makes oath that he fears that the defendant or person in possession thereof, will injure or ill treat such slave, or waste such moveable property, or remove such slave or moveable property out of the county, 4. When any person sues for the title or possession of real property, and makes oath that he fears the defendant or person in possession thereof, may make use of his possession to injure such property, or waste the fruits and revenue produced by the same, or convert them to his own use; 5. When any person sues for the title or possession of any property from which he has been ejected by force or violence, and shall make oath to such facts.

Deeds.

THESE must be sealed, but a scroll by way of seal will answer, if the person making the same shall, in the body of the instrument, recognise such scroll as having been affixed by way of seal. They should be recorded in the office of the clerk of the county court of the county where the lands or some part thereof lie.

To entitle them to be recorded they must be proved by a subscribing witness, or acknowledged by the grantor, if within the state before some notary public or clerk of any county court in the state, if out of the state and within the United States or their territories, before some judge of a court of record having a seal. If out of the United States, before some public minister, chargé d'affaires, or consul of the United States. The certificate of the acknowledgment or proof shall be attested under the official seal of the officer taking the same.

If a married woman convey her separate estate, she must acknowledge the same before a judge of the district court, or chief-justice of the county court, or if she merely release her interest in the estate of her husband, then before any judge of the supreme or district court, or notary public.

The certificate of acknowledgment in either case must state that she had been examined by the officer privily and apart from her husband, and that the conveyance was fully explained to her, and that she acknowledged the same to be her act and deed, and declared that she had willingly signed, sealed, and delivered the same, and that she wished not to retract it.

In other cases the certificate must state that the grantor appeared before the officer and acknowledged that he executed the instrument for the consideration and purposes therein stated.

Mortgages of real estate are not a lien unless recorded in the county where the land lies, within ninety days from the date of the execution of such mortgage.

For RIGHTS OF MARRIED WOMEN, INTEREST, *and* WILLS, *see page* 248.

ARKANSAS.

TEXAS
LOUISIANA
MISSISSIPPI
Caddo Lake
Shreveport
Natchitoches
Red River
Columbia
Monroe
Harrisonburg
Wachita Riv.
Mississippi Riv.
Natchez
Port Gibson
Vicksburg
Princeton
Helena
Little Rock
Benton
Hot Springs
Washington
Lewisville
Camden
Eldorado
Columbia
Arkansas
POLK
SEVIER
PIKE
MONTGOMERY
HEMPSTEAD
CLARKE
HOT SPRING
LAFAYETTE
UNION
WACHITA
DALLAS
ASHLEY
DREW
DESHA
JEFFERSON
ARKANSAS
PHILLIPS
16 Lon. West from 15 Washington
14
32
33
34

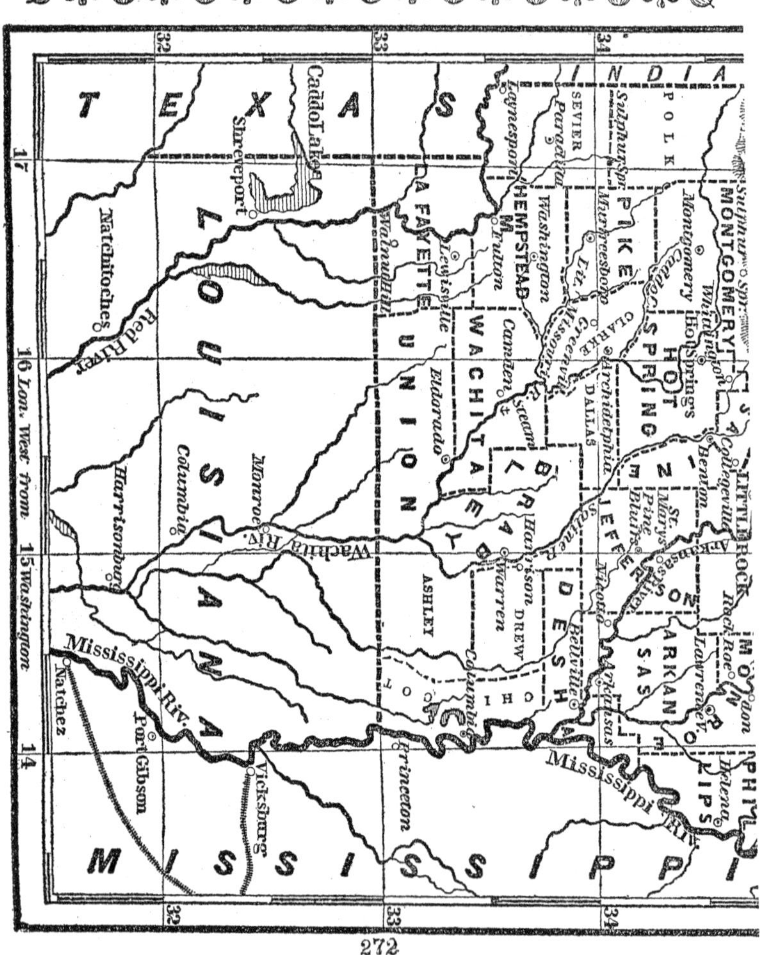

ARKANSAS.

ARKANSAS
Scale of miles
10 30 50 70
MISSOURI
TERRITORY
BENTON
WASHINGTON
CRAWFORD
FRANKLIN
JOHNSON
MADISON
CARROLL
NEWTON
POPE
CONWAY
VAN BUREN
SEARCY
MARION
FULTON
IZARD
INDEPENDENCE
LAWRENCE
RANDOLPH
WHITE
JACKSON
POINSETT
GREENE
ST FRANCIS
CRITTENDEN
MISSISSIPPI
PULASKI
YELL
SCOTT
Gasconade R.
Big Black R.
St. Francis R.
Cache R.

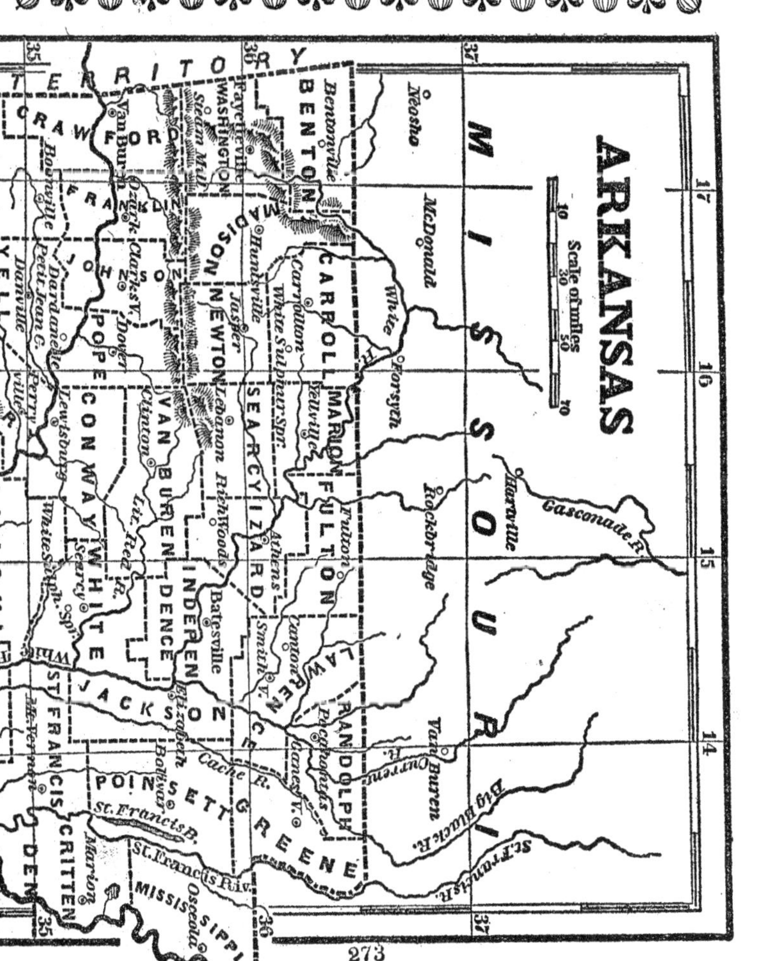

ARKANSAS.

Constitution adopted 1836.—Square Miles, 52,198.—Population in 1850, 198,796

Exemptions.

THERE is exempt from levy and sale on execution, if belonging to any one not the head of a family, his wearing-apparel, except watches, and also the necessary tools and implements of trade of a mechanic while carrying on his trade.

If belonging to a married man with a family, one horse, mule, or yoke of oxen; one cow and calf; one plough, one axe, one hoe, and one set of plough gears, if the person be a farmer: spinning-wheels and cards, one loom and apparatus necessary for manufacturing cloth in a private family; all spun yarn, thread, and cloth, manufactured for family use; any quantity of hemp, flax, cotton, and wool, not exceeding twenty-five pounds; all wearing-apparel of the family; two beds, with the usual bedding; and such other household and kitchen furniture as may be necessary for the family, agreeably to an inventory thereof, to be returned on oath with the execution by the officer; the necessary tools and implements of trade of any mechanic, while carrying on his trade; all arms and military equipments required by law to be kept, and all such provisions as may be on hand for family use.

Mechanics' Lien.

MECHANICS have a lien for all sums over one hundred dollars, for labor and materials, if they file with the clerk of the circuit court of the county where the building is, a true account of their demand and the amount due, verified by oath of the person entitled to the lien, which lien extends to the land appurtenant to the building, not exceeding two acres.

The lien continues in force only one year after the building is finished, unless suit be brought to enforce it.

Law regulating Contracts.

No action shall be brought—

1. To charge any executor or administrator, upon any special promise, to answer for any debt or damage out of his own estate;

2. To charge any person, upon any special promise, to answer for the debt, default, or miscarriage, of another;

3. To charge any person upon an agreement made in consideration of marriage;

4. To charge any person upon any contract for the sale of lands, tenements, or hereditaments, or any interest in or concerning them;

5. To charge any person upon any lease of lands, tenements, or hereditaments, for a longer term than one year;

6. To charge any person upon any contract, promise, or agreement, that is not to be performed within one year from the making thereof; unless the agreement, promise, or contract, upon which such action shall be brought, or some memoran-

sum or note thereof, shall be made in writing, and signed by the party to be charged therewith, or signed by some other person by him thereunto properly authorized.

No contract for the sale of goods, wares, and merchandise, for the price of thirty dollars or upward, shall be binding on the parties, unless, first, there be some note or memorandum, signed by the party to be charged; or, second, the purchaser shall accept a part of the goods so sold, and actually receive the same; or, third, shall give something in earnest to bind the bargain, or in part payment thereof.

Limitation of Actions.

ACTIONS upon promissory notes, and other instruments in writing, not under seal, shall be commenced within five years after the cause of action shall accrue.

Actions upon sealed instruments, judgments, and decrees, within ten years.

All actions of account, assumpsit, or case, founded on any other contract or liability, within three years.

Non-residents are subject to the limitation equally with residents; but when a debtor has absconded from another state into Arkansas, without the knowledge of his creditor, such creditor may sue within the time limited, after he is apprised of such residence of the absconding debtor.

Minors, married women, persons insane, or imprisoned out of the state, have the same times respectively after the removal of their disability.

Any acknowledgment to take a case out of the operation of the statute, or to bind a person for a debt contracted during infancy, must be in writing.

One joint contractor or executor is not bound by the promise of another.

Collection of Debts.

ATTACHMENT.—If a creditor shall, at the time of filing his declaration, file an affidavit of himself, or some other person for him, stating that the defendant is justly indebted to the plaintiff in a sum exceeding one hundred dollars, and stating the amount, and also that the defendant is not a resident of this state, or that he is about to remove out of this state, or that he is about to remove his goods and effects out of this state, or that he so secretes himself that process can not be served on him, an attachment against his property may issue.

Bond, in double the amount claimed, must also be filed, conditioned for the payment of such damages as may be awarded against him.

Justices of the peace may issue an attachment in like cases when the demand is one hundred dollars or less.

Boats running on the navigable waters of the state may be attached for debts contracted by the owner, &c., on account of work or supplies furnished the boat.

ARREST.—Only in case of fraud alleged by the plaintiff, and supported by his affidavit and the affidavit of some disinterested and creditable person, to the facts on which such allegation is founded, can any person be arrested in a civil action.

Deeds.

DEEDS shall be executed in the presence of two witnesses, and SEALED.

They should be acknowledged, if in the state, before the supreme court, the circuit court, or either of the judges thereof, or the clerk of either of said courts, or before the county court, or the presiding judge thereof, or any justice of the peace, or notary public.

If elsewhere in the United States, before any court of the United States, or of any state or territory having a seal, or the clerk of any such court, or the mayor of any city or town, or the chief officer of any city or town, having a seal of office.

If out of the United States, before any court having a seal, or any mayor or chief officer of any city or town having an official seal.

The certificate to be attested under the seal of office; but if he have no such seal, then under his official signature.

If the grantor be not personally known to the officer, he must be satisfactorily proven.

The grantor must acknowledge that he executed the deed for the consideration and purposes therein mentioned and set forth.

Married women must voluntarily appear before such court or officer, and in the absence of her husband declare that she had, of her own free will, executed the instrument in question, or had signed and sealed the relinquishment of dower, for the purposes therein contained and set forth, without compulsion or undue influence of her husband.

Deeds should be recorded by the recorder of the county where the land is situated.

Form of Acknowledgment.

State of Arkansas,
County of *Franklin*, } to wit:

Be it remembered, that on the *first* day of *October*, one thousand eight hundred and *fifty*, before me, JOHN JONES, a *notary public* in and for said county, personally appeared JOHN DOE *and* SUSAN *his wife*, to me personally known to be the persons described in and who executed the foregoing *conveyance*, and severally acknowledged that they executed the same, for the consideration and purposes therein mentioned; *and the said* SUSAN, *having voluntarily appeared before me, in the absence of her husband, declared that she had, of her own free will, executed the said conveyance, and had signed and sealed the relinquishment of her dower, for the purposes therein contained and set forth, without compulsion or undue influence of her husband.*

(Seal.) JOHN JONES, *Notary Public.*

Rights of Married Women.

ANY married woman may become seized and possessed of any property, real or personal, in her own right and as of her own property, provided the same does not come from the husband after marriage.

The slaves and their natural increase, owned by any married woman before marriage, and that she may acquire after marriage, shall be her separate property, exempt from any liability for the debts or contracts of the husband.

But a schedule, under oath, and verified by the oath of some other reputable person, must be made out by the husband and wife, and filed in the recorder's office of the county where the property is, and of the county where they reside.

DOWER.—A widow shall be endowed of the third part of all the lands whereof her husband was seized of an estate of inheritance at any time during the marriage, unless the same shall have been relinquished in legal form.

Rate of Interest.

WHERE no rate is mentioned, it is six per cent. Parties may contract for any rate not exceeding ten per cent. Usurious contracts are void.

Wills.

Every will shall be executed and attested in the following manner:—

1. It must be subscribed by the testator at the end of the will, or by some person for him at his request.
2. Such subscription shall be made by the testator in the presence of each of the attesting witnesses, or shall be acknowledged by him to have been so made to each of the attesting witnesses.
3. The testator, at the time of making such subscription, or at the time of acknowledging the same, shall *declare* the instrument so subscribed to be his will and testament.
4. There shall be at least two attesting witnesses, each of whom shall sign his name as a witness at the end of the will, at the request of the testator.
5. Where the entire body of the will and the signature thereto shall be written in the proper handwriting of the testator or testatrix, such will may be established by the unimpeachable evidence of at least three disinterested witnesses to the handwriting and signature of each testator or testatrix notwithstanding there may be no attesting witnesses to such will; but no will, without such subscribing witnesses, shall be pleaded in bar of a will subscribed in due form as prescribed in this act.

Every person who shall sign the testator's name to any will by his direction, shall write his own name as a witness to such will, and state that he signed the testator's name at his request.

Wills.—Louisiana.

Wills are nuncupative or open, mystic or sealed, and olographic. They must all be in writing, either by the testator himself or by some other person under his direction.

Nuncupative wills may be made by public acts or by act under private signature. If by public acts, it must be received by a notary public, in the presence of three witnesses residing in the place where the will is executed, or of five witnesses not residing in the place. It must be dictated by the testator, and written by the notary as it is dictated. It must be read to the testator in presence of the witnesses, and signed by the testator. All those formalities must be fulfilled at one time, without interruption. It must be signed by the witnesses, or at least by one of them for all, if the others can not write.

If under private signature, it must be written by the testator or by any other person from his dictation, in presence of five witnesses residing in the place where the will is received, or of seven witnesses residing out of the place; or the testator may present the paper on which he has written his testament, or caused it to be written out of their presence, declaring to them that that paper contains his last will. In either case, the will must be read by the testator to the witnesses, or by one of the witnesses to the rest, in presence of the testator. It must be signed by the testator if he is able, and by the witnesses, or at least by two of them in case the others know not how to sign, and those of the witnesses who do not know how to sign must affix their marks.

The mystic or secret testament is made in the following manner: The testator must sign the will, whether he has written it himself or has caused it to be written by another. The will, or the paper serving as its envelope, must be closed and sealed. The testator shall present it thus closed and sealed to the notary and seven witnesses, or he shall cause it to be closed and sealed in their presence. Then he shall declare to the notary, in presence of the witnesses, that that paper contains his testament, written by himself, or by another by his direction, and signed by him the testator. The notary shall then draw up the act of superscription, which shall be written on the will or on the sheet that serves as its envelope, and that act shall be signed by the testator, by the notary, and by the witnesses. Those who know not how or are not able to write, and those who know not how or are not able to sign their names, can not make dispositions in the form of the mystic will. In all cases the act of superscription must be signed by at least two witnesses.

The olographic will is that which is entirely written, dated, and signed, by the hand of the testator. It is subject to no other form, and may be made anywhere, even out of the state.

The following persons are absolutely incapable of being witnesses to wills: Women of what age soever; male children who have not attained the age of sixteen years complete; persons insane, deaf, dumb, or blind; persons whom the criminal laws declare incapable of exercising civil functions; and slaves. Neither can wills be witnessed by those who are constituted heirs or named legatees, under whatsoever title it may be. Mystic wills are excepted from this article.

TENNESSEE.

ILLINOIS
Ohio R.
Salem
Green R.
Cairo
K E N T
Hopkinsville
Franklin
MISSOURI
Mississippi R.
Tennessee R.
Clinton
STEWART
Dover
MONTGOMERY
Clarksv.
ROBERTSON
Springfield
SUMNER
Gallatin
OBION
Troy
Dresden
WEAKLEY
HENRY
Paris
Camden
BENTON
Charlotte
DICKSON
DAVIDSON
NASHVILLE
Lebanon
WILSON
DYER
Reynoldsburg
Dyersburg
Trenton
GIBSON
CARROLL
Huntington
HUMPHREYS
HICKMAN
Centreville
WILLIAMSON
Franklin
Murfreesboro
RUTHERFORD
LAUDERDALE
Ripley
Brownsv.
Covington
HAYWARD
MADISON
Jackson
Lexington
HENDERSON
PERRY
Perrysburg
Columbia
MAURY
MARSHALL
BEDFORD
Shelbyville
Randolph
TIPTON
Lewisv.
SHELBY
Raleigh
Memphis
FAYETTE
Somerville
Bolivar
HARDIMAN
LaGrange
McNAIRY
Purdy
HARDIN
Savannah
Waynesboro
WAYNE
LAWRENCE
Lawrenceburg
Pulaski
GILES
LINCOLN
Fayetteville
Elk R.
ARKANSAS
MISSISSIPPI
Holly Springs
Florence
Huntsville
A L A B A
Decatur
Tennessee R.
TENNESSEE
Scale of Miles.
10 30 50 70
Blountville
37
36
12
11
10
Lon. West from Wa

TENNESSEE.

Mt.Vernon
Manchester
Cumberland R.
Cumberland Mountains
VIRGINIA
CAMPBELL
Jacksboro
CLAIBORNE
Tazewell
HANCOCK
Rogersville
HAWKINS
SULLIVAN
Blountville
CARTER
Elizabeth
OVERTON
Livingston
James T.
FENTRESS
PUTNAM
Monticello
Montgomery
MORGAN
ANDERSON
Clinton
GRAINGER
Rutledge
Jonesboro
GreeneV.
GREENE
WASHINGTON
JEFFERSON
Dandridge
Newport
WHITE
Sparta
Kingston
Knoxville
KNOX
ROANE
BLOUNT
Maryville
SEVIER
SevierV.
UNION
Smoky Mts.
MARION
Dallas
Washington
Decatur
Athens
MONROE
McMINN
Madison V.
POLK
Benton
BRADLEY
Cleveland
Murphy
N. CAROLINA
Henderson V.
Clayton
SOUTH CAROLINA
Spring Place
Dahlonego
GEORGIA
Jefferson
Coosa R.
37
35
8
7
6

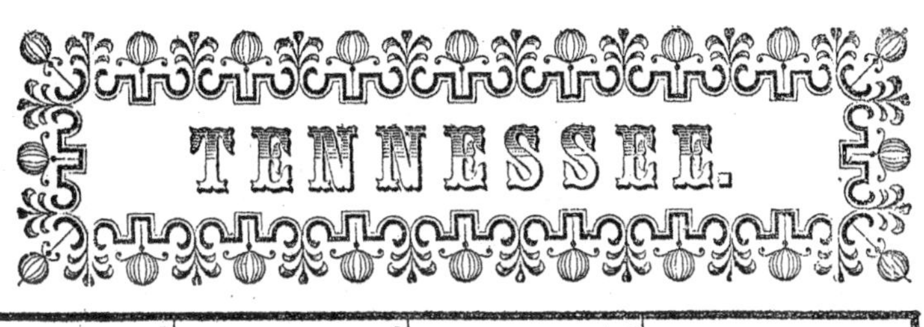

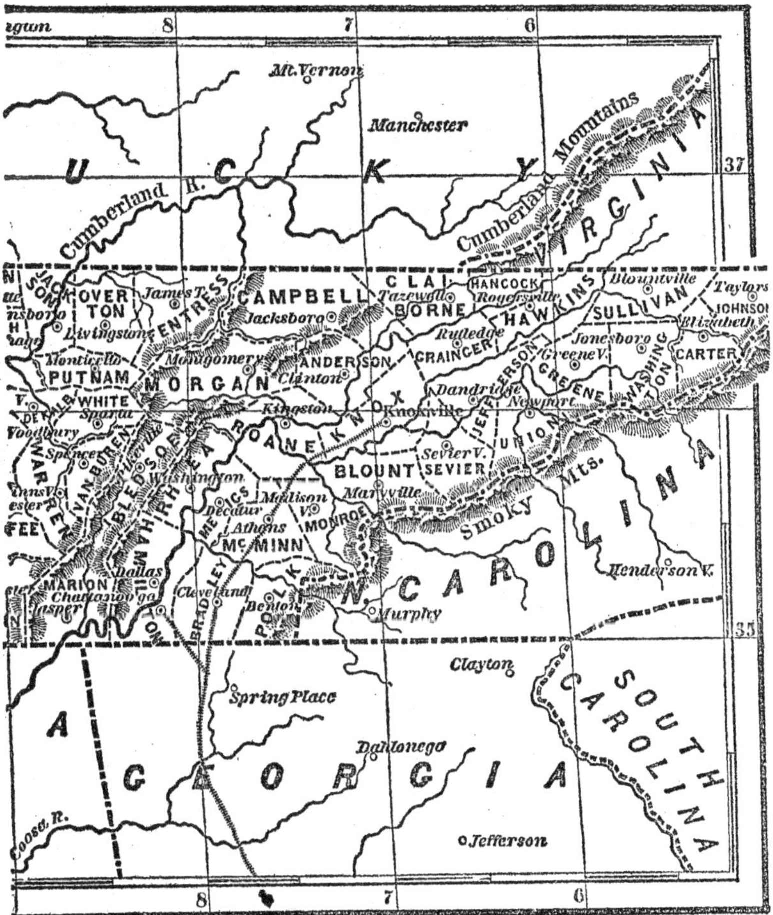

TENNESSEE.

Constitution adopted 1835—Square Miles 45,600—Population in 1850, 1,023,698.

Exemptions.

There is exempted in this state from levy and sale on execution—one cow and calf; one bedstead and bed, containing not more than twenty-five pounds of feathers; two sheets, two blankets, and one counterpane; where the family consists of six or more persons, one additional featherbed, bedstead, and bedclothes, are allowed; one half dozen knives and forks, six plates, one dish, one pot, one Dutch oven; one spinning-wheel; one pair of cotton-cards; one chopping-axe; five head of sheep; ten head of stock hogs; all fowls and poultry; six chairs; one bible and hymn-book; one loom and gear; also ten barrels of corn; and three hundred weight of pork or bacon, as the case may be, if such they have, or so much thereof as they or either of them may have.

Also in the hands of persons engaged in agriculture, one plough, one hoe, one set of gears for ploughing, one iron wedge; and one farm horse, mule, or yoke of oxen; and the workman's one set of mechanical tools, usual and necessary in his trade; any indigent, decrepit, or idiotic person or persons, who are unable by manual labor or physical exertions to obtain a living or support, are exempt from working on public roads, and paying poll tax, when such infirmities shall be made to appear satisfactory to any county court.

The arms and equipments of any militia-man, are exempt from execution at all times. *See page* 154.

Mechanics' Lien.

When any mechanic or undertaker, by special contract with the owner of any lot of ground or tract of land in this state, or his agent, shall construct, build, or repair, either in whole or in part, or furnish materials or any part of materials, in the construction, building, or repairing, of any house, fixtures, or improvements, or shall do any work upon the said house, either by finishing off the same, painting, ornamenting, or otherwise, such mechanic or undertaker shall have and retain a lien upon such building, and the lot of ground thereto attached, in proportion to the amount and value of work done or materials furnished as aforesaid.

A lien hereby created, shall continue one year after the work done, or materials furnished, and until the decision of any suit that may be brought within that time for the debt that may be due said mechanic or undertaker; also said lien shall extend to journeymen, or all who in part build, or in part furnish materials. Provided notice in writing of said lien shall be first given to the owner or proprietor of said lot, tract of land, house, or improvements, or his agent, at the time said work is begun, or materials furnished by said journeymen or other person.

When any debt is contracted by the master, owner, agent, or consignee, of any steam or keel boat within this state, by and on account of any work done, or materials or articles furnished for or toward the building, repairing, fitting, furnishing, or equipping, such steam or keel boat, or for wages due to the hands thereof, such debt shall be a lien upon such steam or keel boat, her tackle and furniture; provided that suit be commenced within three months from the time said work is finished, or said materials or articles are furnished, or said wages fall due.

Chattel Mortgages.

These must be proved and recorded the same as mortgages on land, to make them valid as against *bona fide* creditors and purchasers.

Law Regulating Contracts.

No action shall be brought whereby to charge any executor or administrator, upon any special promise, to answer any debt or damages out of his own estate; or whereby to charge the defendant, upon any special promise, to answer for the debt, default, or miscarriage, of another person; or to charge any person upon any agreement made upon consideration of marriage; or upon any contract for the sale of lands, tenements, or hereditaments, or the making any lease thereof for a longer term than one year; or upon an agreement which is not to be performed within the space of one year from the making thereof, unless the promise or agreement upon which such action shall be brought, or some memorandum or note thereof, shall be in writing, and signed by the party to be charged therewith, or some other person by him thereunto lawfully authorized.

Limitation of Actions.

ACTIONS of account, and upon the case, except such accounts as concern the trade of merchandise between merchant and merchant, their factors or servants; actions of debt for arrearages of rent; actions of detinue, replevin, and trespass, *quare clausum fregit*, must be brought within three years next after the cause of action accrues.

Any contract or lending, without specialty, within six years from the time the cause of action accrues.

Actions of trespass, assault, battery, wounding, and imprisonment, within one year.

Actions of slander, within six months.

The same limitation applies to bonds, bills, and other securities, made transferable by law, after their assignment or endorsement, as is applicable to promissory notes.

There is the usual saving in favor of infants, *femme coverts*, and persons noncompos mentis, imprisoned, or beyond seas, of the term of limitation, after the removal of their respective disabilities.

Collection of Debts.

ATTACHMENT.—When the sheriff shall return that "the defendant is not to be found in his county," in civil cases, an attachment may issue against the property of a defendant who is a resident of the state.

When a creditor makes affidavit that his debtor so absconds or conceals himself that process can not be served on him, or is removing or about to remove himself or his property without the state, or is absconding or concealing himself or his property, or that he is a non-resident, and states therein the amount of his claim, a writ of attachment may issue against the property of the debtor.

Arrest for debt is abolished.

Deeds.

THESE must be sealed, and attested by two subscribing witnesses.

When the wife joins her husband in a conveyance, she must be privately examined, separate from her husband.

Form of Acknowledgment.

State of Tennessee, } ss.
Marion County, }

Personally appeared before me, JOHN JONES, *clerk of the county court of Marion*, the within-named JOHN DOE *with* SUSAN *his wife*, with whom I am personally acquainted, and who acknowledged that he executed the within deed for the purposes therein contained.

Witness my hand at office, this *tenth* day of *February*, one thousand eight hundred and *fifty-one*.

And SUSAN DOE *having also personally appeared before me, privately and apart from her husband, the said* JOHN DOE, *acknowledged the execution of said deed to have been done by her freely, voluntarily, and understandingly, without compulsion or restraint from her said husband, and for the purposes therein expressed.*

Witness JOHN JONES, clerk of said court, at office this *tenth* day of *December*, one thousand eight hundred and *fifty*.

Acknowledgments may be made before the clerk of any county court in the state.

If made out of the state, they may be acknowledged before a notary public under his seal of office, or before a judge of a supreme, circuit, or superior court of any state or territory of the United States. The judge must endorse thereon or append thereto a certificate of such acknowledgment, and the official character of such judge must be certified by the governor of such state or territory under the great seal thereof.

Deeds must be recorded in the office of the register of the county where the lands are situate.

Rights of Married Women.

WHEN any married woman shall, either before or after marriage, become entitled to any interest in any lands, tenements, hereditaments, or other real estate whatever, either by gift, devise, descent, or in any other mode, it shall not be lawful, by virtue of any judgment, decree, or execution against the husband of such married woman to sell or dispose of his interest in the real estate of the wife; or by virtue of the judgment, sentence, or decree, of any court in this state to dispossess or eject the husband and wife from the possession of the real estate of the wife acquired in any manner, either before or after marriage.

The exemption of the husband's interest in his wife's lands, shall not extend beyond his wife's life, nor shall the husband sell the same during his wife's lifetime, without her joining in the conveyance in the manner prescribed by existing laws, in which married women shall convey lands.

When any person shall die intestate, leaving no heirs-at-law capable of inheriting real estate under the laws of the state, but leaving a widow she is entitled in fee simple to all the real estate of which her husband died seized and possessed, after paying the debts of her husband.

DOWER.—A widow is entitled to dower of one third part of the lands, tenements, and hereditaments, of which her husband died seized or possessed.

Rate of Interest.

THE legal rate is six per cent.; and the person exacting more is liable to a fine of not less than the amount usuriously taken.

Wills.

WILLS must be in writing, signed by the testator, or some other person in his presence and by his express direction, and subscribed in the presence of the testator by two witnesses, no one of whom is interested in the will.

KENTUCKY.

Constitution adopted, 1850.—Square Miles, 40,500.—Population in 1850, 993,344.

Exemptions.

THERE is exempt from levy and sale on execution one work-beast, or yoke of oxen; one plough and gear, one axe, one hoe; two cows and calves; two beds, bedding, and furniture; one loom and spinning-wheels, and cards for the same; all the spun yarn and manufactured cloth and carpeting manufactured by the family, necessary for family use; one pot, one oven, half-dozen plates, half-dozen cups and saucers, one coffee-pot, one teapot, half-dozen knives and forks; one table; the family Bible; one saddle and its appendages, one bridle; six chairs, not exceeding eight dollars in value; poultry of their own rearing, or purchased for family use; five head of sheep, and wearing-apparel; and to a mechanic his tools, not exceeding one hundred dollars in value; but the work-beast of any mechanic who claims his tools, shall be liable to execution. The officer is also required to set apart to each defendant by two disinterested housekeepers as much provisions, including breadstuffs and animal food, and as much wood or stone-coal laid in for family consumption as fuel, as will be sufficient for such defendants and his, her, or their family or families, for six months from and after the time of levy.

Mechanics' Lien.

IN the towns of Bowling-Green, Russellville, and Owenborough, the city of Maysville, the town of Brandenburgh, the city of Lexington, and in the town of Paducah, the mechanics have a lien for their labor and materials furnished in the construction or repair of any buildings, upon the building and the lot of land on which it is situate, provided they file their amounts in the county court clerk's office within six months from the time they cease to work, and proceed to enforce their lien by suit.

In Paducah, they may enforce their lien within one year by bill filed in the M'Cracken circuit court.

Chattel Mortgages.

CHATTEL mortgages must be acknowledged and recorded the same as deeds of real estate.

Law regulating Contracts.

NO action shall be brought whereby to charge any executor or administrator, upon any special promise, to answer any debt or damages out of his own estate; or whereby to charge the defendant, upon any special promise, to answer for the debt, default or miscarriage of another person; or to charge any person upon any agreement made upon consideration of marriage; or upon any contract for the sale of lands, tenements, or hereditaments, or the making any lease thereof for a longer term than one year; or upon any agreement which is not to be performed within the space of one year from the making thereof; unless the promise or agreement upon which such action shall be brought, or some memorandum or note thereof, shall be in writing, and signed by the party to be charged therewith, or by some other person by him thereunto lawfully authorized.

KENTUCKY.

KENTUCKY
Scale of miles
10 30 50 70
12
11
10
9
39
38
ILLINOIS
INDIANA
Bloomfield
White Riv.
Wabash R.
Evansville
Fredonia
Benton
Ohio River
Mississippi R.
Tennessee R.
Cumberland R.
Clarksville
Dresden
HENDERSON
UNION
Morganfield
HOPKINS
Madisonville
CRITTENDEN
LIVINGSTON
Smithland
CALDWELL
Princeton
MUHLENBURG
Greenville
OHIO
Hartford
GRAYSON
Litchfield
HANCOCK
BRECKENRIDGE
Hardinsburg
MEADE
Brandenburg
Owensboro
DAVIESS
Green R.
BUTLER
Morgan T.
EDMONSON
Brownsville
WARREN
Bowling Green
Barren R.
ALLEN
Scottsv.
SIMPSON
Franklin
LOGAN
Russellville
TODD
Elkton
CHRISTIAN
Hopkinsville
TRIGG
Cadiz
CALLOWAY
Murray
MARSHALL
Benton
GRAVES
Mayfield
HICKMAN
Clinton
BALLARD
Blandv.
McCRACKEN
Paducah
FULTON
Mills Point
Feliciana
Lon. West from Washing

KENTUCKY.

OHIO
Ohio Riv.
Cincinnati
Covington
Newport
Lawrenceburg
Burlington
Independence
Alexandria
BOONE
KENTON
CAMPBELL
Carrollton
Madison
Warsaw
GALLATIN
PENDLETON
Falmouth
Williams T.
GRANT
Augusta
BRACKEN
Washington
Maysville
Portsmouth
Greenupsburg
Clarksburg
MASON
LEWIS
GREENUP
CARROLL
TRIMBLE
Bedford
New Castle
HENRY
Owenton
OWEN
Clays V.
HARRISON
Cynthiana
NICHOLAS
Carlisle
Flemingsburg
FLEMING
Grayson
CARTER
OLDHAM
FRANKLIN
SCOTT
SHELBY
Shelby V.
George town
BOURBON
Paris
BATH
Owingsville
West Liberty
Louisa
LAWRENCE
Big Sandy R.
FRANKFORT
Versailles
Lexington
Mt. Sterling
Lawrence burg
Taylors V.
WOOD FORD
FAYETTE
CLARK
Winchester
MONTGOMERY
Licking R.
MORGAN
JOHNSON
Paintville
SPENCER
ANDERSON
Nicholas V.
Kentucky R.
JESSAMINE
MADISON
ESTILL
NELSON
MERCER
Harrodsburg
WASHINGTON
Springfield
Danville
GARRARD
Richmond
Irving
Jackson
Prestonburg
Piketon
Proctor
BREATHITT
FLOYD
PIKE
MARION
Lebanon
BOYLE
Lancaster
OWSLEY
Stanford
LINCOLN
ROCKCASTLE
Mt. Vernon
PERRY
Hazard
Greensburg
Liberty
CASEY
LETCHER
Whitesburg
GREEN
CLAY
Columbia
Somerset
London
Manchester
PULASKI
LAUREL
ADAIR
Jamestown
RUSSELL
Barboursville
Mt. Pleasant
HARLAN
Monticello
Williamsburg
KNOX
CUMBERLAND
Albany
Newberry
WAYNE
WHITLEY
CLINTON
VIRGINIA
TENNESSEE
Clinch R.
Holston R.
8
7
6
39
38
37

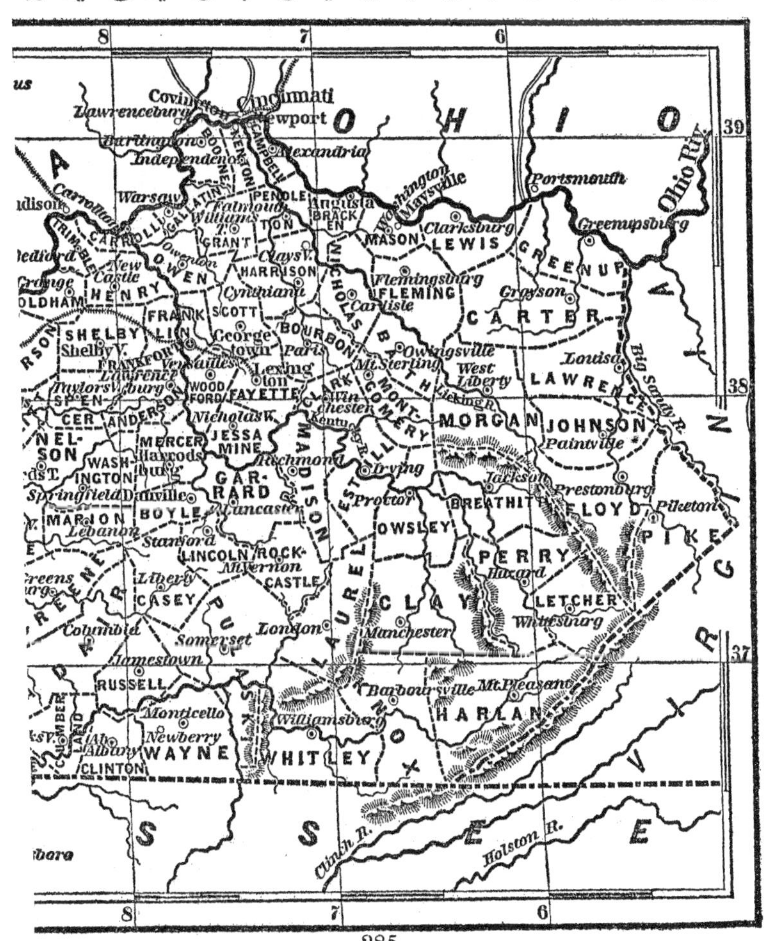

Limitation of Actions.

An action for the recovery of real property can only be brought within fifteen years after the right to bring it first accrued to the plaintiff, or to the person through whom he claims.

If, at the time when the right of any person to bring an action for the recovery of real property first accrued, such person was an infant, married woman, or of unsound mind, then such person, or the person claiming through him, may, notwithstanding the period of fifteen years has expired, bring the action within three years after the time at which the person to whom the right so accrued ceased to be under such disability as existed when the same so accrued, or died—whichever has happened first.

The period within which an action for the recovery of real property may be brought, shall not in any case be extended beyond thirty years from the time at which the right to bring the same first accrued to the plaintiff, or to the person through whom he claimed, by reason of any death, or the existence or continuance of any disability whatever.

An action upon a judgment or decree of any court of the United States, or of any state or territory within the United States, the period to be computed from the date of the last execution regularly issued thereon; and an action upon a recognizance or a written contract other than one for which a different limitation is hereinafter prescribed, must be brought within fifteen years.

An action upon the official bond of a sheriff, marshal, sergeant, clerk, constable, or other public officer or his deputy: an action upon the official bond of a personal representative, guardian, curator, or committee: an action upon a bond for an appeal, supersedeas, attachment, injunction, or order of arrest, or for the delivery of property: or a bond for the forthcoming of property, or to obey or perform an order or judgment of a court in an action; or a bond for costs, or any other bond taken by a court or judge, or by an officer pursuant to the direction of a court or judge in an action, or upon a replevin, sale, or delivery bond taken under an execution or warrant of distress: an action upon an indemnifying bond taken under a statute, or upon a bond to suspend a proceeding or sale under an execution, or distress warrant, must be brought within ten years.

An action against a surety in any recognizance, bond, or contract, except where a shorter period is hereinafter prescribed: an action upon a contract, express or implied, other than one for which a different limitation is herein prescribed: an action upon a liability created by statute other than a penalty or forfeiture: an action for trespass upon real property, for the profits of, or damages for withholding real property; for taking, detaining, or injuring personal property, including actions for the specific recovery thereof; for an injury to the rights of the plaintiff not arising on contract and not hereinafter enumerated: an action upon a bill of exchange, check, draft, or order, or upon a promissory note placed upon the footing of a bill of exchange: an action to enforce the liability of a steamboat or other vessel, in a case in which it is specifically subject, by statute, to the plaintiff's claim: an action upon an account concerning the trade of merchandise between merchant and merchant or their agents: and an action for relief on the ground of fraud, must be brought within five years.

An action for an injury to the person of the plaintiff or of his wife, child, ward, or servant other than a slave; for malicious prosecution or arrest; for seduction, criminal conversation, or breach of promise of marriage; upon a statute for a penalty or forfeiture, other than those for which a different limitation is prescribed in this chapter: an action for libel or slander; for the escape of a prisoner arrested or imprisoned on civil process; to enforce the liability of bail, or of a sheriff or other officer as bail, must be brought within one year after the cause of action accrued.

And an action upon an account for goods, wares, and merchandise, sold and delivered, or for any article charged in a store account, must be brought within one year. In every such action, the limitation shall be computed from the first day of January next succeeding the respective dates or times of delivery of the several articles charged in the account; and judgment shall be rendered for no more than the amount of such articles as were actually charged or delivered within the year preceding that in which the action is brought.

If any merchant or trader shall wilfully post-date any article charged in such account, or the receipt for the delivery thereof, he shall forfeit tenfold the amount of such article, to be recovered by any person, with costs, before a justice, where the penalty does not exceed fifty dollars; and where it does exceed that sum, in the circuit court.

Collection of Debts.

Arrest.—A defendant in a civil action can be arrested and held to bail only when there is filed in the office of the clerk of the court in which the action is brought an affidavit of the plaintiff, showing—

1. The nature of the plaintiff's claim. 2. That it is just. 3. The amount or value which the deponent believes the plaintiff ought to recover. 4. That the deponent believes, either that the defendant is about to depart from this state, and, with intent to defraud his creditors, has concealed or removed from this state his property or so much thereof that the process of the court after judgment can not be executed, or that the defendant has money, or

securities for money, or evidences of debt, in the possession of himself or of others for his use, and is about to depart from this state without leaving property therein sufficient to satisfy the plaintiff's claim.

There must be a bond executed on the part of the plaintiff by one or more sufficient sureties, conditioned to pay to the defendant all damages if the order be wrongfully obtained, not exceeding double the amount of the plaintiff's claim.

ATTACHMENT.—An attachment against the property of the defendant may issue, first, in an action for the recovery of money where the action is against—1. A defendant or several defendants, who, or some one of whom, is a foreign corporation or a non-resident of this state: or—2. Who has been absent therefrom four months: or—3. Has departed from this state with intent to defraud his creditors: or—4. Has left the county of his residence to avoid the service of a summons: or—5. So conceals himself, that a summons can not be served upon him: or—6. Is about to remove his property or a material part thereof out of this state, not leaving enough therein to satisfy the plaintiff's claims: or—7. Has sold, conveyed, or otherwise disposed of his property, or suffered or permitted it to be sold, with the fraudulent intent to cheat, hinder, or delay his creditors: or—8. Is about to sell, convey, or otherwise dispose of his property, with such intent.

But an attachment shall not be granted on the ground that the defendant or defendants, or any of them, is a foreign corporation or a non-resident of this state, for any claim other than a debt or demand arising upon contract.

Secondly, in an action to recover the possession of personal property where it has been ordered to be delivered to the plaintiff, and where the property or part thereof has been disposed of, concealed, or removed, so that the order for its delivery can not be executed by the sheriff.

Deeds.

THESE must be in writing, sealed, and lodged for record in the office of the county court of the county where the land is situate within eight months.

They may be acknowledged in any county court, or in the office of any such court, before the clerk thereof, or proven by two witnesses.

Out of the state, before any judge or justice of a superior or inferior court of the county, district, or place, where they reside.

Form of Acknowledgment.

State of Kentucky,
County of *Livingston*, } to wit:

Be it remembered, that on this *first* day of *October*, one thousand eight hundred and *fifty*, before me, at office, JOHN JONES, *clerk of the county court* of said county, personally came JOHN DOE *and* SUSAN *his wife*: to me known to be the persons described in, and who executed the foregoing *conveyance*, and severally acknowledged that they executed the same; *and the said* SUSAN, *on an examination by me, privily and apart from her husband, declared that she did freely and willingly seal and deliver the said conveyance, which was then by me shown and explained to her, and that she wishes not to retract it, and acknowledged it to be her act, and consented that it may be recorded.*

Witness my hand and seal of court, at office, the day and year above written.

(Seal.) JOHN JONES, *Clerk of the County Court of the County of Livingston.*

Rights of Married Women.

THE slaves of a married woman and the increase thereof, and her real estate owned before or acquired after marriage, shall not be liable for the debts of her husband; but are liable for debts by her and her husband jointly created, in writing, for necessaries furnished her or any member of her family.

The estate and property of the husband shall not be subject to the payment of any contracts, liabilities, damages or debts, incurred by the wife prior to marriage.

Rate of Interest.

THE legal rate *is* six per cent. The usurious excess only is void.

Wills.

WILLS to be in writing, signed by the testator or by some other person in his presence and by his directions; and if not wholly written by himself, must be attested by two or more competent witnesses, subscribing their names in his presence.

OHIO.

OHIO.

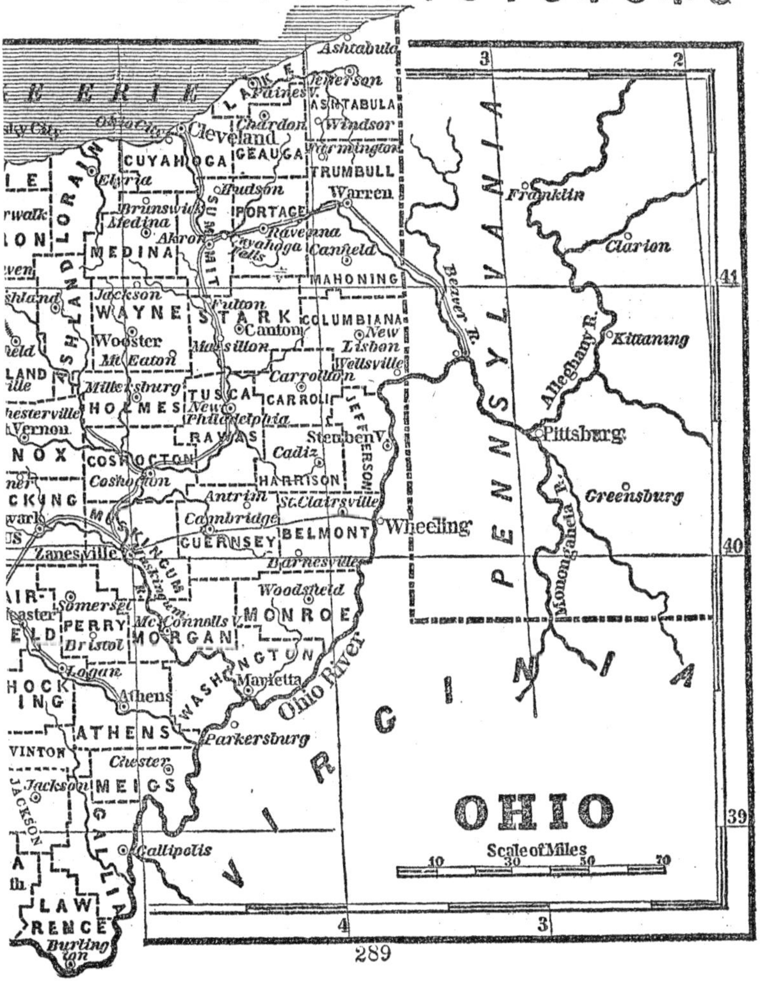

OHIO
Scale of Miles
PENNSYLVANIA
VIRGINIA
Cleveland
Pittsburg
Wheeling
Zanesville
Marietta
Ohio River

OHIO.

Constitution adopted, 1851.—Square miles, 39,964.—Population in 1850, 1,977,032.

Exemptions.

EVERY person who has a family shall hold exempt from execution—

1. The wearing-apparel of such family; the beds, bedsteads, and bedding, necessary for the use of such family; one stove and pipe, used either for cooking or for warming the dwelling-house; an amount of fuel sufficient for the period of sixty days, actually provided and designed for the use of such family.

2. One cow, or, if the debtor own no cow, household furniture, to be selected by the debtor, not exceeding fifteen dollars in value; two swine, or the pork therefrom; or, if the debtor own no swine, household or kitchen furniture, to be selected by the debtor, not exceeding six dollars in value; six sheep, the wool shorn from them, and the cloth or other articles manufactured therefrom; or, in lieu of such sheep, household and kitchen furniture, to be selected by the debtor, not exceeding ten dollars in value, and sufficient food for such animals, when owned by the debtor, for the period of sixty days.

3. The bibles, hymn-books, psalm-books, testaments, and schoolbooks, used in the family, and all family pictures.

4. Any amount of provisions actually prepared and designed for the sustenance of such family, not exceeding forty dollars in value, to be selected by the debtor; and such other articles of household and kitchen furniture, or either, necessary for the debtor and his family, and to be selected by the debtor, not exceeding thirty dollars in value.

5. The tools and implements of the debtor, necessary for carrying on his trade or business, whether mechanical or agricultural, to be selected by him, not exceeding fifty dollars in value.

In all cases arising under the first section of this act, the amount of beds, bedsteads, and bedding, necessary for the use of such family; the amount of fuel sufficient for the period of sixty days, actually provided and designed for the use of such family; the amount of food for the use of the animals exempted from execution for the period of sixty days, shall be determined by two disinterested householders of the county, to be selected by the officer holding the execution. And the value of the provisions, household and kitchen furniture, and the tools and implements of the debtor necessary for carrying on his trade or business, by this act exempt from execution, shall be estimated and appraised by said householders.

Burial-grounds, so recorded in the recorder's office of the county where situate, or used as such for fifteen years, are exempt from execution; notaries' seal, and his registers and official documents, are also exempt.

By the homestead law, which went into effect July 4, 1850, it is provided that "It shall be lawful for any resident of Ohio, being the head of the family, and *not* the owner of a homestead, to hold exempt from execution, or sale as aforesaid (see homestead exemption law), mechanical tools, or a team and farming utensils, not exceeding three hundred dollars in value, *in addition* to the amount of chattel property now exempted.

For MECHANICS' LIEN, see page 294.

Homestead-Exemption Law.

FROM and after July 4th, 1850, the family homestead of each head of a family shall be exempt from sale on execution on any judgment or decree rendered on any cause of action accruing after the taking effect of this act; provided that such homestead shall not exceed five hundred dollars in value.

The sheriff or other officer executing any writ of execution, founded on any judgment or decree such as is mentioned in the first section of this act, on application of the debtor or his wife, his agent, or attorney, if such debtor have a family, and the lands or tenements about to be levied on, or any part or parcel thereof, shall be the homestead thereof, shall cause the inquest of appraisers, upon their oaths, to set off to such debtor, by metes and bounds, a homestead not exceeding five hundred dollars in value, and the assignment of the homestead so made by the appraisers shall be returned by the sheriff, or other officer, along with his writ, and shall be copied by the clerk into the execution docket; and if no complaint be made by either party, no further proceedings shall be had against the homestead, but the remainder of the debtor's lands and tenements, if any more he shall have, shall be liable to sale on execution, in the same manner as if this act had not passed; provided, that upon complaint of either party, and upon good cause shown, the court out of which the writ issued, may order a re-appraisement and re-assignment of the homestead; provided, also, that in case no application be made as aforesaid during the lifetime of the debtor, such application may be made by the widow of the judgment debtor any time before a sale.

On petition of executors or administrators, to sell the lands of any decedent to pay debts, who shall have left a widow and a minor child or children, unmarried and composing part of decedent's family at the time of his death, the appraisers shall proceed to set apart a homestead in the same manner as is provided in the preceding section; and the same shall remain exempt from sale on execution for debts contracted after the taking effect of this act, and exempt from sale under any order of such court so long as any unmarried minor child, or children, shall reside thereon, although the widow may have previously died and the unmarried minor child, or children, actually residing on the family homestead, shall be entitled to hold the same exempt from sale on execution for debts as hereinbefore provided for, although the parent from whom the same descended may have left no wife or husband surviving.

Every widower, or widow, having an unmarried minor child, or children, residing with him, or her, as part of his or her family, shall have the benefit of this act, in the same manner as married persons. And married persons, living together as husband and wife, shall be entitled to the exemption in this act provided, although they have no children.

Any person owning the superstructure of a dwelling-house, occupied by him or her as a family homestead, shall be entitled to the benefit of this act, although the title to the land on which the same may be built shall be in another, and lessees shall be entitled to the benefits of this act, in the same manner as owners of the freehold or inheritance; provided, nothing herein contained shall be construed to prevent a sale of the fee simple subject to such lease.

When the homestead of any debtor in execution shall consist of a house and lot of land, which, in the opinion of the appraisers, will not bear division without manifest injury and inconvenience, the plaintiff in execution shall receive in lieu of the proceeds of the sale of the homestead, the amount, over and above forty dollars annually, which shall be adjudged by the appraisers heretofore mentioned, as a fair and reasonable rent for the same, until the debt, costs, and interest, are paid, the said rent over and above the said forty dollars shall be payable in quarterly payments, commencing three months from the time of the levy of the execution, and the said rent may be paid to the plaintiff in execution or to his assigns, or to the clerk of the court of common pleas of the county in which the said homestead is situated, and the said clerk shall give to the persons paying the same a proper receipt, and enter the same upon the execution docket without charge, and in case the said rent shall not be paid quarter yearly as above provided for or within ten days after each and every payment shall become due, then, in that case, it shall be the duty of the officer to proceed and sell said homestead in the same manner as is provided in other cases for the sale of real estate; provided such homestead shall not be sold for less than its appraised value, and the plaintiff in execution may cause the said homestead to be re-appraised once in two years in the same manner as provided for in the second section of this act, and the said rent shall, after such re-appraisement, be paid in accordance with the said re-appraisement, but in case the said homestead shall not on any such re-appraisement be appraised at least one hundred dollars more than the next previous appraisement, the costs of such re-appraisement shall be paid by the plaintiff in execution.

The provisions of this act shall not extend to any judgment or decree rendered on any contract made before the taking effect of this act, or judgment or decree rendered on any note or mortgage executed by the debtor and his wife, nor any claim for work and labor less than one hundred dollars, nor to impair the lien by mortgage or otherwise of the vender for the purchase-money of the homestead in question, nor of any mechanic or other person, under any statute of this state, for materials furnished or labor performed in the erection of the dwelling-house thereon, nor from the payment of taxes due thereon.

No sale of any real estate made under any mortgage hereafter executed and which shall not have been executed by the wife of such debtor, if he have one, shall in any manner affect the right of said debtor's wife or family to have a homestead set off under the provisions of this act.

Nothing in this act contained shall be so construed as in any way to impair the right of dower, as it now exists, or the mode provided by law for enforcing the right.

Chattel Mortgages.

THESE must be immediately deposited with the county recorder when executed in a shire town, or with the clerk of the township where the mortgager resides, or if he be not a resident, where the property mortgaged is at the time of the execution of the mortgage, or they will be void. Such record is valid for one year only.

Law regulating Contracts.

No action shall be brought whereby to charge the defendant, upon any special promise, to answer for the debt, default, or miscarriage, of another person; or to charge any executor or administrator, upon any special promise, to answer damages out of his own estate; or to charge any person, upon any agreement made upon consideration of marriage; or upon any contract or sale of lands, tenements, or hereditaments, or any interest in or concerning them; or upon any agreement that is not to be performed within the space of one year from the making thereof; unless the agreement upon which such action shall be brought, or some memorandum or note thereof, shall be in writing and signed by the party to be charged therewith, or some other person thereunto by him or her lawfully authorized.

Limitation of Actions.

1. ACTIONS of ejectment, or any other action for the recovery of the title or possession of lands, tenements, or hereditaments, must be brought within twenty-one years.
2. Actions for forcible entry and detainer, or forcible detainer only, within two years.
3. Actions upon the case, covenant, and debt, founded upon a specialty, or any agreement, contract, or promise, in writing, within fifteen years.
4. Actions upon the case and debt, founded upon any simple contract not in writing, and actions on the case for consequential damages, within six years.
5. Actions of trespass upon property, real or personal, detinue, trover, and replevin, within four years.
6. Actions of trespass for any injury done to the person; actions of slander for words spoken or for a libel; actions for malicious prosecutions, and for false imprisonment; actions against officers for malfeasance or nonfeasance in office; and actions of debt *qui tam*, within one year. All other actions not above enumerated within four years after the right of action shall have accrued.

Collection of Debts.

ARREST.—Each and every officer and soldier of the revolutionary war, and each and every female, shall be privileged from arrest or imprisonment on any process, mesne or final, for any debt, claim, or demand, where the cause of the action is founded upon contract.

Any person, desirous of having his body exempted from liability to imprisonment for debt, who shall have resided in this state two years next preceding his application, and in the county where such application is made six months next preceding such application, shall deliver to the commissioner of insolvents an accurate schedule in writing of all debts by him owing, specifying the name of the person to whom due, and the original consideration of such debt, and whether the same is due by bond, note, or other contract, in writing, or by book-account, or otherwise, &c.

The commissioner is empowered to give a certificate, which shall protect the person of the applicant from arrest or imprisonment for any debt or demand in any civil action at the suit of any person named in the schedule, until the second day of that term of the court of common pleas to which the commissioner shall return copies.

§ 1. No person shall be arrested or imprisoned on any mesne or final writ or process issuing out of any court of law or equity, in any suit, action, or proceeding, instituted for the recovery of any debt due on any contract, promise, or agreement, or for the recovery of damages for the non-performance of any contract, promise, or agreement, or for the recovery of damages in any action of trespass, or on any judgment or decree founded upon any such contract, promise or agreement, or damages for the non-performance thereof, or on any judgment in action of trespass, or for consequential damages, except in cases hereinafter specified.

§ 2. The provisions of the first session shall not extend to proceedings for contempts, actions, or judgments, for fines or penalties for crimes, misdemeanors, or offences, prosecuted in the name of the state of Ohio, or on promises to marry, for money collected by any public officer or attorney-at-law, or for any misconduct or neglect in office, or professional employment.

§ 3. If any creditor, his authorized agent or attorney, shall make oath or affirmation in writing before any judge of the supreme court or court of common pleas, justice of the peace. or clerk of either of said courts, that there is debt or demand justly due to such creditor of one hundred dollars or upward, specifying as nearly as may be the nature and amount thereof and establishing one or more of the following particulars:—

1. That the defendant is about to remove his property out of the jurisdiction of the court, with intent to defraud his creditors; or—2. That he is about to convert his property into money, for the purpose of placing it beyond the reach of his creditors; or—3. That he has property or rights in action which he fraudulently conceals; or—4. That he has resigned, removed, or disposed of, or is about to dispose of, his property, with intent to defraud his creditors; or—5. That he fraudulently contracted the debt or incurred the obligation for which suit is about to be brought, and shall file such affidavit with the clerk of the court of common pleas of the proper county, such clerk shall issue a *capias*.

§ 4. After a judgment or decree has been obtained, the defendant may be arrested on *capias ad satisfaciendum*, if the court when in session or any judge thereof in vacation shall be satisfied by the affidavit of the judgment creditor or his lawful attorney, and such other testimony as he shall present, of the existence of either of the following particulars:—1. That the judgment debtor has removed or is about to remove any of his property out of the jurisdiction of the court, with intent to prevent the collection of the money due on the judgment or decree;—2. That he has property, rights in action, evidences of debt, or some interest or stock in some corporation or company, which he fraudulently conceals, or unjustly refuses to apply to the payment of the judgment or decree; or—3. That he has assigned or disposed of, or is about to assign or dispose of his property or rights in action, with intent to defraud his creditors, or give an unfair preference to some of them; or—4. That he has converted or is about to convert his property into money, with intent to prevent its being taken on execution; or—5. That he fraudulently contracted the debt or incurred the obligation on which the judgment or decree was rendered.

If the plaintiff, his agent or attorney, shall make and file his affidavit that the defendant or debtor is about to remove his body out of the jurisdiction of the court; or that he has converted his property into money, for the purpose of placing it beyond the reach of his creditors; or that he is not a citizen or resident of this state, it shall be deemed additional cause to those mentioned in the third and fourth sections to entitle the plaintiff to a *capias ad respondendum or capias ad satisfaciendum.*

ATTACHMENT.—If any creditor, his agent or attorney, shall file an affidavit with any justice of the peace within this state, setting forth that his debtor absconds to the injury of his creditor, or that such debtor is not a resident of the county, as he verily believes, the said justice shall thereupon issue a writ of attachment under his hand and seal, directed to any constable of his proper county, commanding him to execute the same on the goods, chattels, rights, credits, money, and effects, of the defendant, within the county. and make return thereof within twenty days.

A creditor, making the like affidavit, and filing it with the clerk of the court of common pleas, may have an attachment against the lands, tenements, goods, chattels, rights, credits, moneys, and effects, of the debtor.

Deeds.

§ 1. A SCRAWL of the pen may be used instead of a seal.

A conveyance of interest in lands must be signed and sealed by the grantors, and such signing and sealing acknowledged before two witnesses, who shall attest such signing and sealing, and subscribe their names to such attestation and such signing and sealing, also acknowledged by the grantors before a judge of the supreme court, of common pleas, a justice of the peace, notary public, mayor or other presiding officer of any incorporated town or city, who shall certify such acknowledgment on the same sheet on which such deed, &c., may be printed or written.

§ 2. When a husband and wife, she being eighteen years of age or upward, shall execute within this state any deed, &c., for the conveyance or incumbrance of the estate of the wife or her right of dower in any lands, &c., situate within this state, such deed, &c., shall be signed and sealed by the husband and wife, and such signing and sealing shall be attested and acknowledged in the manner prescribed in section first; and in addition thereto, the officer before whom such acknowledgment shall be made shall examine the wife separate and apart from her husband, and shall read or otherwise make known to her the contents of such deed, mortgage, or other instrument of writing; and if, upon such separate examination, she shall declare that she did voluntarily sign, seal, and acknowledge the same, and that she is still satisfied therewith, such officer shall certify such examination and declaration of the wife, together with the acknowledgment as aforesaid on such deed, &c., and subscribe his name thereto.

§ 5. All deeds, powers of attorney, &c., for the conveyance or incumbrance of lands, &c., situate within this state, executed and acknowledged or proved in any other state, territory, or country, in conformity with the laws of such state, &c., or of this state, shall be as valid as if executed within this state, in conformity with this act.

The governor of the state may appoint commissioners to take acknowledgment of deeds, depositions, &c., residing out of the state to convey lands, or to be used in the state.

Form of Acknowledgment.

State of Ohio, } ss.
Cuyahoga County, } *April* 24, 1851.

Personally appeared SAM HILL *and* MARY *his wife*, who acknowledged that they did sign and seal the foregoing instrument, and that the same is their free act and deed.

I further certify that I did examine the said MARY HILL *separate and apart from her said husband, and did then and there make known to her the contents of the foregoing instrument; and upon that examination she declared that she did voluntarily sign, seal, and acknowledge the same, and that she was still satisfied therewith.* *(Seal.)* JOHN ROGERS, *Notary.*

Rights of Married Women.

The interest of any married man in the real estate of his wife, and the interest he may have in any chose in action, demand, legacy, or bequest of his wife unless the same shall have been reduced to possession, together with all articles of furniture of hers given her by bequest or otherwise, or bought with her money, before or after marriage, are exempt from liability for the husband's debts.

DOWER.—A widow is endowed of one full and equal third part of all the lands, tenements, and real estate, of which her husband was seized at any time during the coverture.

Rate of Interest.

THE legal rate is six per cent. On written agreement, any rate as high as ten per cent. If more be reserved, the excess is void.

Wills.

EVERY will shall be in writing (except nuncupative), and signed at the end thereof by the party making the same, or by some other person in his presence and by his express direction, and shall be attested and subscribed in the presence of such party by two or more competent witnesses, who saw the testator subscribe or heard him acknowledge the same.

Mechanics' Lien.

ANY person who shall perform labor, or furnish materials or machinery, for constructing, altering, or repairing, any boat, vessel, or other water-craft, or for erecting or repairing any house, mill, manufactory, or other building or appurtenance, by virtue of a contract or agreement with the owner thereof, shall have a lien to secure the payment of the same, upon such boat, vessel, or other water-craft, and upon such house, mill, manufactory, or other building or appurtenance, and the lot of land upon which the same shall stand.

Every mechanic, or other person, doing or performing any work toward the erection or repair of any house, mill, manufactory, or other building or appurtenance, or the construction, alteration, or repair, of any boat, vessel, or other water-craft, erected under a contract between the owner thereof and the builder, or other person, whether such work shall be performed as journeyman, laborer, carman, sub-contractor, or otherwise, or any person who shall furnish materials for work so done, or materials so furnished, has not been paid and satisfied, may deliver to the owner of such building, or vessel, an attested account of the amount and value of the work and labor thus performed, or the materials thus furnished, and remaining unpaid, and thereupon such owner shall retain out of his subsequent payments to the contractor, the amount of such work or labor, for the benefit of the person so performing the same.

The person wishing to avail himself of the provisions of this law, must make out an account in writing, of the items of labor, skill, materials, &c., against the party owing him, and make oath thereto before a magistrate, and have the account so sworn to deposited with the recorder of the county where the labor was performed, within four months from the time of performing such labor, or furnishing such materals, &c., and file with this account a copy of any written contract, if such there be.

MICHIGAN.

Constitution adopted 1850—Square Miles 56,243—Population in 1850, 395,576.

Exemptions.

THE following property is exempt from levy and sale under any execution or upon any other final process of a court. All spinning-wheels, weaving-looms, with the apparatus, and stoves put up or kept for use in any dwelling-house; a seat, pew, or slip, occupied by any person or family, in any house or place of worship; all cemeteries, tombs, and rights of burial while in use as repositories of the dead; all arms and accoutrements required by law to be kept by any person; all wearing apparel of every person or family; the library and schoolbooks of every individual and family, not exceeding one hundred and fifty dollars, and all family pictures. To each householder, ten sheep with their fleeces, and the yarn or cloth manufactured from the same; two cows, five swine, and provisions and fuel for the comfortable subsistence of such householder and family for six months; to each householder all household goods, furniture, and utensils, not exceeding in value two hundred and fifty dollars; a sufficient quantity of hay, grain, feed, and roots, for properly keeping for six months the animals exempted as aforesaid; and any chattel mortgage, bill of sale, or lien, created on any property exempted, except what is specified in the next section, shall be void unless the same is signed by the wife.

The tools, implements, materials, stock, apparatus, team, vehicle, horse, harness, or other things, to enable any person to carry on the profession, trade, occupation, or business, in which he is wholly or principally engaged, not exceeding in value two hundred and fifty dollars.*

By the constitution, the personal property of every resident of this state, to consist of such property only as shall be designated by law, shall be exempted to the amount of not less than five hundred dollars, from sale on execution or other final process of any court issued for the collection of any debt contracted after the adoption of this constitution, January 1, 1851.

Homestead-Exemption Law.

A HOMESTEAD consisting of any quantity of land not exceeding forty acres, and the dwelling-house thereon and its appurtenances, to be selected by the owner thereof, and not included in any recorded town-plat, or city, or village; or instead thereof, at the option of the owner, a quantity of land not exceeding in amount one lot, being within a recorded town-plat, or city, or village, and the dwelling-house thereon and its appurtenances, owned and occupied by any resident of this state (not exceeding in value fifteen hundred dollars, by the constitution of 1851), shall not be subject to forced sale on execution, or any other final process from a court, for any debt or debts, growing out of or founded upon contract, either express or implied, made after the third day of July, in the year of our Lord, one thousand eight hundred and forty-eight. Said homestead is exempt during the minority of his children, and if no children but widow, it shall be exempt, and rents and profits thereof shall accrue to her during her widowhood, unless she is the owner of a homestead in her own right.

* The property exempted in this division, except mechanical tools, and implements of husbandry, are not exempt from execution in judgment for purchase-money of the same.

MICHIGAN.

42
43
44
9
8
6
5
Lon. West from Washington
INDIANA
OHIO
CANADA
L. ERIE
SAGINAW BAY
VAN BUREN
ALLEGAN
BARRY
KENT
OCEANA
NEWAYGO
MASON
LAKE
OSCEOLA
CLARE
ISABELLA
MIDLAND
GRATIOT
IONIA
EATON
CALHOUN
JACKSON
WASHTENAW
WAYNE
OAKLAND
MACOMB
LAPEER
TUSCOLA
SANILAC
HURON
WEXFORD
ROSCOMMON
IOSCO
ALCONA
ALPENA
OTSEGO
Toledo
Detroit
Ypsilanti
Jackson
Marshall
Hastings
Charlotte
Lansing
Mason
Howell
Pontiac
Flint
Saginaw
Lapeer
Adrian
Tecumseh
Monroe
Niles
Cassopolis
Coldwater
Hillsdale
Paw Paw
Kalamazoo
Grandville
Ionia
Corunna
Sandwich
Amherstburg
Port Huron

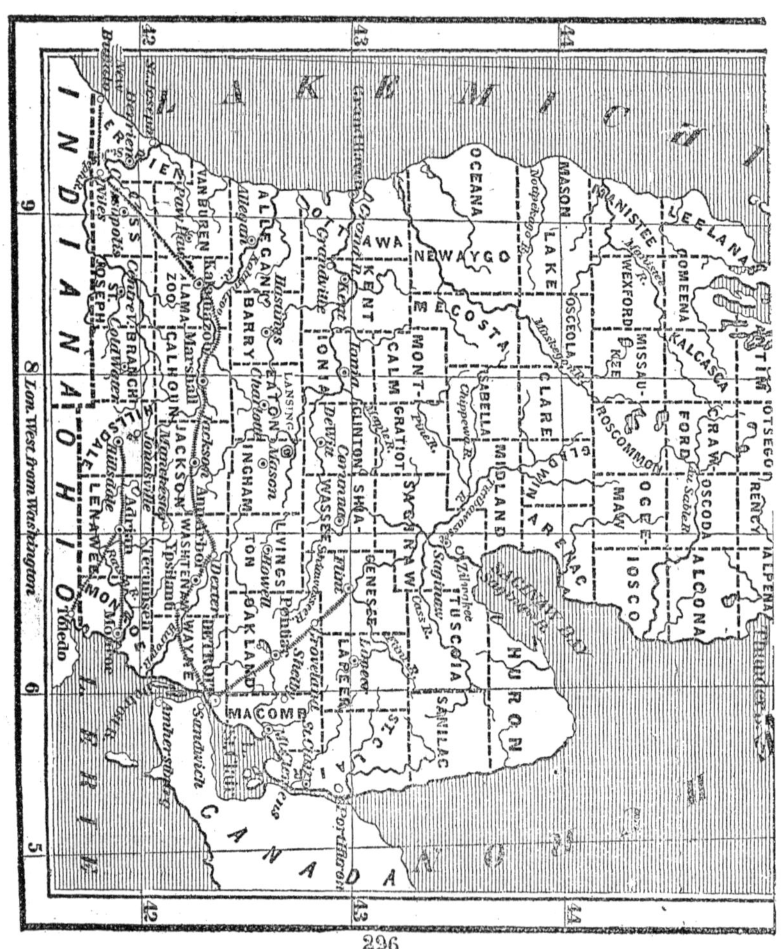

MICHIGAN.

MICHIGAN
10 20 30 40 50 60 Miles
MICHIGAN
WESTERN PART
LAKE SUPERIOR
SCHOOLCRAFT
DELTA
CHIPPEWA
MICHILIMACKINAC
ONTONAGON
MARQUETTE
WISCONSIN
CANADA
White Fish Pt.
Sault St. Mary's
Falls of St. Mary's
St. Josephs I.
Drummonds I.
Great Manitoulin I.
Mackinaw
Manistic R.
Ontonagon R.
Menomonee R.
Kewenaw R.
Kewenaw Pt.
Huron
St. Johns R.
EMMET
CHEBOYGAN
WYANDOT
PRESQUE ISLE

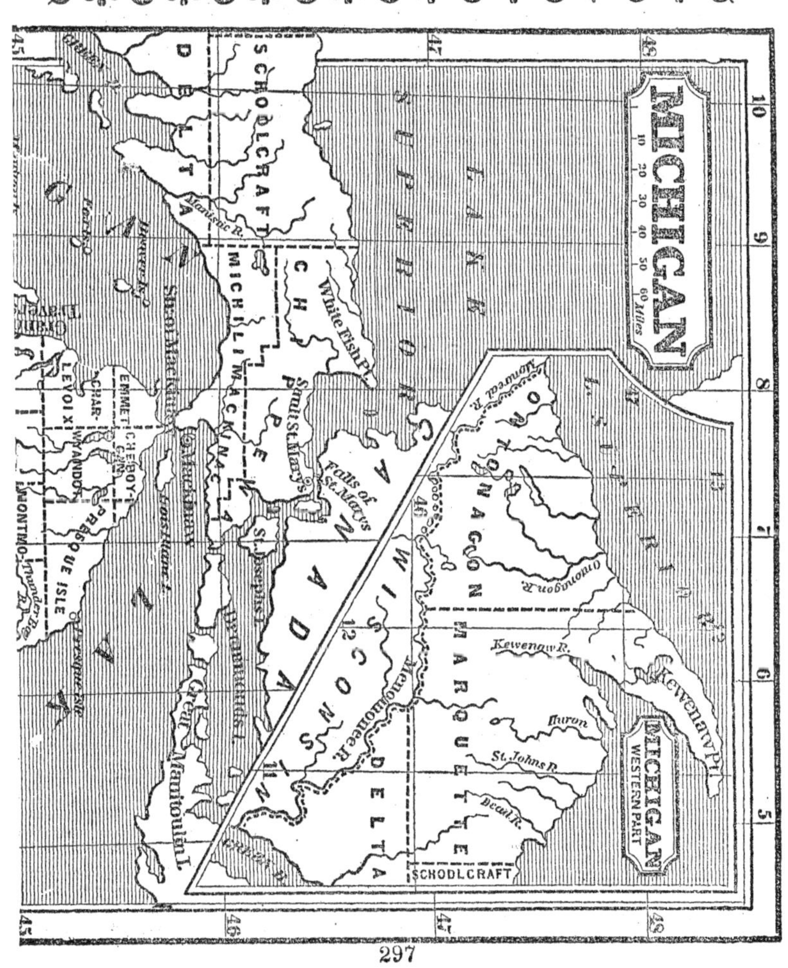

Such exemption shall not extend to any mortgage thereon lawfully obtained; but such mortgage or other alienation of such land by the owner thereof, if a married man, shall not be valid without the signature of the wife to the same, unless such mortgage shall be given to secure the payment of the purchase-money or some portion thereof.

Whenever a levy shall be made upon the lands or tenements of a householder, whose homestead has not been selected and set apart by metes and bounds, such householder may notify the officer, at the time of making such levy, of what he regards as his homestead, with a description thereof, within the limits above prescribed, and the remainder alone shall be subject to sale under such levy.

If the plaintiff in execution shall be dissatisfied with the quantity of land selected and set apart as aforesaid, the officer making the levy shall cause the same to be surveyed, beginning at a point to be designated by the owner, and set off in a compact form, including the dwelling-house and its appurtenances, the amount specified in the first section of this act, and the expense of said survey, shall be chargeable on the execution, and collected thereupon.

After the survey shall have been made, the officer making the levy may sell the property levied upon, and not included in the set-off, in the same manner as provided in other cases for the sale of real estate on execution; and in giving a deed of the same, he may describe it according to his original levy, excepting therefrom by metes and bounds, according to the certificate of the survey, the quantity set off as aforesaid.

Any person owning and occupying any house on land not his own, and claiming such house as his homestead, shall be entitled to the exemption as aforesaid.

Nothing in this act shall be considered as exempting any real estate from taxation or sale for taxes.

Mechanics' Lien.

EVERY building shall be subject to the payment of the debts contracted for work or material in the erection and construction thereof, when the building or any part thereof, is constructed under contract entered into by the owner with any person to do work or furnish materials; provided such lien shall not attach unless the contract is made in writing and signed by the owner of such building or by some person duly authorized by him, and recorded in the registry of deeds for the county where the land lies.

Every person furnishing labor or materials for erecting or repairing any building or the appurtenances thereof by contract with the owner of any piece of land, shall have a lien on the whole piece of land, not exceeding one hundred and sixty acres, for the amount due him therefor; provided the contract is in writing, and signed by the owner of the land or some one duly authorized by him, and recorded in the registry of deeds for the county where the land lies.

The lien ceases at the expiration of six months after the time when the money or the last instalment shall become payable, unless a suit shall have been commenced to enforce such lien within said six months.

Chattel Mortgages.

No chattel mortgage is valid as against creditors and purchasers and mortgagees in good faith, unless the mortgage or a true copy thereof shall be filed in the office of township clerk of the township, or city clerk of the city where such mortgagor resides. Every such mortgage shall cease to be valid as against creditors, subsequent purchasers, and mortgagees in good faith, after the expiration of one year from filing the same, unless within thirty days next preceding expiration of the year, the mortgagee, his agent or attorney, shall make and annex to the instrument on file, an affidavit setting forth the interest which the mortgagee has by virtue of such mortgage in the property therein mentioned, and the mortgage must be renewed from year to year, in manner aforesaid.

Law Regulating Contracts.

In the following cases, every agreement, contract, and promise, shall be void, unless the same, or some note or memorandum thereof, be in writing, and signed by the party to be charged therewith, or by some person thereunto by him lawfully authorized:—

1. Every agreement that, by its terms, is not to be performed in one year from the making thereof. 2. Every special promise to answer for the debt, default, or misdoings of another person. 3. Every agreement, promise, or undertaking, made upon consideration of marriage, except mutual promises to marry. 4. Every special promise made by an executor or administrator to answer damages out of his own estate.

No contract for the sale of any goods, wares, or merchandise, for the price of fifty dollars or more, shall be good or valid, unless the purchaser shall accept and receive part of the goods so sold, or shall give something in earnest to bind the bargain, or in part payment, or unless some note or memorandum in writing of the bargain be made and signed by the party to be charged thereby or by some person thereunto by him lawfully authorized.

No action shall be brought to charge any person upon or by reason of any favorable representation or assurance made concerning the character, conduct, credit, ability, trade, or dealings, of any other person, unless such representation or assurance be made in writing, and signed by the party to be charged thereby, or by some person thereunto by him lawfully authorized.

The consideration need not be expressed in such written contract, note, or memorandum.

Limitation of Actions.

The following actions must be brought within six years after the cause of action accrues:—

1. All actions of debt, founded upon any contract or liability not under seal, except such as are brought upon the judgment or decree of some court of record of the United States, or of this or of some other of the United States. 2. All actions upon judgments rendered in any court other than those above excepted. 3. All actions for arrears of rent. 4. All actions of assumpsit or upon the case, founded on any contract or liability, express or implied. 5. All actions of waste. 6. All actions of replevin and trover, and all other actions for taking, detaining, or injuring, goods or chattels. 7. All other actions on the case, except actions for slanderous words or for libels.

All actions for trespass upon land, or for assault and battery, and for false imprisonment, and slanderous words and libels, shall bo commenced within two years.

All personal actions upon other contracts must be brought within ten years, and not after.

Infants, *femme coverts*, persons insane, imprisoned, or absent from the United States, at the time any cause of action accrues on their behalf, may bring the same within the times respectively limited after the removal of their disability.

The foregoing limitations do not apply to bills or notes issued by a bank.

In cases of mutual account, the cause of action shall be deemed to have accrued at the time of the last item proved.

When any person is absent from the state at the time a cause of action accrues against him, or subsequently leaves the state, such period of absence is not to be computed.

In actions upon any contract, no promise or acknowledgment shall take a case out of the operation of the statute, unless the same is made or contained by or in some writing; nor can one of two or more joint contractors or executors deprive the other of the benefit of the statute, by any written acknowledgment.

Collection of Debts.

ARREST.—No person shall be arrested on demand arising out of contract, except promises to marry, or for moneys collected by any public officer, or for any misconduct or neglect in office or in any professional employment, unless satisfactory evidence is adduced by the affidavit of the plaintiff or some other person, that there is a debt due the plaintiff from the defendant, specifying the nature and amount thereof as near as may be, for which the defendant can not be arrested, and establishing—

1. That the defendant is about to remove any of his property out of the jurisdiction of the court in which suit is brought, with intent to defraud his creditors; or, 2. That the defendant has property, or rights in action, or some interest in any public or corporate stock, money, or evidence of debt, which he unjustly refuses to apply to the payment of such judgment or decree as shall have been rendered against him, or which he fraudulently conceals; 3. That he has assigned, removed, or disposed of, or is about to dispose of, any of his property or rights in action, with the intent to defraud his creditors; or, 4. That the defendant fraudulently contracted the debt or incurred the obligation respecting which suit is brought.

ATTACHMENT.—Upon an affidavit being made by the creditor or some person in his behalf, stating that the defendant is justly indebted to the creditor in a sum therein mentioned according to the belief of the deponent, and being more than one hundred dollars, and that the same is due upon a contract, express or implied, or a judgment rendered on such contract; and further, that, deponent knows or has good reason to believe, either—

1. That the defendant has absconded, or is about to abscond, from this state, or that he is concealed therein to the injury of his creditors; 2. That defendant has assigned, disposed of, or concealed, or is about to assign, dispose of, or conceal, any of his property, with intent to defraud his creditors; 3. That defendant has removed, or is about to remove, any of his property out of this state, with intent to defraud his creditors; 4. That he fraudulently contracted the debt, or incurred the obligation, respecting which, suit is brought; 5. That the defendant does not reside in this state, and has not resided therein for three months immediately preceding the time of making application for such attachment; or, 6. That defendant is a foreign corporation.

The clerk of the circuit court shall issue an attachment against the goods, chattels, lands, tenements, rights, credits, moneys, and effects, of the defendant.

Deeds.

CONVEYANCES of lands, or of any estate or interest therein, may be made by deeds, signed and sealed by the person from whom the estate or interest is intended to pass, being of lawful age, or by his lawful agent or attorney, and acknowledged or proved and recorded as directed (below), without any other act or ceremony whatever.

A husband and wife may, by their joint deed, convey the real estate of the wife, in like manner as she might do by her separate deed, if she were unmarried; but the wife shall not be bound by any covenant contained in such joint deed.

Deeds executed within this state, of lands, or any interest in lands therein, shall be executed in the presence of two witnesses, who shall subscribe their names to the same as such, and the persons executing such deeds may acknowledge the execution thereof before any judge or commissioner of a court of record, or before any notary public, justice of the peace, or master in chancery within the state, and the officer taking such acknowledgment, shall endorse thereon a certificate of the acknowledgment, and the time and date of making the same, under his hand.

If any such deed shall be executed in any other state, territory, or district, of the United States, such deed may be executed according to the laws of such state, territory, or district, and the execution thereof may be acknowledged before any judge of a court of record, notary public, justice of the peace, master in chancery, or other officer authorized by the laws of such state, territory, or district, to take the acknowledgment of deeds therein, or before any commissioner appointed by the governor of this state for such purpose.

In the cases provided for in the last preceding section, unless the acknowledgment be taken before a commissioner appointed by the governor of this state for that purpose, such deed shall have attached thereto a certificate of the clerk, or other proper certifying officer of a court of record of the county or district within which such acknowledgment was taken, under the seal of his office, that the person whose name is subscribed to the certificate of acknowledgment was at the date thereof, such officer as he is therein represented to be, that he believes the signature of such person subscribed thereto to be genuine, and that the deed is executed and acknowledged according to the laws of such state, territory, or district.

If such deed be executed in any foreign country it may be executed according to the laws of such country, and the execution thereof may be acknowledged before any notary public therein, or before any minister plenipotentiary, minister extraordinary, minister resident, chargé d'affaires, commissioner, or consul of the United States, appointed to reside therein; which acknowledgment shall be certified thereon by the officer taking the same, under his hand, and if taken before a notary public, his seal of office shall be affixed to such certificate.

When any married woman residing in this state, shall join with her husband in a deed of conveyance of real estate, situate within this state, the acknowledgment of the wife shall be taken separately, and apart from her husband, and she shall acknowledge that she executed such deed freely and without any fear or *compulsion from any one.*

When any married woman not residing in this state, shall join with her husband in any conveyance of real estate, situate within this state, the conveyance shall have the same effect as if she were sole, and the acknowledgment or proof of the execution of such conveyance by her, may be the same as if she were sole.

Deeds must be recorded by the register of deeds in the county where the lands lie. A scrawl of the pen may be used as a seal.

Form of Acknowledgment.

State of Michigan,
County of *Wayne,* } ss.

Be it remembered, that on this *eighteenth* day of *March,* one thousand eight hundred and *fifty-one,* before me, JOHN JONES, a *notary public* in and for said county, personally came the *above* (or *within*) named JOHN DOE, *and* SUSAN DOE *his wife,* known to me to be the *persons* who executed the *foregoing* instrument, and acknowledged the same to be *their* free act and deed; *and the said* SUSAN, *wife of the said* JOHN DOE, *on a private examination, before me, separate and apart from her said husband, acknowledged that she executed the same freely, and without any fear or compulsion from any one.*

(Seal of Officer.) JOHN JONES, *Notary Public.*

Rights of Married Women.

ALL property acquired by any female before marriage, or to which she may be entitled afterward, continues her separate property, and is not liable for her husband's debts, but is liable for her own debts contracted before marriage. She can not give, grant, or sell, the same without consent of her husband, except by order of court.

The constitution of 1851, provides that, "The real and personal estate of every female acquired before marriage, and all property to which she may afterward become entitled by gift, grant, inheritance, or devise, shall be and remain the estate and property of such female, and shall not be liable for the debts, obligations, or engagements, of her husband, and may be devised and bequeathed by her as if she were unmarried."

DOWER.—The wife is entitled to dower in all lands of which her husband was seized of an estate of inheritance during coverture.

Rate of Interest.

THE legal rate is seven per cent., with permission to agree upon any rate not higher than ten per cent. for a loan of money. Contracts are not void for usury beyond the usurious excess.

Wills.

WILLS must be in writing, subscribed by the testator or by some person in his presence and by his express direction, attested and subscribed in the presence of the testator by two or more competent witnesses.

INDIANA.

INDIANA
Scale of Miles
10 20 30 40 50
10 Longitude West from 9 Washington 8
K E N T U C K Y
I L L
O
Wabash River
Ohio River
White R.
E. Branch of White R.
W. Branch
Louisville
POSEY
VANDERBURG
GIBSON
PIKE
WARRICK
SPENCER
PERRY
DUBOIS
CRAWFORD
HARRISON
FLOYD
CLARKE
ORANGE
WASHINGTON
SCOTT
JEFFERSON
SWITZERLAND
KNOX
DAVIES
MARTIN
LAWRENCE
JACKSON
SULLIVAN
GREENE
MONROE
BROWN
BARTHOLOMEW
JENNINGS
RIPLEY
DEARBORN
DECATUR
FRANKLIN
OWEN
VIGO
CLAY
PARKE
PUTNAM
HENDRICKS
MORGAN
JOHNSON
MARION
SHELBY
RUSH
UNION
VERMI
Princeton
Vincennes
Washington
Evansville
Rockport
Troy
Rome
Jasper
Corydon
New Albany
Jeffersonville
Charlestown
Madison
Vevay
Salem
Paoli
Bedford
Bloomington
Columbus
Greensburg
Rushville
Brookville
Indianapolis
Terre Haute
Rockville
Danville
Fairfield
Lawrenceburg
Aurora
Versailles
Carlisle
Spencer
Franklin
Shelbyville
Connersville
Centreville

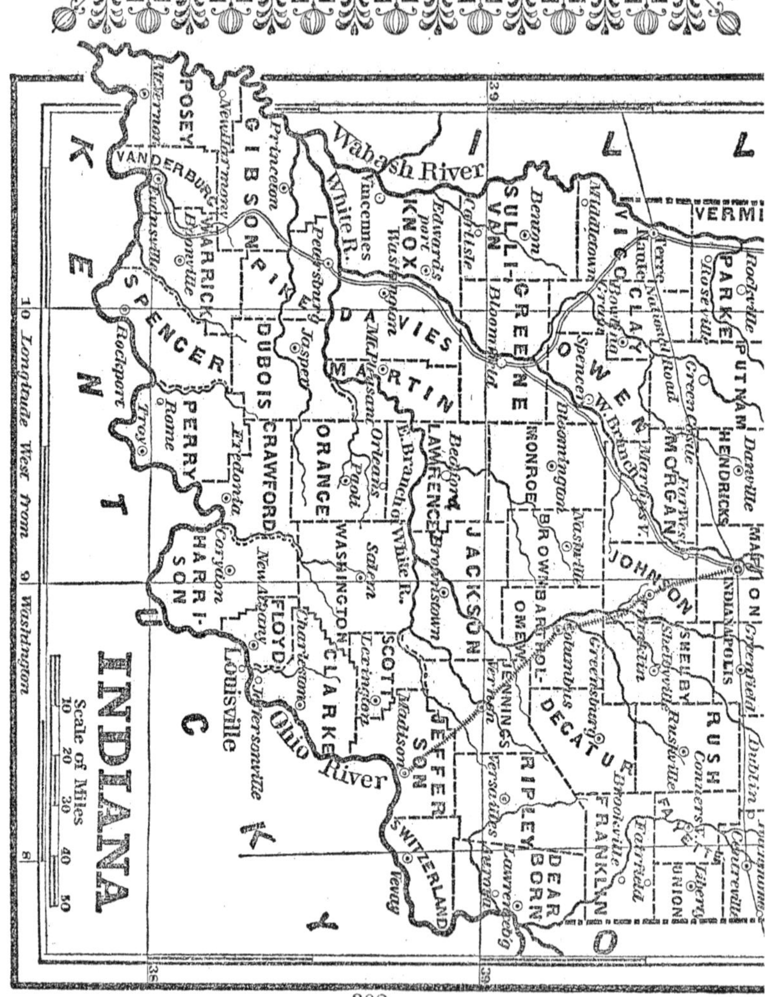

INDIANA.

ILLINOIS
MICHIGAN
OHIO
LAKE MICHIGAN
Chicago
Michigan City
Berrien
Branch
LAKE
Crown Pt.
Valparaiso
PORTER
LAPORTE
LaPorte
ST. JOSEPH
South Bend
St. Joseph R.
ELKHART
Elkhart
Goshen
LA GRANGE
Lima
STEUBEN
Angola
NEWTON
Kankakee R.
Montgomery
Rensselaer
Iroquois R.
STARK
English L.
MARSHALL
Plymouth
KOSCI USKO
Warsaw
Milford
NOBLE
Augusta
DEKALB
Auburn
BENTON
Oxford
WHITE
Monticello
West Bedford
PULASKI
Winnemac
New Boston
FULTON
Rochester
Tippecanoe R.
WHITLEY
Columbia
Perry
ALLEN
Fort Wayne
Maumee R.
WARREN
Williamsport
TIPPE- CANOE
LaFayette
CARROLL
Delphi
Logansport
Eel R.
Peru
WABASH
Wabash
HUNTINGTON
Huntington
WELLS
Bluffton
ADAMS
Decatur
FOUNTAIN
Covington
Newport
MONT- GOMERY
Crawfordsville
Danville
CLINTON
Frankfort
TIPTON
RICHARDVILLE
Kokomo
GRANT
Marion
BLACKFORD
Hartford
JAY
Portland
BOONE
Lebanon
Jamestown
HAMIL- TON
Noblesville
MADI- SON
DELAWARE
Muncie T.
RANDOLPH
Winchester
HENRY
WAYNE

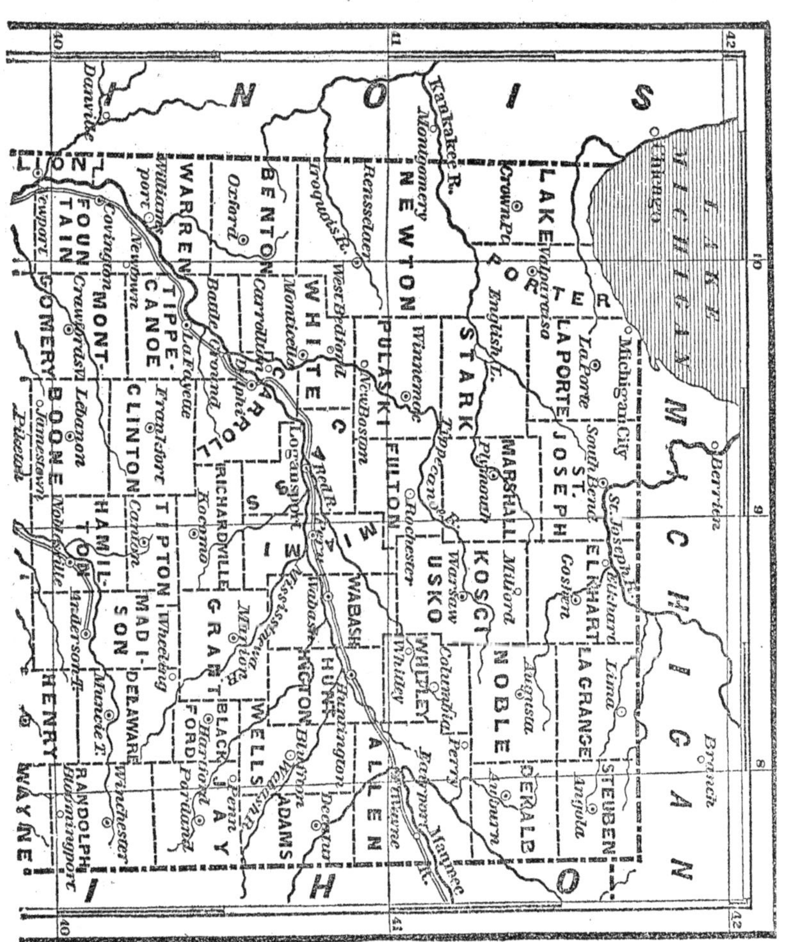

INDIANA.

Constitution adopted, 1816.—Square Miles, 33,809.—Population in 1850, 988,416

Household and Homestead Exemptions.

1. An amount of property not exceeding in value three hundred dollars, owned by any resident householder, shall not be liable to sale on execution or any other final process from a court, for any debt growing out of or founded upon contract, express or implied, after the fourth of July, 1852.

2. The said property may be real or personal, or both, as the debtor may elect.

3. No mortgage or sale of any real estate exempted under the provisions of this act, shall be valid, if executed by a married man, unless the deed be acknowledged by the wife in due form of law.

4. Such exemption shall not affect any laborer's or mechanic's lien, nor lien for purchased money of real estate exempted under this act.

5. For the appraisement of any property to be exempted under the provisions of this act, two disinterested householders of the neighborhood shall be chosen, one by the plaintiff, his agent, or attorney, and one by the execution debtor, and these two in cases of disagreement, shall select a third; and in case either party fails to select an appraiser, the same shall be selected by the officer holding the execution.

6. Such appraisers shall proceed forthwith to make a schedule of the real and personal property selected by the debtor, describing the real estate by metes and bounds, and the personal property by separate items, affixing to each the value they agree upon; and they, or a majority of them, shall affix to the schedule so made an affidavit in substance as follows: "We the undersigned. swear that in our opinion, the above is a just cash valuation of the property therein described."

7. Such schedule shall be delivered to the officer holding the execution or other process, and shall be by him returned with such execution, or other process, and made part of such return.

8. Each appraiser, for his services, shall be allowed the sum of fifty cents to be paid by the execution debtor.

9. If any execution debtor shall claim property as exempted by virtue of this act, he shall elect whether he will claim personal or real property, or both, and shall designate the property so claimed.

10. If such claim include personal property only, the officer holding such execution shall cause the same to be appraised and set apart to the debtor, and shall proceed to sell such other property, if any, as may be liable to said writ, according to law.

11. If any such claim include both personal and real property, the officer shall proceed to have such personal property valued and shall set the same apart to the debtor; he shall then cause the real property claimed as aforesaid to be valued; and if the same together with the personal property set apart, shall exceed three hundred dollars, the debtor shall within sixty days thereafter, pay such excess, or enough to satisfy the execution; and if he fail to do so, the officer shall proceed to sell the same as other lands are sold on execution if his writ shall authorize the sale of real property; but making such sale, he shall receive no bid therefor, unless it exceed the difference between three hundred dollars and the personal property so valued and set apart; and if he shall sell said property, he shall pay over to the debtor the amount of said difference, and apply so much of the remainder on the execution as shall satisfy the same, and the overplus, if any shall be paid to the debtor or other party having the next right.

12. If the claim include real property only, the same shall be valued, and if it exceed three hundred dollars, it shall be dealt with as is specified in respect to real property in the last preceding section.

13. In all cases in which real property is sought to be exempted from sale on execution if such real property is susceptible of division by metes and bounds, without material injury thereto, it shall be so divided as to exempt the principal dwelling-house or homestead of the debtor.

14. Nothing in this act shall be considered as exempting any property from taxation or from sale for taxes.

Only one hundred and twenty-five dollars' worth of property is exempt from execution for debts contracted *before* July 4th, 1852.

For MECHANICS' LIEN, see page 308.

Chattel Mortgages.

No assignment of goods and chattels, by way of mortgage or security, or upon any condition whatever, shall be valid against any other person than the parties thereto, where the possession of such goods and chattels is not delivered to the mortgagee or assignee, and retained by him, unless such assignment shall be proved or acknowledged as provided in cases of deeds of conveyance, and recorded in the recorder's office of the county where the mortgager or assignor resides, within ten days after the execution thereof.

Law regulating Contracts.

No action shall be brought—

1. To charge an executor or administrator, upon a special promise, to answer damages out of his own estate ; or—

2. To charge any person, upon any special promise, to answer for the debt, default, or miscarriage, of another ; or—

3. To charge any person upon any agreement or promise made in consideration of marriage ; or—

4. To charge any person upon any contract for the sale of lands, tenements, or hereditaments, or any interest in or concerning them ; or—

5. Upon any agreement that is not to be performed within one year from the making thereof; unless the promise, contract, or agreement, upon which such action shall be brought, or some memorandum or note thereof, shall be in writing, and signed by the party to be charged therewith, or by some person thereunto by him lawfully authorized, excepting leases not exceeding the term of three years.

The consideration need not be expressed in the writing.

No action shall be maintained to charge any person upon or by reason of any representation or assurance made concerning the character, conduct, credit, ability, trade, or dealings, of any other person, when such action is brought by the person to whom such representation or assurance was made, unless such representation or assurance be made in writing, and signed by the party to be charged thereby, or by some person thereunto by him lawfully authorized.

No contract for the sale of any goods, wares, or merchandise, for the price of fifty dollars or more, shall be good or valid, unless the purchaser shall accept and receive part of such property so sold, or shall give something in earnest to bind the bargain or in part payment, or unless some note or memorandum in writing of the bargain be made and signed by the party to be charged thereby, or by some person thereunto by him lawfully authorized.

Limitation of Actions.

The following actions shall be commenced within six years next after the cause of action shall accrue :—

1. All actions of debt founded upon any contract or liability, except as provided in the next section.

2. All actions upon judgments rendered before a justice of the peace, or in any court not being a court of record.

3. All actions for arrears of rent.

4. All actions of assumpsit, or upon the case, founded on a contract or liability, express or implied, except as provided in the next section.

5. All actions for waste and for trespass upon land.

6 All actions of replevin, and for taking, detaining, or injuring goods or chattels.

7. All other actions on the case, except actions for slanderous words and for libels.

None of the provisions of the foregoing section shall apply to any action brought upon any bond, promissory note, or contract in writing, nor to any action brought upon any bills, notes, or other evidences of debt, issued by any bank, where the suit is against such bank, nor to any action brought on the judgment or decree of any court of record of this state or of the United States, or of any state or territory of the United States.

All actions for assault and battery, and for false imprisonment, shall be commenced within three years.

All actions for slanderous words, and for libels, shall be commenced within one year.

In all actions of debt or assumpsit, where there are mutual and open accounts current between the parties, the cause of action shall be deemed to have accrued at the time of the last item proved in such account.

All personal actions on any contract not limited above shall be brought within twenty years after the accruing of the cause of action.

Minors, married women, persons insane, imprisoned, or absent from the United States, may bring action within one year after the disability is removed.

Absence from the state of the defendant is not to be computed.

Actions for the recovery of lands must be brought within twenty years.

A widow shall not recover dower after the expiration of twenty years from the death of her husband. If, at the time of his death, she be a minor or insane, the time of such disability is not to be computed.

Collection of Debts.

ARREST.—Actions brought for the recovery of any debt, or for damages only, may be commenced either by the issuing of a *capias ad respondendum* or by a summons.

Special bail shall not be required in any case until the plaintiff, his agent or attorney-at-law, shall make and file, with the clerk or court where suit is instituted, an affidavit specifying the plaintiff's rights to recover an existing debt or damages from the defendant, and also stating that he believes the defendant is about to leave the state of Indiana, taking with him property subject to execution, or money or effects which should be applied to the payment of the plaintiff's debt or damages, with intent to defraud said plaintiff.

No *capias ad respondendum* shall be delivered to any officer to be executed until an order for special bail has been obtained and endorsed on such writ.

ATTACHMENT.—The real and personal property of a debtor, being an inhabitant of this state, may be attached for the payment of his debts, whenever such debtor shall be secretly leaving the state, or shall have left the state, with intent to defraud his creditors, or to avoid the service of civil process, or shall keep himself concealed so that process can not be served upon him, with intent to delay or defraud his creditors.

No writ of attachment shall issue against any debtor while the wife and family of such debtor shall be and remain *bona fide* settled within the county where his usual place of residence may have been prior to his absence, if such debtor shall not continue absent from the state more than one year after he shall have absented himself, unless an attempt shall be made to conceal such debtor's absence, or unless such debtor shall be secretly transferring, conveying, or removing his property or effects, by which the payment of his debts may be evaded.

If the wife or family of such debtor shall refuse to give an account of the cause of his absence, or of the place where he may be, or shall give a false account of either, or shall be unable to account for his absence, or to tell where he may be found, such refusal, false accounts, or inability to account for his absence, or to tell where he may be found, shall be deemed and construed an attempt to conceal his absence.

Deeds.

A SCRAWL of the pen may be used fur a seal.

To entitle any deed, conveyance, mortgage, or instrument in writing, to be recorded, it shall be acknowledged by the party or parties executing the same, or shall be proved by a subscribing witness thereto, &c., before any supreme judge, judge of a circuit court, justice of the peace, recorder, notary public, or mayor of a city, within this state, or before any judge of a supreme or circuit court or court of common pleas, justice of the peace, or mayor or recorder of a city, or notary public of any other state, or before any commissioner appointed by the governor of this state in another state for such purpose, or before any minister charge d'affaires, or consul of the United States, in any foreign country.

Form of Acknowledgment.

State of Indiana,
County of *Harrison*, } to wit:

Be it remembered, that on this *tenth* day of *October*, one thousand eight hundred and *fifty*, before me, JOHN JONES, a *notary public* in and for said county, personally appeared JOHN DOE *and* SUSAN *his wife*, and severally acknowledged the foregoing instrument to be their act and deed; *and the said* SUSAN, *on a private examination, separate and apart from and without the hearing of her husband, I having first freely made known to her the contents and purport thereof, acknowledged to me that she executed the same of her own free will and accord, and without any coercion or compulsion from her said husband.*

Witness my hand and notarial seal of office, the day and year first above written.

(Seal.) JOHN JONES, *Notary Public.*

The acknowledgment of the execution of any deed or conveyance by which a married woman releases her dower in any lands conveyed or assigned by her husband, or by which the husband and wife convey the real estate of the wife, may be taken before any officer herein authorized to take the acknowledgment of deeds; but such officer shall first make known to her the contents and purport of such deed or conveyance, and she acknowledge on a private examination, separate and apart from, and without the hearing of her husband, that she executed such deed or conveyance of her own free will and accord, and without any coercion or compulsion from her husband; all of which shall be certified by such officer in his certificate of such acknowledgment.

Without such acknowledgment and certificate, her dower will not be barred, nor her interest conveyed.

The deed must be recorded in the county where the land is situate, within ninety days. It is better to record it at once.

Rights of Married Women.

No real estate whereof any married woman was or may be seized or other wise entitled to, at the time of her marriage, or which she has or may fairly acquire during her coverture, or any interest therein, shall be liable for the debts of her husband; but the same, and all interest therein, and all rents and profits arising therefrom, shall be deemed and taken to be her separate property, free and clear from any and all claim or claims of the creditors or legal representatives of her husband, as fully as if she had never been married; provided this law shall not be so construed as to apply to debts contracted by such married woman before such marriage, but in all cases her said property shall be first liable therefor.

DOWER.—The widow shall be endowed of one full and equal third part of all the lands the legal title to which was in her husband, or in any person to and for his use and benefit at any time during the coverture, unless such right of dower has been legally barred.

Rate of Interest.

THE legal rate of interest is six per cent. Usurious interest can not be recovered; and if paid, may be recovered back, but usury does not render the entire contract void.

Wills.

THESE must be in writing, and signed by the testator, or by some person in his presence and by his express direction, and attested and subscribed in the presence of the testator by two or more competent witnesses.

For form of attestation, see page 163.

Mechanics' Lien.

ALL persons performing labor on or furnishing materials for the construction of any [new] building, or repair of any building, under any contract entered into with the owner, and not with the tenant, may have a lien on the same for his services or materials, or both.

Sub-contractors and laborers, giving notice to the owner of their claim, may make him liable for it, if he be indebted to their employer in that amount; if not, then to the amount due from the owner to their employer.

Within sixty days after the completion of the building or repairs, notice of the intention to hold a lien on the property, specifying the amount claimed, must be filed in the recorder's office of the county.

Lien may be enforced by filing a bill in chancery.

Boats and vessels of all descriptions built, repaired, or equipped, within the jurisdiction of this state, and those built, repaired, or equipped, out of such jurisdiction, by citizens of this state, who shall afterward come within such jurisdiction, shall be liable for all debts contracted by the master, owner, or consignee thereof, on account of work done and supplies or materials furnished by any person for, on account of, or toward the building, repairing, fitting, furnishing, or equipping such boats or vessels; and the debts so contracted shall be a lien on such boats or vessels, their tackle, apparel, and furniture, and shall have preference to any and all debts due from the owners, masters, or consignees thereof, except mariners' and boatmen's wages.

Attachment may issue to enforce such lien.

After a boat or vessel of any description shall have started on her voyage, if any person shall sell to the captain, commandant, master, consignee, or any officer of said boat or vessel, materials for her repair or equipment, or wood or coal for fuel, or provisions to be made use of by the crew or passengers during said voyage, or any articles not being freight or cargo, and which are designed merely to enable said boat or vessel to prosecute her voyage, said person making affidavit of the truth and justice of his demand, shall have the same remedy.

Boatmen and mariners, for their wages, may proceed under these provisions

ILLINOIS.

Constitution adopted, 1848.—Square Miles, 55,405.—Population in 1850, 858,234.

Exemptions.

THE wearing-apparel of every person shall be exempt from sale on execution, writ of attachment, or distress for rent, necessary for use.

The following property, when owned by any person being the head of a family and residing with the same, shall be exempt from levy and sale on any execution, writ of attachment, or distress for rent, and such articles of property shall continue so exempt while the family of such person or any of them are removing from one place of residence to another in this state, viz.:—

1. Necessary beds, bedsteads, and bedding; the necessary utensils for cooking; necessary household furniture, not exceeding in value fifteen dollars; one pair of cards, two spinning-wheels, one weaving-loom and appendage, one stove and the necessary pipe therefor, being in use or put up for ready use in any house occupied by such family.

2. One milch-cow and calf; two sheep for each member of the family, and the fleeces taken from the same, or the fleeces of two sheep for each member of a family which may have been purchased by any debtor not owning sheep, and the yarn and cloth that may be manufactured from the same; and sixty dollars' worth of property suited to his or her condition or occupation in life, to be selected by the debtor.

3. The necessary provisions and fuel for the use of the family for three months, and necessary food for the stock hereinbefore exempted from sale, or that may be held under the provisions of this act.

When any lot not exceeding ten acres shall be appropriated and used as a burying-ground, and shall be recorded as such in the recorder's office of the county, it shall be exempt from all taxes; and when sold in lots for burying the dead, the said lots shall not be subject to execution or attachment; provided that no person shall hold more than one eighth of an acre exempt from execution.

When in any case the head of a family dies, deserts or ceases to reside with the same, the said family shall be entitled to retain the property above exempted, free from levy and sale on execution.

Mechanics' Lien.

PERSONS furnishing labor or materials in repairing or erecting any building, shall have a lien on the building and lot or tract of land on which the same shall be erected.

To enforce such lien, suit must be brought within six months from the time that the last payment should have been made.

Landlords have a lien on growing and grown crops for their rent.

ILLINOIS.

ILLINOIS
Scale of Miles
10 30 50 70
Longitude West from Washington
Mississippi River
Missouri River
Ohio Riv
Wabash R.
Kaskaskia R.
St. Louis
KENTUCKY
Cairo
MADISON
ST. CLAIR
MONROE
RANDOLPH
WASHINGTON
CLINTON
BOND
MARION
JEFFERSON
FRANKLIN
PERRY
JACKSON
UNION
ALEXANDER
PULASKI
MASSAC
JOHNSON
POPE
HARDIN
GALLATIN
WILLIAMSON
HAMILTON
WHITE
WAYNE
EDWARDS
WABASH
CLAY
RICHLAND
LAWRENCE
CRAWFORD
JASPER
EFFINGHAM
FAYETTE
MONTGOMERY
SHELBY
CUMBERLAND
CLARK
COLES
EDGAR
MOULTRIE
CHRISTIAN
GREENE
JERSEY
SCOTT
PIKE
Alton
Edwardsville
Belleville
Waterloo
Kaskaskia
Pinckneyville
Nashville
Carlyle
Greenville
Vandalia
Salem
Mt. Vernon
Benton
Marion
Jonesboro
Vienna
Golconda
Shawneetown
Equality
Carmi
Fairfield
Albion
Mt. Carmel
Lawrenceville
Olney
Newton
Palestine
Charleston
Paris
Marshall
Shelbyville
Hillsboro
Carrollton
Jerseyville
Pittsfield
Winchester
Jacksonville
Auburn
Edinburg
Metropolis City
Caledonia
Unity

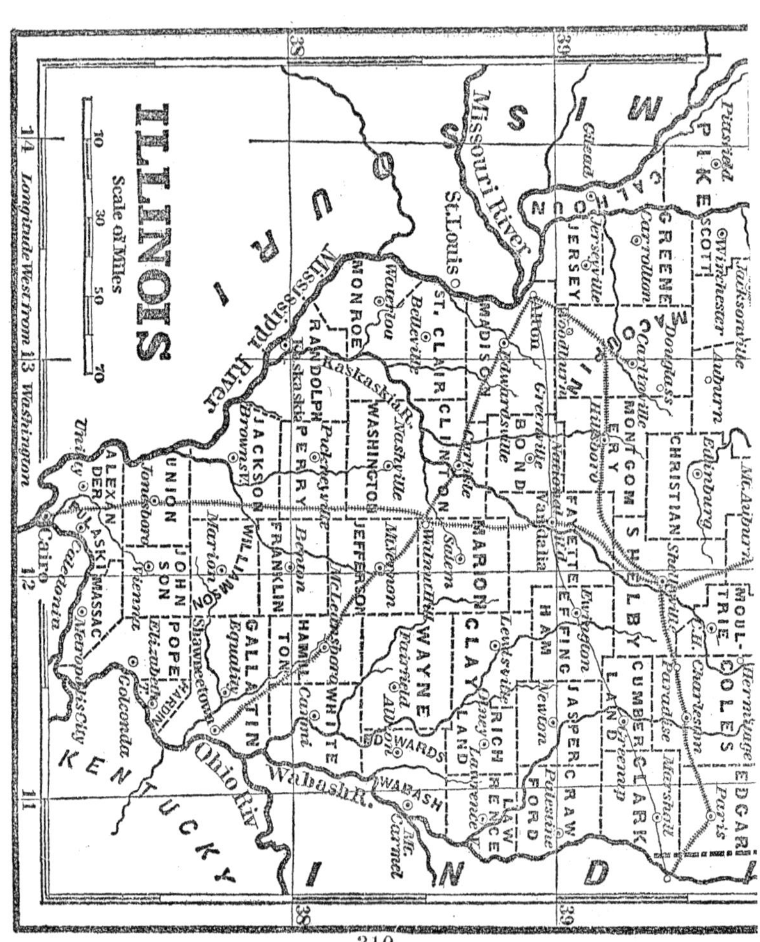

ILLINOIS.

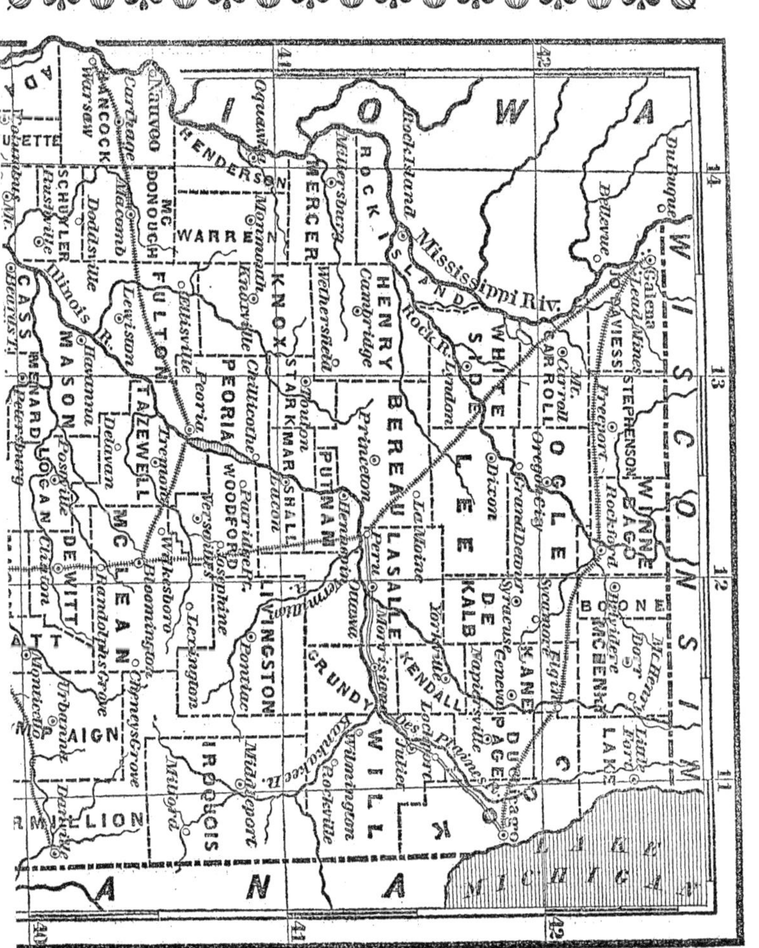

Homestead Exemption.

In addition to the property now exempt by law from sale under execution, there shall be exempt from levy and forced sale, under any process or order from any court of law or equity in this state, for debts contracted from and after the fourth day of July, A. D. 1851, the lot of ground and the buildings thereon occupied as a residence, and owned by the debtor, being a householder and having a family, to the value of one thousand dollars. Such exemption shall continue after the death of such householder, for the benefit of the widow and family, some or one of them continuing to occupy such homestead until the youngest child shall become twenty-one years of age, and until the death of such widow; and no release or waiver of such exemption shall be valid, unless the same shall be in writing, subscribed by such householder, and acknowledged in the same manner as conveyances of real estate are, by law, required to be acknowledged.

No property shall, by virtue of this act, be exempt from sale for non-payment of taxes on assessments, or for a debt or liability incurred for the purchase or improvement thereof, or prior to the recording of the aforesaid conveyance or notice.

If, in the opinion of the creditors or officer holding an execution against such householder, the premises claimed by him or her as exempt are worth more than one thousand dollars, such officer shall summon six qualified jurors of his county, who shall, upon oath, to be administered to them by the officer, appraise said premises, and if, in their opinion, the property may be divided without injury to the interest of the parties, they shall set off so much of said premises, including the dwelling-house, as in their opinion shall be worth one thousand dollars, and the residue of said premises be advertised and sold by such officer.

In case the value of the premises shall, in the opinion of the jury, be more than one thousand dollars, and can not be divided, as is provided for by this act, they shall make and sign an appraisal of the value thereof, and deliver the same to the officer, who shall deliver a copy thereof to the execution debtor, or to some one of the family of suitable age to understand the nature thereof, with a notice thereto attached, that, unless the execution debtor shall pay to said officer the surplus over and above one thousand dollars on the amount due on said execution, within sixty days thereafter, that such premises will be sold.

In case such surplus, or the amount due on said execution, shall not be paid within the said sixty days, it shall be lawful for the officer to advertise and sell the said premises, and out of the proceeds of such sale to pay to such execution debtor the said sum of one thousand dollars, which shall be exempt from execution for one year thereafter and apply the balance on such execution: *Provided,* That no sale shall be made unless a greater sum than one thousand dollars shall be bid therefor; in which case the officer may return the execution for the want of property.

The costs and expenses of settling off such homestead as provided herein, shall be charged and included in the officer's bill of costs upon such execution.

Chattel Mortgages.

No mortgage on personal property hereafter executed shall be valid as against the rights and interests of third persons, unless possession of the property shall be delivered to and remain with the mortgagee, or the said mortgage be acknowledged and recorded in the office of the recorder of the county in which the mortgager shall reside.

Any mortgager must first acknowledge, before any justice of the peace in the justice's district in which he may reside, such mortgage, and the said justice must certify to such acknowledgment and enter the same upon his docket.

It shall then be valid for two years, provided that such mortgage shall provide for the possession of the property so to remain with the mortgager.

Law regulating Contracts.

No action shall be brought whereby to charge any executor or administrator, upon any special promise, to answer any debt or damages out of his own estate; or whereby to charge the defendant, upon any special promise, to answer for the debt, default, or miscarriage, of another person; or to charge any person upon any agreement made upon consideration of marriage; or upon any contract for the sale of lands, tenements, or hereditaments, or any interest in or concerning them for a longer term than one year; or upon any agreement that is not to be performed within the space of one year from the making thereof, unless the promise or agreement upon which such action shall be brought, or some memorandum or note thereof, shall be in writing, and signed by the party to be charged therewith, or some other person thereunto by him lawfully authorized.

Limitation of Actions.

ALL actions of trespass *quare clausum fregit*, trespass, detinue, trover, and replevin, for taking away goods and chattels; all actions for arrearages of rent due on a parol demise; and all actions of account, and upon the case, except actions for slander and malicious prosecution, and such as concern the trade of merchandise between merchant and merchant, their factors or agents, shall be commenced within five years next after the cause of action accrued.

Actions of trespass for assault, battery, wounding, and imprisonment, shall be commenced within two years next after the cause of action accrued.

Actions on the case for words shall be commenced within one year; and for malicious prosecution shall be commenced within two years.

Every action of debt, or covenant for rent or arrearages of rent, founded upon any lease under seal, and of debt or covenant founded upon any single or penal bill, promissory note, or writing, obligatory for the direct payment of money, or the delivery of property, or the performance of covenants, or upon any award under the hands and seals of arbitrators, for the payment of money only, shall be commenced within sixteen years after the cause of action accrued; and when any payment has been made upon such instrument, then within sixteen years from the time of such payment.

Judgments of any court of record of this state may be revived by action of *scire facias* or action of debt within twenty years next after the rendition of the same.

Right of entry and actions to recover lands are barred by the lapse of twenty years.

Infants, married women, persons insane and absent from this state, may make such entry and bring such actions within the times respectively limited after the removal of their disability.

The absence of a defendant from the state is not to be computed in the limitation.

Collection of Debts.

ARREST.—When any debtor shall refuse to surrender his estate, lands, goods, or chattels, for the satisfaction of any execution which may be issued against the property of any such debtor, it shall and may be lawful for the plaintiff or his attorney or agent to make affidavit of such fact before any justice of the peace of the county; and upon filing such affidavit with the clerk of the court from which the execution issued, or with the justice of the peace who issued such execution, it shall be lawful for such clerk or justice of the peace, as the case may be, to issue a *capias ad satisfaciendum* against the body of such defendant in execution.

The defendant may board out his debt in jail at one dollar and fifty cents per day.

ATTACHMENT.—If any creditor or his agent shall make complaint, on oath or affirmation, to the clerk of the circuit court of any county in this state, that his debtor is about to depart from this state, or has departed from this state, with the intention in either case of having his effects and personal estate removed without the limits of this state, to the injury of such creditor, or stands in defiance of any officer authorized to arrest him on civil process, so that the ordinary process of law can not be served on such debtor, and that the debtor is indebted to him in a sum exceeding twenty dollars, specifying the amount and nature of such indebtedness, such creditor may sue out a writ of attachment against the debtor's lands and tenements, goods and chattels, rights and credits, moneys and effects, of what nature soever, or so much as will satisfy the debt sworn to, with interest and costs.

When any creditor, his agent or attorney, shall make oath or affirmation before any justice of the peace in this state, that any person, being a non-resident of this state, is indebted to such creditor in a sum not exceeding fifty dollars, such justice may issue an attachment against his personal estate.

Attachment may issue, in the case of a non-resident, against all his property for a sum exceeding twenty dollars, from the clerk of the circuit court of any county.

Deeds.

A SCRAWL of the pen may be used as a seal. Deeds should be witnessed by two subscribing witnesses.

Form of Acknowledgment.

State of Illinois,
County of *Hancock*, } *ss.*

Be it remembered, that on this *first* day of *April*, one thousand eight hundred *and fifty-one*, before me, JOHN JONES, a *notary public*, personally appeared JOHN DOE *and* SUSAN *his wife*, to me known to be the real persons whose names are subscribed to the foregoing *conveyance*, and severally acknowledged that they executed the same; *and the said* SUSAN, *on an examination separate and apart from her husband, having had the contents thereof fully made known to her by me, acknowledged that she executed the same, and relinquished her dower to the lands and tenements therein mentioned, voluntarily, freely, and without any compulsion of her said husband.*

In witness whereof, I have hereunto set my hand and notarial seal of office, the day and year first above written.

(*Seal of Office.*) JOHN JONES, *Notary Public.*

Deeds may be acknowledged or proved before any judge or justice of the supreme or district court of the United States; any commissioner to take acknowledgment of deeds; any judge or justice of the supreme, superior, or circuit court of any of the United States or their territories; any clerk of a court of record, mayor of a city, or notary public: but when made before a clerk, mayor, or notary public, it shall be certified by such officer under his seal of office.

When any married woman, not residing in this state, being over eighteen years, shall join with her husband in the execution of a deed or mortgage of lands in the state, she shall thereby be debarred from all interest, estate, or dower therein, as if she were sole and of full age.

The officer taking the acknowledgment must certify that the person offering to make such acknowledgment is personally known to him to be the real person whose name is subscribed to the deed as having executed the same, or that he was proved to be such by a credible witness (naming him).

In case of married women, in addition to the above, he shall acquaint her with the contents of the deed, and shall examine her separately and apart from her husband, whether she executed the same, and relinquished her dower to the lands and tenements therein mentioned, voluntarily, freely, and without compulsion of her said husband, and shall certify the same on or annexed to the deed.

Rights of Married Women.

DOWER.—A widow shall be endowed of the third part of all the lands whereof her husband was seized of an estate of inheritance at any time during marriage, unless the same shall have been relinquished in legal form.

Rate of Interest.

FROM and after January 30, 1849, money *may be loaned* at such rate of interest, not exceeding ten per cent. per annum on each hundred dollars, as the parties may agree upon. In the trial of any action brought upon a promissory note or writing obligatory in any of the courts of this state, wherein is reserved a higher rate of interest than six per cent. per annum, it shall be lawful for the defendant to set up and plead, as a defence in any such suit, that the consideration of said note or writing obligatory, upon which such suit is brought, was not "*money loaned;*" upon which issue it shall be lawful for the debtor, the creditor being alive, to become a witness, and his testimony shall be received as evidence; and the creditor, if he shall offer his testimony, shall be received as a witness, together with any other legal evidence that may be introduced by either party; and if, upon the trial of the said issue, it shall be found that the said note or writing obligatory upon which such suit is brought was not given for money loaned, then the said court shall render judgment for the principal sum in said promissory note or writing obligatory, and six per cent. interest thereon.

Wills.

THEY must be in writing, signed by the testator, or by some one in his presence and by his direction, and attested by two credible witnesses.

For form of attestation, see page 163.

MISSOURI.

Constitution adopted, 1820.—Square Miles, 67,380.—Population in 1850, 684,132.

Exemptions.

THERE is in this state exempted from sale on execution, the wearing-apparel of all persons, and the necessary tools, implements of trade, of any mechanic while carrying on his trade, and the following articles, being the property of any person being a householder, namely: ten head of choice hogs, ten head of choice sheep, two cows and calves; one plough, one axe, one hoe, and one set of plough-gears; working-animals, of the value of sixty-five dollars; the spinning-wheels and cards, one loom and apparatus, necessary for manufacturing cloth in a private family; all the spun yarn, thread, and cloth, manufactured for family use; flax, hemp, and wool, twenty-five pounds of each; all wearing-apparel of the family; two beds, with the usual bedding; and such other household and kitchen furniture necessary for the family, not exceeding in value twenty-five dollars; all arms and military equipments required by law to be kept; all provisions on hand for family use, not exceeding twenty-five dollars in value. All lawyers, physicians, and ministers, may select such books necessary to their profession in the place of other property, at their option; doctors of medicine, in lieu of property exempt, may select their medicines.

Instead of ten hogs, ten sheep, two cows and calves, one plough, one axe, one hoe, one set of plough-gears, and working-animals of the value of sixty-five dollars, the debtor, if the head of a family, may select any other property, real or personal, not exceeding in value, one hundred and fifty dollars.

The wife's property is exempt from sale on execution against her husband, if the debt was contracted before marriage, before she came into possession, or if it was a security debt. It is also exempt from execution for fine or costs in any criminal case against her husband.

The husband's property is exempt from all debts and liabilities contracted by the wife before marriage.

Mechanics' Lien.

CONTRACTORS, sub-contractors, artisans, and laborers, shall have a lien for work and materials on the buildings.

Every person, except sub-contractors, must file with the clerk of the circuit court of the county in which the building is, within six months after the materials are furnished or the work is done, a true account of his demand, verified by his oath, and a correct description of the property.

Sub-contractors must give notice to the owners of their intention to furnish materials or labor, and the probable value thereof; and having settled the amount afterward with the contractor, must, within ten days after the labor is done or the materials are furnished, file in the like office a copy of such settlement, and a correct description of the property charged with the lien.

The lien to bind the building for twelve months after it is finished.

The owner not to settle with the contractor until the sub-contractors' liens are discharged.

Lien to extend to the land on which the building is erected, and not exceeding five hundred square feet clear of the building.

MISSOURI.

IOWAS
Foxes & Sacs
DELAWARES
KANSAS
Kansas River
Missouri River
INDIAN TERRITORY
SHAWNEES
Osage River
POTAWATOMIES
Neosho R.
OSAGES
CHEROKEES
Arkansas R.
ATCHISON
NODAWAY
Maryville
HARRISON
Dallas
GENTRY
Athens
HOLT
Oregon
ANDREW
Savannah
DE KALB
BUCHANAN
PLATTE
Weston
Platte City
CLINTON
Platsburg
CLAY
Liberty
CALDWELL
Kingston
RAY
Richmond
MERCER
Princeton
GRUNDY
Trenton
SULLIVAN
LINN
Linneus
LIVINGSTON
Chillicothe
CARROLL
Carrollton
CHARITON
SALINE
Marshall
HOWARD
Fayette
Lexington
Independence
LAFAYETTE
JACKSON
JOHNSON
Warrensburg
Harrisonville
PETTIS
Georgetown
COOPER
CASS
Clinton
HENRY
BENTON
Warsaw
MORGAN
Osage R.
Batesville
Osceola
ST. CLAIR
HICKORY
Hermitage
BATES
CEDAR
POLK
Bolivar
DALLAS
Buffalo
JASPER
DADE
Greenfield
Springfield
GREENE
Carthage
Mt. Vernon
LAWRENCE
NEWTON
Neosho
BARRY
Cassville
TANEY
Forsyth
White R.
ARK
20
19
18
17
16
40
39
38
37
Lon. West from Washing

MISSOURI.

MISSOURI
Scale of miles
10 30 50 70
ILLINOIS
SPRINGFIELD
Illinois R.
Mississippi R.
Mississippi Riv.
Kaskaskia R.
Ohio River
Tennessee R.
KENTUCKY
TENNESSEE
Alton
Vandalia
St. Louis
Herculaneum
Kaskaskia
Shawneetown
Cairo
St. Francisville
Memphis
Waterloo
SCOTLAND
CLARK
KNOX
Edina
Monticello
LEWIS
Palmyra
MARION
SHELBY
MONROE
Paris
RALLS
New London
PIKE
Bowling Green
AUDRAIN
Mexico
BOONE
LINCOLN
Troy
MONTGOMERY
Danville
CALLAWAY
Fulton
Warrenton
WARREN
St. Charles
ST. CHARLES
Hermann
COLE
OSAGE
Linn
GASCONADE
Union
FRANKLIN
ST. LOUIS
JEFFERSON
Hillsboro
Steelville
Potosi
Lead M.
WASHINGTON
St. Genevieve
ST. GENEVIEVE
ST. FRANCIS
Farmington
Perry V.
PERRY
Waynesville
PULASKI
CRAWFORD
Iron Mt.
Fredericton
MADISON
CAPE GIRARDEAU
Jackson
Ellsworth
C.H.
TEXAS
SHANNON
REYNOLDS
Copper Mines
WAYNE
Greenville
Benton
SCOTT
Charleston
MISSISSIPPI
STODDARD
Bloomfield
Van Buren
RIPLEY
BUTLER
OREGON
St. Francis R.
New Madrid
NEW MADRID
New Market
DUNKLIN
ARKANSAS
40
39
38
37
14
13
12
11
15

Chattel Mortgages.

THE property must be delivered to and retained by the mortgagee, or the mortgage must be acknowledged or proved and recorded in the county in which the mortgager resides, the same as deeds of real property.

Law regulating Contracts.

ALL contracts which, by common law, are joint only, shall be construed to be joint and several.

A joint debt or contract survives against the heirs, executors, and administrators of the deceased obligor or promisor, as well as against the survivor, also against the heirs, executors, and administrators of all the joint obligors, if all are dead.

Suit may be prosecuted against any one or more copartners, in case of copartnership, obligation, or assumption.

No action shall be brought to charge any executor or administrator, upon any special promise, to answer any debt or damages out of his own estate; or to charge any person, upon any special promise, to answer for the debt, default, or miscarriage, of another person; or to charge any person upon any agreement made upon consideration of marriage; or upon any contract for the sale of lands, tenements, or hereditaments, or any interest in or concerning them, or any lease thereof for a longer term than one year; or upon any agreement that is not to be performed within one year from the making thereof, unless the agreement upon which the action shall be brought, or some memorandum or note thereof, shall be in writing, and signed by the party to be charged therewith, or some other person by him thereto lawfully authorized.

No contract for the sale of goods, wares, and merchandise, for the price of thirty dollars or upward, shall be allowed to be good, except the buyer shall accept part of the goods so sold, and shall actually receive the same, or give something in earnest to bind the bargain or in part payment, or unless some note or memorandum in writing be made of the bargain, and signed by the parties to be charged with such contract, or their agents lawfully authorized.

Actions shall not be brought to charge any person for representations of the character, conduct, credit, ability, trade, or dealings, of another person, unless such representation is in writing, and subscribed by the person to be charged thereby, or by some person by him thereunto lawfully authorized.

Limitation of Actions.

ALL actions founded upon any writing, whether sealed or unsealed, for the direct payment of money or property, must be commenced within ten years after the cause of such action accrued—also, actions on covenants of seizin and actions for relief, not otherwise provided for. Actions on covenants of warranty, within ten years after final decision against title of warrantor.

Actions upon contracts, &c., express or implied, except upon judgments or decrees of courts of record, and except where a different time is limited; actions upon a liability created by statute, other than a penalty or forfeiture; actions for trespass on real estate, actions for taking, detaining, or injuring goods and chattels, or for the recovery of specific personal property; actions for criminal conversation or other injury to the rights of persons, not otherwise limited, within five years. Actions for relief on the ground of fraud, within five years, the cause of action accruing at the discovery of the fraudulent acts.

Actions against sheriffs or coroners, and actions for penalty or forfeiture, where the penalty is given to the party aggrieved, or to him, or to the state, within three years.

Actions for libel, assault, battery, or false imprisonment, and actions for penalty or forfeiture to the state, within two years.

Actions against sheriffs, &c., for escape, one year.

On a current account, the cause of action accrues at the time of the last item in the account on the adverse side.

Qui tam actions, within one year after the commission of the offence, or within two years if not brought by a private party, if commenced by the attorney-general or circuit attorney in behalf of the state.

Limitations apply to actions brought by the state or for its benefit.

Infants, married women, persons insane or imprisoned, have the same periods respectively after their disability is removed.

A promise in writing is necessary to revive action barred by this act.

Bonds, judgments, and decrees, are presumed to have been paid after the lapse of twenty years; such presumption being liable to be repelled by proof of payment in part, or written acknowledgment of the indebtedness.

Collection of Debts.

ATTACHMENT.—Attachment may issue—1. Where the debtor does not reside within the state; 2. Or conceals himself so that process can not be served upon him; 3. Or the debtor has absconded or absented himself from his usual place of abode in this state, so that process can not be served on him; 4. Or is about to remove his property out of the state, with the intent to defraud, hinder, or delay, his creditors; 5. Or has fraudulently conveyed or assigned his property, so as to hinder or delay his creditors. 6. Or has fraudulently concealed or disposed of his property, so as to hinder or delay his creditors; 7. Or is about fraudulently to convey or assign his property or effects, so as to hinder or delay his creditors; 8. Or is about fraudulently to conceal or dispose of his property, so as to hinder or delay his creditors; 9. Where the debt was contracted out of this state, and the debtor has absconded or secretly removed his property into this state, with the intent to defraud, hinder, or delay, his creditors. In the fourth, fifth, sixth, seventh, eighth, and ninth cases, attachment may issue though the debt be not due.

Before attachment can issue, affidavit must be made by the plaintiff, or some person for him, stating that the defendant is justly indebted to the plaintiff in the sum claimed, after allowing all just credits and off-sets: stating, also, on what account the debt was incurred and that affiant has good reason to believe and does believe the existence of one or more of the above causes, which entitle him to an attachment. Bond must also be given, with one or more securities, resident householders of the county in which the action is to be brought, in a sum at least double the amount of the demand sworn to. If the defendant puts in issue the truth of the affidavit, the plaintiff must prove the facts therein alleged as grounds of attachment.

N. B. Non-resident parties wishing to sue their debtors in this state by attachment, should send, with the demand, an affidavit setting out the above facts, and should also take measures to provide the requisite security.

Imprisonment for debt is abolished.

Deeds.

EVERY conveyance of freehold estate must be subscribed and sealed by the grantor and acknowledged or proved (if in this state) before some court having a seal, or some judge, justice, or clerk thereof, or some notary public or justice of the peace of the county in which the land lies; if in the United States and out of this state before any court of the United States or of any state or territory having a seal or the clerk of any such court or commissioner for this state residing at the place where the acknowledgment is taken; and in foreign countries, before any court of such country having a seal, or the mayor of any city having an official seal. Relinquishments of dower may be taken by the same officers, but acknowledgments of married women, when conveying their separate estate, can be taken only by some court, judge, or clerk, authorized to take acknowledgments in other cases.

A certificate thereof must be endorsed on the deed, under the hand and seal of the officer.

The deed should be recorded in the county where the land is situate. No deed is valid except between the parties thereto and such as have *actual* notice thereof, until the same is filed for record.

The person acknowledging must be personally known to the officer or one judge of the court, to be the person whose name is subscribed as a party thereto, or shall be proved to be such by two credible witnesses, which shall be stated in the certificate.

In addition, a married woman, upon relinquishing her dower, shall be made acquainted with the contents of the deed, and shall acknowledge, on an examination apart from her husband, that she executed the same, and relinquishes her dower in the real estate therein mentioned, freely and without compulsion or undue influence of her husband; all which must be stated in the certificate.

Form of Acknowledgment, with Relinquishment of Dower.

State of Missouri,
County of *Benton*, } ss.

Be it remembered, that on the *first* day of *March*, one thousand eight hundred and *fifty-one*, before me, JOHN JONES, a *justice of the peace* in and for said county, personally appeared

JOHN DOE *and* SUSAN *his wife*, to me personally known to be the persons whose names are subscribed to the foregoing deed, as parties thereto, and acknowledged that they executed the same for the purposes therein mentioned; *and the said* SUSAN, *being by me examined apart from her husband, and made fully acquainted with the contents of the foregoing deed, acknowledged that she executed the same [and relinquished the dower in the real estate therein mentioned], freely and without fear, compulsion, or undue influence, of her said husband.*

Witness my hand, the day and year first above written.

JOHN JONES, *Justice of the Peace.*

A scrawl of the pen may be used instead of a seal.

A married woman may convey any of her real estate by a conveyance executed by herself and husband. The husband *must* join in the conveyance. Her acknowledgment is to be taken by some court, judge, or clerk, as above stated, she having first been made acquainted with the contents of the deed, by the officer, and on an examination separate and apart from her husband. The certificate of acknowledgment must be precisely similar to that given above, excepting that the words "and relinquished her dower in the real estate therein mentioned" *must* be omitted.

Rights of Married Women.

PROPERTY owned by a woman before marriage, or in any way acquired subsequent to her marriage, and the use and profits thereof, are exempt from debts and liabilities of her husband contracted before marriage or before the wife came into possession of such property. Such property is absolutely exempt from the husband's security debts, whenever contracted, and also from fines or costs, imposed on the husband in any criminal case.

DOWER.—The wife is endowed of one third of all the lands of which her husband, or any one to his use, was seized, of an estate of inheritance, at any time during the marriage; also, of leasehold estate for the term of twenty years or more.

The widow is also entitled to have and keep as her absolute property, all her implements of industry, and all the beds, bedding, wearing apparel, provisions, &c., requisite for the family; also, kitchen furniture to the value of twenty dollars, and any other personal property to the value of two hundred dollars. In addition, she is entitled as follows, viz.:—

1st. If the husband leaves descendants—to a child's share of the personal estate, absolutely, or at her option, or to one third of the slaves for her life, and one third of the other personal property, absolutely, subject to her husband's debts.

2d. If the husband leaves no descendants—to all the real and personal estate which came to the husband in right of the marriage, remaining undisposed of, absolutely, and to one half of the real and personal estate belonging to the husband at the time of his death, absolutely, subject to the husband's debts.

3d. If the husband leaves descendants, but not by his last marriage, his widow may, in lieu of dower, take the real estate and personal property in possession of the husband which came to him in right of his wife, by means of the marriage—subject to the husband's debts.

Rate of Interest.

THE rate of interest is six per cent. If plea of usury be sustained, judgment shall be rendered for legal interest only, which interest shall be paid to the common-school fund. In addition, a usurer shall, upon information to any justice of the peace or court having jurisdiction, forfeit and pay to the common schools the whole interest agreed upon.

Wills.

THEY must be in writing, signed by the testator, or by some person in his presence and at his request, and attested by two competent witnesses, who shall subscribe their names as witnesses in the presence of the testator.

Wills must be recorded within thirty days after probate. If lands in different counties are devised, a copy of the will shall be recorded in the recorder's office in each county, within six months after probate.

IOWA.

Constitution adopted, 1846.—Square Miles, 50,914.—Population in 1850, 192,264.

Exemptions.

DEFENDANTS in execution, if he, she, or they, have families, may claim as exempt from execution the following property, to wit: One bible; one cow and calf; one horse, or yoke of cattle; twelve sheep, and the wool shorn from them; five head of hogs, and all pigs under six months old; all the flax in the possession of the family, and the yarn or thread manufactured therefrom; one bedstead and the necessary bedding therefor, for every two in the family; the cloth manufactured by the family, not exceeding one hundred yards; household and kitchen furniture, not exceeding in value fifty dollars; one stove and pipe; all spinning-wheels and looms put up and kept for use; all farming utensils not exceeding in value fifty dollars; the necessary food for all animals exempt from execution; four months' provision for the family, and fuel for sixty days; the surgical instruments and medical library of every practising physician, and the library of every practising lawyer or counsellor; all private libraries not exceeding one hundred dollars in value, and all family portraits; all mechanics' tools necessary in their peculiar calling; the astronomical and mathematical instruments of every teacher or schoolmaster, and the instruments of every practical surgeon, in their profession: and all property exempt from execution is exempt from attachment or other process of law.

In addition to the above, it is lawful for the defendant to claim as exempt from process founded upon contracts made after the passage of the act, fifty head of sheep and the wool shorn therefrom.

Homestead-Exemption Law.

ANY quantity of land, not exceeding forty acres, used for agricultural purposes, the dwelling-house thereon, and the appurtenances, not included in any town plat, or city, or village, or instead thereof not exceeding one fourth of an acre, being within a recorded town plat, city, or village, the dwelling-house thereon and the appurtenances, owned and occupied by any resident of the state, is exempt from forced sale on execution or any other final process from any court, for any debt or liability contracted after the fourth day of July, one thousand eight hundred and forty nine; provided that such exempted homestead or town-lot and dwelling-house thereon shall in no case exceed in value five hundred dollars. This exemption is not to affect any laborer's or mechanic's lien, or mortgage lawfully obtained. Defendant must notify the officer of what he regards as his homestead.

Mechanics' Lien.

CONTRACTORS to build or repair a house or other building, mill, or machinery, or their appurtenances, or for furnishing labor or materials for such purposes, and every other person furnishing materials used in their construction, by agreement with the owner of any tract of land or town-lot, or the lessee of either with the owner's knowledge or consent, have a lien upon the house, &c., and the tract of land or lot on which the same is erected, in proportion to the labor or materials furnished, which can not be avoided, or sold so as to avoid said lien, unless upon judgment rendered before such house, &c., was commenced.

Suit must be brought within one year from the time of payment fixed by the contract upon which the lien is claimed, or within six months after the decision of any suit brought within that time; and if brought in the district court, must be by bill or petition, describing with common certainty the tract of land, house, &c., upon which the lien is intended to operate, the nature of the contract or indebtedness, with a bill of particulars, which together are to be filed in lieu of a declaration. The execution upon a judgment in a suit of this nature must be levied upon the property specified, and no other property of defendant is bound for the payment of such judgment.

Miners have a lien, by this act, upon a sufficient quantity of mineral to pay any just demand for labor performed upon it.

IOWA.

M I N N E S
Spirit L.
Plateau du Coteau des Prairies
Moingonan R.
Moingonan Brother R.
L. Boone
Sioux River
Floyds R.
L. Sioux R.
Boone R.
INDIAN TERRITORY
Soldier R.
Missouri River
Boyers R.
Raccoon Fork
Elk Horn R.
Des M
Ft. Des Moines
Up. Three R.
SACS AND FOXES
Platte River
2d. Three R.
Lower 3 R.
Barrel C.
Nishnabottona R.
Nodaway R.
Saline R.
Tarkio R.
L. Platte R.
Muddy C.
E. Fork Grand R.
M I S S
20
19
18
17
43
42
41

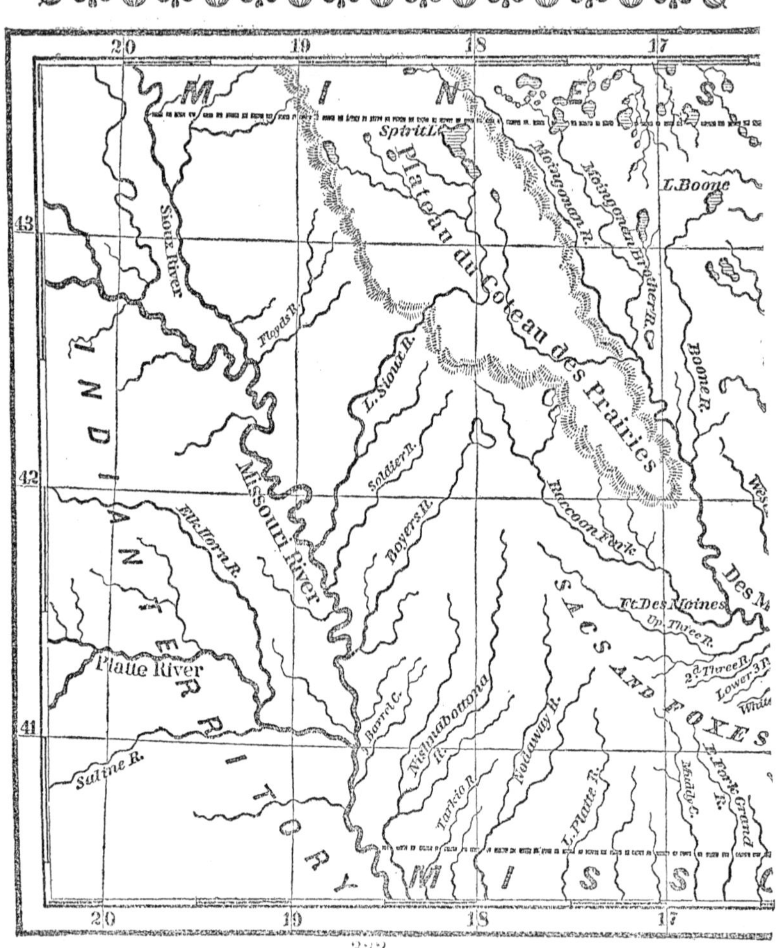

IOWA.

IOWA
Scale of miles
10 20 30 40 50 60
Mississippi River
Wisconsin R.
Upper Iowa R.
Turkey R.
Red Cedar R.
Shell Rock C.
Lime C.
L. Alber Lea
East Fork
Iowa River
Red Cedar R.
English R.
Skunk R.
Rock R.
Fox R.
CLAYTON
Prairie la Porte
FAYETTE
BLACK HAWK
BUCHANAN
DELAWARE
DUBUQUE
DuBuque
Peru
Galena
Lancaster
Mineral Point
Monroe
JACKSON
Bellevue
Andrew
LINN
Marion
JONES
Edinburg
TAMA
BENTON
CLINTON
DeWitt
Camanche
CEDAR
Tipton
SCOTT
Davenport
Rock Island
POWASHIEK
IOWA
JOHNSON
IOWA CITY
MUSCATINE
Bloomington
MAHASKA
KEOKUCK
WASHINGTON
Washington
LOUISA
Wapello
Millersburg
KISHKEKOSH
Ottumwa
WAPELLO
JEFFERSON
Fairfield
HENRY
Mt. Pleasant
DES MOINE
Burlington
APPANOOSE
DAVIS
VAN BUREN
Van Buren
LEE
Madison
Nauvoo
Montrose
C.H.
16
15
14
13
43
42
41

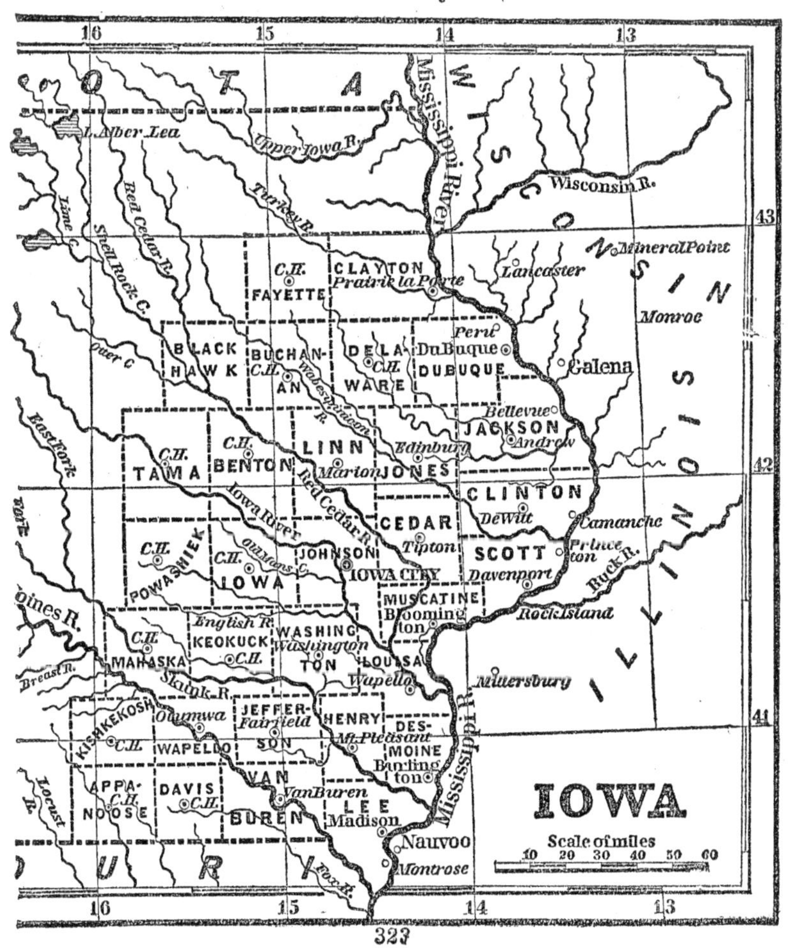

Chattel Mortgages.

Bills of sale, or other conveyances of personal property, where the vender retains the actual possession of the property so conveyed, are not valid in law against creditors or subsequent purchasers, unless acknowledged before some justice of the peace for the county where the same is executed, and recorded in the office of the recorder of deeds (who keeps a separate book for this purpose) within ten days, in the county where the holder of the property resides.

Law regulating Contracts.

All interests or estates in lands and hereditaments, made or created by livery and seisin only, or by parol, and not put in writing, shall have the force and effect of leases or estates at will only, excepting leases for a term not exceeding three years, upon a yearly reserved rent equal to two thirds of what the premises are really worth: and no estate in lands or hereditaments is assignable, except in writing, or by act and operation of law.

No action shall be brought whereby to charge any executor or administrator, or upon any special promise, to answer damages out of his own estate; or whereby to charge the defendant upon any special promise to answer for the debt, default, or miscarriage, of any other person; or to charge any person upon any agreement in consideration of marriage; or upon any contract or sale of lands, tenements, or hereditaments, or any interest in or concerning them; or upon any agreement which is not to be performed within one year from the making thereof, unless the agreement upon which such action shall be brought, or some note or memorandum thereof, shall be in writing, and signed by the party to be charged thereby, or some person by him thereunto lawfully authorized.

Declarations or creations of trust in lands and hereditaments must be in writing, signed by the party, or by his last will. Trusts arising by implication of law are exempt from the operation of the act.

Judgments in the district or supreme courts are liens upon the real estates of the parties against whom they may be rendered from the day of rendition thereof in the county within which such judgments may be rendered. Attested copies of such judgments, filed with the clerk of the district court of any other county, recorded, and entered upon the judgment docket of said county also, are made liens upon the estates of defendants therein situate, but no execution can issue upon such attested copy.

No contract for the sale of any goods, wares, or merchandise, for the price of thirty dollars or upward, shall be binding, except the buyer accept part of the goods so sold, and actually receive the same, or give something in earnest, or in part payment, or that some note or memorandum in writing of said bargain, be made and signed by the parties to be charged thereby, or their agents thereunto lawfully authorized.

Limitation of Actions.

All actions of trespass, detinue, trover, and replevin, for taking away goods, &c.; actions for arrearages of rent due on parol demise; actions of account and upon the case, except for slander and malicious prosecution, and such actions as concern the trade of merchandise between merchant and merchant, their factors or agents, must be commenced within five years after the cause of action accrues. Actions of trespass for assault and battery, wounding, and imprisonment, must be commenced within two years. Actions on the case for slanderous words must be commenced within one year after the words spoken, and actions for malicious prosecution within two years after the cause of action accrues. Actions of debt or covenant for rent or arrearages of rent founded upon lease, of debt upon any single or penal bill, promissory note, or writing, obligatory for the direct payment of money or the delivery of property, or the performance of covenants, or upon the award of arbitrators for the payment of money only, and every action of assumpsit, must be commenced within six years after cause of action accrues, or after any partial payment may have been made.

Judgment of any court of record may be revived by scire facias, or an action of debt may be brought within twenty years. The right of entry into any lands, tenements, or hereditaments, is barred after twenty years from the accruing of the right. Every real, possessory, ancestral, or mixed action, or writ of right, or action of ejectment, must be brought within twenty years after the right or title accrued, but in case of disability then within twenty years after the disability is removed.

If the person or persons against whom any of the foregoing actions, except real or possessory actions, are brought, shall be absent from the state at the time the cause of action accrued, or at any time during which said action might have been brought, such period of absence shall not be accounted part of the time limited by the act. The plaintiff, in certain cases, may bring a new suit within one year after judgment is reversed or given against him.

Collection of Debts.

ARREST.—The person of a debtor can not be taken in execution upon any civil contract.

ATTACHMENT.—When any action founded on contract is commenced or is about to be commenced, writ of attachment may be issued by the clerk of the district court, upon an affidavit that something is due the plaintiff from the defendant; that affiant believes the defendant is a non-resident, or that he is about to dispose of or remove his property, with intent to defraud his creditors; or that he has absconded, so that ordinary process can not be served upon him. Such writ may be levied upon any lands, tenements, goods, chattels, rights, credits, moneys, or effects, of said debtor, which may be found in the county, or so much thereof as may be sufficient to pay the debt, together with interests and costs of suit.

Deeds.

EVERY instrument of writing conveying any real estate, or whereby any real estate may be affected in law or equity, must be proved and acknowledged, and recorded in the office of the recorder of the county in which such real estate is situate. Such recording is notice to all the world, and no such instrument is valid except between the parties thereto, until deposited with the recorder for record.

Deeds and conveyances may be acknowledged before any court having a seal, justice or clerk thereof, a justice of the peace, or notary public. If before a justice of the peace in a county different from that in which the property is situate, it must be accompanied by the certificate of the clerk of the district court of the county, that the justice was, at the time of taking said acknowledgment, an acting justice of the peace for such county. The certificate of acknowledgment must state that the person making such acknowledgment was personally known to the officer to be the same whose name is subscribed to the instrument as party thereto, or was proved to be such by at least one witness, whose name must be inserted.

The certificate of acknowledgment of a married woman must state that she was personally known to the officer taking the same, to be the person whose name is subscribed to such conveyance; that she was made acquainted with the contents of such conveyance, and acknowledged on examination, apart from her husband, that she executed the same, and relinquished her dower in the real estate therein mentioned, freely and without compulsion or undue influence of her husband.

(The form of acknowledgment is the same as in MISSOURI, page 320.)

Rights of Married Women.

ANY married woman may become seized or possessed of any real estate by descent, bequest, demise, gift, purchase, or distribution, in her own name, and as of her own property, provided that the same does not come from her husband, and is not purchased with the funds or property of the husband during coverture. Property so held by any married woman is in no case liable for the debts of her husband. The control and management of such estate, the annual products, and rents and profits of the same, remain to the husband. Suits in relation to the property must be in the joint name of the husband and wife. Such real estate may be conveyed by the joint deed of the husband and wife, executed, proved, acknowledged, and recorded, as above.

DOWER.—The common-law right of dower exists in this state.

Rate of Interest.

THE legal rate of interest, when no other is agreed upon, and upon all judgments, is six per cent.; but parties may agree upon any rate not exceeding ten per cent. Illegal interest may be recovered by the proper suit.

Wills.

ALL wills, except nuncupative, must be in writing, signed by the testator, or by some person in his presence and by his express direction, and attested and subscribed in his presence by two or more competent witnesses. Subsequent incompetency of the witness will not invalidate the will. Nuncupative wills, proved by two competent witnesses, when the value of the estate does not exceed three hundred dollars, are valid.

Soldiers being in actual service, and mariners being at sea, may dispose of their wages and other personal property by nuncupative will.

WISCONSIN.

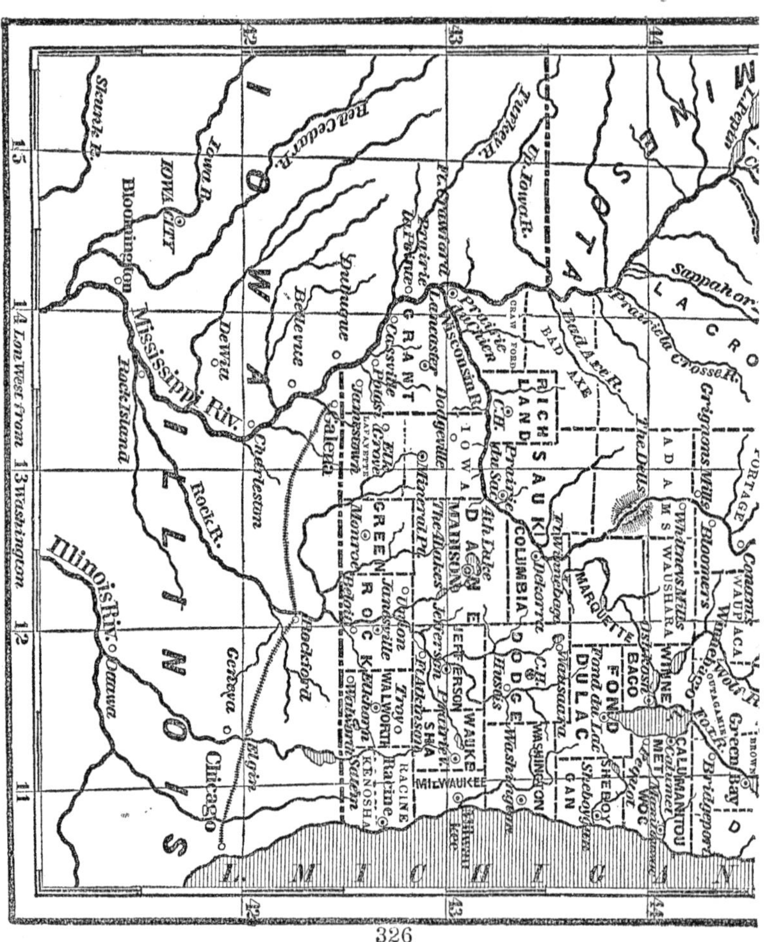

WISCONSIN.

WISCONSIN
10 30 50 70 Miles
St. Louis R.
Fond du Lac
Poplar R.
Burnt Wood R.
Red Cedar R.
St. Croix R.
Chippewa
Manidowish R.
Montreal R.
La Pointe
Apostles Islands
Marathon
Wisconsin R.
Pine R.
Big Bull Falls
Oconto
Oconto R.
Peshtigo R.
Menomonee R.
Kewenaw R.
Huron R.
Kewenaw Bay
Ft. Wilkins
Point Kewenaw
I. Royal

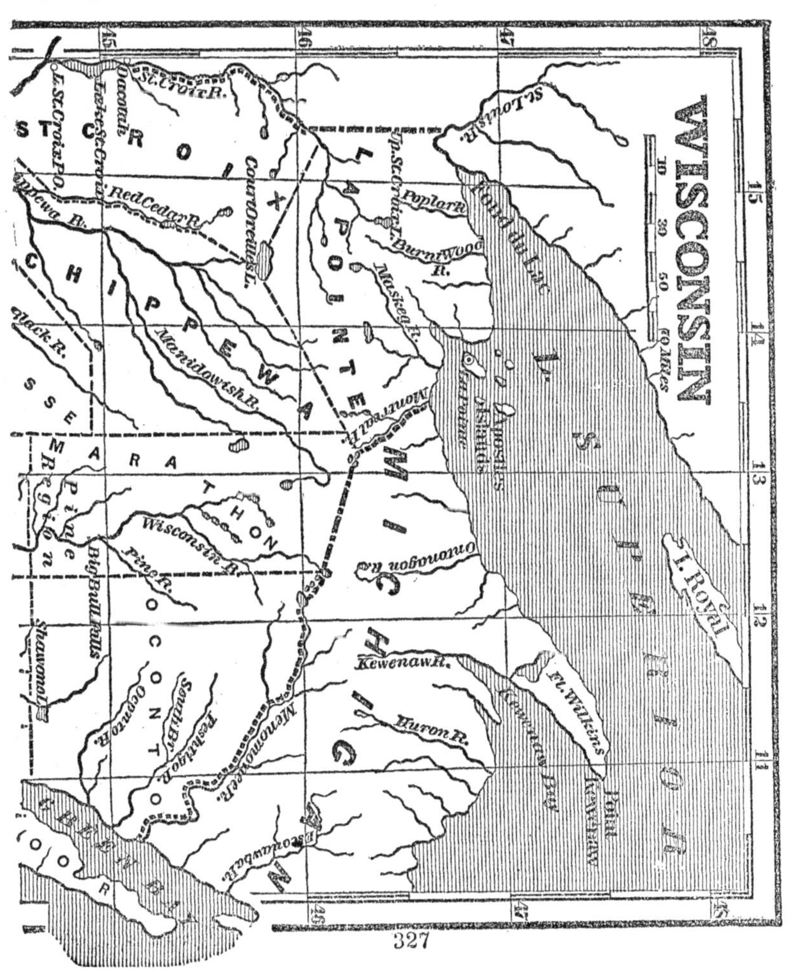

WISCONSIN.

Constitution adopted, 1848.—Square Miles, 53,924.—Population in 1850, 304,121.

Exemptions.

No property hereinafter mentioned or represented shall be liable to attachment, execution, or sale, on any final process issued from any court of this state:—

1. The family Bible.
2. Family pictures, schoolbooks, or library.
3. A seat or pew in any house or place of public worship.
4. The rites of burial of the dead.
5. All wearing-apparel of the debtor and his family; all beds, bedsteads, and bedding, kept and used for the debtor and his family; all stoves and appendages put up or kept for the use of the debtor and his family; all cooking-utensils, and all other household furniture not herein enumerated, not exceeding two hundred dollars in value.
6. Two cows, ten swine, one yoke of oxen, and one horse; or, in lieu of one yoke of oxen and a horse, a span of horses; ten sheep, and the wool from the same, either in the raw material or manufactured into yarn or cloth; the necessary food for all the stock mentioned in this section for one year's support, either provided or growing, or both, as the debtor may choose; also one wagon, cart, or dray; one sleigh, one plough, one drag, and other farming utensils, including tackle for teams, not exceeding fifty dollars in value.
7. The provisions for the debtor and his family necessary for one year's support, either provided or growing, or both, and fuel necessary for one year.
8. The tools and implements, or stock in trade, of any mechanic, miner, or other person, used and kept for the purpose of carrying on his trade or business, not exceeding two hundred dollars in value; the library and implements of any professional man, not exceeding two hundred dollars in value: all of which articles, hereinbefore intended to be exempt, shall be chosen by the debtor, his agent, servant, clerk, or legal representatives, as the case may be.

Homestead-Exemption Law.

A HOMESTEAD, consisting of any quantity of land not exceeding forty acres, used for agricultural purposes, and the dwelling-house thereon and its appurtenances, to be selected by the owner thereof, and not included in any town-plot, or city, or village; or instead thereof, at the option of the owner, a quantity of land not exceeding in amount one fourth of an acre, being within a recorded town-plot, or city, or village, and the dwelling-house thereof and its appurtenances, owned and occupied by any resident of the state, shall not be subject to forced sale on execution, or any other final process from a court, for any debt or liability contracted after the first day of January, one thousand eight hundred and forty-nine.

Such exemption shall not affect any laborers' or mechanics' lien, or extend to any mortgage thereon lawfully obtained; but such mortgage or other alienation of such land by the owner thereof, if a married man, shall not be valid without the signature of the wife to the same.

Any person owning and occupying any dwelling-house on land not his own, which land he shall be rightfully in possession of by lease or otherwise, and claiming such house as his homestead, shall be entitled to the exemption of such house.

Mechanics' Lien.

All and every dwelling-house hereafter constructed and erected in the state of Wisconsin, with the right, title, and interest of the person or persons owning such dwelling-house or other buildings in and to the land upon which the same shall be situated, not exceeding forty acres; or if erected within the limits of any city, town, or village plot, the lot on which such dwelling-house or other building shall be situated, not exceeding in extent one acre, shall be subject to the payment of the debts contracted for or by reason of any work done, or materials found and provided, by any brickmaker, bricklayer, stonecutter, mason, lime-merchant, carpenter, painter and glazier, ironmonger, plasterer, and lumber-merchant, or any other persons employed in erecting or furnishing materials for and in the erection and construction of such house or other building, before any other lien which originated subsequent to the commencement of such house or other building.

Sub-contractors must give notice to the owner within thirty days after the work is done or materials furnished to the owner, or be debarred from their lien. Lien to continue only one year.

Chattel Mortgages.

No mortgage of personal property hereafter made shall be valid against any other person than the parties thereto, unless possession of the mortgaged property be delivered to and retained by the mortgagee, or unless the mortgage be filed in the office of the town-clerk where the mortgager resides; or, in case he does not reside in the state, in the town where the property mortgaged may be at the time of executing the same.

Law regulating Contracts.

In the following cases, every agreement shall be void, unless such agreement, or some note or memorandum thereof, expressing the consideration, be in writing, and subscribed by the party charged therewith:—

1. Every agreement that by the terms is not to be performed within one year from the making thereof.

2. Every special promise to answer for the debt, default, or miscarriage, of another person.

3. Every agreement, promise, or undertaking, made upon consideration of marriage, except mutual promises to marry.

Every contract for the sale of any goods, chattels, or things in action, for the price of fifty dollars or more, shall be void, unless—

1. A note or memorandum of such contract be made in writing, and be subscribed by the parties to be charged therewith.

2. Unless the buyer shall accept and receive part of such goods, or the evidences, or some of them, of such things in action.

3. Unless the buyer shall, at the time, pay some part of the purchase-money.

Limitation of Actions.

ACTIONS for the recovery of lands must be brought within twenty years after the cause of action accrued.

Infants, persons insane, imprisoned, and married women, have ten years after the removal of their disability.

The following actions shall be commenced within six years next after the cause of action shall accrue, and not afterward:—

1. All actions of debt founded upon any contract or liability not under seal, except such as are brought upon the judgment or decree of some court of record of the United States, or of any state or territory of the United States.
2. All actions upon judgments rendered in any court not being a court of record.
3. All actions for arrears of rent.
4. All actions of assumpsit, or on the case, founded on any contract or liability, express or implied.
5. All actions for waste and for trespass on land.
6. All actions of replevin, and all other actions for taking, detaining, or injuring, goods or chattels.
7. All other actions on the case, except actions for slanderous words and libels.

All actions for assault and battery, and for false imprisonment, and all actions for slanderous words and for libels, shall be commenced within two years.

None of the foregoing provisions shall apply to any action brought upon a promissory note which is signed in the presence of an attesting witness, provided the action be brought by the original payee, or by his executor or administrator: nor to an action brought upon any bills, notes, or other evidences of debt, issued by any bank.

In all actions brought to recover the balance due upon a mutual and open account current, the cause of action shall be deemed to have accrued at the time of the last item proved in such account.

It shall be lawful for any person against whom any action shall be commenced in any court of this state, when the cause of action accrued without the state, upon a contract or agreement, express or implied, more than six years before the commencement of the action, or upon any sealed or attested instrument in writing, a judgment or decree of any court more than ten years before the commencement of the action, to plead the same, and give the same in bar of the plaintiff's right of action.

All personal actions on any contract not limited by the foregoing or by any other law of this state, shall be brought within twenty years after the accruing of the cause of action.

Persons under age, insane, imprisoned, or absent from the United States, and married women, may have the same periods respectively after the removal of their disability.

Collection of Debts.

ATTACHMENT.—An attachment may issue against the property of a debtor when the plaintiff, or some one on his behalf, shall make an affidavit, stating that the defendant is indebted to the plaintiff, and specifying the amount of such debt over and above all set-offs, and that the same is due on contract, express or implied. or upon judgment or decree; and containing, further, a statement that the deponent knows or has good reason to believe, either—

1. That the defendant has absconded or is about to abscond from this state, or that he is concealed therein, to the injury of his creditors; or—
2. That the defendant has assigned, disposed of, or concealed, or is about to assign, dispose of, or conceal, any of his property, with intent to defraud his creditors; or—
3. That the defendant has removed or is about to remove any of his property out of this state, with intent to defraud his creditors; or—
4. That he fraudulently contracted the debt or incurred the obligation respecting which the suit is brought; or—
5. That the defendant is not a resident of this state; or—
6. That the defendant is a foreign corporation; or—
7. That the defendant has fraudulently conveyed or disposed of his property,

or a part of it, or is about fraudulently to convey or dispose of the same, or a part of it, with intent to defraud his creditors.

ARREST.—No person shall be imprisoned for debt arising out of or founded on a contract, express or implied.

Deeds.

CONVEYANCES of lands, or of any estate, or interest therein, may be by deed, signed and sealed by the person from whom the estate or interest is intended to pass, being of lawful age, or by his lawful agent or attorney, and acknowledged or proved and recorded as directed (below), without any other act or ceremony whatever.

Deeds executed within this state of lands or any interest therein, shall be executed in the presence of two witnesses, who shall subscribe their names to the same as such; and the persons executing such deeds may acknowledge the execution thereof before any judge or commissioner of a court of record, or before any notary public or justice of the peace within the state; and the officer taking such acknowledgment shall endorse thereon a certificate of the acknowledgment thereof, and the true date of making the same, under his hand.

If executed in any other state, territory, or district of the United States, such deed may be executed according to the laws of such state, territory, or district; and the execution thereof acknowledged before any judge of a court of record, notary public, justice of the peace, master in chancery, or other officer authorized by the laws of such state, territory, or district, to take the acknowledgment of deeds therein, or before any commissioner appointed by the governor of this state for such purpose.

In the cases provided for in the last preceding section, unless the acknowledgment be taken before a commissioner appointed by the governor of this state for that purpose, such deed shall have attached thereto a certificate of the clerk or other proper certifying officer of a court of record of the county or district within which such acknowledgment was taken, under the seal of his office, that the person whose name is subscribed to the certificate of acknowledgment, was, at the date thereof, such officer as he is therein represented to be; that he believes the signature of such person subscribed thereto to be genuine; and that the deed is executed and acknowledged according to the laws of such state, territory, or district.

If in a foreign country, then before a notary public, or minister plenipotentiary, or minister resident, or consul, appointed to reside therein.

When any married woman residing in this state, shall join with her husband in any deed of conveyance of or relating to real estate, situate within this state, or when she alone without joining with her husband, shall execute a release of dower, her acknowledgment or the proof of the execution of such deed, conveyance, or release, may be taken and certified the same as if she were sole, and if so taken and certified shall entitle such deed, conveyance, or release, to be recorded.

Form of Acknowledgment.

State of Wisconsin,
County of *Dodge*, } *ss.*

Be it remembered, that on this *tenth* day of *March*, one thousand eight hundred and *fifty-one*, before me, JOHN JONES, a *notary public*, in and for said county, personally appeared JOHN DOE *and* SUSAN *his wife*, to me known to be the persons described in and who executed the foregoing deed, and severally acknowledged that they executed the same.

(Seal.) JOHN JONES, *Notary Public.*

Deeds must be recorded in the office of the register of deeds of the county where the lands lie.

A scroll or device, used as a seal, shall have the same effect as a seal; but this does not apply to official seals.

Rights of Married Women.

THE widow shall be entitled to dower of one third of all the lands whereof her husband was seized of an estate of inheritance at any time during the marriage, unless she is lawfully barred.

Rate of Interest.

ANY rate of interest, not exceeding twelve per cent., agreed upon by the parties in contract, specifying the same in writing, is legal and valid; if more be taken the whole debt is forfeited.

When no rate of interest is agreed upon or specified in a note or other contract, seven per cent. per annum shall be the legal rate.

Wills.

WILLS must be in writing, and signed by the testator, or by some person in his presence and by his express direction, and attested and subscribed in the presence of the testator by two or more competent witnesses.

CALIFORNIA.

Constitution adopted 1849.—Square Miles, 188,981.—Population in 1849, 125,000.

Mechanics' Lien.

ALL master-builders, mechanics, lumber-merchants, and all other persons performing labor or furnishing materials for the construction or repair of any building or wharf, shall have a lien, separately or jointly, upon the building or buildings, or wharf, which they may have constructed or repaired, or for which they may have furnished materials of any description, to the extent of the labor done or materials furnished, or for both.

Any such contractor, journeyman, or laborer, who may be employed in the construction or repairing of any building or wharf, or in furnishing any materials for the same, may give to the owner or owners of the building or buildings, or wharf, on which he may have worked, or for the construction of which he may have furnished materials, notice in writing, particularly setting forth the amount of his claim, and the service rendered, for which his employer is indebted to him, and that he holds said owner or owners responsible for the same; and the owner is hereby made liable for the amount so claimed, if indebted to the employer to the amount; if not, then to the amount due from him to said employer at the time such notice was served.

When any such contractor, journeyman, or laborer, shall have given the notice prescribed in the preceding section, he shall present to his employer a copy of such notice for his endorsement. If such employer endorse thereon that the claim is correct, the owner or other person liable shall pay the same, if indebted to the employer in the amount; if not, then the amount due from him to said employer at the time the notice was served. If he fail or refuse so to pay, such sub-contractor, journeyman, or laborer, shall, within thirty days after the service of the notice, commence an action in the proper court to enforce his lien. If, by the terms of the contract between the owner and the contractor, the money be payable at some future day, such sub-contractor, journeyman, or laborer, may file the copy of the notice, with the endorsement thereon, in the recorder's office of the county in which the building or wharf is situated; and shall have thirty days after the money becomes due in which to commence his action. If he fail to commence his action as prescribed in this section, his lien shall be lost.

If the employer fail or refuse to make the endorsement required by the preceding section, such sub-contractor, journeyman, or laborer, shall lose his lien for the amount claimed, unless he shall, within thirty days after the service of the notice, commence an action in the proper court against his employer to establish the amount of the claim. If he obtain judgment against his employer, he shall lose his lien for the amount thereof, unless, within thirty days thereafter, he shall commence an action against the owner for the amount established by the judgment, if the money be then due from the owner to the contractor; if not, then he shall file in the recorder's office of the county in which the building or wharf is situated, a notice of said claim and judgment; and shall commence his action against the owner within thirty days after the money is due from the owner to the contractor.

The owner or other person made liable, as aforesaid, for the amount admitted to be due, or established by judgment, may set off the same in any action brought against him by the contractor or person otherwise entitled to recover the same, under the contract.

The land upon which any building shall be erected, together with the space around the same, not exceeding five hundred square feet, clear of the building, shall also be subject to the above lien, if the said land shall have been at the time of the erecting of the building the property of the person or persons, corporation or association, contracting for the erection or repair of the same.

Any person wishing to avail himself of the provisions of the first section of this act, whether his claim be due or not, shall file in the recorder's office of the county in which the building or wharf is situated, at any time before the expiration of sixty days after the completion of the building or repairs, notice of his intention to hold a lien upon the

CALIFORNIA.

120
115
Tlamath L.
Christmas L.
Scale of Miles.
100
200
O R E G O
Rhett L.
Tlamath R.
Mt.Tsashti
Great Salt Lake
Mud L.
Fremont 1845
Marys or Humbolts R.
City of the Gr.S.
C.Mendocino
Humbolts L.
Utah
Mt.Linn
Pyramid L.
Sacramento
American R.
Carson R.
Carson L.
Nicolet L.
U T
Yuba C.
Fremont
Walker L.
Sacramento City
Benicia
Stockton
Fremont Mts.
San Francisco
S.Jose
S.Cruz
Monterey Bay
S.Juan
Monterey
Soledad
Owens L.
S.Miguel
R. Buenaventura
L.Tulares
Rio Virgin
Colora
S.Luis Obispo
Kern L.
La Purissima
S.Ynes
Mohave R.
Pt.Conception
S.Buenaventura
S.Barbara
S.Gabriel
P.de los Angelos
S.Anna
S.Juan
Warners Ranch
S.Luis Rey
San Pasqual
Gila R.
San Diego
UTAH
NEW MEXICO
AND
CALIFORNIA
LOWER
S.Miguel
CALIFORNIA
M E
120
Long. We

CALIFORNIA.

110
105
Sweetwater R.
Keha Paha R.
South Pass
Ft. Laramie
Ft. Bridger
Black F.
Mary R.
Platte R.
Laramie R.
N. Fork Platte R.
Pole Cr.
S. Fork Platte R.
Yampah R.
Longs Peak
Uintah R.
St. Vrains Ft.
40
White R.
PAWNEES
H
Eagle R.
Pikes Peak
Pueblo
Bents Ft.
Gen. Kearney
Arkansas R.
Campadre R.
Spanish Peaks
Cimarone R.
R. St. John
NAVAHOES
Taos
N. Fk. Canadian R.
Red R.
Joya
Santa Fe
Algodones
Canadian R.
S. Miguel
Greggs route 1840
Albuquerque
Tome
35
MEXICO
APACHES
Gibilleta
Socorro
Salt Fk.
South Fk.
Rio Salinas
Sholeys Z.
Valverde
Fra Cristobal
Big Wichita R.
San Diego
Robleró
Brazito
Rio Pecos
Tueson
El Paso
SIERRA MADRE
COMANCHES
from 110 Greenwich.
105

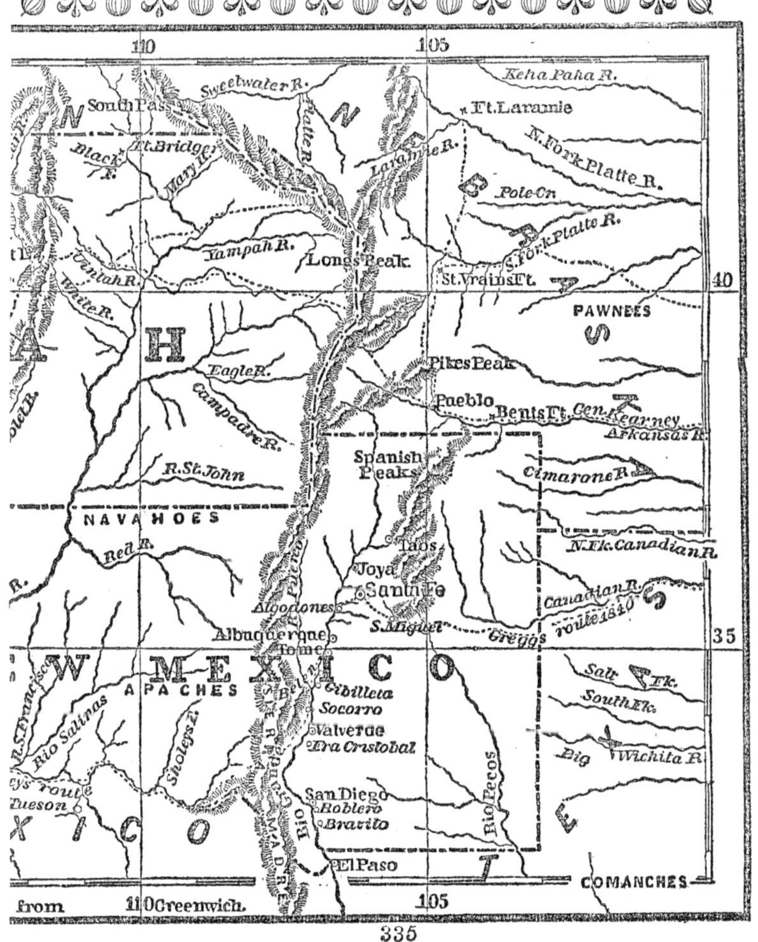

property declared by this act liable to such lien, for the amount due, or to become due to him, specifically setting forth the amount claimed; upon his failure to do so, the lien shall be lost.

No such lien shall bind any building or wharf for a longer time than one year after the work is done, or the materials have been furnished, unless suit be brought in a proper court to enforce the same within that time, or if a credit be given, within one year from the expiration of the credit; but no lien shall be continued in force for a longer term than two years from the time the work is completed, or the materials furnished, by any agreement to give credit.

The lien for work or materials, given by this act, shall be preferred to every other lien or incumbrance which attached upon the property subsequent to the time at which the work was commenced or the materials were furnished.

Any mechanic or artisan who shall make, alter, or repair, any article of personal property, at the request of the owner or legal possessor of such property, shall have a lien on such property so made, altered, or repaired, for his just and reasonable charges, for his work done and materials furnished; and may hold and retain the possession of the same until such just and reasonable charges shall be paid; and if not paid for within the space of two months after the work shall have been done, such mechanic or artisan may proceed to sell the property by him so made, altered, or repaired, at public auction, by giving three weeks' public notice of such sale, by advertisement, in some newspaper published in the county in which the work may be done; or if there be no such newspaper, then by posting up notices of such sale in three of the most public places in the town where such work was done: and the proceeds of said sale shall be applied, first, to the discharge of such lien, and the costs and expenses of keeping and selling such property, and the remainder, if any, shall be paid over to the owner thereof.

LIEN ON VESSELS.

Every boat and vessel used in navigating the waters of this state shall be liable—

1. For all debts contracted by the master, owner, agent, or consignee thereof, on account of supplies furnished for the use of such boat or vessel; on account of work done or services rendered on board of such boat or vessel; on account of labor done or materials furnished by mechanics, tradesmen, or others, in and for the building, repairing, and fitting out, furnishing or equipping such boat or vessel.
2. For all sums due for the wharfage or anchorage of such boat or vessel within the state.
3. For demands or damages accruing from the non-performance or mal-performance of any contract touching the transportation of persons or property, entered into by the master, owner, agent, or consignee, of the boat or vessel on which such contract is to be performed; and—
4. For all injuries done to persons or property by such boat or vessel: provided the wages of mariners, boatmen, and others, employed in the service of such boats and vessels, shall have the preference, and be first paid.

Any person having a demand as aforesaid, instead of proceeding for a recovery thereof against the master, agent, owner, or consignee, of a boat or vessel, may, at his option, institute suit against such boat or vessel by name.

All actions against a boat or vessel, under the provisions of this act, shall be commenced and sued within fifteen days after the cause of such action shall have accrued.

Chattel Mortgages.

No mortgage of personal property hereafter made shall be valid against any other persons than the parties thereto, unless possession of the mortgaged property be delivered to and retained by the mortgagee.

Law regulating Contracts.

In the following cases, every agreement shall be void, unless such agreement, or some note or memorandum thereof, expressing the consideration, be in writing, and subscribed by the party charged therewith:—

1. Every agreement that by the terms is not to be performed within one year from the making thereof.

2. Every special promise to answer for the debt, default, or miscarriage, of another.
3. Every agreement, promise, or undertaking, made upon consideration of marriage, except mutual promises to marry.

Every contract for the sale of any goods, chattels, or things in action, for the price of two hundred dollars or over, shall be void, unless—

1. A note or memorandum of such contract be made in writing, and be subscribed by the parties to be charged therewith; or—
2. Unless the buyer shall accept or receive part of such goods, or the evidences, or some of them, of such things in action; or—
3. Unless the buyer shall at the time pay some part of the purchase-money.

Whenever any goods shall be sold at auction, and the auctioneer shall, at the time of sale, enter in a sale-book, a memorandum, specifying the nature and price of the property sold, the terms of the sale, the name of the purchaser, and the name of the person on whose account the sale is made, such memorandum shall be deemed a note of the contract of sale within the meaning of the last section.

No estate or interest in lands, other than for leases for a term not exceeding one year, nor any trust or power over or concerning lands, or in any manner relating thereto, shall hereafter be created, granted, assigned, surrendered, or declared, unless by act or operation of law, or by deed, or conveyance in writing, subscribed by the party creating, granting, assigning, surrendering, or declaring the same, or by his lawful agent thereunto authorized by writing.

Every instrument required by any of the provisions of this act to be subscribed by any party, may be subscribed by the lawful agent of such party.

Limitation of Actions.

No action for the recovery of real property, or for the recovery of the possession thereof, shall be maintained, unless it appear that the plaintiff, his ancestor, predecessor, or grantor, was seized or possessed of the premises in question, within five years before the commencement of such action.

No cause of action, or defence to an action founded upon the title to real property, or to rents or services out of the same, shall be effectual, unless it appear that the person prosecuting the action, or making the defence, or under whose title the action is prosecuted, or the defence is made, or the ancestor, predecessor, or grantor of such person, was seized or possessed of the premises in question, within five years before the commencement of the act in respect to which such action is prosecuted or defence made.

No entry upon real estate shall be deemed sufficient or valid as a claim, unless an action be commenced thereupon within one year after making such entry, and within five years from the time when the right to make such entry descended or accrued.

If a person entitled to commence any action for the recovery of real property, or to make an entry or defence, founded on the title to real property, or to rents or services out of the same, be, at the time such title shall first descend or accrue, either—

1. Within the age of twenty-one years; or—
2. Insane; or—
3. Imprisoned on a criminal charge, or in execution upon conviction of a criminal offence, for a term less than for life; or—
4. A married woman—

The time during which such disability shall continue shall not be deemed any portion of the time in this act limited for the commencement of such action, or the making of such entry or defence; but such action may be commenced, or entry or defence made, within the period of five years after such disability shall cease, or after the death of the person entitled, who shall die under such disability: but such action shall not be commenced, or entry or defence made, after that period.

Actions, other than those for the recovery of real property, can only be commenced as follows:—

Within five years: an action upon a judgment or decree of any court of the United States, or of any state or territory within the United States.

Within four years: an action upon any contract, obligation, or liability, founded upon an instrument of writing, except those mentioned in the preceding section.

Within three years: 1. An action upon a liability created by statute, other than a penalty or forfeiture. 2. An action for trespass upon real property. 3 An action for taking, detaining, or injuring, any goods or chattels, including actions for the specific recovery of personal property. 4. An action for relief on the ground of fraud, the cause of action in such case not to be deemed to have accrued until the discovery, by the aggrieved party, of the facts constituting the fraud.

Within two years: 1. An action upon a contract, obligation, or liability, not founded upon an instrument of writing, except an action on an open account, for goods, wares, and merchandise, and an action for any article charged in a store account. 2. An action against a sheriff, coroner, or constable, upon the liability incurred by the doing of an act in his official capacity, and in virtue of his office, or by the omission of an official duty, including the non-payment of money collected upon an execution. But this section shall not apply to an action for an escape.

Within one year: 1. An action upon a statute for a penalty or forfeiture, where the action is given to an individual, or to an individual and the state, except where the statute imposing it prescribes a different limitation. 2. An action for libel, slander, assault, battery, or false imprisonment. 3. An action upon a statute for a forfeiture or penalty to the people of this state. 4. An action against a sheriff or other officer for the escape of a prisoner, arrested or imprisoned on civil process. 5. An action on an open account, for goods, wares, and merchandise, sold and delivered. 6. An action for any article charged in a store account.

In an action brought to recover a balance due upon a mutual, open, and current account, where there have been reciprocal demands between the parties, the cause of action shall be deemed to have accrued from the time of the last item proved in the account on either side.

If a person, entitled to bring an action mentioned in the last preceding chapter, except for a penalty or forfeiture, or against a sheriff or other officer for an escape, be, at the time the cause of action accrued, either—first, within the age of twenty-one years; or, second, insane; or, third, imprisoned on a criminal charge, or in execution under the sentence of a criminal court, for a term less than his natural life; or, fourth, a married woman: the time of such disability shall not be a part of the time limited for the commencement of the action.

When a person shall be an alien subject, or citizen of a country at war with the United States, the time of the continuance of the war shall not be part of the period limited for the commencement of the action.

No acknowledgment or promise shall be sufficient evidence of a new or continuing contract, whereby to take the case out of the operation of this statute, unless the same be contained in some writing, signed by the party to be charged thereby.

Collection of Debts.

Arrest.—No person shall be arrested in a civil action except as prescribed by this act; but this provision shall not apply to proceedings for contempt.

The defendant may be arrested in the following cases:—

1. In an action for money received, or property embezzled or fraudulently misapplied, by a public officer, or by an attorney or counsellor, or by an officer or agent of a corporation, in the course of his employment as such, or by any factor, agent, broker, or other person in a fiduciary capacity.

2. When the defendant has been guilty of a fraud in contracting the debt or incurring the obligation for which the action is brought, or in concealing or disposing of the property for the taking, detention, or conversion of which, the action is brought.

3. When the defendant has removed or disposed of his property, or is about to do so, with intent to defraud his creditors. But no female shall be arrested in any action.

Attachment.—Any creditor shall be entitled to proceed, by attachment in the district court, against the property of his debtor, in the manner provided in this act.

Before any writ of attachment shall be issued, the plaintiff, his agent or attorney, shall take and subscribe an affidavit in writing that the defendant is indebted to the plaintiff in the sum of two hundred dollars or over, specifying the amount of such indebtedness as near as may be, over and above all legal set-offs, and that the sum is due upon contract, express or implied, and that the deponent knows, or has good reason to believe, either—

1. That the defendant has absconded, or is about to abscond from this state, or that he is concealed therein, to the injury of his creditors; or—

2. That the defendant has removed or is about to remove any of his property out of this state, with intent to defraud his creditors; or—

3. That he fraudulently contracted the debt, or incurred the obligation, respecting which the suit is brought; or—

4. That the defendant is a non-resident of the state; or—

5. That the defendant has fraudulently conveyed, disposed of, or concealed his property, or a part of it, or is about fraudulently to convey, dispose of, or conceal the same, or a part of it, with intent to defraud his creditors.

No writ of attachment shall be issued under the provisions of this act in the district court, unless the amount stated in such oath or affidavit as due to the plaintiff, over and above legal set-offs, shall exceed the sum of two hundred dollars.

At the time of filing the affidavit, and before the issuance of any writ of attachment, the plaintiff, or some responsible person in his behalf, shall execute a bond with sufficient surety, in a sum at least double the amount of the demand sworn to, payable to the defendant, and conditioned that the plaintiff shall pay to the defendant all damages that he may incur, by reason of the wrongful suing out of the writ of attachment.

Attachment may issue, although the debt or demand of the plaintiff be not due, when it is shown by the affidavit—

1. That the defendant is about to abscond from the state, or that he is concealed therein, to the injury of his creditors; or—

2. That the defendant is about to remove any of his property out of the state, or that he is about fraudulently to convey, dispose of, or conceal the same, with intent to defraud his creditors:

In this case no judgment shall be rendered until the debt becomes due, but the attachment shall give a lien as in other cases.

Deeds.

CONVEYANCES of lands, or of any estate or interest therein, may be made by deed, signed by the person from whom the estate or interest is intended to pass, being of lawful age, or by his lawful agent or attorney, and acknowledged or proved and recorded as hereinafter directed.

A husband and wife may, by their joint deed, convey the real estate of the wife in like manner as she might do by her separate deed if she were unmarried.

Every conveyance in writing, whereby any real estate is conveyed or may be affected, shall be acknowledged, or proved and certified, in the manner hereinafter provided.

The proof or acknowledgment of every conveyance affecting any real estate shall be taken by some one of the following officers:—

1. If acknowledged or proved within this state, by some judge or clerk of a court having a seal, or some notary public, or justice of the peace, of the proper county.

2. If acknowledged or proved without this state, and within the United States, by some judge or clerk of any court of the United States, or of any state or territory having a seal, or by any commissioner appointed by the government of this state for that purpose.

3. If acknowledged or proved without the United States, by some judge or clerk of any court of any state, kingdom, or empire, having a seal, or by any notary public therein, or by any minister, commissioner, or consul of the United States, appointed to reside therein.

Every officer that shall take the proof or acknowledgment of any conveyance affecting any real estate, shall grant a certificate thereof, and cause such certificate to be endorsed or annexed to such conveyance. Such certificate shall be—

1. When granted by any judge or clerk, under the hand of such judge or clerk, and the seal of the court.

2. When granted by an officer who has a seal of office, under the hand and official seal of such officer.

No acknowledgment of any conveyance whereby any real estate is conveyed or may be affected, shall be taken, unless the person offering to make such acknowledgment shall be personally known to the officer taking the same, to be the person whose name is subscribed to such conveyance as a party thereto, or shall be proved to be such by the oath or affirmation of a credible witness.

The certificate of such acknowledgment shall state the fact of acknowledgment, and that the person making the same was personally known to the officer granting the certificate to be the person whose name is subscribed to the conveyance as a party thereto, or was proved to be such by the oath or affirmation of a credible witness, whose name shall be inserted in the certificate. Such certificate shall be substantially in the following form, to wit:—

Forms of Acknowledgment.

State of California,
County of *Sutter*, } *ss.*

On this *thirtieth* day of *December*, A. D. one thousand eight hundred and *fifty*, personally appeared before me, JOHN JONES, a *notary public* [or *judge*, or *officer*, as the case may be] in and for the said county, JOHN DOE *and* SUSAN *his wife*, known to me to be the persons described in and who executed the foregoing *instrument*, who acknowledged to me that they executed the same freely and voluntarily, and for the uses and purposes therein mentioned; *and the said* SUSAN, *having been by me first made acquainted with the contents of such conveyance, acknowledged, on an examination by me had apart from and without the hearing of her husband, that she executed the same freely and voluntarily, without fear, or compulsion, or undue influence, of her husband, and that she does not wish to retract the execution of the same.* JOHN JONES, *Notary Public.*

When the grantor is unknown to the court or officer taking the acknowledgment, the certificate may be in the following form, to wit: State of California, County of *Sacramento*: On this *tenth* day of *December*, A. D. one thousand eight hundred and *fifty*, personally appeared before me, JOHN JONES, a *notary public* [or *judge*, or *officer*, as the case may be] in and for the said county, JOHN DOE, satisfactorily proved to me to be the person described in, and who executed the within *conveyance*, by the oath of JOHN SMITH, a competent and credible witness for that purpose, by me duly sworn; and he, the said JOHN DOE, acknowledged that he executed the same freely and voluntarily, for the uses and purposes therein mentioned. JOHN JONES, *Notary Public.*

Rights of Married Women.

ALL property, both real and personal, of the wife, owned by her before marriage, and that acquired afterward by gift, bequest, devise, or descent, shall be her separate property; and all property, both real and personal, owned by the husband before marriage, and that acquired by him afterward by gift, bequest, devise, or descent, shall be his separate property.

All property acquired after the marriage by either husband or wife, except such as may be acquired by gift, bequest, devise, or descent, shall be common property.

A full and complete inventory of the separate property of the wife shall be made out and signed by the wife, acknowledged or proved in the manner required by law for the acknowledgment or proof of a conveyance of land, and recorded in the office of the recorder of the county in which the parties reside.

If there be included in the inventory any real estate lying in other counties, the inventory shall also be recorded in such counties.

The filing of the inventory in the recorder's office shall be notice of the title of the wife; and all property belonging to her, included in the inventory, shall be exempt from seizure or execution for the debts of her husband.

The husband shall have the management and control of the separate property of the wife, during the continuance of the marriage; but no sale or other alienation of any part of such property can be made, nor any lien or incumbrance created thereon, unless by an instrument in writing, signed by the husband and wife, and acknowledged by her upon an examination separate and apart from her husband, before a justice of the supreme court, judge of the district court, county judge, or notary public, or if executed out of the state, then so acknowledged before some judge of a court of record, or before a commissioner appointed under the authority of this state to take acknowledgment of deeds.

The husband shall have the entire management and control of the common property, with the like absolute power of disposition as of his own separate estate. The rents and profits of the separate property of either husband or wife shall be deemed common property.

Upon the dissolution of the community by the death of either husband or wife, one half of the common property shall go to the survivor, and the other half to the descendants of the deceased husband or wife, subject to the payment of the debts of the deceased. If there be no descendants of the deceased husband or wife, the whole shall go to the survivor, subject to such payment.

In case of the dissolution of the marriage, by the decree of any court of competent jurisdiction, the common property shall be equally divided between the parties, and the court granting the decree shall make such order for the division of the common property, or the sale and equal distribution of the proceeds thereof, as the nature of the case may require.

The separate property of the husband shall not be liable for the debts of the wife contracted before the marriage, but the separate property of the wife shall be and continue liable for all such debts.

In every marriage hereafter contracted in this state, the rights of husband and wife shall be governed by this act, unless there is a marriage contract, containing stipulations contrary thereto.

DOWER.—No estate shall be allowed to the husband as tenant by courtesy upon the decease of his wife, nor any estate in dower be allowed to the wife upon the decease of her husband.

Rate of Interest.

WHEN there is no express contract in writing, fixing a different rate of interest, interest shall be allowed at the rate of ten per cent. per annum, for all moneys after they become due on any bond, bill, promissory note, or other instrument of writing, on any judgment, recovered before any court in this state, for money lent, for money due on the settlement of accounts, from the day on which the balance is ascertained, and for money received to the use of another. Parties may contract for any rate as high as eighteen per cent., but principals and endorsers are held responsible, under heavy penalties for receiving a higher rate of interest.

Wills.

No will, except such nuncupative wills as are mentioned in the following section, shall be valid, unless it be in writing, and signed by the testator or by some person in his presence, and by his express direction, and attested by two or more competent witnesses subscribing their names to the will, in the presence of the testator.

No nuncupative will shall be good, when the estate bequeathed exceeds the value of five hundred dollars; nor unless the same be proved by two witnesses, who were present at the making thereof; nor unless it be proved that the testator, at the time of pronouncing the same, did bid some one present to bear witness that such was his will, or to that effect; nor unless such nuncupative will was made at the time of the last sickness and at the dwelling-house of the deceased, or where he or she had been residing for the space of ten days or more, except where such person was taken sick from home, and died before his or her return. Nothing contained herein shall prevent any soldier being in actual service, nor mariner being on shipboard, from disposing of his wages and other personal estate by a nuncupative will.

Any married woman may dispose of all her estate by will, and may alter or revoke the will, in like manner as a person under no disability might do; provided that no such will, alteration, or revocation, shall be of any validity, without the consent of the husband, in writing, annexed to such will, alteration, or revocation, and attested and subscribed, and to be proven and recorded in like manner as a will is required to be witnessed, proven, and recorded, unless the wife has power to make a will, conferred by marriage contract or authority in writing, executed by her husband before marriage.

Homestead-Exemption Law.

THE homestead, consisting of a quantity of land, together with the dwelling-house thereon and its appurtenances, and not exceeding in value the sum of five thousand dollars, to be selected by the owner thereof, shall not be subject to forced sale on execution, or any other final process from a court, for any debt or liability contracted or incurred after June first, 1851, or if contracted or incurred at any time in any other place than in this state.

This exemption does not extend to mechanics' or venders' liens, or to any mortgage lawfully obtained; but no mortgage, sale, or alienation, by a married man, is valid without the signature of the wife, acknowledged by her apart from her husband, unless it be to secure the payment of purchase-money. Neither is it exempt from liability for taxes.

Appraisers may be appointed to value the homestead if the plaintiff requires it. If the lot selected as a homestead contain 2500 square yards or less, and the appraisers value the land and improvements at more than $5,000, the excess or the whole may be sold; if the whole, the amount exempt must be paid to the defendant, and no bid can be received for less than $5,000. If the land selected as a homestead exceed 2500 square yards, and $5,000 in value, the appraisers must set off such portion in compact form, including the dwelling-house, as will be of the value of $5,000. The defendant may also designate such articles of personal property as are exempt by law from levy and forced sale. The same benefits accrue to the wife and his own legitimate children, upon the death of the head of a family

UNITED STATES.

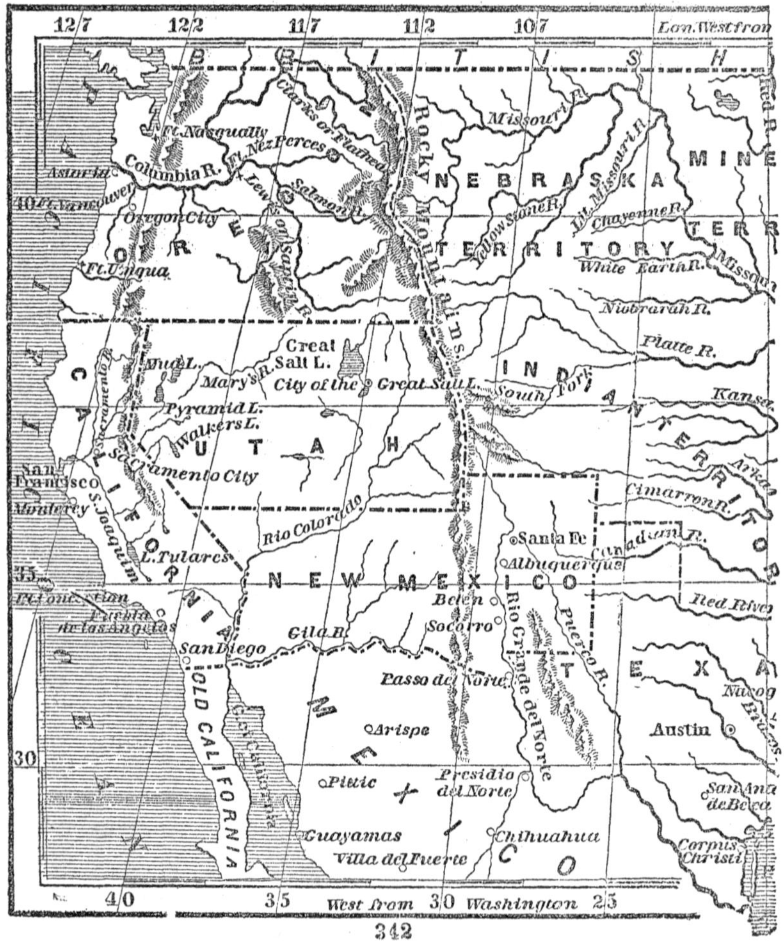

UNITED STATES.

UNITED STATES AND FOREIGN POSTAGE.

UNITED STATES INLAND POSTAGE—New Rates.

The following abstract contains all the provisions relating to letters and printed matter of the new postage law, passed March 3, 1851, and which goes into operation on and after *July* 1, 1851.

LETTER POSTAGE.—For a letter not exceeding *half an ounce* in weight, (avoirdupois,) sent not more than 3,000 miles, if *prepaid, three cents*; if *not paid* before depositing in the postoffice, *five cents.* For any distance *over* 3,000 miles, *double* the above rates. Each additional weight of half an ounce or fraction of half an ounce, is charged with an additional single postage, according to the conditions of distance and mode of payment before specified. These rates apply only to places within the United States. Drop letters one cent each.

A letter, when conveyed wholly or in part by sea, and to or from a foreign country, *over* 2,500 miles, *twenty cents*; and *under* 2,500 miles, *ten cents*, except all cases where the postages have been or shall be adjusted at different rates by postal treaty or convention. Each half ounce or fraction of half an ounce to be rated at a single postage. This law does not effect the old rates of postage to England, but reduces the postage to California and Oregon to *six cents* if prepaid, or *ten cents* if not paid in advance. On letters sent to the continent of Europe (not sent through England), the postage will be 20 cents the single rate, without regard to distance the same are carried in the United States.

NEWSPAPER POSTAGE.—All newspaper not exceeding *three ounces* in weight, sent from the office of publication to actual and bonafide subscribers, are charged with the following rates of postage :—

Newspapers per Quarter, published—

Payable in advance.	Monthly.	Semi-Monthly.	Weekly.	Semi-Weekly.	Tri-Weekly.	Daily.
Not exceeding 50 miles.........	1¼	2½	5	10	15	25
From 50 to 300 miles...........	2½	5	10	20	30	50
From 300 to 1,000 miles........	3¾	7½	15	30	45	75
From 1,000 to 2,000 miles......	5	10	20	40	60	100
From 2,000 to 4000 miles......	6¼	12½	25	50	75	125
Exceeding 4,000 miles.........	7½	15	30	60	90	150

Newspapers less than 300 square inches *one fourth* these rates.

Weekly newspapers only, sent to subscribers in the *County* where published, are *free* of postage.

Other newspapers, and each circular not sealed, handbill, engraving, periodical, magazine, bound book not exceeding thirty-two ounces in weight, and every other description of printed matter, unconnected with any manuscript or written matter, not exceeding one ounce in weight, pay the following rates:—

500 miles, or less..........	1 cent	2,500 to 3,500 miles......	4 cents
500 to 1,500 miles.........	2 "	Exceeding 3,500 miles...	5 "
1,500 to 2,500 miles......	3 "		

Each additional ounce is charged an additional rate. The postage on all printed matter (other than newspapers and periodicals sent to subscribers) must be prepaid; but if sent without prepayment, it will be charged double these rates.

Bona-fide subscribers to periodicals published at intervals not exceeding three months, are required to pay one quarter's postage in advance; and in all such cases the postage is *one half* the foregoing rates.

Publishers of pamphlets, periodicals, magazines, and newspapers, which do not exceed sixteen ounces in weight, are allowed to exchange a single copy free. They can also enclose in their publications the bills for subscriptions without any additional charge for postage.

Postage will be charged according to the regular mail-route, although it may not be the shortest distance. Newspapers are *not* considered as periodicals, and are *not* entitled to the reduced rates as such by prepayment. Subscribers to periodicals, to obtain the benefit of the prepaid rates, must pay the full quarter's postage *before* the delivery of the first number for the quarter. Payments in advance on newspers and periodicals can only be made by subscribers at the postoffice where delivered. Publishers have no deduction for prepayment.

POSTAGE WITH FOREIGN COUNTRIES.

FOREIGN POSTAGE.—Between any office in the United States (Oregon and California excepted) and any office in Great Britain and Ireland, the entire postage is 24 cents the single letter, which may be prepaid or sent unpaid. Payment of anything less than the entire postage, goes for nothing.

Between the offices of California and Oregon and those of Great Britain and Ireland, the entire postage is 29 cents the single letter, which may be prepaid or sent unpaid.

On all correspondence between the United States and the following-named countries, the United States postage, and that only, *must* be collected in the United States by prepayment when sent, and on delivery when received, at the rate of 5 cents the single letter when conveyed by British packet (unless from or to Oregon or California, then 10 cents), and 21 cents the single letter when conveyed by United States packet (unless, as aforesaid, from or to Oregon or California, then 26 cents); newspapers each 4 cents, to be prepaid, to wit:—

Alexandria, city of, via Marseilles.
Algeria.
Austria, and the Austrian states.
Baden, Bavaria, Belgium.
Bremen, free city of Brunswick.
Beyroot, city of, via Marseilles.
Dardanelles, the, "
Denmark, France.
German states, Gibraltar.
Greece, via Marseilles.
Hamburg and Cuxhaven.
Hanover, Holland.
Hong-Kong (China), island of.
Ionian islands.
Lubec, free city of.
Malta, island of. "
Mecklenburg-Schwerin.
Mecklenburg-Strelitz.
Moldavia.
Naples, kingdom of, via Marseilles.
Norway, Oldenburg.
Poland, Prussia.
Roman or Papal states.
Russia, Saxony.
Scutari, city of, via Marseilles.
Smyrna, " "
Sweden, Switzerland.
Turkey in Europe.
Tuscany, via Marseilles.
Venetian states.
Wallachia, Wurtemberg.
West Indies, &c., British, viz.: Antigua, Barbadoes, Bahamas, Berbice, Cariacou, Demerara, Dominica, Essequibo, Granada, Honduras, Jamaica, Montserrat, Nevis, St. Kitts, St. Lucia, St. Vincent, Tobago, Tortola, Trinidad.

This leaves, in those cases, the British and foreign postage to be collected at the other end of the route. But no British inland postage is to be charged in such cases.

On all correspondence between the United States (Oregon and California excepted) and the following-named countries, through the United Kingdom, and by the routes here specified, there *must* be prepaid when sent, and collected when received, the following rates the single letter, not exceeding a half-ounce (unless to or from Oregon or California, then 5 cents is to be added to each rate), viz.:—

(Half-ounce Letters.)	CENTS.
Aden, Asia, island of Ceylon, China, East Indies, New Granada, Philippine islands, Sierra Leone, Venezuela, via Southampton	45
Australia, Bourbon, islands of, Borneo, Java, Labuan, Moluccas, New South Wales, New Zealand, island of Sumatra, Van Dieman's Land, via Southampton and India	53
Australia, New South Wales, New Zealand, any British colony or foreign country, when conveyed to or from the United Kingdom by private ships	37
Canary islands, Cape de Verde islands, island of Madeira	65
Egypt, Greece, Syria	57
Azores islands, via Southampton and Lisbon	63
Brazils, via Falmouth	87
Buenos Ayres, "	83
Heligoland, island of, via London	33
Lucca and Modena, via France	31
Mauritius, via Southampton and India.	45
Montevideo, via Falmouth	83
Parma and Placentia, via France	31
Portugal, via Southampton	63
Spain, via Southampton	73
West Indies (foreign), viz., Cuba, via Southampton	75
Guadaloupe, Hayti, Martinique, Porto Rico, St. Croix, St. Eustatius, St. Martin, St. Thomas, via Southampton	55

Places	For single letters, which must be less than one fourth of an ounce in weight.	Cents.
Aden, Asia, East Indies; Ceylon, island of; China; Hong-Kong, island of; Mauritius; Philippine islands. To be sent by closed mail, via Marseilles	British and sea	50
	Foreign	10
	American inland	5
	Total	65
Australia; New Zealand; Van Dieman's Land; Bourbon, Borneo; Java, Labuan; Moluccas, Sumatra; Or any other place in the Indian Archipelago. By closed mail, via Marseilles	British and sea	58
	Foreign	10
	American inland	5
	Total	73
Egypt; Syria. By closed mail, via Marseilles	British and sea	46
	Foreign	10
	American inland	5
	Total	61
Egypt; Syria; Sicily, island of; Tunis, Africa. By French packet, via Marseilles	British and sea	26
	Foreign	20
	American inland	5
	Total	51
Sardinia; Spain. Via France	British and sea	26
	Foreign	10
	American inland	5
	Total	41

NOTE.—The *foreign* portion of the above rates is to be charged according to the following scale, viz.:—

Weighing under a ¼ ounce	1 rate.
" ¼ ounce, and under ½ ounce	2 rates.
" ½ " " " ¾ "	3 rates.
" ¾ " " " 1 "	4 rates.
" 1 " " " 1¼ "	5 rates.

And so on, an additional rate being charged for each *quarter of an ounce.*

Postage by the New York, Southampton, and Bremen Line of Steamers.

The postage on letters and packages sent by this line, from or to any part of the United States (except Oregon and California when 5 cents will be added) to or from the Continent, not exceeding half an ounce in weight, is 20 cents; and for every additional fraction of an ounce, 20 cents.

On letters addressed to the following countries and places, the foreign postage, to the place of destination, may be *added* to the United States postage of 20 cents, and the whole prepaid—or the American postage alone may be prepaid—or the whole postage may be left unpaid, at the option the sender, viz:—

(Half-Ounce Letters.)	CENTS.	*(Half-Ounce Letters.)*	CENTS.
Altona	6	Mecklenburg-Scherwin	12
Bremen	Nothing	Mecklenburg-Strelitz	12
Brunswick	6	Nassau	12
Cassel	12	Oldenburg	2
Coburg	12	Prussia (kingdom and provinces)	12
Darmstadt	12	Reuss	12
Frankfort-on-the-Maine	12	Saxe-Altenberg	12
Gotha	12	Saxe-Meningen	12
Hamburg	6	Saxe-Weimar	12
Hanover	6	Saxony (kingdom)	12
Hesse-Homburg	12	Schaumburg-Lippe	12
Kiel	11	Schwartzburg-Rudolstadt	12
Lippe-Detmold	12	Schwartzburg-Sondershausen	12
Lubec	9	Wurtemberg (kingdom)	12

United States postage of 20 cents, *only* should be paid on letters addressed to the following places. Letters to these places can be sent wholly unpaid, by the *Bremen* line.

Copenhagen, and farthest parts of Denmark; Bergen, Christina, and farthest parts of Norway: St. Petersburgh or Cronstadt, Russia; Stockholm, and farthest parts of Sweden; Alexandria; empire and provinces of Austria; Baden; Basle, and other parts of Switzerland; Bavaria; Cairo in Egypt; Constantinople; Greece; and eastern towns of Italy.

To Havre (France), or any other port or place on the coast of France, Germany, or any other port on the continent of Europe where the United States steam-packets touch (Great Britain and Ireland excepted), the postage is 20 cents, which must be prepaid when sent from, and collected when received in the United States.

Other Foreign Letter-Postage.

Between any place in the United States (not over 3000 miles from the line of crossing), and Canada, the provinces of New Brunswick, Nova Scotia. Newfoundland, and Cape Breton, on a letter not exceeding half an ounce, the postage is 10 cents; over 3000 miles from the line of crossing, 15 cents; an additional rate for each half ounce or less; prepayment is optional.

On letters to Havana (Cuba), Antigua, Barbadoes, Bahamas, Berbice, Carioco, Demerara, Dominica. Essequibo, Grenada, Honduras, Jamaica, Montserrat, Nevis, St. Kitt's, St. Lucia, St. Vincent, Tobago, Tortola, and Trinidad, if the distance from the mailing office does not exceed 2,500 miles, the postage is ten cents: if it exceeds 2,500 miles, 20 cents. The above postage must be *prepaid* on letters sent from, and *collected* on those received in the United States. On letters from the West India islands (*not British*), Mexico, ports or points on the gulf of Mexico, or places on the Atlantic coast of South America, *not* in British possessions, the postage is 35 cents, if less than 2,500 miles, or 45 cents if over; which must be prepaid on letters sent *from* the United States, but on letters *received*, only 10 or 20 cents according to distance, will be collected in the United States.

The postage on letters *sent* from the United States to the following places on the Pacific coast of South America, will be 50 cents, which must be prepaid; on letters *received*, only 25 cents will be collected in the United States. Southwest coast of South America; Buenaventura, Bogota, New Grenada; Guayaquil, Quito, Ecuador; Payta, Lambayeque, Huanchaco, Casma, Huacho, Callao, Lima, Pisco, Islay, Arica, Iquique, Peru; Cobija, La Paez, Bolivia; Copiapo, Huasco, Coquimbo, Valparaiso, St. Iago, Chili.

Letters sent from the United States to foreign countries by *private* vessels, are chargeable with inland postage which must be prepaid. Letters are sent in this way from California to the Sandwich islands, China, and New South Wales; and also from other places in the United States to foreign countries.

Newspaper and Pamphlet Postage.

The regular United States rates to and from the line, are collected on newspapers to or from Canada. The postage between the United States and Great Britain and Ireland, is 2 cents; when sent to the continent *through* England, 4 cents; to places on the continent when sent through the *Bremen line*, to the *British* West Indies and Havana, 2 cents; to be *prepaid when sent, and collected when received in the United States.* To the West India islands, and places on the Atlantic coast of South America, *not* in British possession, and Mexico, 4 cents when *sent*, and 2 when received, to be prepaid. To places on the Pacific coast of South America, the postage to be paid is 8 cents when *sent* from, and 4 cents when received in the United States.

Newspapers and periodicals to foreign countries (particularly to the continent of Europe), must be sent in narrow bands, open at the sides or end; otherwise they are chargeable there with letter-postage.

PERIODICALS.—Periodical works and pamphlets are not entitled to transit conveyance *through* Great Britain and Ireland, but they may be sent from the United States to the United Kingdom, and *vice versa*, at 2 cents United States postage each, if they do not exceed 2 ounces in weight; and at 1 cent per ounce, or fraction of an ounce, when they exceed that weight, to be collected in all cases in the United States; and the same will be subject to an additional like charge in the United Kingdom when not exceeding 2 ounces; but the third ounce raises the British charge to sixpence, with an additional charge of twopence for each additional ounce. When sent to or received from foreign countries, *without passing through the United Kingdom*, they will be chargeable with the regular United States rates, to be prepaid when sent, and collected when received.

BOOK-KEEPING.

THE art of Book-keeping teaches to record systematically the various transactions of business in any occupation in which a person may be engaged, so that he may know his pecuniary situation, possess ability to substantiate his claims, and protect his property, and at death leave behind him evidence that will enable his friends to understand his business relations and engagements, and settle his affairs in a satisfactory manner. For these reasons no one should fail to keep a book record, instead of relying on his memory or loose papers for evidence.

There are two methods of book-keeping, Single and Double Entry; the last is employed in extensive and complicated mercantile business, where a check is required upon each entry, to prove that it has been properly recorded. The first is generally used by persons engaged in ordinary business, as it is more simple and sufficiently correct for such purposes. It requires but three books—the Day-Book, Ledger, and Cash-Book; to these may be added, a Bill-Book, in which all notes, received or given, are recorded, showing when drawn, by whom, in whose favor, length of time, when due, amount of note, and any explanatory remarks required; also, a Sales-Book, in which orders for goods or the details of sales are entered, and a Receipt-Book where receipts can be permanently kept.

DAY-BOOK.

The Day-book should contain statements of every business transaction, which gives rise to persons owing us or to our owing them, properly arranged under the head of debtor or creditor. The accounts should be entered in this book at the time they were created, or in the order in which they occurred in business.

The book should be commenced by stating the name of the owner and his residence. The day, month, and year, should then be written, and repeated at the head of each page corresponding with the date of the first transaction on the page, the subsequent dates on the page may stand above the transaction to which they belong. In making an entry the name of the person with whom we deal is written, with Dr. or Cr. at the right of the name, to show whether he becomes debtor or creditor by the transaction. Then a statement should follow of the business done, specifying the articles bought or sold, and the price of each. The total amount should be added up and entered in the dollar and cent columns. The person with whom you deal is debtor for whatever he receives of you, and creditor for whatever you receive of him, is the rule for determining how an entry must be made. The entries in the Day-book are transferred to the Ledger, where all the transactions relating to an individual are recorded on a page devoted to his account. The figure at the left of an entry indicates the page of the Ledger to which it has been carried. (See posting accounts.)

If a mistake is made in an account, it should not be corrected by altering the original entry, but a new entry made debiting or crediting the amount of the error, thus, "John Smith, Cr. by [or Dr. to] error in account of Oct. 6, $1.50." This will enable a person to swear before a court that his book contains his original entries without an alteration.

LEDGER.

The Ledger is employed for collecting the scattered accounts of the Day-book. The accounts which relate to the same individual are brought together on one page, showing all the debits and credits, thus enabling the owner to tell at a glance the state of his account with any person. The Dr. accounts are placed on the left hand of the page, and the Cr. on the right. The Ledger may be ruled according to the example on page 351. Every Ledger should have an index, in which all the names it contains are alphabetically arranged, with the page of the Ledger on which the account can be found.

Posting Accounts.—Transferring accounts from the Day-book to the Ledger is called posting. Commence with the first name in the Day-book, which in our example is William Smith; begin by writing his name in a fair hand at the top of the page, with his residence if different from your own, placing Dr. on the left, and Cr. on the right of the name. As he is debtor to us we commence at the left hand, writing in the first column the year, month, and day, in the second the page of the Day-book on which the original entry can be found, in the third the name of the article, or if several articles are recorded under one date, they may be entered with the general designation of sundries or merchandise, and in the fourth column the total amount of the transaction. Against the account in the Day-book mark the page of the Ledger to which it has been posted; a mark can also be made to show that it has been transferred to the Ledger. Now take the second transaction in the Day-book, and if it is another name take a new page in the Ledger, and proceed in the same manner as the first. In this way all the entries in the Day-book are posted to each person's account, every week or month as opportunity may occur. By subtracting one side from the other the balance which is due will be found. The specimen page represents three pages of a Ledger, to correspond with the three persons who have transactions in the Day-book.

Balance-Sheet.—This may be made to accomplish a double purpose, as it will exhibit the state of the owner's accounts, by determining the amounts owing him and that he may owe, and also prove that the accounts have been correctly posted and added. The method is as follows: rule a sheet of paper similar to ledger page, for debtor and creditor; add up all the items of credit on a page of the Day-book, and enter the amount on the sheet, then add the debits in the same manner, and proceed in this way for whatever time it is wished the proof should cover, add up the two columns and subtract one total from the other, and the difference will be the balance of the Day-book. Turn to the Ledger and obtain the balance of each person's account, and place it under its proper head; add these up, and the difference will be the Ledger balance. If the two balances agree, it proves the entries have been correctly posted.

A complete balance sheet should be made out once or twice a year, when an inventory of stock on hand is taken and added to the debtor balances of accounts, and the original capital is added to the credit balances, (or balances we owe,) these compared will give the amount of profit or loss. It will be remembered that this sheet is an account between ourselves and our books.

All the accounts in the Ledger ought to be balanced twice a year. To do this add up each column and find the difference, and make an entry of this balance on the side that is smallest (this should be made with red ink to distinguish it from other entries); both sides now being equal, draw a line under them to show the fact. Now place the balance on the opposite side, so that it will exhibit the true state of the account. (See Wm. Smith's account on the Ledger page.)

CASH-BOOK.

The Cash-book records the payment and receipt of cash. Cash is made debtor to the cash on hand and cash received, and credited with what is paid out. At the close of each day or week, the cash on hand is counted, and the amount entered on the credit side. This should make the debits and credits equal; the amount of cash on hand is then entered on the debtor side. If money is paid to or received from a person who has an account with us it is also entered in the Day-book; the total receipts and expenditures are carried to the Day-book as often as the Cash-book is balanced. (See form of Cash-book.)

Farmers and mechanics who make but few entries, and therefore require but one book for their accounts, can adopt the plan of the Ledger, omitting the column for day-book page, and make their original entries on a page devoted to each person with whom they deal. It should have an index like the Ledger.

Day-Book.

PETER STONE, GENEVA, NEW YORK, OCTOBER 2, 1850. 1

	William Smith	Dr.		
	To 8 yds. of muslin at 9 cts. a yd.	$ 0.72		
× 1	To 4 yds. of cloth, at $3 a yd.	12.00		
	To 1 scythe	1.10	$13	82
	“			
	Henry Jones	Dr.		
× 2	To 1 pr. of shoes	$1.40		
	To 1 lb. of tea	.75	2	15
	“			
	Charles Johnson	Cr.		
× 3	By 1 yoke of oxen		115	00
	3			
	Henry Jones	Dr.		
	To 14 lbs. nails, at 6 cts.	$0.84		
× 2	To 5 galls. molasses, at 32 cts.	1.60		
	To 12 lbs. cheese, at 10 cts.	1.20	3	64
		Cr.		
	By 8 lbs. wool, at 36 cts.		2	88
	“			
	William Smith	Cr.		
× 1	By 1 load of hay	$6.00		
	By 12 lbs. butter, at 9 cts.	1.08	7	08
	“			
	Charles Johnson	Dr.		
× 3	To Cash		50	00
	4			
	William Smith	Dr.		
	To 1 stove	$14.00		
× 1	To 8 yds. cloth, at $3	24.00		
	To 1 horse	42.00	80	00
	“			
	Charles Johnson	Dr.		
× 3	To 1 set of harness	$20.00		
	To 1 wagon	64.00	84	00
	5			
	Henry Jones	Dr.		
	To 28 lbs. sugar, at 8 cts.	$2 24		
× 2	To 1 barrel of flour	7.00		
	To 3 brooms, at 14 cts.	.42	9	66
	“			
	Charles Johnson	Cr.		
	By 20 bushels corn, at 62 cts.	$12 40		
× 3	By cash	30.00		
	By order on Peter Wilkins	21.00	63	40
	7			
	Charles Johnson	Dr.		
× 3	To check to balance account		44	40
	10			
	Henry Jones	Cr.		
× 2	By Cash to balance account		12	57
	12			
	William Smith	Cr.		
× 1	By his note at 3 months from date		75	00

Ledger.

1 Dr. WILLIAM SMITH. (Waterloo.) Cr. 1

1850.					1850.				
Oct. 2	1	To Sundries	$ 13	82	Oct. 3	1	By hay and butter	$ 7	08
" 4	1	" Sundries	80	00	" 12	1	" note at 3 mos.	75	00
							" *Balance*	11	74
			93	82				93	82
" 12		To Balance	11	74					

2 Dr. HENRY JONES. Cr. 2

1850.					1850.				
Oct. 2	1	To Sundries	$ 2	15	Oct. 3	1	By wool	$ 2	88
" 3	1	" Sundries	3	64	" 10	1	" cash	12	57
" 5	1	" Sundries	9	66					
			15	45				15	45

3 Dr. CHARLES JOHNSON. Cr. 3

1850.					1850.				
Oct. 3	1	To Cash	$50	00	Oct. 2	1	By oxen	$115	00
" 4	1	" harness & wagon	84	00	" 5	1	" sundries	63	40
" 7	1	" check to balance.	44	40					
			178	40				178	40

Cash-Book.

1 Dr. CASH. Cr. 1

1850.				1850.			
Oct. 2	To cash on hand	$150	00	Oct. 2	Paid rent of store 6 mos.	$ 75	00
" 5	Received of C. Johnson	30	00	" 3	" Charles Johnson	50	00
" 5	Order on P. Wilkins	21	00	" 7	" Charles Johnson	44	40
" 9	Receipts of store	106	75	" 9	" expenses in store	8	20
				" 9	*Cash on hand*	130	15
		307	75			307	75
Oct. 9	To cash on hand	$130	15				
" 10	Received of H. Jones	12	57				

INTEREST.

Principal is the sum on which interest is paid. *Interest* is the compensation charged by the lender to the borrower for the use of the principal, and is the real meaning of the word *usury*, though this term is *now* understood as a rate above legal interest: usurious interest, therefore, is the amount above the legal rate established by the state. *Amount* is the principal and interest added together, or the whole sum of several items. *Per cent.* is a rate on a hundred dollars, cents, or pounds, allowed by the lender for the use of money. *Per annum* signifies by the year. *Per cent. per annum* means the rate of interest on a hundred for one year, as six per cent. per annum means six dollars to be charged for the use of one hundred dollars for one year. *Discount* is a deduction of the interest from the principal at the time the money is lent; or an allowance of interest on a sum paid before it is due; or a sum less than par value. *Commission* or *brokerage* is the percentage allowed for services in buying, selling, or transacting business, for another. *Par* or *nominal value* is the sum expressed on the face of a stock certificate, note, coin, &c. *Premium* is a sum charged for insurance, or is the sum exceeding the par value of anything.

INTEREST TABLE,

AT SIX PER CENT., IN DOLLARS AND CENTS, FROM ONE DOLLAR TO TEN THOUSAND.

	1 day.	7 days.	15 days.	1 mo.	3 mos.	6 mos.	12 mos.
$	$ c.	$ c.	$ c.	$ c.	$ c.	$ c.	$ c.
1	00	00	00¼	00½	01½	03	06
2	00	00¼	00½	01	03	06	12
3	00	00¼	01¾	01½	04½	09	18
4	00	00½	01	02	06	12	24
5	00	00½	01¼	02½	07½	15	30
6	00	00¾	01½	03	09	18	36
7	00	00¾	01¾	03½	10½	21	42
8	00	01	02	04	12	24	48
9	00	01	02¼	04½	13½	27	54
10	00	01¼	02½	05	15	30	60
20	00¼	02½	05	10	30	60	1 20
30	00½	03½	07½	15	45	90	1 80
40	00¾	04½	10	20	60	1 20	2 40
50	01	06	12½	25	75	1 50	3 00
100	01½	11¾	25	50	1 50	3 00	6 00
200	03	23½	50	1 00	3 00	6 00	12 00
300	05	35	75	1 50	4 50	9 00	18 00
400	07	46½	1 00	2 00	6 00	12 00	24 00
500	08	58½	1 25	2 50	7 50	15 00	30 00
1000	17	1 16½	2 50	5 00	15 00	30 00	60 00
2000	33	2 33½	5 00	10 00	30 00	60 00	120 00
3000	50	3 50	7 50	15 00	45 00	90 00	180 00
4000	67	4 66½	10 00	20 00	60 00	120 00	240 00
5000	83	5 83½	12 50	25 00	75 00	150 00	300 00
10000	1 67	11 66½	25 00	50 00	150 00	300 00	600 00

INTEREST TABLE,

AT SEVEN PER CENT., IN DOLLARS AND CENTS, FROM ONE DOLLAR TO TEN THOUSAND.

	1 day.	7 days.	15 days.	1 mo.	3 mos.	6 mos.	12 mos.
$	$ c.	$ c.	$ c.	$ c.	$ c.	$ c.	$ c.
1	00	00	00¼	00½	01¾	03½	07
2	00	00¼	00½	01¼	03½	07	14
3	00	00½	00¾	01¾	05¼	10½	21
4	00	00½	01	02⅓	07	14	28
5	00	00¾	01½	03	08¾	17½	35
6	00	00¾	01¾	03½	10½	21	42
7	00	01	02	04	12¼	24½	49
8	00	01	02¼	04⅔	14	28	56
9	00	01¼	02½	05¼	15¾	31½	63
10	00¼	01¼	03	05¾	17½	35	70
20	00⅜	02¾	06	11⅔	35	70	1 40
30	00½	04	09	17½	52½	1 05	2 10
40	00¾	05½	12	23⅓	70	1 40	2 80
50	01	06¾	15	29¼	87½	1 75	3 50
100	02	13½	29	58⅓	1 75	3 50	7 00
200	04	27¼	58	1 16⅔	3 50	7 00	14 00
300	06	40¾	87½	1 75	5 25	10 50	21 00
400	08	54½	1 17	2 33⅓	7 00	14 00	28 00
500	10	68	1 46	2 91⅔	8 75	17 50	35 00
1000	19½	1 36	2 92	5 83⅓	17 50	35 00	70 00
2000	39	2 72¼	5 83	11 66⅔	35 00	70 00	140 00
3000	58	4 08¼	8 75	17 50	52 50	105 00	210 00
4000	78	5 44½	11 67	23 33⅓	70 00	140 00	280 00
5000	97	6 80½	14 58	29 16⅔	87 50	175 00	350 00
10000	1 94	13 61	29 17	58 33	175 00	350 00	700 00

TABLE FOR BANKING AND EQUATION,

Showing the number of Days from any Date in one Month to the same Date in any other Month. Example: How many Days from the 2d of February to the 2d of August? Look for February at the left hand, and August at the top—in the angle is 181. *In leap-year, add one day if February be included.*

From / To	Jan.	Feb.	Mar.	April.	May.	June.	July.	Aug.	Sept.	Oct.	Nov.	Dec.
January	365	31	59	90	120	151	181	212	243	273	304	334
February	334	365	28	59	89	120	150	181	212	242	273	303
March	306	337	365	31	61	92	122	153	184	214	245	275
April	275	306	334	365	30	61	91	122	153	183	214	244
May	245	276	304	335	365	31	61	92	123	153	184	214
June	214	245	273	304	334	365	30	61	92	122	153	183
July	184	215	243	274	304	335	365	31	62	92	123	153
August	153	184	212	243	273	304	334	365	31	61	92	122
September	122	153	181	212	242	273	303	334	365	30	61	91
October	92	123	151	182	212	243	273	304	335	365	31	61
November	61	92	120	151	181	212	242	273	304	334	365	30
December	31	62	90	121	151	182	212	243	274	304	335	365

CALCULATION OF INTEREST.

To find the Interest on any number of Dollars for one Year.—Multiply the sum by the rate per ct., and divide by 100, or cut off the two right-hand figures, and the answer will be the interest in dollars: but if the original sum be dollars and cents, proceed in the same manner, and the answer will be the interest in cents. To find the interest for more than one year, multiply the answer by the number of years. What is the interest on $550.50 for one year at 5 per cent.?

$550.50 cts.
5

Divisor 100)275250($27, 52 cts., 5 mills.

To find the Interest on any number of Dollars and Cents for any number of Days.—Multiply the sum by the number of days; divide the product by 6; cut off the two right-hand figures, and the answer will be in dollars, cents, and mills.

What is the interest on $3,469.32 for 25 days, at 6 per cent. per annum? *Ans.* $14, 45 cts., 5 mills.

$3,469.32
25

1734660
693864

Divisor 6)8673300

1445550

Although the rate of interest may vary from 6 per cent., this method can still be used, by adding when it is more and substracting when it is less than 6 per cent. First find the interest at 6 per cent., as in the preceding example, and then—

Add	one sixth of itself	....	for 7 per cent.
Add	one third	"	" 8 per cent.
Add	one half	"	" 9 per cent.
Add	two thirds	"	" 10 per cent.
Subtract	one sixth	"	" 5 per cent.
Subtract	one third	"	" 4 per cent.

MENSURATION.

To find the Superficial Number of Feet a Board contains.—Multiply the length of the board in feet by the breadth in inches, and divide the product by 12: the quotient is the contents in square feet. If the board is wider at one end than the other, add the breadths of the two ends together, and take half the amount for the mean breadth; then multiply this by the length, and divide by 12 as before. If the length be feet and inches, reduce the whole to inches, multiply it by the breadth, and divide by 144, when the answer will be feet.

To find the Cubic Contents of Square Timber.—Multiply the width and thickness in inches together, and this amount by the length in feet: then divide the product by 144—the answer will be cubic feet. If the length be feet and inches, reduce the length to inches, and multiply as before, dividing the product by 1728: the answer will be cubic feet.

For Round Timber.—Take the mean diameter of the log clear of the bark; deducting from this diameter one fourth, will give the square of the log; multiply the square thus found in inches into itself, and this product by the length in feet; divide the amount by 144, which will give the cubic contents in feet.

What are the contents of a board 9 feet 8 inches long and 15 inches wide?

9 ft. 8 inches=116 inches.
15

580
116

144)1740(12 feet 1 inch.
144

300
282

12

WEIGHTS AND MEASURES.

In 1837, Congress passed a law for regulating the weights and measures of the Union, by which the secretary of the treasury was directed to supply standards of weights, of length, and of capacity, according to the standards of Great Britain, to the governors of states and revenue collectors. The measure of time and circular motion is the same in America and Europe. The Troy weight of England was adopted by the U S. for weighing coin and bullion. Apothecaries compound their medicines by the Troy lb. and a subdivision of their own. The avoirdupois weight used in England is also our legal standard for weighing all other articles bought and sold by weight. The British and the United States statute acre, square yard, square foot, and square inch, and the mile, yard, foot, and inch, are the same.

Congress retained the *old* English wine gallon, as a measure for liquids, and the Winchester bushel for grain, &c.; though England has abandoned both, and substituted what she terms the imperial measure, whether for wines, beer, and other liquids, or dry articles sold by measure; her imperial gallon is exactly 1 1-5th of our wine gallon, and measures 277.274 solid inches; our Winchester gallon measuring 268.8, or about 8½ cubic inches less; her new bushel is equal to 1.032 of ours; heaped measure was abolished by law in Scotland 200 years ago, though not always in practice. England recognises it in recent laws and the United States have sometimes ordered duties to be collected by it.

Apothecaries' Weight.—20 grains make 1 scruple ℈, 3 scruples 1 dram ʒ; 8 drams 1 ounce ℥; 12 ounces 1 pound ℔.

(U. S.) Troy Weight.—24 grains make 1 pennyweight; 20 pennyweights, 1 ounce; 12 ounces 1 pound. 1 lb. Troy is to 1 lb. avoirdupois as 144 is to 175; or, 5,760 grains make 1 lb. Troy, and 7,000 grains 1 lb. Avoirdupois.

(U. S.) Avoirdupois Weight.—[1 dram or 27 11-32 grains equal 1.7712 grammes]—16 drams make 1 ounce [equal to 28.334 grammes]; 16 ounces, 1 pound; 28 pounds, 1 quarter; 4 quarters, 1 hundred weight; 20 hundred weight, or 2,240 pounds, 1 ton.

In Philadelphia, and many other places 2,240 lbs. are generally considered a ton. In the state of New York, unless by special bargain, 2,000 lbs. are a ton. Sales by the lb. are the most common; nothing is sold by the cwt. of 112 lbs. In Avoirdupois, 7 lbs. make 1 clove of wool, and 14 lbs. 1 stone. A pack of wool is 240 lbs. In Ohio, when sales are made by the bushel, without a *special* agreement, the following are the legal weights of a bushel—wheat 60 lbs.; Indian corn 50; barley 48; oats 39; rye 56; flaxseed 56; cloverseed 64. Corn is usually sold in the Western States 56 lbs. to the bushel. In Boston, 53 lbs. are considered a bushel of Western corn. 36 bushels, or 57½ cubic feet, of English coal make 1 chaldron.

In freights, by the rules of the N. Y. Chamber of Commerce, a ton is composed of 8 barrels of flour; 22 bushels of grain, peas, or beans, in casks, or 36 in bulk; 36 bushels European, or 31 bushels W. I. salt; 6 barrels of beef, pork, tallow, or pickled fish; 200 gallons, wine measure, of oil, wine, brandy, or other liquids; 29 bushels of sea-coal; 40 cubic feet of square timber, oak-plank, pine, cotton, wool, and bale goods; 2,000 lbs. of bar or pig iron, ashes, and all other heavy goods.

(U. S.) Linear Measure.—3 barley-corns make 1 inch; 12 inches 1 foot; 3 feet 1 yard; 5½ yards 1 rod or pole; 40 rods 1 furlong; 8 furlongs 1 mile. A hand is 4 inches; a fathom 6 feet; 120 fathoms 1 cable's length; a cubit 1½ feet; 69½ statute, or 60 sea miles, 1 degree; 360 degrees a great circle of the earth; 3 miles are a league; 1 link is equal to 7.92 inches; 100=792 inches, or 66 feet, or 4 rods, or 1 chain; 80 chains=320 rods, or 1 mile.

An English or American mile is 5280 feet; A Dutch mile 24303 feet; a Roman 4884 feet; an Arabian 6444 feet; a Persian Parasang 18108 feet; 4½ English miles make 1 German; 2½ English 1 French league; the Spanish and Polish mile is about 3½ English miles; the Russian mile or verst is about three fourth of an English mile; the Hungarian, Danish, and Swiss mile is between five and six English miles; the Swedish nearly seven.

Cloth Measure.—4 nails or 9 inches make 1 quarter; 4 quarters, 1 yard.

(U. S.) Square Measure.—144 square inches make 1 square foot; 9 sq. feet, 1 sq. yard; 30¼ sq. yards, 1 sq. rod; 40 sq. rods, 1 rood; 4 roods, or 43560 feet, 1 acre; 640 acres, 1 sq. mile; 16 square rods or 10 square chains make an acre.

(U. S.) Solid Measure.—1,728 cubic inches make 1 cubic foot, 27 cubic feet, 1 cubic yard; 42 cubic feet, 1 ton of shipping; 40 cubic feet, 1 ton of unhewn timber; 50 cubic feet 1 ton squared timber. A pile of wood 8 feet long, 4 feet wide, and 4 feet high (or 128 cubic feet), make 1 cord.

(U. S.) Wine Measure.—4 gills make 1 pint; 2 pints, 1 quart; 4 quarts, 1 gallon; 31½ gallons, 1 barrel; 63 gallons, 1 hogshead; 2 hogsheads, 1 pipe; 2 pipes, 1 tun.

(U. S.) Dry, or Winchester Measure.—4 gills make 1 pint = 33.6 cubic inches = 0.55053 French litres; 2 pints 1 quart = 67.40 cubic inches = 1.10107 litres, 4 quarts 1 gallon = 268.8 cub. in. = 4.40428 litres; 2 gallons 1 peck = 537.6 cub in. = 8.808 litres; 4 pecks 1 bushel = 2150.42 cub. in. = 35.2343 litres; 5 quarters 1 wey or load.

The Winchester bushel is 18½ inches wide and 8 inches deep; it contains 2150 2-5 solid inches, being 47 1-5 less than the imperial bushel. Of wheat the bushel is 60 lbs. The barrel of flour contains 5 Winchester bushels, and weighs, net, 196 lbs. The barrel of Indian corn contains 3 1-8 bushels. The weight of a gallon of molasses is usually 11 lbs. but sometimes 10 or 12.

British Imperial (new) Standard Measure, compared with Winchester and Wine Measure.—Our extensive dealings with England make it useful for business-men to have an explanation of the difference between the imperial measure for liquids and dry articles, and our Winchester and wine measures, which latter were formerly used in England.

By the imperial standard, adopted in England in 1826, 1 gill is = 8.665 solid inches; 4 gills = 1 pint; 2 pints 1 quart; 4 quarts 1 gallon, or 277.274 solid inches; 2 gallons 1 peck; 4 pecks 1 bushel, or 2218.191 inches; 4 bushels are 1 coomb; 2 coombs (8 bushels) 1 quarter.

The quarter of wheat is equal to the quarter of a ton of 2240 lbs. or 560 lbs.; 70 lbs. in weight are an English bushel wheat, while 60 lbs. of wheat make our bushel; so that the U. S. wheat bushel is just 6-7ths of the English or imperial, and a quarter of wheat in England is equal to 9⅓ bushels in the United States, though in capacity to only 8¼ bushels.

The U. S. grain gallon measures 268.8 solid inches; the wine gallon 231 inches; the imperial measures 277¼ inches; 36 of our wine gallons are very nearly equal to 30 imperial gallons. The *obsolete* English ale and beer gallon measured 282 cubic inches.

The imperial standard gallon is a measure that will hold 10 lbs. avoirdupois of pure (distilled) water, weighed in air at 62° Fahrenheit, the barometer being at 30°.

This is the unit standard in Britain of capacity, for liquids, ale, beer, wine, spirits, and dry articles not measured by heaped measure. Our Winchester gallon weighs 9 lbs. 10 oz. and 1 3-4 drams of pure water.

1 Winchester quarter = 0.96945 of an imperial quarter; 33 Winchester quarters = 31.99175 imp.; 98 W. = 95.00581 imp.; 100 W. = 96.94470 imp.

To Reduce the Price of Wheat, in Sterling, per Imperial Quarter, to Dollars and Cents.—Reduce the shillings per quarter into dollars and cents, at 24.2 cts. per shilling, and divide by 9⅓, the number of U. S. bushels in an imperial quarter.

Example—Required the price of wheat per U. S. bushel in Liverpool, when it fetches 58s. 6d. per imperial quarter. 58s. 6d. equals $14.15, which, divided by 9⅓, gives $1.51½ the price per bushel.

TABLE OF FOREIGN WEIGHTS AND MEASURES,

REDUCED TO THE STANDARD OF THE UNITED STATES.

(The two right hand figures are the hundredth parts of a whole number.)

FRANCE.	
Metre	3·28 feet.
Decimetre (1-10th metre)	3·94 inches.
Velt	2·00 galls.
Hectolitre	26·42 galls.
Decalitre	2·64 galls.
Litre	2·11 pints.
Kilolitre	35·32 feet.
Hectolitre	2·84 bush.
Decalitre	9·08 quarts.
Millier	2·205 lbs.
Quintal	220·54 lbs.
Kilogramme	2·21 lbs.

AMSTERDAM.	
100 lbs. 1 centner	108·93 lbs.
Last of grain	85·25 bush.
Ahm of wine	41·00 galls.
Amsterdam foot	0·93 foot.
Antwerp foot	0·94 foot.
Rhineland foot	1·03 feet.
Amsterdam ell	2·26 feet.
Ell of the Hague	2·28 feet.
Ell of the Brabant	2·30 feet.

NETHERLANDS.	
Ell	3·28 feet.
Mudde of Zak	2·84 bush.
Vat hectolitre	26·42 galls.
Kan litre	2·11 pints.
Pond kilogramme	2·21 lbs.

HAMBURG.	
Last of grain	89·64 bush.
Ahm of wine	38·25 galls.
Hamburg foot	0·96 foot.
Ell	1·92 feet.

PRUSSIA.	
100 lbs. of 2 Cologne marks each	103·11 lbs.
Quintal, 110 lbs	113·42 lbs.
Sheffel of grain	1·56 bush.
Eimar of wine	18·14 galls.
Ell of cloth	2·19 foot.
Foot	1·03 feet.

DENMARK.	
100 lbs. 1 centner	110·28 lbs.
Barrel or toende of corn	3·95 bush.
Viertel of wine	2·04 galls.
Copenhagen or Rhineland foot	1·03 feet.

SWEDEN.	
100 lbs. or 5 lispunds	73·76 lbs.
Kan of corn	7·42 bush.
Last	75·00 bush.
Cann of wine	69·09 galls.
Ell of cloth	1·95 feet.

RUSSIA.	
100 lbs. of 32 laths each	90·26 lbs.
Chertwert of grain	5·95 bush.
Vedro of wine	3·25 galls.
Petersburgh foot	1·18 feet.
Moscow foot	1·10 feet.
Pood	36·00 lbs.

SPAIN.	
Quintal, or 4 arrobas	101·44 lbs.
Arroba	25·36 lbs.
Arroba of wine	4·43 galls.
Fanega of grain	1·60 bush.

PORTUGAL.	
100 lbs.	101·19 lbs.
22 lbs. (1 arroba)	22·26 lbs.
4 arrobas of 22 lbs. (1 quintal)	89·05 lbs.
Alquiere	4·75 bush.
Mojo of grain	23·03 bush.
Last of salt	70·00 bush.
Almude of wine	4·37 galls.

SICILY.	
Cantaro groso	192·50 lbs.
Cantaro sottile	175·00 lbs.
100 lbs.	70·00 lbs.
Salma grossa of grain	9·77 bush.
Salma generale	7·85 bush.
Salma of wine	23·06 galls.

NAPLES.	
Cantaro groso	196·50 lbs.
Cantaro picolo	106·00 lbs.
Carro o grain	52·24 bush.
Carro of wine	264·00 galls.

ROME.	
Rubbio of grain	8·36 bush.
Barih of wine	15·31 galls.

GENOA.	
100 lbs. or peso groso	76·87 lbs.
100 lbs. or peso sottile	69·89 lbs.
Mina of grain	3·43 bush.
Mezzarola of wine	39·22 galls.

FLORENCE AND LEGHORN.	
100 lbs. or 1 cantaro	74·86 lbs.
Moggio of grain	16·59 bush.
Barile of wine	12·04 galls.

VENICE.	
100 lbs. peso groso	105·18 lbs.
100 lbs. peso sottile	64·04 lbs.
Moggio of grain	9·08 bush.
Anfora of wine	137·00 galls.

TRIESTE.	
100 lbs.	123·60 lbs.
Stajo of grain	2·34 bush.
Orna or eimer of wine	14·94 galls.
Ell for woollens	2·22 feet.
Ell for silk	2·10 feet.

MALTA.	
100 lbs. 1 cantar	174·50 lbs.
Salma of grain	8·22 bush.
Foot	0·85 foot.

SMYRNA.	
100 lbs. (1 quintal)	129·48 lbs.
Oke	2·83 lbs.
Quillot of grain	1·46 bush.
Quillot of wine	13·50 galls.

CHINA.	
Tail	1·33 oz.
16 tails 1 catty	1·33 lbs.
100 catties 1 picul	133·25 lbs.

TABLE OF GOLD AND SILVER COINS

WITH THEIR VALUE, ACCORDING TO WEIGHT.

GOLD COINS.

	$ cts.
United States Double Eagle	20 00
United States Eagle (since 1834)	10 00
United States Eagle (before 1834)	10 50
United States Half-Eagle (since 1834)	5 00
United States Half-Eagle (before 1834)	5 25
United States Quarter Eagle	2 50
California Half-Eagle	4 90 to 5 00
United States Gold Dollar	1 00
Doubloon, Mexico, Central America, New Granada, Ecuador, Colombia, Peru, Bolivia, Chili	15 60
Doubloon, Spain	16 00
Half-Doubloon, Bolivia, Peru, &c.	7 75
Half-Doubloon, Spain	8 00
Quarter-Doubloon, Mexico, Colombia, Peru, Bolivia, Chili, &c.	3 75
Quarter-Doubloon, Spain	4 00
Eighth-Doubloon, Spain	2 00
Sixteenth-Doubloon, Mexico, Central America, New Granada, &c.	90
Sixteenth-Doubloon, Spain	1 00
Half-Joe, Brazil	8 50
Half-Joe, Portugal	6 to 8 50
Eighth-Joe, Portugal	1 75
Moidore, Brazil and Portugal	4 75 to 6 00
Tenth-Moidore, Brazil and Portugal	50
Crown, Portugal	5 75
Dobraon, Portugal	34 00
Five Sovereigns, England	24 20
Double Sovereign	9 67
Sovereign	4 80 to 4 83
Half-Sovereign	2 41
Guinea	5 00
Half-Guinea	2 50
Third of a Guinea	1 66
One Mohur, East India Company	6 75
Double Louis d'or, France	9 00
Louis d'or	4 50
Forty Francs	7 66
Twenty Francs	3 83
Six Francs	1 12
Ten Thalers, Germany	7 80
Five Thalers	3 90
Frederick d'or, Prussia	3 90
Double Frederick d'or	7 80
Sovereign	6 50
Half-Sovereign	3 25
Ten Gilders	3 98
Five Gilders	1 98
Carolin	4 75
Half-Carolin	2 85
Quarter-Carolin	1 18
Twelve Marks	1 55
Ducat	2 20
Quadruple Ducat, Austria	8 80
Twenty-Five Francs	4 75
Imperial, Russia	7 78
Half-Imperial, or Five Roubles	3 90
Hundred Lire, Italian States	19 15
Eighty Lire	15 32
Forty Lire	7 66
Twenty Lire	3 83
Ten Lire	1 90
Sequin	2 20
Ten Scudo	10 00
Twenty Drachms, Greece	3 30
Turkish Gold Coin	24

SILVER COINS.

	$ cts.
United States Dollar	1 00
Half-Dollar	50
Quarter-Dollar	25
One Dime	10
Half-Dime	5
Dollar, Mexico, Central America, New Granada, Colombia, Peru, Chili, Argentine Confederation, &c.	1 00
Base Dollar, New Granada	65
Base Dollar, Bolivia	90
960 Reis, Brazil and Portugal	98
1,200 Reis	1 00
One Real, South American states	6 to 12
Half-Dollar	30 to 50
Quarter-Dollar	22 to 24
Spanish Dollar	1 00
Half-Dollar	40 to 50
Quarter-Dollar	23 to 24
Head-Pistareen	18
Pistareen	16
Half-Pistareen	8
Five Pecetas	90
One Peceta	16
Crusado, Portugal	50
Six Vintems	12
Testoon	6
Crown, England	1 00 fo 1 12
Half-Crown	50 to 56
Shilling	23
Sixpence	11
Rupee, East India Company	40
Crown, France	1 06
Five Francs	93
Two Francs	34
One Franc	17
Crown, Italy	93 to 97
Scudo	86 to 97
One Livre	17
Rix-Dollar	93
Florin	20
Crown, Germany	1 00 to 1 02
Thaler	66 to 1 02
Florin	40 to 45
Gilder	36
Six Stivers	6
Six Kreutzers	2
Ducatoon, Germany	1 15
Ducatoon, Belgium	93
Crown, Switzerland	1 00
Rix-Dollar, Denmark, Sweden, Norway, &c.	75 to 1 10
Rouble, Russia	73

LAW OF COPYRIGHT.

Any person or persons, being a citizen or citizens of the United States, or resident therein, who shall be the author or authors of any book or books, map, chart, or musical composition, which may be now made or composed, and not printed and published, or shall hereafter be made or composed, or who shall invent, design, etch, engrave, work, or cause to be engraved, etched, or worked, from his own design, any print or engraving, and the executors, administrators, or legal assigns of such person or persons, shall have the sole right and liberty of printing, re-printing, publishing, and vending, such book or books, map, chart, musical composition, print, cut, or engraving, in whole or in part, for the term of twenty-eight years from the time of recording the title thereof, in the manner hereinafter directed.

No person shall be entitled to the benefit of this act, unless he shall, before publication, deposite a printed copy of the title of such book, or books, map, chart, musical composition, print, cut, or engraving, in the clerk's office of the district court of the district wherein the author or proprietor shall reside; and no person shall be entitled to the benefit of this act, unless he shall give information of copyright being secured, by causing to be inserted, in the several copies of each and every edition published during the term, secured on the title-page, or the page immediately following, if it be a book, or, if a map, chart, musical composition, print, cut, or engraving, by causing to be impressed on the face thereof, or if a volume of maps, charts, music or engravings, upon the title or frontispiece thereof, the following words, viz.: "Entered according to Act of Congress, in the year ——, by *A. B.*, in the Clerk's Office of the District Court of ——," (naming the district in which it was entered). There is a fine of one hundred dollars for putting on a false copyright notice.

If any person from and after the recording the title of any book, shall print, publish, or import, or cause to be printed, published, or imported, any copy of such book, without the consent of the person legally entitled to the copyright thereof, first had and obtained in writing, signed in presence of two or more credible witnesses, or shall, knowing the same to be so printed or imported, publish, sell, or expose to sale, or cause to be published, sold, or exposed to sale, any copy of such book without such consent in writing; then such offender shall forfeit every copy of such book to the person legally, at the time, entitled to the copyright thereof; and shall also forfeit and pay fifty cents for every such sheet which may be found in his possession, either printed, or printing, published, imported, or exposed to sale, contrary to the intent of this Act, the one moiety thereof to such legal owner of the copyright as aforesaid, and the other to the use of the United States, to be recovered by action of debt in any court having competent jurisdiction thereof.

The penalty for violating the copyright on engravings, maps, &c., by copying either on the whole, or by varying, adding to, or diminishing the main design with intent to evade the law, or by printing, importing, or selling, or causing either to be done, is forfeiture of the plates or engraving, with all the sheets copied or printed, besides a forfeit of one dollar for every sheet of such map, chart, musical composition, print, cut, or engraving, which may be found printed, published, or exposed for sale, one half to the proprietor, and the other half to the United States. An action must be brought within two years after the cause of action shall arise.

A copyright can be renewed for fourteen years by re-entering it six months before the expiration of the first term, but the renewal must be published four weeks in one or more newspapers printed in the United States, within two months from the date of the renewal. The fee for entering a copyright is fifty cents, and a like sum for a certified copy of the record.

A copy of the book, or whatever is copyrighted, must be deposited in the clerk's office where it has been entered, within three months from the publication of the same, and also a copy delivered to the librarian of the Smithsonian Institution and another copy to the Librarian of the Congress library, at Washington.

An assignment of copyright, to be good against a subsequent purchaser, must be acknowledged and recorded in the office where the original copyright was taken out, within sixty days after its execution.

NOTICES OF BEADLE'S AMERICAN LAWYER & FORM-BOOK.

From the Hon. JOHN W. EDMONDS, *Judge of the Supreme Court, New York:* "I have examined with some care, the American Lawyer and Form-Book, and it affords me pleasure to bear testimony to its general accuracy and value. It must be of great service to almost every man of business; and from the manner in which it has been prepared it may be fully relied upon."

From the Hon. Judge WM. KENT, *of New York:* "I have looked over your work and like it exceedingly. It seems to me an admirable compend, and of great use to men of business."

From the Hon. HENRY CLAY, *of Kentucky:* "I have received the copy of the American Lawyer and Business-Man's Form-Book, which you did me the favor to send me, and for which I thank you. Upon looking into it, I find it contains a great variety of well-arranged matter, and adapted to almost every vocation of life. Every man of business would find it useful to resort occasionally to the work. I am respectfully your obedient servant, H. CLAY."

From the Hon. Judge ELLIS LEWIS, *of the Supreme Court, Pennsylvania:* "I have examined Beadle's American Lawyer and Business-Man's Form-Book, and know of no work which contains, in so small a space, so much useful information concerning the varied business-interests of society."

JEFFERSON F. JACKSON, Esq., United States District Attorney for *Alabama,* writes: "Your book will be of great value to our profession."

"The highly practical character of the information comprised in this volume, its great scope, and undoubted accuracy, adapt it alike to the convenience of the merchant and the professional man. The author is a young member of the bar, in excellent standing in his profession. From intimate knowledge we do not hesitate to commend his industry, precision, and sound judgment. In order to secure the highest degree of accuracy, the author is in correspondence with jurists of each state, submitting to them his labors, and obtaining the latest enactments on each subject. The Maps of each state, bound in the volume, showing the county boundaries, will often be found of great convenience for reference."—*Journal of Commerce.*

"A form-book of some kind is almost indispensable to every man doing business, who dreads, as every man ought to dread, the lawyer's office. A thousand occasions occur in which it becomes necessary to observe legal accuracy in the drawing of instruments and papers, and yet are not of sufficient moment to justify seeking legal advice This work steps in at this point to assist. The proper forms and directions for the transaction of all kinds of business, when straightforward and free from intricacy, are given in a systematic manner. Besides, the laws of the various States on questions apt to come up in practical business, are digested so as to prevent mistakes. A great variety of tables, such as tariff of postage, interest tables, equation of time, mensuration rules, value of coin, weights and measures, are added, of great utility. A map of each State of the Union accompanies the description of the laws and usages of the State. The book shows research, comprehensiveness, and practical tact; and possesses that brevity and clearness of style, and explicitness of directions, which the business man desires. We should suppose that merchants, tradesmen, and householders generally, would be apt to find great saving and benefit in the use of it."—*New York Evangelist.*

"A useful volume this, not attempting to make every man his own lawyer and give him a fool for his client, but presenting a great variety of forms for legal and business instruments, with the laws of the different states on exemptions, deeds, mechanics' lien, debts, interest, wills, and other topics of every-day importance. With the large amount of information, which is condensed within a narrow compass, this work must prove a highly valuable manual for reference to all classes of business-men."—*N. Y. Tribune.*

"This is one of the most useful aids that a business-man can employ, containing as it does, besides other instructions, correct forms of all legal instruments in use, from a due-bill to a full-covenant deed. We believe it to be highly deserving the confidence and patronage of the business community, and that every man belonging to the same should possess a copy."—*Orleans Democrat.*

"A book for everybody—truly a comprehensive work."—*Philad. American Courier*

www.ingramcontent.com/pod-product-compliance
Lightning Source LLC
LaVergne TN
LVHW010149110826
845151LV00002B/469

9781425538293